Methods of Physical Examination in Archaeology

Studies in Archaeological Science

Consulting editor G. W. DIMBLEBY

Other titles in the Series

The Study of Animal Bones from Archaeological Sites
R. E. CHAPLIN

Ancient Skins, Parchments and Leathers
R. REED

Land Snails in Archaeology
J. G. EVANS

Methods of Physical Examination in Archaeology

M. S. TITE

Department of Physics,
University of Essex,
Colchester, Essex, England

1972

SEMINAR PRESS · London and New York

SEMINAR PRESS LTD.
24–28 Oval Road,
London NW1

U.S. Edition published by
SEMINAR PRESS INC.
111 Fifth Avenue,
New York, New York 10003

Library of Congress Catalog Card Number: 76–183476
ISBN: 0–12–916450–X

Printed in Great Britain by
William Clowes & Sons, Limited
London, Beccles and Colchester

Preface

The aim of this book is to provide a description and assessment of the multifarious methods of physical examination which are now playing an increasingly important role in archaeology. Firstly geophysical prospecting techniques, which are used to locate buried features on archaeological sites, are described. Secondly the physical methods of age determination, which provide the archaeologist with an essentially absolute and world-wide chronology, are discussed. Finally the wide range of physical techniques, which are employed in the examination of archaeological artefacts and which can provide information on trade and technology, are described. In each case, the general physical principles and experimental procedures associated with the technique are outlined and an attempt is made to assess the relative merits and limitations of the different techniques. In addition, an indication of their impact on archaeology is provided through the presentation and discussion of typical applications to archaeological sites and material.

The presentation is such that the majority of the text, and in particular the discussion of the relevance of the techniques to archaeology, can be read and understood without a specialist knowledge of physics and chemistry. However some general knowledge of the concepts of physics and chemistry is desirable and obviously the scientific reader will achieve a fuller understanding of certain sections. It is therefore hoped that the book will enable the archaeologist to gain an insight into the contributions that the physical sciences are now making to archaeology and to assess the relevance of a particular technique to his specific archaeological problem. At the same time, the book should be of interest to those physical scientists who have either been involved in applying a specific technique to archaeology or who are considering the possible relevance of their current research techniques to the study of archaeological material.

Acknowledgements

For assistance in obtaining the photographs which are used to illustrate this book, I am grateful to: E. Adair, Dr M. J. Aitken, L. Alcock, Dr R. H. Brill, J. A. Charles, A. J. Clark, H. Cleere, Dr A. S. Darling, Professor G. W. Dimbleby, I. F. Freeman, Dr I. Friedman, Dr R. G. Newton, Dr D. P. S. Peacock, Dr J. K. St Joseph, Professor F. W. Shotton, Dr D. J. Smith, H. Thompson and Dr R. F. Tylecote. I also thank my wife and Miss J. Sanderson for translating my handwriting into typescript.

Finally I wish to record my permanent debt to Dr M. J. Aitken, who first introduced me to this general area of scientific research, and to D. Britton and Dr P. R. S. Moorey, from whom I have gained much of my admittedly limited knowledge of and insight into archaeology. Without their past help and stimulation, I feel certain that I would not have been in a position to write this book.

M. S. TITE

September, 1972.

Units and Fundamental Constants

The SI system (i.e. rationalized M.K.S. system) of units is used in this book. In this system, the unit of length is the *metre* (m), the unit of time is the *second* (sec), the unit of mass is the *kilogram* (kg), the unit of force is the *newton* (N), the unit of work or energy is the *joule* (J) and the unit of power is the *watt* (W). The prefixes employed to indicate the multiples and submultiples of these units, and the other units in the SI system, are as follows:

Prefix	Value	Symbol
mega-	$\times 10^6$	M
kilo-	$\times 10^3$	k
centi-	$\times 10^{-2}$	c
milli-	$\times 10^{-3}$	m
micro-	$\times 10^{-6}$	μ

The *angstrom* (Å), which is equal to 10^{-10} metre, is also used as a unit of length, particularly in the context of the wavelength of electromagnetic radiation. The units of surface area and volume are the *square metre* (m^2) and the *cubic metre* (m^3) respectively, while for liquid measure the *litre* (l), which equals 10^{-3} m^3 (i.e. 10^3 cm^3), and the millilitre (ml) are also employed. The unit of frequency (i.e. the rate of repetition of a periodic phenomenon such as an oscillation or pulse) is the *hertz* (Hz), one hertz being one cycle per second.

In the context of magnetic phenomena, the following units are employed, their relationship to the corresponding C.G.S. units being given in brackets:

magnetic field intensity (H) *ampere/metre* (A m^{-1})

$$(1 \text{ A } m^{-1} = 4\pi \times 10^{-3} \text{ oersted } = 4\pi \times 10^2 \text{ gamma})$$

magnetic flux density (B)   *weber/metre*^{2} (Wb m^{-2}) or *tesla* (T)
      (1 Wb m^{-2} = 10^4 gauss)
magnetization (i.e. magnetic   *weber-metre/kilogram* (Wb m/kg)
      moment per unit mass)   (1 Wb m/kg = 10^7/4π emu/g)
magnetic susceptibility (χ)   *SI units/kilogram* (SI/kg)
      (1 SI/kg = 10^3/4π emu/g)

The approximate values for the fundamental constants referred to in the text are as follows:

c velocity of light *in vacuo*   3 × 10^8 m s^{-1}
e electronic charge   1·6 × 10^{-19} C (coulomb)
m electron rest mass   9·1 × 10^{-31} kg
h Planck's constant   6·6 × 10^{-34} J s
eV   electron volt   1·6 × 10^{-19} J
μ° permeability of free space   4π × 10^{-7} H m^{-1} (henry/metre)

Contents

1

Introduction   **1**

References 5

2

Location   **7**

Magnetic surveying 9
  general principles 9
  instruments 18
  survey logistics 23
Resistivity surveying 25
  general principles 25
  instruments 28
  field procedures 29
Electromagnetic surveying 32
  metal detectors 33
  location of archaeological features 35
Induced polarization techniques 39
Presentation and analysis of survey data . . . 41
Applications 43
  hill-forts and camps 43
  farmsteads and villas 46
  villages and towns 47
  burial sites 50
  industrial sites 51
Conclusions 53
  prospecting techniques 54
  applications 55
References 56

3

Age Determination – Introduction   58

Radioactive methods 59
  radiocarbon dating 61
  geological methods 61
  thermoluminescent dating 64
Magnetic dating 65
Dating by chemical change 66
Natural rhythmic processes 68
  dendrochronology 68
  varves 70
Dating by flora and fauna 70
Applications 73
References 74

4

Age Determination – Radioactive Methods   76

Radiocarbon dating 76
  general principles 77
  experimental procedures 78
  selection of samples 81
  fossil fuel effect and nuclear weapon tests . . . 82
  fluctuations in the ^{14}C concentration of the exchange reservoir   83
  results 88
Potassium – argon dating 90
  general principles 91
  experimental procedures 92
  selection of rock samples 96
  results 97
Fission track dating 99
  general principles 100
  experimental procedures 101
  results 103
Deep sea sediments 106
  temperature measurements 106
Age determination 109
  results 111
Thermoluminescent dating 114

general principles 115
experimental procedures 119
complications 123
results 126
References 129

5

Age Determination – Non-Radioactive Methods   134

Magnetic dating 134
theory of thermoremanent magnetism 135
principles of age determination 138
experimental procedures 141
results 147
Dating of bone 150
general principles 150
experimental procedures 151
results 151
Obsidian dating 154
general principles 155
experimental procedures 157
results 158
Glass layer counting 161
general principles 161
results 162
References 164

6

Age Determination – Archaeological Results   167

Pleistocene 168
East Africa 169
Western Europe 171
New World 175
Postglacial 176
Neolithic 178
Copper and Bronze Ages 184

Conclusions 191
References 193

7

Physical Examination of Artefacts and Biological Material – Introduction   195

Techniques 197
  microscopy and radiography 198
  physical methods of analysis 201
  chromatography 203
Artefacts 206
  stone artefacts 208
  pottery 208
  metals 209
  glass, glaze and faience 209
  colorants and pigments 210
  artefacts derived from biological material . . . 210
Biological materials 211
  plants and animals 211
  Man 212
Select bibliography 213

8

Microscopy and Radiography   215

Petrological microscopy 215
  experimental procedures 215
  principles of mineral and rock identification . . . 217
  stone artefacts 222
  pottery 224
Metallographic microscopy 230
  experimental procedures 230
  non-ferrous metals and alloys 232
  iron and steel 238
Electron microscopy 242
  transmission electron microscope 242
  scanning electron microscope 246

applications 249
Radiography 252
  microradiography 253
References 254

9
Physical Methods of Analysis — Techniques 256

Chemical analysis: general discussion 257
Optical emission spectrometry 260
  experimental procedures 261
  advantages and limitations 263
Atomic absorption spectrometry 264
  experimental procedures 264
  advantages and limitations 266
X-ray fluorescence spectrometry 267
  experimental procedures 267
  advantages and limitations 270
  X-ray milliprobe 272
Neutron activation analysis 273
  experimental procedures 275
  advantages and limitations 278
Electron probe microanalyser 278
  experimental procedures 279
  applications 281
Beta-ray backscattering 281
Specific gravity determinations 283
X-ray diffraction 285
  powder-diffraction method 286
  back reflection diffraction method 287
Infra-red absorption spectrometry 288
Mössbauer spectroscopy 291
Thermal analysis 295
  differential thermal analysis 295
  thermogravimetric analysis 297
  thermal expansion measurements 298
  colour analysis 300
Isotopic analysis 301
References 304

10

Physical Methods of Analysis — Applications 306

Stone artefacts 307
  flint 307
  obsidian 309
Pottery 314
  source of raw materials 315
  technology 323
Metal artefacts 328
  copper and bronze artefacts 328
  iron and steel artefacts 333
  lead 334
  coins 337
Glass, glaze and faience 345
  glass 346
  glaze 350
  faience 352
Pigments and paintings 355
Amber and mollusc shells 358
  amber 358
  mollusc shells 360
Conclusions 364
References 366
Author index 371
Subject index 377
Index of Sites 387

Section of plates . . . . between pp: 192 and 123

List of Illustrations

Figure   *page*

1. Acquisition of thermoremanent magnetism in the Earth's magnetic field   10

2. Histograms showing the distribution of values for susceptibility and fractional conversion for soil samples from pits and ditches on archaeological sites and for samples of normal agricultural topsoil   13

3. Idealized magnetic anomaly   17

4. Typical magnetic anomalies produced by a kiln and a pit along a traverse through the centre of the feature   .   18

5. Gyrations performed by a proton in a magnetic field and a spinning top in a gravitational field   20

6. Proton signal (after amplification) associated with a proton gradiometer   22

7. Typical electrode arrangement for resistivity surveying .   26

8. Idealized resistivity profiles associated with a stone wall surrounded by low resistivity soil   27

9. Resistivity profiles associated with ditches   .   .   .   28

10. Electrode configurations for resistivity surveying .   .   30

11. Coil arrangement for electromagnetic surveying   .   .   33

12. Waveforms for the pulsed induction metal detector   .   35

13. Plot of equivalent values for magnetic susceptibility and resistivity such that the in-phase component from homogeneous magnetic topsoil has the same magnitude as the 90° out-of-phase component from homogeneous conducting topsoil   36

14. Profile associated with a road and a ditch obtained using an electromagnetic instrument, the traverse being perpendicular to the line of the features   .   .   .   37

15. Waveforms for the induced polarization technique.   .   40

16. Induced polarization and resistivity profiles associated with a ditch and bank, the positions of which are marked by arrows   40

17. Magnetic survey results for the Iron Age hill-fort at Rainsborough, Northants 42

18. Magnetic and electromagnetic survey results for a typical area at Cadbury Castle (Camelot), Somerset . . 45

19. Resistivity survey results, in the form of a simplified contour diagram, for the Roman villa at Barnsley Park, Gloucs. 47

20. Magnetic survey results for a typical area of the Iron Age-cum-Roman settlement at Dragonby, Lincs.. . . 48

21. Resistivity survey results in the form of a dot density diagram, for a typical area of the Iron Age cemetery at Burton Fleming, Yorks. 51

22. Magnetic survey results, in the form of a simplified contour diagram, for a typical area of the Etruscan cemetery at Cerveteri, Italy 52

23. Radioactive decay (graph of Eq. 3.1) 60

24. Idealized diagram representing the principles of dendro-chronology 69

25. Simplified pollen diagram during the Hoxnian interglacial for which four major vegetational stages can be identified 71

26. Production process for ^{14}C and the carbon exchange reservoir 77

27. (a) Fluctuations in the ^{14}C concentration of the atmosphere over the past 7000 years, as determined from tree-ring data. (b) Fluctuations in the Earth's magnetic moment over the past 9000 years as determined from the thermo-remanent magnetism measurements on fired clay from Europe, Central America and Japan 84

28. Fluctuations in the ^{14}C concentration of the atmosphere over the past 13 000 years 85

29. Comparison of the fluctuations in the ^{14}C concentration of the atmosphere as determined from tree-ring data, and the sunspot number per year over the past 1000 years . 87

30. Relationship between the radiocarbon age of tree-ring dated wood and the true calendar tree-ring age as determined from tree-ring studies on the bristlecone pines and other long-lived trees 89

31. Block diagram of a mass spectrometer . . . 93

32. Hypothetical 'age spectra' obtained with the $^{40}Ar/^{39}Ar$ method of potassium–argon dating, the ages associated with outgassing over a series of heating steps towards complete fusion being determined   95

33. Results from $^{40}Ar/^{39}Ar$ method of potassium–argon dating for felspar phenocrysts from volcanic deposit at Lake Rudolf in Kenya   98

34. Comparison of the fission track ages with the known ages of the man-made glass and the ages determined by other radioactive methods (e.g. potassium–argon dating) in the case of the natural minerals (e.g. tektites, micas and obsidian)   105

35. Comparison of fission track ages with the estimated archaeological ages of pottery, tiles and fired clay from Japan   106

36. Palaeotemperature curves from deep-sea sediments   .   107

37. Generalized isotopic temperature curve for the surface water of the central Caribbean, together with an earlier tentative correlation between the oceanic stages and the continental glacial and interglacial phases for North America and Britain   112

38. Generalized climatic curve based on the variations in the abundance of various temperature-sensitive planktonic foraminifera   114

39. Electron energy levels for an inorganic non-conducting solid   115

40. Thermoluminescent history of a clay sample   .   .   117

41. Annual radiation dose received by a fragment of pottery with typical concentrations of radioactive impurities buried in soil with the same radioactivity .   .   .   117

42. Block diagram of apparatus for thermoluminescence measurements   120

43. (a) Thermoluminescent glow curves for a typical specimen of ancient pottery. (b) 'Plateau' test   121

44. Supralinear growth of thermoluminescence with radiation dose   124

45. Idealized curves for the acquisition and removal of thermoremanent magnetism in fired clay .   .   .   137

46. Secular variation of the declination and the angle of dip for London, the dates being shown in years AD .   .   139

47. Changes in the polarity of the Earth's magnetic field during the past 2·5 million years 141

48. Scatter in the values of the declination and the angle of dip for groups of samples taken from mediaeval kilns at Grimston, Norfolk and West Cowick, Yorks . . 143

49. Typical results obtained using the double-heating method for determining the ancient magnetic field intensity . 144

50. Astatic magnetometer 146

51. Variation in the Earth's magnetic field intensity for Europe, central America and Japan 149

52. Fluorine dating results for bones from western Germany 154

53. Variation in the thickness of the hydration layer for obsidian artefacts of known age under different climatic conditions 156

54. Variation in the thickness of the hydration layer for obsidian artefacts from Japan whose age is known from radiocarbon dating 158

55. Thickness of hydration layers of obsidian artefacts from various depths within the refuse deposits at the Chorrera site on the coast of Ecuador 160

56. Radiocarbon dates for the Palaeolithic period in France 174

57. Graph showing the difference between the historically derived dates and the radiocarbon dates for the beginning of the pottery Neolithic in different parts of Europe and the Near East 179

58. Sketch map of Europe and the Near East showing the earliest known agricultural settlements as determined by radiocarbon dating 180

59. Radiocarbon dates for the Neolithic period in southern England 182

60. Radiocarbon dates for the Aegean and the Balkans from the Late Neolithic through to the Early Bronze Age . 187

61. Radiocarbon dates for archaeological material related to the Wessex culture 190

62. Spectrum of electromagnetic radiation . . . 198

63. Paper chromatography 204

64. Gas chromatography record showing the volume of sample gas emerging from the liquid column versus time 205

65. Schematic diagram showing the principal components of a petrological microscope 216
66. Identification of minerals in thin section . . . 218
67. Examination of minerals in thin section between crossed polars 220
68. Sketch map of south-western Britain, showing the distribution of stone axes originating from Cornwall and the fine 'Hembury' ware made from the gabbroic clay on the Lizard peninsula 226
69. Schematic diagram showing the principal components of a metallurgical microscope 231
70. Reflection of light and the contrast pattern observed for polished etched metal surfaces 232
71. Polished etched surfaces of a non-ferrous alloy observed under reflected light using a metallurgical microscope . 235
72. Schematic representation of the structure and the surface appearance of a typical 'pattern-welded' sword . . 241
73. Block diagram showing the principal components of a transmission electron microscope 243
74. Replication method of transmission electron microscopy 244
75. Schematic representation of the interaction between the primary electron beam and the specimen in a scanning electron microscope 246
76. Detection systems for the backscattered and the secondary electrons in the scanning microscope . . . 247
77. Schematic diagram showing the principal components of an optical emission spectrometer 262
78. Schematic diagram showing the principal components of an atomic absorption spectrometer 265
79. Schematic diagram showing the principal components of an X-ray fluorescence spectrometer 268
80. X-ray fluorescence spectrum for a gold–silver–copper alloy 269
81. Schematic diagram showing the principal components of an X-ray milliprobe 272
82. Neutron activation analysis: nuclear reactions involved in the emission of a gamma ray whose energy is effectively characteristic of the element gold 274
83. Gamma ray spectrum (partial) for a typical pottery sample, obtained using a high resolution semiconductor counter 277

84. Schematic diagram showing the principal components of the electron probe microanalyser 279

85. Schematic diagram of the beta ray backscatterer . . 282

86. Specific gravity data for gold–silver alloy discs containing known percentages of gold 284

87. Diagram illustrating the Bragg relationship for X-ray diffraction 285

88. Schematic diagram of an X-ray power-diffraction camera 287

89. Schematic diagram of an X-ray back reflection diffraction camera 288

90. Schematic diagram showing the principal components of an infra-red absorption spectrometer 289

91. Infra-red absorption spectra for calcite and gypsum . 290

92. The energy spectrum associated with the emission and absorption of gamma rays by a nucleus for both the normal process and the recoil-free Mössbauer effect . 292

93. Schematic diagram showing the principal components of a Mössbauer effect spectrometer 293

94. Mössbauer spectrum for a typical pottery sample . 294

95. Hypothetical differential thermal analysis curve illustrating the principal reactions that can occur in a pottery sample 296

96. Thermogravimetric curves for typical clay minerals 297

97. Schematic diagram of a fused silica extension rod dilatometer 298

98. Thermal expansion curves during heating and cooling for typical pottery samples 299

99. Variation in the $^{18}O/^{16}O$ ratio for various natural materials, including the raw materials used in making glass . . 303

100. Trace element concentrations for flint from seven major axe factories and mines in southern Britain and continental Europe 308

101. Sketch map of the Near East showing the principal obsidian sources and the settlement sites on which obsidian from these sources was employed during the seventh and sixth millennia BC 310

102. Barium and zirconium concentrations for obsidian samples from the Near East showing the division of the obsidian into six major groups 311

103. Variations in the percentage of obsidian in the total chipped stone industry with distance from the source for the Near East during the seventh and sixth millennia BC .   312

104. Average concentrations of five elements for groups of Romano-British mortaria from typical kiln sites .   .   318

105. Ranges of concentrations of nine elements for Mycenaean pottery from the Peloponnese and Minoan pottery from Knossos on Crete   319

106. Comparison of the concentration ranges of nine elements for Theban stirrup jars and Minoan pottery from Crete .   322

107. Histograms showing the variation in the concentrations of arsenic andtin in the alloys used to make copper/bronze artefacts during the Early Bronze Age in the British Isles   329

108. Histogram showing the difference between the lead concentrations in bronzes of the British Middle and Late Bronze Ages   331

109. Lead isotope ratios for lead ores and lead artefacts produced from ores of known origin   .   .   .   335

110. Lead isotope ratios for samples of lead extracted from bronze coins and Mesopotamian red and yellow opaque glasses   336

111. Variation in the concentration ratios for gold to silver, and silver to copper with the depth below the surface for a Roman coin made from a silver–copper alloy   .   .   338

112. Comparison of the results obtained for the gold concentrations in gold–silver coins using specific gravity measurements, neutron activation analysis and the X-ray milliprobe   339

113. Histograms showing the variation in the copper concentrations in Greek silver coins minted at Syracuse at different periods during the fifth century BC   .   .   340

114. Histograms showing the variation in the gold concentrations in Greek silver coins minted at (a) Athens during the sixth century BC, (b) Athens during the fifth century BC and (c) Corinth during the fifth century BC   342

115. Concentration ranges for gold and silver in Dark Age coins from western Europe   343

116. Histograms showing the variation in the silver concentrations in English silver pennies minted during the periods (a) 1050–1087 AD and (b) 1087–1125 AD . 345

117. Average concentrations of various metal oxides in the five main categories of Western ancient glass . . 347

118. Oxygen isotope ratios for a selection of ancient glass . 348

119. Concentration ratios for manganese to cobalt in the blue cobalt pigment used in the decoration of Chinese blue-and-white porcelain manufactured during the period 1300–1900 AD 351

120. Magnesium/tin concentration ratio versus aluminium concentration for a selection of faience beads . . . 354

121. Tin/copper concentration ratios for faience beads from (a) Scotland and Wessex and (b) Egypt, XVIIIth and XIXth dynasties 354

122. Concentration profiles for the four major elements in the green pigment (glauconite) employed in a provincial Roman wall painting 357

123. Infra-red absorption spectra for Baltic and Sicilian amber 359

124. Oxygen and carbon isotopic ratios for cockle shells from the Neolithic settlement site of Nea Nikomedeia in Greece 363

List of Plates

Plates appear between pages 192 and 193

1. Experimental earthwork constructed at Overton Down, Wiltshire in 1960. Upper: immediately after completion. Lower: four years later, by which time considerable silting of the ditch and erosion of the rampart had occurred. (By permission of the Research Committee on Archaeological Field Experiments of the British Association for the Advancement of Science.)
2. The experimental firing of a pottery kiln of Romano-British type at Boston, Lincs. in 1962
3. Aerial photographs. Left: crop-marks associated with huts, enclosures and ditches of a pre-Roman or Roman Iron Age settlement near to Lockington, Leics. Right: differences in relief (i.e. shadow-marks) associated with the houses and streets of the deserted mediaeval village at Argam, Yorks. (By permission of the Committee for Aerial Photography, University of Cambridge. Copyright reserved. Ph.: J. K. St Joseph.)
4. The proton magnetometer in operation with one person moving the detector bottle and the second person reading the instrument. (Photo courtesy of Thomas-Photos, Oxford.)
5. The square array resistivity probe system in operation. A single person can both move the probe system and subsequently read the instrument. (Photo courtesy of A. Clark.)
6. Typical electromagnetic surveying instrument in operation. A single person can both carry the coil system and read the instrument.
7. Excavated area at Cadbury Castle, Somerset showing the pits, the circular wall trench or drainage gulley of an Iron Age hut, the mediaeval boundary ditch and the foundation trenches of the cruciform building (see Fig. 18 for the

associated magnetic and electromagnetic survey results). (By permission of the Camelot Research Committee and the Society of Antiquaries of London.)

8. Excavated area at the Iron Age-cum-Roman settlement at Dragonby, Lincs. showing the remains of the road (foreground) and the soil fillings of various pits and ditches which appear dark in contrast to the light-coloured sand subsoil.

9. Photomicrograph of a polished etched surface of a modern glass showing the etch pits developed from artificially-induced fission tracks

10. Typical pottery kiln (Romano-British type: Dragonby, Lincs.) used to provide samples for magnetic dating. (By permission of the Society of Antiquaries of London.)

11. Magnetic dating samples showing both an isolated stump of fired clay and several completed samples which have been encased in plaster of Paris and are ready for detachment.

12. Spinner magnetometer coil system showing a pottery vessel in position on the table which is rotated at 5 revolutions per sec. (Photo courtesy of Thomas-Photos, Oxford.)

13. Photomicrographs of a thin section of an obsidian artefact showing the hydration layer, (left) as viewed in ordinary light and (right) as viewed between crossed polarizers. (Photo courtesy of I. Friedman.)

14. Weathering crust which has formed on the surface of a fragment of a glass wine bottle recovered at Port Royal, Jamaica. (By permission of the Corning Museum of Glass.)

15. Photomicrographs of sections through the weathering crusts of ancient glass samples showing their fine laminar structure. Upper: uniform laminar structure with a human hair (dark central band) placed across the layers to illustrate the magnification. Lower: non-uniform weathering with randomly located intrusions or 'plugs', each containing a different number of layers. (Upper by permission of the Corning Museum of Glass; lower by permission of the Society of Glass Technology. Ph.: R. G. Newton.)

16. Photomicrographs of a selection of pollen grains. (a) Elm. (b) Alder. (c) Hazel. (d) Birch. (e) Lime. (f) Rye. (g) Wave hairgrass. (h) Field maple. (i) Fat hen. (j) Ragged robin.

(k) Ribwort plantain. (l) Sheep's-bit. (m) Common fumitory. (n) Persicaria. (o) Hornbeam. (Photo courtesy of G. W. Dimbleby.)

17. Photomicrographs of thin sections of stone axes viewed between crossed polarizers. Left: Group VI (Great Langdale): dark isotropic matrix embedded with small angular shattered fragments which are largely felspathic. Right: Group XII (Montgomeryshire): intergrowth of large crystals of olivine, pyroxene and felspar. (Photo courtesy of F. W. Shotton.)

18. Photomicrographs of thin sections, viewed between crossed polarizers, of Iron Age pottery showing the different types of temper added to the clay (dark isotropic matrix). (a) Fragment of quartz diorite (b) Fragment of meta-morphic rock.
(c) Fragments of limestone. (d) Single large fragment of sandstone (no clay matrix visible). (Photo courtesy of D. P. S. Peacock.)

19. Photomicrograph of a polished etched section of the head of a rivet from a Minoan dagger showing the silver–copper eutectic layer (b) which provides the bonding between the copper rivet (c) and the silver capping (a). The deformed grains of the cold-worked copper in the rivet and the primary silver dendrites growing into the eutectic layer from the interface with the silver are also visible. (Photo courtesy of J. A. Charles and Antiquity Publications Ltd.)

20. Photomicrograph of a polished etched section of a wrought iron specimen showing the ferrite grains and fibrous inclusions of slag (dark streaks). (Photo courtesy of H. Cleere.)

21. Scanning fluorescent X-ray images, obtained using the electron probe microanalyser, for (upper) silver and (lower) copper across a section through the head of a rivet from a Minoan dagger. (a) Silver capping; (b) eutectic layer; (c) copper rivet. (Photo courtesy of J. A. Charles and Antiquity Publications Ltd.)

22. Backscattered electron image, obtained using the scanning electron microscope, for a Greek electrum coin showing the gold-rich dendrites. (a) Gold deficient areas; (b) gold-rich dendrites; (c) 'valleys' filled with dirt. (By permission of Macmillan Journals Ltd. *Nature*.)

23. Radiograph of the hilt end of a pattern-welded iron sword dating from the third century AD and found at South Shields showing the bronze inlay of Mars (on one side) and an eagle with palm branches (on the other side). (By permission of South Shields Corporation.)

24. X-ray diffraction patterns (power method) for typical pottery samples, the bright lines on the print corresponding to the dark lines on the original photographic film. The principal minerals which can be identified from these diffraction patterns are: (upper) quartz, (middle) quartz and mica and (lower) quartz and calcite.

25. Photomicrographs of the surface topography of unfired and fired clay specimens obtained using the scanning electron microscope (backscattered/secondary electron image). Left (upper) Carboniferous shale: unfired; (lower) Carboniferous shale: fired at 875°C. Right, London Clay: fired at 1025C°. (By permission of the Director of the Building Research Establishment and the Controller of Her Majesty's Stationery Office. Crown copyright.)

List of Tables

Table	page
1. Magnetic susceptibility of soil from archaeological sites	14
2. Magnetic anomalies produced by 'spherical' kilns (mass 500 kg)	16
3. Magnetic anomalies produced by cylindrical pits (diameter 1 m)	16
4. Electrical resistivities of rocks, clay and soil (ohm m)	26
5. Detection depth for electromagnetic instruments	38
6. Radioactive isotopes used for age determination	62
7. Potassium–argon results for Lake Rudolf artefact site	98
8. Fission track dating: minimum sample age	103
9. Uranium decay series used for dating deep-sea sediments	110
10. Fluorine, nitrogen and uranium contents of bones from Europe and North Africa	152
11. Results for layer counting on ancient glass	163
12. Potassium–argon dates for Bed I at the Olduvai Gorge, Tanzania	170
13. Stages and absolute chronology for the European Pleistocene	172
14. Archaeological sequence during the European Pleistocene	175
15. Principal techniques appropriate to the physical examination of archaeological artefacts	207
16. Simplified classification of igneous rocks	222
17. Heavy mineral analysis of Romano-British black-burnished pottery	227
18. The development of the microstructure in non-ferrous metals and alloys	237
19. The development of the microstructure in iron and steel	240
20. Comparison of the physical methods of chemical analysis	259
21. Lead isotope ratios for lead ores from different mining regions	302
22. Fission track data for obsidian samples	314

23. Concentrations of selected elements, determined using neutron activation analysis, in pottery from diverse sources 316

24. Variation in the composition of pottery sherds as a result of burial conditions 316

25. Comparison of the elements analysed in Greek pottery using optical emission spectrometry and neutron activation analysis 320

26. Firing temperatures for calcareous pottery from the Mediterranean area, estimated on the basis of the mineral phases present 324

27. Firing temperatures for pottery, estimated on the basis of thermal expansion measurements 326

28. Mössbauer spectrum parameters for pottery and clay samples from Cheam, Surrey 327

29. Silver concentrations in twelfth-century Byzantine trachy 344

30. Oxygen isotopic data for *Spondylus* shells from Neolithic sites 361

1

Introduction

Archaeology seeks to reconstruct and explain the past developments of human culture through the study of the material remains. Although the application of archaeological techniques extends to and throws valuable light on quite recent periods of history in highly literate societies, the most important and exciting contributions from archaeology relate to the vast phases of human prehistory which are unilluminated by the written word.

The reconstruction of human cultural development involves both establishing a chronological framework and studying the biological aspects of man himself, his natural environment, his means of subsistence and his material culture (i.e. his artefacts). From this data inferences concerning the economic, political, social and ideological systems of the human culture can be made. Having thus established the pattern of culture in both time and space, it is then necessary to explain the changes that have occurred either using invasion, migration and diffusion models or in terms of the internal interaction of all aspects of a culture. Finally, since the explanation of development in archaeology employs general theories of socio-cultural development, derived from anthropology and the social sciences, the archaeological data provides a means of testing these theories and possibly generating new theories (Trigger, 1970).

In order to achieve this aim it is obvious that the archaeologist must extract the maximum possible amount of information from the available material and must therefore adopt a wide-ranging, multi-disciplinary approach to his study of human culture. Consequently the natural sciences must inevitably play an extremely important role in archaeology since they can assist in the location of sites, in the provision of an absolute world-wide chronology and in the description of the bio-cultural system.

Geophysical prospecting techniques are used to locate buried features (e.g. kiln, pit, ditches) on archaeological sites, thus suggesting fruitful areas for excavation and helping to extend the range of material available for study. In addition, when financial considerations prevent complete excavation, these techniques can be used to establish the limits of the site and the density of buried features, thus providing, in the case of a settlement site, data for estimating the total population.

Physical techniques of age determination, and in particular those based on radioactive decay (e.g. radiocarbon and potassium–argon dating), provide the archaeologist with an essentially absolute, world-wide chronological framework. This is of fundamental importance since a precise knowledge of the temporal relationship between human cultures, spread throughout the world, is obviously essential for understanding and explaining cultural developments.

In the study of the bio-cultural system a wide range of natural sciences are involved. Soil scientists, botanists and zoologists, for example, provide essential information on the natural environment in which man existed. Information on soil fertility, climate, flora and fauna is of vital importance since these environmental factors provide the basis for man's subsistence in terms of food, shelter and clothing. Furthermore, not only does the environment influence man's pattern of life, but with increasing cultural progress, man is instrumental in modifying the environment and these modifications must be appreciated and understood.

Experts in the various branches of human anatomy and physiology provide information on the biological aspects of man himself. Study of the physical remains (i.e. bones) of prehistoric man provide information on the evolution of the earlier hominids to *Homo sapiens* as well as on the subsequent development of different races from *Homo sapiens*. Furthermore within a particular culture, it is possible to establish the relative frequency of ages at death, the sex ratios, the variations in stature, the general health and nutritional level achieved as well as the range of diseases experienced.

The study of the artefacts (i.e. structures, tools, weapons, domestic utensils, ornaments etc) provide the traditional focus of attention in archaeology; early cultures having been largely defined by the artefacts or artefactual assemblies that they employed. Although originally studied only from a typological point of view, a wide range of physical techniques are now employed in the examination of artefacts. Information on the identity and source of the raw materials and the techniques used in their manufacture is thus obtained. These data, in turn, help to establish the extent of trade or exchange of artefacts between cultural groups and also provide information on their technological capabilities and development.

In addition to the direct employment of the natural sciences in the study of material remains, the attitudes, instilled in archaeology through this extensive contact, have encouraged the development of archaeological experiments. For example, experimental earthworks have been built in Britain (Plate 1) in order to study the processes involved in the natural erosion and silting of ramparts and ditches together with the progressive deterioration of buried materials (Jewell, 1963; Jewell and Dimbleby, 1966). Other experiments include the reconstruction and firing of various types of pottery kiln (Plate 2) in order to establish their technological and economic efficiency (Mayes, 1961, 1962).

Associated with the extensive use of the natural sciences, together with the development of high-speed electronic computers, is the increasing employment of quantitative assessment and mathematical techniques in archaeology. Thus it is valuable to obtain a quantitative estimate of, for example, the relative meat weights associated with the various types of food debris (e.g. animal and fish bones, shells), the population of a settlement, the man-hours involved in the construction of a monument or the quantity of imported materials (e.g. obsidian, pottery, metal). However, of perhaps greater significance is the use of mathematical techniques, such as cluster analysis and seriation, to provide a more objective classification of artefacts and artefactual assemblages (Hodson, 1970; Kendall, 1970). These techniques involve firstly the selection of a group of variables or attributes which describe the artefact or artefactual assemblage. In the case of a specific type of artefact (e.g. Beaker pottery or La Tène brooches), the variables could include the physical dimensions and the style of decoration while in the case of an assemblage (e.g. group of flint tools or a grave group), they could be the numbers of each artefact type within the assemblage. Using an electronic computer, the variables can then be subjected to mathematical analysis in order either to group together similar artefacts or artefactual assemblages (i.e. cluster analysis) or to arrange them in an ordered series representing, for example, a chronological sequence (i.e. seriation).

The employment of the natural sciences and mathematical analysis in archaeology has increased dramatically during the past two or three decades and has radically changed the philosophy of archaeological research (Isaac, 1971; Neustupný, 1971). In particular, the traditional emphasis placed on artefacts when defining human cultures has decreased and instead greater importance is now attached to ecological considerations and the fact that man forms part of a closely interacting man/plant/animal system.

These changes in emphasis, together with the provision of a tentative absolute chronology, has also modified the concepts used in explaining cultural development.   For example, in the case of Britain, the transition to a Neolithic way of life and the introduction of metallurgy by the Beaker Culture were undoubtedly the result of invasions or migrations from Europe. However the interpretation of the subsequent cultural development in terms of a series of invasions is now questioned (Clark, 1966). In particular, the explanation of the Wessex culture in terms of invasion by a group who had been in contact with the Mycenaean civilization is now questioned since recalibration of the radiocarbon dates suggests that the Wessex culture pre-dates the Mycenaean civilization (Renfrew, 1968). Similarly the diffusion model, which explains change in terms of strong influences from higher cultures and which was extensively employed by Childe (1957) in describing the prehistory of Europe, is no longer necessarily accepted as the dominant cause of cultural development. In particular, the associated hypothesis that each invention has been made but once is now questioned especially with respect to the early development of metallurgy (Renfrew, 1969a). Instead, cultural change is now frequently explained in terms of the internal interactions of the environmental or economic subsystems of the society, such as climatic conditions, the subsistence occupations (e.g. hunting, agriculture), technology (e.g. metallurgy, ceramics) and trade (Binford 1965). Thus for the Palaeolithic period, changes in climate with their consequent modification of the subsistence occupations are dominant causes of development. In contrast, the cultural contacts and requirements associated with trade, which itself could be dependent on the development of a new technology (e.g. metallurgy), are probably of primary importance in explaining the more rapid cultural development subsequent to the Neolithic "revolution" (Renfrew, 1969b).

The intrusion of science and mathematics into archaeology is still feared by some archaeologists who see these techniques as a "monster" which will devour and dehumanize the subject (Hawkes, 1968). This fear is expressed especially with respect to the use of mathematical techniques in the classification of artefacts and artefactual assemblages since typological classification is regarded as the prime concern of the archaeologist himself: the more subservient natural scientist is less feared since he is seen to be adding information in an essentially new dimension. However these fears are both damaging to the subject and unjustified since, in the first place, it is essential that the archaeologist makes full use of the information provided by the natural sciences and mathematics if he is to achieve an accurate reconstruction of the human past. Secondly, in spite of the increased range of data made available, the archaeologist should still remain in full control of the final co-ordination and interpretation of this accumulated data and it is at this fundamental stage that the subject retains its humanistic aspects.

It is, however, accepted that this multidisciplinary approach to the subject does place a considerable burden on the individual archaeologist since it is essential that he understands something of the general principles of the scientific and mathematical techniques employed. Otherwise he will find it difficult either to ask the appropriate questions or to appreciate the potentialities and limitations of the techniques.

The present volume is concerned with the description of those techniques, derived from the physical sciences, which can be used for the location of buried features on archaeological sites (Chapter 2), for age determination (Chapters 3–6) and for the study of artefacts and biological material (Chapters 7–10). A wide range of examples of the application of these techniques to archaeology is presented, except in the case of the physical examination of biological material where the interpretation of the resulting data remains the province of the associated specialist (i.e. botanist, zoologist, anatomist, pathologist, soil scientist), rather than the physical scientist who has provided the basic equipment.

References

Binford, L. R. (1965). Archaeological systematics and the study of culture process. *Am. Antiq.* **31**, 203–210.
Childe, V. G. (1957). "The Dawn of European Civilisation," Routledge and Kegan Paul, London.

Clark, J. G. D. (1966). The invasion hypothesis in British prehistory. *Antiquity* **40**, 172–189.

Hawkes, J. (1968). The proper study of mankind. *Antiquity* **42**, 255–262.

Hodson, F. R. (1970). Cluster analysis and archaeology: some new developments and applications. *Wld Archaeol.* **1**, 299–320.

Isaac, G. Ll. (1971). Whither archaeology? *Antiquity* **45**, 123–129.

Jewell, P. A. (Ed.) (1963). "The Experimental Earthwork on Overton Down, Wiltshire, 1960", *Br. Ass. Adv. Sci., London.*

Jewell, P. A. and Dimbleby, G. W. (Eds.) (1966). The experimental earthwork on Overton Down, Wiltshire: the first four years. *Proc. prehist. Soc.* **32**, 313–342.

Kendall, D. G. (1970). A mathematical approach to seriation. *Phil. Trans. R. Soc. Lond.* A**269**, 125–135.

Mayes, P. (1961). The firing of a pottery kiln of a Romano-British type at Boston, Lincs. *Archaeometry* **4**, 4–30.

Mayes, P. (1962). The firing of a second pottery kiln of Romano-British type at Boston, Lincs. *Archaeometry* **5**, 80–92.

Neustupný, E. (1971). Whither archaeology? *Antiquity* **45**, 34–39.

Renfrew, C. (1968). Wessex without Mycenae. *Ann. Br. Schl. Archaeol., Athens* **63**, 277–285.

Renfrew, C. (1969a). The autonomy of the South-east European Copper Age. *Proc. prehist. Soc.* **35**, 12–47.

Renfrew, C. (1969b). Trade and culture process in European prehistory. *Curr. Anthropol.* **10**, 151–169.

Trigger, B. G. (1970). Aims in prehistoric archaeology. *Antiquity* **44**, 26–37.

2

Location

Archaeological sites become buried to depths varying between a few inches and tens of feet by the accumulation of soil through the action of wind, water or worms. Evidence for their existence can occur through the chance discovery of a scatter of pottery fragments on the surface following ploughing or through the chance exposure of walls or ditches when the topsoil is removed prior to road building, for example. Alternatively, many new sites have been found by the deliberate visual examination of a region, either at ground level or from the air. Apart from the existence of obvious man-made features such as the ramparts and ditches surrounding an Iron Age hill-fort, a series of shallow mounds and hollows, visible at ground level, could indicate the presence of a deserted mediaeval village. It is, however, aerial photography which provides the most powerful visual technique for the location of archaeological sites (Plate 3. In this case the visual evidence consists of crop-marks, soil-marks and slight differences in relief (shadow-marks) which only appear when viewed from above, preferably at an oblique angle. Typically crop-marks result from the different moisture conditions in the vicinity of buried features. Because of the lower moisture content of the soil, the crop above a buried wall ripens prematurely and therefore produces a lighter line on the photograph. In contrast, because of the higher moisture content above a ditch, the crop is richer in growth and is therefore darker in appearance.

Having established the existence of an archaeological site by one of the above methods, geophysical prospecting techniques can then be used to locate specific buried features such as kilns, pit, ditches, roads and walls within the site (Aitken, 1961; Hesse, 1966; Keller and Frischknecht, 1966; Parasnis, 1962). For example, where a ditch or wall system is revealed by aerial photography, geophysical techniques can be used to establish its precise position on the ground and also detect any associated features such as pits and kilns which do not normally show up on aerial photographs. In addition to locating features for immediate excavation, these techniques can provide an indication of the overall pattern of occupation on the site and can help to define the limits of the site.

Consequently, although not removing the need for excavation, geophysical prospecting techniques do indicate those areas which are likely to prove most rewarding as well as supplementing the archaeological results obtained from the excavated areas. These techniques have therefore been increasingly exploited during the past decade since, with the threatened destruction of many important archaeological sites by urban expansion, road building and quarrying as well as the increasing cost of manual labour, the rapid and cheap location of buried features has become imperative.

The location of buried archaeological features using geophysical techniques depends on the differences between the physical properties of the feature itself and those of the soil or subsoil surrounding it. Magnetic surveying (p. 9), which involves detecting the small localized changes in the intensity of the Earth's magnetic field associated with buried features, has been of prime importance following its first successful application on an archaeological site in 1958 (Aitken *et al.*, 1958). Resistivity surveying (p. 25), which involves the insertion of electrodes into the ground and the measurement of its electrical resistance, was first employed on an archaeological site in 1946 (Atkinson, 1952) and although its popularity waned with the advent of the more rapid magnetic surveying techniques, it still provides a valuable alternative in many instances. Various electromagnetic instruments (p. 32) have recently been used to detect buried features in addition to their more normal application as metal detectors while induced polarization techniques (p. 39), which are in many ways related to resistivity surveying, have also been adapted for the location of archaeological features. The possibility of using seismic techniques for the location of archaeological features has also been investigated (Carson, 1962; Linington, 1963). In spite of their great importance in geological exploration, these techniques, which involve studying the transmission through the ground of elastic waves, generated by a hammer blow or explosion at the surface, have proved to be of limited value for the location of the small-scale features of interest in archaeology and are therefore not considered further.

The presentation and analysis of survey data is discussed on p. 41 while the results obtained with geophysical prospecting techniques on a range of archaeological sites are presented on p. 43.

Magnetic Surveying

Magnetic surveying involves the measurement of the Earth's magnetic field intensity to an accuracy of $\pm 10^{-3}$ A m^{-1} (1 A m^{-1} = $4\pi \times 10^{-3}$ oersted = $4\pi \times 10^2$ gamma) using, typically, a proton magnetometer. Buried archaeological features can then be located because they produce a localized change of between 2×10^{-3} and 2×10^{-1} A m^{-1} in the magnetic field intensity which for England is approximately 38 A m^{-1}.

The magnetic disturbance associated with metallic iron is well known, the deflection of a compass needle when placed near to an iron object being an obvious illustration. In contrast, the magnetic disturbance associated with archaeological features is very much weaker and arises because of subtle variations in the condition of the few per cent of iron oxide present in most soils, clays and rocks. Fired structures (e.g. pottery kilns, furnaces, hearths and ovens) produce a localized increase in the magnetic field intensity because they have acquired a weak permanent magnetism, referred to as thermoremanent magnetism, as a result of the firing. Pits and ditches produce a similar localized increase because their fillings have a higher magnetic susceptibility than that of the subsoil into which they have been cut. Walls and roads, in contrast, normally produce a localized decrease since the subsoil material (e.g. rock or gravel) from which they have been constructed has a lower susceptibility than that of the soil surrounding them.

General Principles

Since the average iron oxide content of the Earth's crust is approximately 6·8 per cent, most soils, clays and rocks can be expected to contain between 1 and 10 per cent of iron oxide. In the context of magnetic surveying, the relevant oxides are haematite (αFe_2O_3), magnetite (Fe_3O_4) and maghaemite (γFe_2O_3), all of which are ferrimagnetic: ferrimagnetism being related to the ferromagnetism which produces the permanent magnetism associated with metallic iron. The

oxidized form, haematite, is weakly magnetic (saturation magnetization = 6 × 10^{-7} Wb m/kg) while the reduced form, magnetite, and
the oxidized form, maghaemite, are both strongly magnetic
(saturation magnetization = 1·2 × 10^{-4} and 1·0 × 10^{-4} Wb m/kg
respectively). Maghaemite, although having the same chemical
formula as haematite and being converted to haematite when heated
to high temperatures, is strongly magnetic because its crystal
structure is more similar to that of magnetite.

The iron oxides exist in soil, clay or rock as very small well-dispersed
grains which are each spontaneously magnetized and can be satisfactorily discussed in terms of isolated sub-microscopic magnets, that is
single magnetic domains (Chapter 5, p. 135).

Thermoremanent magnetism. The location of fired structures is possible
because of the thermoremanent magnetism acquired as a result of the
firing. In unfired clay, the magnetic domains which represent the dispersed iron oxide grains point in random directions (Fig. 1a) so that

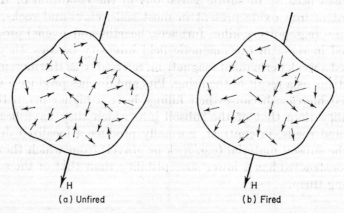

(a) Unfired   (b) Fired

Figure 1. Acquisition of thermoremanent magnetism in the Earth's magnetic field (H).
(a) In unfired clay, the magnetic domains are randomly orientated so that the nett
magnetic moment is zero. (b) At elevated temperatures the direction of the magnetic
domains can reverse so that they have a component parallel rather than antiparallel
to the magnetic field (*H*). Hence in the fired clay, there is a nett magnetic moment
parallel to *H*.

the resultant permanent magnetic moment is zero. However, when the
clay is heated to high temperatures, reversal of the direction of magnetization can occur as a result of thermal agitation. Since the direction
parallel to the Earth's magnetic field is favoured, there then exists a

fractional excess of grains whose magnetization is parallel, rather than antiparallel, to the Earth's magnetic field direction. During subsequent cooling, this fractional excess remains frozen in position (Fig. 1b), thus leaving the clay with a nett permanent magnetic moment in the direction of the Earth's magnetic field. The existence of this thermo-remanent magnetism in fired clay can be readily demonstrated by holding a modern brick close to a compass needle when a deflection of half a degree or more is normally observed.

The specific remanent magnetization (i.e. the permanent magnetic moment per kg) of fired clay depends on the concentration of iron oxide, the crystalline form of the iron oxide (i.e. haematite or magne-tite), the temperature to which it was fired and the intensity of the magnetic field in which cooling occurred. Although the maximum effect occurs when the clay is heated to above the Curie temperature for the iron oxide (i.e. 580°C for magnetite and 650°C for haematite), any elevated temperature produces some thermoremanent magnetiza-tion. Typically for clays cooled from approximately 650°C in the Earth's magnetic field, the specific remanent magnetization varies between 10^{-10} and 10^{-7} Wb m/kg (1 Wb m/kg = $10^{7}/4\pi$ emu/g). The lower limit applies to red highly oxidized clays in which the con-version of the iron oxide to haematite is nearly complete and the upper limit to grey reduced clays in which magnetite is predominant.

In addition to providing a means of locating fired structures, the direction of the thermoremanent magnetism provides a record of the direction of the Earth's magnetic field at the time of firing and thus forms the basis for magnetic dating. This method of age determination is discussed in Chapter 5 (p. 134) where the theory of thermoremanent magnetism is also described in more detail.

Magnetic susceptibility of soils. The magnetic disturbances which per-mit the location of unfired features (i.e. pits, ditches, walls, etc.) arise from differences in magnetic susceptibility. The magnetic suscepti-bility expresses the magnetic moment *induced* in 1 kg of sample when it is placed in a magnetic field of 1 A m^{-1}. This induced magnetization occurs without heat treatment since even at ordinary temperatures some rotation of the magnetic domains, representing the iron oxide grains, towards the direction of the applied magnetic field occurs and a small magnetization results. In contrast to the thermoremanent magnetism, the induced magnetization is essentially temporary in that if the magnetic field is removed, the magnetization disappears while if the sample is rotated, the magnetization remains in the direction of the magnetic field. In the context of magnetic surveying on archaeological sites, the applied field is of course the Earth's magnetic field, so that the specific magnetization is obtained by multiplying the susceptibility by the Earth's magnetic field intensity and the permeability of free space ($\mu_0 = 4\pi \times 10^{-7}$ H m^{-1}).

The enhanced magnetic susceptibility of natural soils compared to that of the subsoil from which they have been derived was first observed and studied by Le Borgne (1955, 1960). This increase in susceptibility results from the conversion of the iron oxide from its weakly magnetic form, haematite, to the strongly magnetic form, maghaemite; the conversion proceeding via reduction to magnetite followed by re-oxidation to maghaemite. Two possible mechanisms for the conversion have been suggested. The first, which is thought to be of primary importance, is associated with the cumulative effects of fires on the soil, the fires possibly occurring during the clearance of the ground prior to cultivation. When vegetable matter is burnt, air is excluded from the underlying soil so that reduction of the iron oxide occurs while when the fires cool, air reaches the soil and results in the re-oxidation of the iron oxide. Consequently, a thin layer of soil underlying the fire acquires an enhanced susceptibility and subsequent disturbance of the soil through cultivation, followed by further fires, will ultimately produce enhancement throughout the topsoil: at the same time cultivation destroys the thermoremanent magnetism acquired during the fire. The second mechanism occurs at ordinary temperatures and is associated with the decay of organic material during periods of humidity and dryness. Reduction of the iron oxide occurs in the anaerobic conditions provided during wet periods while re-oxidation occurs in the aerobic conditions associated with subsequent dry periods.

On archaeological sites a similar enhancement in the susceptibility of the topsoil and the filling of pits or ditches is observed. In this case the enhancement is achieved through the action of domestic fires and decaying organic rubbish associated with human habitation; either of the mechanisms outlined above being possible. The susceptibility (χ) of soils depends first on the fraction of the iron oxides which has been converted to the strongly magnetic form, maghaemite, and secondly on the concentration of iron oxide in the soil which is available for conversion. High fractional conversion of the iron oxide, and hence high susceptibility soils, will be found on those sites which have been intensively occupied over a large period of time since these conditions provide the necessary large number of fires and high concentration of organic material. The concentration of iron oxide in the soils depends on the geological strata from which they were derived. A figure, representative of the iron oxide content of the soil, is provided by the magnetic susceptibility (χ_H) after the iron oxides have been converted to magnetite by heating the soil in a reducing atmosphere (e.g. hydrogen)

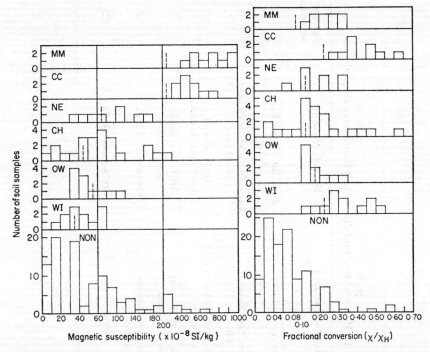

Figure 2. Histograms showing the distribution of values for (a) susceptibility (χ) and (b) fractional conversion (χ/χ_H) for soil samples from pits and ditches on archaeological sites (see Table 1) and for samples of normal agricultural topsoil (NON). The values for the topsoil from archaeological sites are indicated by the dashed vertical lines. Note changes in scale at 60×10^{-8} and 200×10^{-8} SI/kg for susceptibility and at 0·10 for fractional conversion.

in the laboratory; the fractional conversion is then given by the ratio χ/χ_H (Tite and Mullins, 1971).

The range of soil susceptibilities (χ) and fractional conversions (χ/χ_H) observed on typical sites in England is illustrated in Fig. 2 while the associated archaeological and geological data are presented in Table 1. Differences in the susceptibility of soils from a particular site reflect

Table 1. Magnetic susceptibility of soil from archaeological sites

Code	Site	Archaeological data	Subsoil geology	Susceptibility ($\times 10^{-8}$ SI/kg) Subsoil (χ)	Soil (χ_H)
MM	Madmarston, Oxon.	Iron Age hill-fort	Jurassic–Upper Lias (clay)	5	3000
CC	Cadbury Castle, Somerset	Iron Age–Saxon hill-fort	Jurassic–Inferior Oolite (limestone)	3	1200
NE	N. Elmham, Norfolk	Saxon–post Mediaeval settlement	Drift–glacial (sand, gravel, clay)	15	500
CH	Colchester, Essex	Iron Age–Roman settlement	Drift–Postglacial (sand, gravel)	2	400
OW	Owlesbury, Hants.	Iron Age–Roman settlement	Cretaceous–chalk	6	300
WI	Winchester	Mediaeval town	Cretaceous–chalk	12	130

differences in fractional conversion due presumably to variations in the localized burning to which the various individual features were subjected. In contrast the different ranges of susceptibility observed on different sites (e.g. site WI compared to site MM) are due principally to variations in the iron oxide content of the soils derived from different geological strata. Thus the ranges of fractional conversion observed on different sites are similar except in the case of a site, such as Cadbury Castle (CC), which has been very intensively occupied over a long period. Further it can be seen from Fig. 2b that, as a result of the fires and organic rubbish associated with human habitation, the fractional conversion for soils from archaeological sites tends to be higher than that for normal agricultural soils.

Hence, although the magnetic susceptibility of soil (i.e. topsoil, pit and ditch fillings) is normally greater than that of the subsoil, the extent of the enhancement varies widely: typical subsoils have susceptibilities in the range 2×10^{-8} to 25×10^{-8} SI/kg while for soil the range is 5×10^{-8} to 1200×10^{-8} SI/kg (1 SI/kg $= 10^3/4\pi$ emu/g.). Since the location of buried features by magnetic surveying depends essentially on a large susceptibility contrast between the soil and subsoil, the technique is most appropriate on sites that have been intensively occupied and whose soil has been derived from geological strata containing a high concentration of iron oxide. From the data presented in Table 1 it is apparent that sites situated on chalk or the glacial and Postglacial deposits of East Anglia are less suitable than those situated on the Jurassic strata (Lias and Inferior Oolite) which extend across England from Dorset through Oxfordshire to Lincolnshire.

Magnetic anomalies. As indicated above, the presence of buried archaeological features produces a localized increase or decrease in the Earth's magnetic field intensity, this localized change being referred to as the magnetic anomaly. In order to calculate the magnetic anomaly associated with a particular feature it is convenient to make a number of simplifying approximations, in particular uniform magnetization of the feature and a simplified shape is assumed.

Kilns are assumed to be spherical so that the magnetic anomaly is equal to that produced by a dipole with the same magnetic moment and placed at the centre of sphere. The values calculated for the maximum magnetic anomaly associated with a kiln containing 500 kg of fired clay with specific remanent magnetization in the range 10^{-11} to

10^{-7} Wb m/kg are presented in Table 2, various values for the depth below the present ground surface being considered. Pits are assumed to be cylindrical and only the component of magnetization along the axis is considered (i.e. the component due to the vertical component

Table 2. Magnetic anomalies produced by "spherical" kilns (mass 500 kg)

Specific remanent magnetization (Wb m/kg)	Magnetic anomaly[a] ($\times 10^{-3}$ A m^{-1})			
	$h^b = 0.6$ m	$h = 0.9$ m	$h = 1.2$ m	$h = 1.5$ m
10^{-10}	7·0	3·0	1·5	0·9
10^{-9}	70	30	15	8·8
10^{-8}	700	300	150	88
10^{-7}	7000	3000	1500	880

[a] The magnetic anomaly is calculated for an angle of dip of 60 degrees.
[b] h is the distance from the ground surface to the centre of the sphere representing the kiln. The height of the detector (e.g. proton magnetometer bottle) above the ground surface is taken as 0·3m.

of the Earth's magnetic field). Table 3 contains the values for the maximum magnetic anomaly calculated for cylindrical shallow and deep pits of diameter, 1 m, for which the difference in susceptibility ($\Delta\chi$)

Table 3. Magnetic anomalies produced by cylindrical pits (diameter 1 m)

Susceptibility contrast ($\Delta\chi$) ($\times 10^{-8}$SI/kg)	Pit depth[a] (m)	Magnetic anomaly[b] ($\times 10^{-3}$ A m^{-1})			
		$h^c = 0.3$ m	$h = 0.6$ m	$h = 0.9$ m	$h = 1.2$ m
10	0·3	0·4	0·2	0·1	<0·1
	1·0	0·6	0·3	0·2	0·1
100	0·3	3·7	1·7	0·9	0·5
	1·0	6·5	3·3	1·8	1·1
1000	0·3	37	17	9·0	5·2
	1·0	65	33	18	11

[a] Pit depth refers to the depth of the pit below the surface of the low susceptibility subsoil.
[b] In calculating the magnetic anomaly it is assumed that, as a result of magnetic viscosity phenomena, the magnetic susceptibility of the soils in situ is twice the value ($\Delta\chi$) measured in the laboratory.
[c] h is the distance from the ground surface to the top of the pit (i.e. topsoil thickness), the height of the detector (e.g. proton magnetometer bottle) above the ground surface being taken as 0·3 m.

between the pit filling and surrounding subsoil is in the range 10^{-7} to 10^{-5} SI/kg (i.e. specific magnetization in the approximate range 5×10^{-12} to 5×10^{-10} Wb m/kg).

We can see from the data presented in Tables 2 and 3, that the magnetic anomalies associated with typical archaeological features are in the range 10^{-4} to 1 A m^{-1}. In addition to these anomalies, essentially random variations in the magnetic field strength of between 10^{-3} and 10^{-2} A m^{-1} are observed as a result of small variations in the thickness and magnetic properties of the topsoil. These variations, referred to as "soil noise", will therefore mask the anomaly due to buried features unless the latter is greater than approximately 2×10^{-3} to 5×10^{-3} A m^{-1}. Consequently, in interpreting the results of a magnetic survey, the possibility that the feature is too deep or has too low a magnetization to produce a detectable magnetic anomaly must always be considered. The calculated magnetic anomaly

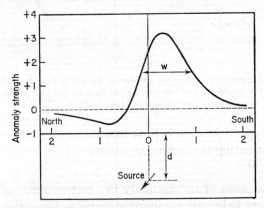

Figure 3. Idealized magnetic anomaly. The source (kiln or pit) is assumed to be equivalent to a magnetic dipole at a depth, d. The angle of dip is taken to be 60 degrees. The anomaly strength represents the deviation (in arbitrary units) from the normal magnetic field intensity. The horizontal scale, representing a north–south traverse through the centre of the anomaly, is in units of depth, d.

data further indicates that kilns and other fired clay structures, as a result of their thermoremanent magnetism, normally produce stronger anomalies than pits. However, on sites where the soil susceptibility is exceptionally high, it is sometimes difficult to distinguish between these two types of feature. The smaller anomalies, and hence the increased problems of location, associated with shallow pits as compared to deep pits should also be noted.

The shape of the magnetic anomaly along a line passing over the centre of the buried feature can be calculated if a uniformly magnetized spherical feature is again assumed (Smellie, 1956). Since the measured field is the vector sum of the Earth's magnetic field and the magnetic field due to the feature, the shape of the anomaly depends on the geomagnetic latitude; the angle of dip (i.e. direction of the Earth's magnetic field with respect to the horizontal) varying from 0 degrees at the equator to 90 degrees at the magnetic poles. For northwest Europe, where the angle of dip is in the range 60–70 degrees, the idealized anomaly is as shown in Fig. 3, while actual anomaly profiles

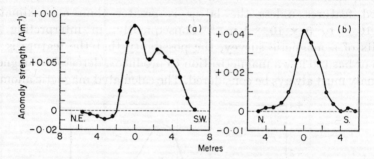

Figure 4. Typical magnetic anomalies produced by (a) a kiln and (b) a pit along a traverse through the centre of the feature. In the case of the kiln profile, the secondary peak to the S.W. is associated with the kiln stoke-hole.

obtained for typical kilns and pits, located in England, are shown in Fig. 4. In interpreting the anomalies obtained in Europe, the following rules are helpful.

(a) The maximum of the anomaly lies to the south of the feature, the displacement being approximately equal to 1/3 of the depth to the centre of the feature.

(b) The separation (W) between the two points, in a straight line traverse, at which the anomaly has half its maximum value is approximately equal to the depth or width of the feature, whichever is greater.

(c) A reverse anomaly (i.e. decrease in magnetic field intensity) may occur to the north of the feature at a distance equal to the depth; the reverse anomaly does not exceed 10 per cent of the maximum normal anomaly except in the case of metallic iron.

Instruments

For the measurement of magnetic field intensity on archaeological sites an instrument capable of detecting changes in field of less than

5×10^{-3} A m^{-1} is normally essential. In addition portability, speed and simplicity of operation are important factors. Of the instruments which satisfy these criteria, the proton magnetometer has been used most extensively on archaeological sites up to the present time. In addition the fluxgate magnetometer, which has the advantage of providing a continuous measurement of the magnetic field strength, has been employed while trials with the more sensitive rubidium vapour magnetometer have recently been carried out.

All three instruments can in principle be operated in two distinct modes. In the first, a single detector element (e.g. proton source, fluxgate, etc.) is used to provide an absolute value for the Earth's magnetic field intensity. In the second, two detector elements, carried at opposite ends of a vertical staff, are employed and the field difference or gradient between them is determined. Zero field difference is observed except in the vicinity of a buried feature when the associated magnetic anomaly has a larger effect on the field at the lower detector. This latter differential mode has a number of advantages over the absolute magnetometer. In the first place it does not record changes in field strength associated with regular diurnal variations (approximately 5×10^{-3} A m^{-1} per hour), magnetic storms (10^{-2} A m^{-1} per minute) or d.c. electrical trains. It also tends to ignore the spacially more extensive anomalies associated with geological features. Finally with a differential instrument it is possible to determine directly the sign of the magnetic anomaly whereas with the absolute instrument the average undisturbed field strength for the site must first be ascertained and on a complex site this is sometimes difficult. Thus the normal anomalies (i.e. increase in field strength) associated with kilns, pits and ditches can be readily distinguished from the reverse anomalies (i.e. decrease in field strength) associated with walls and roads.

Proton magnetometer (Waters and Francis, 1958). The proton which is an elementary particle identical with the nucleus of the hydrogen atom, can be regarded as a tiny bar magnet spinning about its longitudinal axis. Because of its magnetic moment, the proton tends to align itself in the direction of the Earth's magnetic field but as a result of its spin, it performs gyrations while in the process of achieving this direction; these gyrations being similar to those of a spinning top under the influence of gravity (Fig. 5). The frequency of precession (i.e. the speed of gyration) of the proton is exactly proportional to the magnetic field intensity, this frequency being approximately 2000 Hz in a field of 38 A m^{-1} (i.e. the average value for the Earth's field intensity in England).

The detector for the proton magnetometer typically consists of a 200 cm^3 bottle of water or alcohol around which is wound a 1000 turn coil; the nuclei of the hydrogen atoms in the water or alcohol providing the source of protons. An essential preliminary to measurement of the field intensity is the polarizing period (3 sec) during which a current of 1 A is passed through the coil. This provides a magnetic field of several thousand A m^{-1} along the axis of the coil and therefore aligns a fraction of the protons in this direction. When the polarizing field is switched off, the protons gyrate (i.e. precess) about the direction of

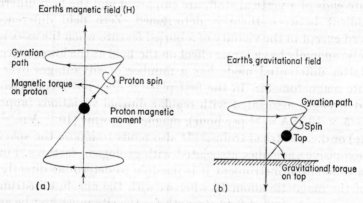

Figure 5. Gyrations performed by (a) a proton in a magnetic field and (b) a spinning top in a gravitational field.

the Earth's magnetic field and induce an alternating voltage of approximately 1 μV in the coil around the bottle. This voltage is then amplified and its frequency measured in the instrument itself which is normally attached to the detector bottle by 30 m of flexible cable. The electronic circuitry permits measurement of the frequency to an accuracy of 1 part in 50 000 within half a second and this corresponds to the required sensitivity for the field intensity of 10^{-3} A m^{-1}. The polarizing period is necessary before each measurement because internal magnetic inhomogeneities within the liquid cause the gyrating protons to lose phase coherence. Hence the signal decays to zero within a few seconds. External magnetic field gradients such as exist close to iron objects can further reduce the duration of the signal.

A typical instrument suitable for archaeological prospecting (Plate

4) is manufactured by the Littlemore Scientific Instrument Co., Oxford. In this the sequence of polarization and measurement is carried out automatically so that the only action required for operation is to read the five meters displaying the frequency. The electrical circuit is fully transistorized so that the instrument is portable and weighs less than 10 kg, including built-in accumulators with sufficient capacity for a full day's work. The major drawback of the absolute proton magneto-meter is the complexity of the electrical circuits and its consequent high cost (typically more than £800). This problem is overcome, with some loss in sensitivity, through the development of a proton "gradio-meter".

In the proton gradiometer (Aitken and Tite, 1962a), two detector bottles carried at either end of a vertically-held staff, which is 2 m or more in length, are used. In the absence of a magnetic anomaly, the two bottles experience the same field intensity and the proton pre-cession frequency in the two bottles is therefore identical. Conse-quently, if the two signals are fed in series to the amplifier, the re-sultant signal is twice the amplitude of the individual signals and decays away in a few seconds as normal. However, in the presence of a buried feature, the two bottles experience slightly different field in-tensities so that the two frequencies are slightly different and the two signals gradually get out of step. The resultant signal therefore decays to zero more rapidly and if the anomaly is sufficiently strong, it in-creases again, exhibiting a series of maxima and minima referred to as "beats" (Fig. 6). The resultant signal, after amplification, is nor-mally displayed on a meter on which the more rapid decay or "beats" associated with an anomaly can be readily observed. A field difference of 5×10^{-3} A m^{-1} between the two bottles can easily be measured since this corresponds to the signal decaying to zero in approximately 2·3 sec whereas in the absence of any field difference, the signal still retains 40 per cent of its original amplitude at that time. By applying a field difference of known sign, using a small coil placed between the bottles, the sign of the magnetic anomaly associated with the buried feature can be determined.

Although less sensitive than the absolute magnetometer, this is not normally a limitation and in any case is outweighed by the significant reduction in cost achieved through the use of much simpler elec-tronics. Commercial instruments (Wardle and Davenport, Staffs.) cost approximately £100 while, with some knowledge of electronics, it is possible to make a gradiometer for considerably less. In addition, the gradiometer possesses all the advantages of a differential instrument outlined above.

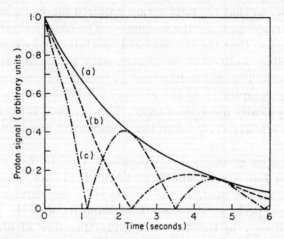

Figure 6. Proton signal (after amplification) associated with a proton gradiometer when the magnetic field difference between the two bottles is (a) zero (exponential decay with time constant, 2·5 sec), (b) 5×10^{-3} A m^{-1} (beat frequency = 0·215 Hz) and (c) 10^{-2} A m^{-1} (beat frequency = 0.430 Hz).

Differential fluxgate magnetometer (Alldred, 1964). The fluxgate detector contains, typically, mu-metal wires having high magnetic permeability and around which primary and secondary coils are wound. A pure sine wave voltage (frequency 1kHz) is applied to the primary coil so that the mu-metal is continuously taken round its hysteresis loop. When a steady (i.e. d.c.) external field, such as the Earth's magnetic field, is present, the voltage induced in the secondary coil contains harmonics of the drive frequency. The amplitude of the second harmonic (i.e. twice the drive frequency) is proportional to the strength of the component of the external field parallel to the axis of the detector and is sensitive to its direction (i.e. sign). As with the proton gradiometer, two fluxgate detectors are carried vertically above one another and the difference in field intensities between them, such as occurs in the presence of a buried feature, is displayed on a meter.

This type of magnetometer has a sensitivity of between 2×10^{-3} and 5×10^{-3} A m^{-1}. In comparison with the proton magnetometer, the operation of which involves a polarization period followed by an individual measurement of field intensity, the major advantage of the fluxgate magnetometer is that measurements of the field intensity are obtained continuously; thus the area to be surveyed can be covered at a higher speed. In addition, it has all the advantages associated with differential instruments. Unfortunately, because of complex electronics and the need for accurate alignment of the fluxgate detectors, the cost of commercially available instruments (Plessey Co., Havant) is comparable to that of the absolute proton magnetometer.

Rubidium vapour magnetometer (Langan, 1966). The operational principle of the rubidium vapour magnetometer is analogous to that of the proton magnetometer in that both involve measurement of a precession frequency which is proportional to the magnetic field intensity. In this case, however, the magnetic moment precessing about the direction of the magnetic field is associated with the atomic electrons of the rubidium vapour.

The precessing magnetic moments cause a modulation, at the precession frequency, of the intensity of a light beam passing through the rubidum vapour and measurement of the modulation frequency provides a value for the magnetic field intensity.

The precession frequency in the Earth's magnetic field in England is approximately 200 kHz compared to 2 kHz for proton precession and consequently measurements of the magnetic field intensity can in principle be made to an accuracy of 10^{-5} A m^{-1}. As with the proton magnetometer, this instrument can be used in either the absolute or differential mode.

The cost of commercially available instruments (Varian Assoc., California, U.S.A.) is very high, even when compared to the absolute proton magnetometer. In addition, its increased sensitivity is not normally of any value on archaeological sites since "soil noise" causes random variations in the magnetic field intensity of between 2×10^{-3} and 5×10^{-3} A m^{-1}. The rubidium magnetometer has therefore found only limited application for the location of archaeological features (Ralph, 1964).

Survey Logistics

Since random measurements of magnetic field intensity tend to produce extremely misleading information, systematically spaced measurements over the area to be surveyed are essential. To achieve this end, the area is typically marked out with wooden pegs (free from iron nails) so as to form a grid of 50 ft squares. Each square is then covered in turn by a net with 10 ft mesh size so that field intensity measurements can be taken over the square at 5 ft intervals, thus involving 100 measurements per square. Closer spacing between measurements would of course provide more information but would necessarily increase the time taken over the survey. In any case abnormal field readings are subsequently investigated with more closely spaced measurements in order to determine the maximum strength of the anomaly, its spacial extent and to pin-point its centre on the ground. Using this technique it is possible to survey an area of between 1 and 2 acres per day.

In considering the suitability of a site for magnetic surveying, the primary factors are of course the extent to which the soil susceptibility has been enhanced and the depth at which the features are buried. In addition, several possible hazards must be considered. Trees, undergrowth, long grass, nettles and thistles may impede the movement of the cable between the detector and instrument such as to seriously reduce the speed of the survey. The proximity of a.c. electrical power cables or radio transmitting stations is liable to cause interference with the operation of the instrument. Iron fences, buildings, buried water pipes and gas mains produce their own magnetic anomalies which may mask or simulate the anomalies associated with buried archaeological features.

Surface iron litter also produces strong localized magnetic anomalies. These can, however, normally be distinguished from the anomalies associated with pits and kilns by detailed measurements since being small and close to the surface, the half-width of the anomaly is typically less than 0·4 m. In addition, surface iron tends to produce a strong reverse anomaly (i.e. a decrease in magnetic field strength) to its north and also because of the associated high magnetic field gradient, the proton signal decays to zero more rapidly than normal. However, large quantities of iron litter, as found near to modern habitation, significantly reduce the speed of the survey.

More fundamental difficulties can arise on sites located on some geological strata. The thermoremanent magnetism acquired by igneous and metamorphic rocks on cooling from the molten state, is sometimes sufficiently strong to mask the archaeological anomalies. This applies particularly to recent basalts of the Tertiary period, while on older basalts and granites, the thermoremanent magnetism is much weaker and magnetic surveying is normally possible. In addition, natural depressions in the subsoil filled with soil of higher susceptibility can frequently produce anomalies similar in magnitude and dimensions to those associated with pits.

Finally, as mentioned above, the presence of d.c. power lines or the occurrence of magnetic storms can create difficulties when an absolute magnetometer is used but these problems are readily overcome with a differential instrument.

Resistivity Surveying

Resistivity surveying involves applying a voltage to the ground via metal electrodes inserted into it and measuring its resistance to the flow of electric current. Buried archaeological features can then be detected because they have a different water content, and hence a different electrical resistance, to that of the soil or subsoil surrounding them. Although in principle the method can be used to locate both linear features (wall, roads and ditches) and isolated features (pits, kilns), because of the comparatively slow speed of operation and difficulties with interpretation, it has principally been used for the detection of linear features.

The advantages of resistivity surveying in comparison to magnetic surveying include the simplicity and consequent cheapness of the instrumentation and the fact that measurements are unaffected by buildings, power cables and surface iron, thus permitting operation in the middle of towns and close to modern habitation.

General Principles

With the exception of certain mineral bodies which conduct electricity because of their metallic content, soils and rocks when completely dry are non-conductors of electricity. When they contain water, the resistivity drops considerably and they must then be considered as conductors, although very poor compared with metals. The resistivity of soil and rocks is therefore determined by the quantity of water retained in the interstices and by the concentration of dissolved salts and humic acids of biological origin in the water. The conduction process is electrolytic, the electric current being carried by the positive and negative ions in the solution. Hard compact rocks, such as granite and sandstone, are poor conductors while the more porous limestones are much better, though still poor by comparison with soil, sand and clays. Representative values for electrical resistivity are given in Table 4. In terms of archaeological applications, it can be assumed that stones and rocks have a high resistivity compared to soils and clays, the latter group showing wide variations depending on their water content. Consequently, stone walls and roads intruding into soil will normally produce a region of high electrical resistance while soil-filled ditches cut into rocky subsoil will produce a region of low resistance.

Table 4. Electrical resistivities of rocks, clay and soil (ohm m)

Granite	5000–1 000 000
Sandstone	100–10 000
Limestone	100–1000
Sand and gravel	60–1000
Clay	1–1000
Soil	1–1000

A typical system for resistivity surveying consists of four equally spaced metal electrodes inserted into the ground as shown in Fig. 7. An a.c. power source provides current flow (I) between the two outer electrodes and the resultant voltage difference (V) between the two inner electrodes is measured, the resistance of the ground being given

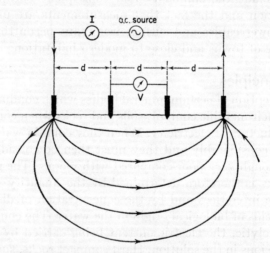

Figure 7. Typical electrode arrangement (Wenner array) for resistivity surveying. The current paths through homogeneous earth are also shown.

by V/I. The use of four electrodes together with an a.c. power source satisfactorily overcomes difficulties associated with variable contact resistance between the electrode and the soil, electrode polarization, contact voltages and natural earth currents.

For a linear array of four equally spaced electrodes (i.e. the Wenner array) in homogeneous earth, the current paths are as shown in Fig. 7 and the resistance measured (R ohm) is related to the specific resistivity (ρ ohm m) of the earth by the equation:

$$\rho = 2\pi d . R \qquad (2.1)$$

where d is the spacing between the electrodes in metres. The value of resistivity thus obtained is representative of the earth beneath the inner electrodes down to a depth of approximately $1 \cdot 5d$. If, however, the ground consists of two layers of widely differing resistivity, such as wet topsoil above impervious rock, then the current paths are distorted so that the majority of the current flows through the low resistivity topsoil and equation (2.1) is no longer applicable.

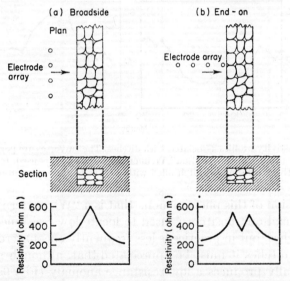

Figure 8. Idealized resistivity profiles associated with a stone wall surrounded by low resistivity soil. The traverses, which are in the directions indicated by the arrows, are perpendicular to the line of the wall. (a) "Broadside" and (b) "end-on" electrode positions are used.

The changes in resistance observed in the vicinity of a buried linear archaeological feature depend critically on the alignment of the electrodes with respect to the feature. Two alignments, the "broadside" position, with the line of electrodes parallel to the feature, and the "end-on" position, with the line of electrodes perpendicular to the feature, must be considered. From Fig. 8, which shows the idealized resistance profiles over a stone wall buried in low resistivity soil for the two alignments, it can be seen that the "broadside" position provides the anticipated single high resistance peak whereas, with the "end-on" position, two separate high resistance peaks are obtained. The occurrence of this "M" pattern depends on the overall electrode separation compared to the depth and width of the feature and can be explained in terms of the greater distortion of the current lines when either outer electrode is above the feature. Although the "M" pattern is replaced by a single peak when the electrode separation is increased, its possible presence must be kept in mind when interpreting resistivity results otherwise misleading conclusions, such as the prediction of two separate walls, could arise.

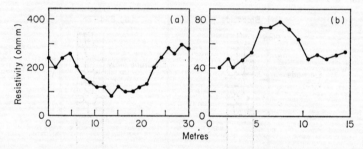

Figure 9. Resistivity profiles associated with ditches. The traverses are perpendicular to the line of the ditch and the "end-on" Wenner electrode array is used. (a) Ditch filled with low resistivity soil and (b) ditch filled with high resistivity rock rubble.

An inversion of this phenomenon, that is a "W" pattern, can occur when the "end-on" position is used to locate low resistance features, such as ditches, but in practice is less frequently encountered. Instead in locating ditches it must be appreciated that, although a soil-filled ditch normally produces a low resistance anomaly (Fig. 9a), a ditch filled with rock rubble can produce a high resistance anomaly (Fig. 9b) since water can sometimes drain away through the rubble more easily than through the solid subsoil.

Instruments

The majority of the instruments currently used for resistivity surveying are of the null-balancing type. An alternating voltage (100–500 Hz), generated by either a transistor oscillator or a vibrating relay, is applied through a low variable resistance (S) to the outer current electrodes. The voltage developed across S, which equals S times the current (I) flowing through the ground, is compared via a transformer with the voltage (V) across the inner electrodes and its value is adjusted until the voltage difference, observed on a meter, is zero. The value for S then provides a measure of the resistance (R) of the ground between the inner electrodes, a calibrated scale normally giving R directly.

A wide range of commercial instruments are available of which the M-C Resistivity Meter (Martin Clark Instruments, Guildford, Surrey) has been developed specifically for archaeological prospecting.

Mild steel rods, of diameter 1 cm and sharpened at one end, provide suitable electrodes for resistivity surveying. A crank at the lower end of the electrodes is valuable in that it permits easy insertion to a constant depth of, for example, 5 cm.

Field Procedures

In contrast to magnetic surveying, resistivity surveying provides the user with considerable choice in his mode of operation, especially with respect to electrode separation and configuration. Although this is advantageous in that modifications can be made to suit the particular site under consideration, the technique probably requires more skill and experience in order to obtain satisfactory and unambiguous results than does magnetic surveying. Again, as with magnetic surveying, systematically spaced measurements, either along a series of parallel traverses or over a gridded area are essential.

The choice of electrode separation is governed by the depth and size of feature to be detected. An accepted guide is that with the equally spaced Wenner array, the electrode separation (d) should be approximately equal to the anticipated depth of the feature. If the electrode separation is too small, very little current will reach the feature so that it will not be detected. In contrast, if the electrode separation is too great, small features will not be located because they will form only a small fraction of the total volume which is penetrated by the current. On typical sites an electrode separation of 1 m is normally appropriate for preliminary measurements and this can subsequently be modified according to the results obtained, a larger separation being required for the location of ditches cut into the subsoil than for the location of walls protruding into the topsoil.

In selecting an electrode configuration for surveying on archaeological sites, the speed of operation, the sensitivity (i.e. the fractional change in resistance observed in the vicinity of the feature) and the shape of the resistivity anomaly (i.e. single peak or "M" and "W" anomalies) must be taken into consideration. Several configurations have been suggested and employed, each of which has its accompanying advantages and disadvantages. In order to achieve a high speed of operation and at the same time maintain a high sensitivity, an "end-on" Wenner array (Fig. 10a) incorporating five electrodes con-

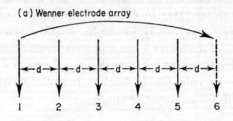

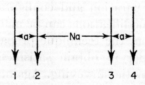

Figure 10. Electrode configurations for resistivity surveying. (a) Wenner array employed in the "end-on" position so that electrode 1 can be moved to position 6 while measurements are made using electrodes 2 to 5. (b) Palmer array in which the electrode pairs, 1–2 and 3–4, are linked together mechanically. *N*, which determines the separation of the two pairs, is typically in the range 2 to 5.

nected to the instrument via a rotary switch has frequently been used. For the first measurement electrodes 1–4 are employed, electrode 5 being spare; rotation of the switch permits electrodes 2–5 to be employed for the second measurement while electrode 1 is being moved to position 6 in readiness for the third measurement. Thus both the instrument operator and electrode handler work simultaneously without time-wasting intervals. However, this "end-on" arrangement can produce the somewhat confusing "M" and "W" shaped anomalies. Therefore, in order to produce more easily interpretable results, the "broadside" position is often preferred even though the necessity of moving four electrodes between each measurement does significantly reduce the speed of the survey. In order to increase the speed of operation with the "broadside" position, Palmer (1960) suggested that two equally spaced pairs of electrodes (1–2 and 3–4) should be employed (Fig. 10b). The two electrodes making up each pair are sufficiently close (e.g. $a = 0.4$ m) for them to be linked together mechanically so that effectively only two electrode movements are necessary between each measurement. Adequate depth penetration is achieved by the choice of the separation between the two pairs, typical values for N being in the range 2 to 5.

Aspinall and Lynam (1970) have also employed two equally spaced pairs of electrodes but in their configuration the separation between the two pairs (i.e. Na) is significantly increased. When N is greater than 30, further increases in separation only produce very small changes in the measured resistance of homogeneous earth. Thus rapid surveying can be achieved by leaving one pair at a fixed station and moving the second pair over the area under investigation, the distance between the fixed station and the survey area being greater than $30a$. Furthermore, since at these large separations the measured resistance is insensitive to the alignment of the electrode pairs, readily interpretable, single peak anomalies are observed. The major disadvantage of this system is that the fractional change in resistance observed in the vicinity of a buried feature is considerably smaller than that which would be observed using either the Wenner or Palmer configurations.

As an alternative to linear electrode arrays, Clark (1968) has developed and extensively used a square array (Plate 5), the four electrodes forming the legs of a table to which the instrument can be attached. Since the four electrodes can be moved as a single unit, the system requires only one person to operate it. Furthermore, since opposite pairs of legs act as current and voltage electrodes respectively, resistance measurements can be made in two directions, equivalent to the "end-on" and "broadside" positions, at each point by incorporating an appropriate switch. The major disadvantage of the square array is that the electrode separation is effectively fixed at approximately 1 m and cannot be readily increased when deep features are to be located: however, for features at depths of up to 1 m, its sensitivity is similar to that of the Wenner configuration.

The suitability of an archaeological site for resistivity surveying is considerably influenced by the recent rainfall, the geology and the vegetation on the site since each of those factors can significantly affect the difference in moisture content between the buried feature and the surrounding soil or subsoil which is required for location of the feature. Recent rainfall can be advantageous for the location of walls since the resulting high moisture content of the topsoil contrasts with the low moisture content of the impermeable walls. However, the possibility of rainwater collecting on the top of the impermeable masonry and thus producing a region of low resistance must be considered. In contrast the location of ditches can be hindered by heavy rainfall since the current flow will tend to be concentrated at the surface within the moist topsoil, thereby reducing the effect of the buried ditch on the measured resistance.

Geological effects which can seriously hamper resistivity surveying include inhomogeneities in either the subsoil or the topsoil. For example, if the subsoil is glacial in origin, changes from clay to gravel to sand, each of which have different resistivities, can occur over a small area, thus providing a complex resistivity background from which it can be difficult to separate the anomalies associated with archaeological features. Similarly if, as is often the case in limestone, the topsoil contains a significant quantity of rock fragments, then these can produce random fluctuations in resistivity which again tend to mask the anomalies associated with buried features. In addition, it should be noted that for the location of buried ditches, a well-drained subsoil such as chalk or gravel is preferable to a clay subsoil whose resistivity is similar to that of a typical ditch fill.

Uniformity in the surface condition of the ground is also advantageous for resistivity surveying. For example, a change in vegetation from grass to ploughed soil could produce a resistivity change since the vegetation determines the protection against evaporation afforded to the topsoil and hence its moisture content and resistivity. Similarly, the well compacted soil associated with a modern path will exhibit a different resistivity to that of the adjacent uncompacted soil.

Electromagnetic Surveying

A typical electromagnetic surveying instrument (Fig. 11; Plate 6) consists of a vertical transmitter coil, fed with a continuous alternating current, and a receiver coil which is mounted at a distance of approximately 1 m on the axis of and perpendicular to the transmitter coil. With this coil arrangement, there is no direct energy transfer to the receiver coil so that in the absence of any external disturbance, zero voltage is induced in the receiver coil. Buried objects can then be detected because the eddy currents, flowing in the metal as a result of the alternating magnetic field (H_p) from the transmitter coil, induce an alternating voltage in the receiver coil. Electromagnetic metal detectors of this general type have been extensively used by the army to locate mines, by civil engineers to locate buried pipes, by treasure hunters to locate "gold bullion" and to a lesser extent by archaeologists to locate coins and other metal artefacts.

In addition to their use as metal detectors, electromagnetic instruments can, in principle, be used to locate buried archaeological features (e.g. pits, ditches, walls), location being achieved as a result of either the electrical resistivity or magnetic susceptibility contrast between the archaeological feature and the surrounding soil or subsoil. In the

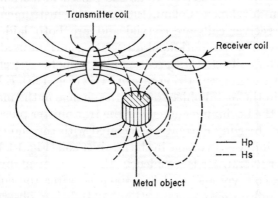

Figure 11. Coil arrangement for electromagnetic surveying. The primary magnetic field. (H_p), generated by the transmitter coil, passes through the metal object and induces eddy currents which flow around the circumference of the object. The eddy currents produce a secondary magnetic field (H_s) which passes through the receiver coil in which it induces a voltage. No primary magnetic field lines pass through the receiver coil because it is perpendicular to the transmitter coil.

former case the possibility of electromagnetic prospecting is extremely attractive since this type of instrument would avoid the tedious business of electrode insertion necessary with the conventional resistivity method.

Metal Detectors

In addition to the instrument described above, a wide range of coil systems have been developed for the location of buried metal. In all these instruments a continuous alternating current, in the frequency range 2–200 kHz, is fed to the transmitter coil and the coil geometry is chosen so that there is no direct energy transfer between the transmitter and receiver coils. For the location of metal artefacts on archaeological sites, detection at depths of 1 m is frequently necessary and this requires either coil diameters or a coil separation of at least 1 m. However, when such large coil dimensions are involved, the maintenance of the precise coil alignment, necessary to achieve zero direct energy transfer, becomes difficult; the sensitivity of the instrument is therefore reduced and consequently the location of small objects (e.g. coins, jewelry) of interest to archaeologists is no longer possible.

In order to increase the sensitivity when using the large coils necessary to achieve an adequate detection depth, a new type of electromagnetic instrument, referred to as the pulsed induction meter, has recently been developed (Colani, 1966). In this instrument the transmitter and receiver coils are coaxial and are both laid flat on the ground. Instead of the continuous alternating current used previously, the transmitter coil is fed with rectangular unipolar current pulses of duration 500 μsec at a repetition rate of 11Hz (Fig. 12a). Eddy currents are induced in the metal object due to the change in the magnetic field occurring at the beginning and end of the transmitter pulse (Fig. 12b). The decay of the eddy currents, associated with the end of the transmitter pulse, induces a voltage in the receiver coil (Fig. 12c). The effect of direct energy transfer is avoided in this instrument by measuring the receiver coil voltage at least 100 μsec after the cut-off of the transmitter pulse, zero voltage (Fig. 12d) being observed at this time in the absence of a metal object. Since accurate alignment of the coils is no longer necessary a high sensitivity is achieved even when large coils (e.g. transmitter = 1 m × 1 m, receiver = 0·4 m × 0·4 m) are employed.

In addition, the decay rate of the eddy currents, and hence the decay rate of the voltage induced in the receiver coil, depends only on the size, shape and electrical conductivity of the metal object. Therefore measurement of the induced voltage at various times after the cut-off of the transmitter pulse (e.g. 100, 200 and 300 μsec) provides information on these parameters (Bean et al., 1959). Further, it is sometimes possible to distinguish between non-ferrous and ferrous metals since the receiver coil voltage only exhibits a pure exponential decay in the former case.

The pulsed induction meter therefore represents a significant advance in the development of metal detectors for systematic use on archaeological sites. Its applications include the detection of coins (Foster and Hackens, 1969) and metal artefacts in graves. In the latter case, the instrument is also valuable after the topsoil has been removed to reveal the overall plan of a cemetery since it can establish, prior to detailed excavation, which of the graves contain potentially fragile metal objects.

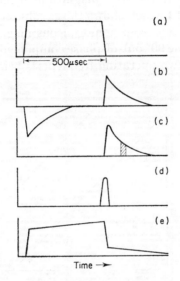

Figure 12. Waveforms for the pulsed induction metal detector. (a) Primary magnetic field pulse produced by the transmitter coil. (b) Eddy currents induced in the metal object and therefore the form of the secondary magnetic field at the receiver coil due to the metal object. (c) Voltage induced in the receiver coil (only the effect of the cut-off of the transmitter pulse is shown) in the presence of metal object. The shaded area indicates the time during which the receiver voltage is measured. (d) Voltage induced in the receiver coil when no metal object is present. (e) Magnetic moment induced in the soil by the primary magnetic field pulse. The increase in magnetic moment while the primary field is present and the decrease after the cut-off of the primary field is referred to as "magnetic viscosity".

Location of Archaeological Features

An electromagnetic instrument of the type illustrated in Fig. 11 can be used for the location of buried archaeological features (Howell, 1966). Application of electromagnetic theory (Tite and Mullins, 1970) to this system shows that the voltage induced in the receiver coil due to the presence of the soil contains two components. The first arises from alternating magnetic moment induced in the soil by the magnetic field generated by the transmitter coil. This component is in-phase with the transmitter voltage, proportional to the magnetic susceptibility (χ) of the soil and independent of the operating frequency (ν). The second component, which is due to the eddy currents induced in the soil, is 90° out-of-phase with the transmitter voltage and proportional to the ratio ν/ρ where ρ equals the resistivity of the soil. An indication of the relative magnitude of these two components is provided by Fig. 13 which shows those values of χ and ρ for which the in-phase component from homogeneous magnetic topsoil has the same magnitude as the 90° out-of-phase component from homogeneous conducting topsoil, two operating frequencies being considered.

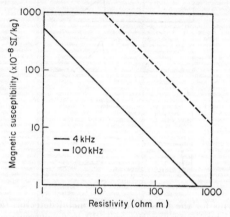

Figure 13. Plot of equivalent values for magnetic susceptibility (χ) and resistivity (ρ) such that the in-phase component from homogeneous magnetic topsoil has the same magnitude as the 90° out-of-phase component from homogeneous conducting topsoil. Two frequencies, 4 kHz and 100 kHz, are considered.

From these data it is apparent that, with an instrument operating at low frequencies (e.g. 4 kHz), the magnetic component dominates and the in-phase voltage provides a measure of the magnetic susceptibility of the topsoil while, with an instrument operating at high frequencies (e.g. 100 kHz), the eddy current component dominates and the out-of-phase voltage provides a measure of the topsoil resistivity. In both cases the induced voltage also increases with increasing thickness of topsoil; with a 1 m coil separation, the increase continues up to a topsoil thickness of approximately 0·8 m, above which the induced voltage remains essentially constant. Consequently, the detection of buried features depends on the fact that the effective topsoil thickness above the feature is either less than normal in the case of roads and walls or more than normal in the case of pits and ditches; thus a decrease or increase in the induced voltage occurs in the vicinity of these features as is illustrated, for a low frequency instrument responding to the magnetic properties, in Fig. 14.

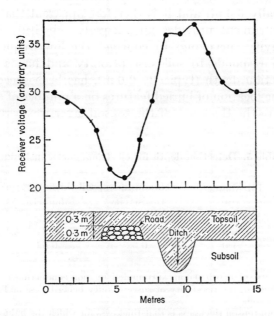

Figure 14. Profile associated with a road and a ditch obtained using an electromagnetic instrument, the traverse being perpendicular to the line of the features. The decrease in receiver voltage over the road and the increase over the ditch are principally due to the decrease and increase in the thickness of the high susceptibility soil (i.e. topsoil) respectively.

An important parameter in comparing electromagnetic surveying with the other available techniques is the depth at which buried features can be located. Because electromagnetic instruments are active devices, transmitting and receiving an alternating magnetic field, their sensitivity falls off as the sixth power of depth (d^{-6}), whereas in the passive measurement of the magnetic field intensity using a magnetometer, the sensitivity falls off as the third power of depth (d^{-3}). Consequently, electromagnetic instruments have an inherently smaller detection depth than that possible in magnetic surveying, the induced voltage due to the topsoil tending to mask any induced voltage from buried features at relatively modest depths. Values for the maximum topsoil thickness under which typical pits can be detected with an electromagnetic instrument, employing a coil separation of 1 m, are presented in Table 5.

The practical application of the high frequency instrument, which responds to soil resistivity, is severely limited by the small detection depth (typically 0·3 m) and it is therefore apparent that no electromagnetic instrument provides an adequate substitute for conventional resistivity surveying. In contrast the low frequency instrument, which responds to soil susceptibility and has a somewhat greater detection depth (typically 0·6 m), has been successfully employed for the location of buried features on a number of archaeological sites where the thickness of the topsoil layer was less than 0·5 m

Table 5. Detection depth for electromagnetic instruments

Pit[a] diameter (m)	Maximum topsoil thickness[b] (m)	
	Resistivity	Magnetic
0·6	0·15	0·45
1·0	0·32	0·62

[a] Cylindrical pits, of depth 0·6 m, surrounded by non-conducting or non-magnetic subsoil are considered, the resistivity or susceptibility being the same for both the pit filling and the topsoil.

[b] The maximum topsoil thickness is that thickness for which the induced voltage due to the pit is 5 per cent of that due to the homogeneous topsoil layer.

(Musson, 1968). In addition, the information that the lower frequency instrument provides on the magnetic susceptibility of the topsoil itself can be archaeologically significant since high susceptibility topsoil is associated with areas of intensive occupation or industrial activity, such as iron smelting and pottery kilns (Tite and Mullins, 1969). Since electromagnetic instruments provide a continuous response, they can thus be used to rapidly define the limits of a large occupation site or the areas of industrial activity: specific features within the areas can subsequently be located using the more sensitive magnetic surveying techniques.

Finally, it should be noted that the pulsed induction meter, described on p. 34, also responds to the magnetic properties of the soil through the phenomenon referred to as "magnetic viscosity" (Colani and Aitken, 1966). Thus the magnetic moment, induced in the soil by the magnetic field produced by the transmitter pulse, continues to increase in magnitude while the magnetic field is maintained (Fig. 12e). Similarly, when the magnetic field is removed at the end of the transmitter pulse, a small magnetic moment remains and the subsequent decay of this magnetic "viscosity" induces a voltage in the receiver coil. Since, to a first approximation, the magnetic viscosity is proportional to the magnetic susceptibility, the pulsed induction meter can also be used to locate buried archaeological features. However, the limitation of comparatively small detection depth, discussed in the case of the continuous alternating current instrument, is still applicable. Furthermore, no measurement of the resistivity of the soil is possible, since the eddy currents induced in the soil decay to zero in less than 50 μsec; that is, before it is possible to measure any voltage induced in the receiver coil.

Induced Polarization Techniques

Induced polarization techniques involve the measurement of the transient voltage which follows the termination of direct, rather than alternating, current flow through the ground and which decays to zero in a few seconds. This transient voltage is due to induced polarization (i.e. the separation of electric charges) and can arise from a group of phenomena, all of which are electrochemical in origin (Wait, 1959). For example, when a good electrical conductor (e.g. metal) is immersed in an electrolytic solution, a double layer of electric charge is created at the metal-electrolyte interface. When current is passed through the electrolyte, the equilibrium state at the interface is temporarily disturbed resulting in the movement of the electric charges. As a result of this induced polarization, a small voltage, in opposition to the applied voltage which drives the current through the electrolyte, is generated. When the current flow is terminated, the charges return to their original equilibrium position and the voltage associated with the induced polarization decays to zero. Alternatively, in disseminated clays, induced polarization can occur as a result of ion-exchange phenomena at the interface between the clay and the electrolyte; an equivalent transient voltage is observed after the termination of the current flow.

For induced polarization measurements (Aspinall and Lynam, 1970), four electrodes are inserted into the ground, as in the case of resistivity surveying. Unipolar current pulses (Fig. 15a), typically of 10 sec duration, are passed through the ground via the two outer electrodes and the resulting transient induced polarization voltage (Fig. 15b) between the two inner electrodes is measured after the termination of the current pulses. The field procedures and electrode configurations are essentially the same as those employed in resistivity surveying. However, non-polarizable electrodes, consisting typically of porous pots filled with copper sulphate gel, must be used instead of metal electrodes otherwise the electrode polarization would mask the induced polarization in the ground.

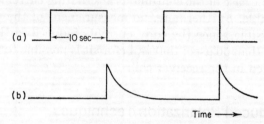

Figure 15. Waveforms for the induced polarization technique. (a) Current pulses passed through the ground between the two outer electrodes. (b) Transient induced polarization voltage measured between the two inner electrodes after the termination of the current pulse.

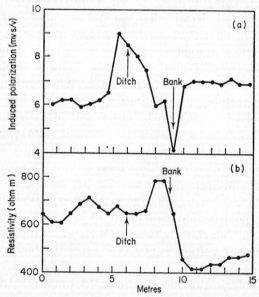

Figure 16. Induced polarization and resistivity profiles associated with a ditch and bank, the positions of which are marked by arrows. The traverses are perpendicular to the line of the features and a "Palmer type" array, with N greater than 30, is used (after Aspinall and Lynam, 1970).

Since induced polarization requires the presence of an electrolytic solution, buried archaeological features are detected principally because they have a different water content to that of the surrounding soil or subsoil. Figure 16 shows both the induced polarization (i.e. transient voltage) and resistivity results obtained for a traverse across a bank and ditch. The low water content over the bank produces a region of low induced polarization and high resistivity while the high water content of the ditch results in an increase in the induced polarization response although the anticipated decrease in resistivity is not very evident. Thus in this instance, the induced polarization changes associated with the archaeological features are significantly greater than the resistivity changes. It therefore seem probable that the induced polarization techniques could be extremely valuable in supplementing resistivity surveying, even though the two techniques are responding to somewhat similar physical properties of the buried features.

Presentation and Analysis of Survey Data

The numerical data obtained from the geophysical survey of an archaeological site must be presented in such a way that the anomalies associated with the buried archaeological features can be clearly identified. In addition, analytical treatment of the numerical data is often desirable in order to remove the anomalies associated with slight surface irregularities and large scale geological variations, which might otherwise mask the archaeological anomalies.

A wide range of methods have been employed for the visual presentation of survey data, the majority of these being illustrated in the figures associated with the applications of geophysical prospecting to archaeological sites (p. 43). An obvious method is to plot the contours of, for example, equal magnetic field intensity or equal electrical resistivity (Figs. 19 and 21). However, this method is extremely time-consuming and, on a complex site, interpretation of the contour pattern can be very difficult. A more satisfactory technique is to use symbols which represent specific values of anomaly strength. By choosing an appropriate range of symbols, such as dots or circles of increasing size, one obtains a darkening over areas of high anomaly strength which is clearly visible to the eye (Fig. 17). A natural extension of this technique is to replace the symbols by a series of dots which are randomly placed in the immediate vicinity of the survey points and whose number is proportional to the anomaly strength. In the resulting "dot density plot" (Figs. 18 and 21), the anomaly strengths are presented to the eye like a half-tone picture and the ability of the eye to distinguish vague geometrical shapes associated with the archaeological features, in a confused field of dots, is fully utilized.

In some instances, the anomalies associated with archaeological features are obscured either by a gradual change in, for example,

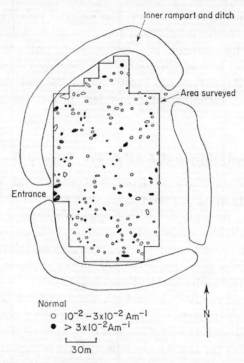

Figure 17. Magnetic survey results for the Iron Age hill-fort at Rainsborough, Northants. Only normal anomalies (i.e. increase in magnetic field strength) are shown.

magnetic field intensity over long distances as a result of geological disturbances or alternatively by abrupt changes associated with small surface irregularities (e.g. stones, surface iron, variations in topsoil thickness). When this problem occurs the archaeological anomalies can be clarified, and interpretation made easier, by subjecting the numerical survey data to various types of analytical treatment using a computer. The analytical treatments are all essentially "filtering" techniques in which the long-range geological disturbances (i.e. long wavelength and low frequency) and short-range surface disturbances (i.e. short wavelength and high frequency) are removed to leave the intermediate-range archaeological anomalies: the term, "filtering", being employed because of the analogy to electrical filters which pass alternating voltages within a defined range of frequencies. Scollar (1969 and 1970) has employed a wide range of techniques, including linear digital filtering and the Fourier transform method, for the treatment of survey data from archaeological sites and has proved that they can be of considerable value in some circumstances. However, it should be emphasized that such sophisticated techniques are not always necessary and that a dot density plot, for example, of the *untreated* data can normally be adequately interpreted.

Applications

Geophysical prospecting techniques have been used on a wide range of archaeological sites extending in age from the Neolithic period to the post-Mediaeval period; the earlier Palaeolithic and Mesolithic sites not normally providing suitable features for location by these techniques. On prehistoric sites, the techniques have principally been used to locate pits, ditches and hearths associated with farmsteads, camps, hill-forts and burials. On later sites (e.g. Roman), their use has been extended to determine the occupation pattern (i.e. buildings and roads) in villages and towns and to locate the pottery kilns and iron smelting furnaces in industrial complexes.

In considering these applications, it is convenient to discuss the various types of site separately; the emphasis being placed on sites in Western Europe, particularly England.

Hill-forts and Camps

Probably the most important application of magnetic surveying on prehistoric sites has been the location of pits, hearths, gullies, etc. within the visually blank interiors of Iron Age hill-forts. The rampart and ditch defences of the hill-fort frequently enclose an area of several acres and consequently complete excavation is rarely possible. The magnetic survey results, in addition to indicating fruitful areas for immediate excavation, provide the archaeologist with an estimate of the total number of pits and their distribution within the hill-fort. This information is important since the total number of pits, when combined with an estimate of the length of time of occupation, can provide an indication of the intensity of occupation. It therefore helps to establish whether the hill-fort was a permanently occupied centre or merely a refuge place in times of stress.

The results obtained at the 6 acre hill-fort of Rainsborough, Northants (Tite, 1967), provides an indication of the value of magnetic surveying on this type of site. In an almost complete survey of the interior (Fig. 17), approximately 100 isolated magnetic anomalies, varying in intensity from 10^{-2} to 5×10^{-2} A m^{-1} and in diameter from 1 to 3 m, were detected and these were distributed fairly uniformly over the entire site. Excavations in two small areas indicated that typical anomalies were produced by small rubbish pits, shallow hollows of industrial or domestic use, hearths and gullies which possibly formed the foundation trenches for hut walls. Magnetic measurements also provided further information on the defences of the hill-fort. An outer ditch, in addition to the well-preserved inner rampart and ditch, was revealed during excavation and this was subsequently traced around the perimeter of the camp by the detection of its associated magnetic anomaly. The fact that this ditch proved to be continuous, except in the region opposite a break in the rampart on the western side, provided further evidence that, of three breaks now present, the western one provided the original entrance. The strength of the magnetic anomaly associated with the ditch varied from 5×10^{-3} A m^{-1}, where the ditch was mainly refilled with material excavated during its construction, to 5×10^{-2} A m^{-1} near to the entrance, where it was refilled with occupation debris. In addition, excavation of the west entrance indicated that the areas of magnetic disturbance just inside the entrance were due to two guard chambers, containing hearths and burnt occupation debris. Finally, it should be noted that excavation indicated that the hill-fort defences were probably maintained for a total of approximately 100 to 150 years during the fifth and second centuries BC. Consequently, the existence of only 100 buried features (i.e. pits, hollows, etc.) suggests that the occupation of the site, during this period, was either spasmodic or was confined to the inhabitants of one or two farmsteads.

Other Iron Age hill-forts where magnetic surveying has been employed (Aitken and Tite, 1962b) include Madmarston, Oxon., where a similar concentration of isolated anomalies, again associated with pits and gullies, were located and Dane's Camp, Worcs., where several dozen magnetic anomalies were found. In the latter case, the anomalies were all situated in the main camp, the lack of anomalies in the associated annexe indicating that the occupation was confined to the main camp itself. In contrast, at Castle-an-Dinas, Cornwall, a survey of the 5 acre interior revealed no magnetic anomalies which could be associated with pits. Although in this case, excavations (Wailes, 1963) indicated that the occupation of the hill-fort was extremely sparse, it must be remembered that the absence of magnetic anomalies does not necessarily mean that no pits exist. Instead, their absence could be due to the fact that the magnetic susceptibility of the pit filling is too low to produce a detectable magnetic anomaly.

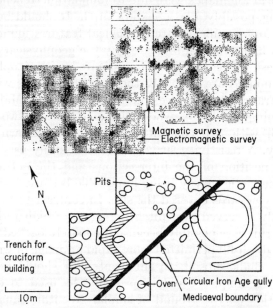

Figure 18. Magnetic and electromagnetic survey results for a typical area at Cadbury Castle (Camelot), Somerset. The dot density presentation is employed so that areas of high density are associated with strong normal anomalies (i.e. increase in magnetic field strength) for the magnetic survey and with large receiver voltages (i.e. increase in the thickness of high susceptibility soil) for the electromagnetic survey. The positions of those excavated features (i.e. pits, ditches, gullies) whose presence was indicated by the survey results are shown on the lower diagram (after Alcock, 1968).

The results obtained at Cadbury Castle (Camelot), Somerset (Alcock, 1968) can also be considered in this section since, although extensively re-used during the post-Roman period, the defences were first built and the hill-fort intensively occupied during the Iron Age. Virtually the whole of the interior has been surveyed using the proton magnetometer and two electromagnetic instruments (Fig. 18), these latter instruments being successfully employed on this site because of the exceptionally shallow layer of topsoil (15–30 cm). In addition to the very high concentration of isolated magnetic anomalies associated with pits of Bronze Age, Neolithic and Iron Age origin, the surveys clearly revealed a number of circular, penannular and linear anomalies. Excavation (Plate 7) established that the circular and penannular anomalies were associated either with the wall trenches of Iron Age huts or with drainage gullies surrounding them, that the long linear anomalies were due to mediaeval or later boundary ditches and that the other linear anomalies were due to foundation trenches for a cruciform building, possibly a late Saxon church. It should be added however that many significant archaeological features found during the excavations had not been indicated by the geophysical survey.

The earliest settlement sites investigated with geophysical prospecting techniques are probably the Neolithic camps with enclosing ditches in France. A typical example is that of Les Matignons, near Cognac (Linington, 1966), where the existence of two intersecting camps, each with two concentric ditches, was known from aerial photography. A resistivity survey was successfully used to establish the precise position of the intersections and the entrances on the ground; a magnetic survey being impossible because iron fences supporting the vineyards covered the site. In contrast to the low resistivity normally observed over ditches, regions of high resistivity were observed in this case possibly because the loosely packed chalk blocks forming the ditch-fill permitted more rapid drainage of water than the surrounding chalk subsoil. In this context it should be noted that geophysical techniques could in principle be used to establish the precise position on the ground of similar Neolithic causeway camps (e.g. Windmill Hill) occurring in England and again revealed by aerial photographs.

Farmsteads and Villas

Although no results have been published, geophysical prospecting could be used to establish the precise position on the ground of the enclosure ditches to Bronze Age and Iron Age farmsteads which are revealed in aerial photographs. In addition, storage pits and hearths within the enclosure could be located by means of magnetic surveying. However, because of their small dimensions, the post holes associated with the huts could not normally be located.

In the case of Roman farmsteads or villas, detailed resistivity surveying has been extensively used to locate the position of the stone walls of the main buildings. However, since excavation is essential in order to establish their frequently complex chronological relationship, this rather laborious operation is not always worthwhile. Consequently, at the Barnsley Park villa, Glouc. (Rees and Wright, 1969), resistivity measurements were made along the sides of a grid of 20 ft squares covering approximately 1 acre. Although individual walls could not be traced with this wide spacing between traverses, areas of high resistivity were approximately defined (Fig. 19). These high resistivity

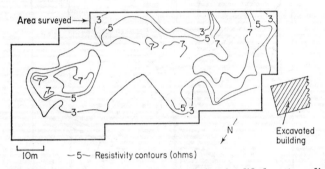

Figure 19. Resistivity survey results, in the form of a simplified contour diagram, for the Roman villa at Barnsley Park, Gloucs. The areas of high resistivity, as defined by the 3 ohm contour, indicate the positions of the main buildings on the site (after Rees and Wright, 1969).

areas were associated with building rubble and paving, as well as walls, and therefore indicated the general position and extent of the main buildings on the site.

Villages and Towns

The determination of the overall plan of the villages, which first occur in England with the increase of population during the Iron Age, and the towns, which are first developed during the Roman period, provides a further extremely important application of geophysical prospecting.

The results obtained from a magnetic survey at Dragonby, a complex Iron Age-cum-Roman settlement near Scunthorpe, Lincs. (May, 1970), illustrates both the value and limitation of the technique on this type of site. Approximately 14 acres of the site were surveyed using a proton magnetometer and an extremely complex pattern of magnetic anomalies was obtained. Both normal (increase in field strength) and reverse (decrease in field strength) anomalies with intensities up to 10^{-1} A m^{-1} were observed. The survey results for a typically area are shown in Fig. 20, the method of presentation being such as to emphasize the major linear and isolated anomalies. On the basis of limited excavation (Plate 8), it was established that the normal anomalies were produced by ditches (linear) and pits, wells or kilns (iso-

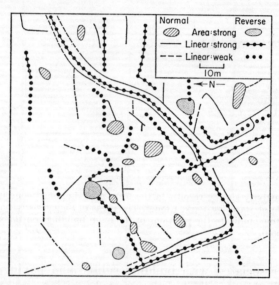

Figure 20. Magnetic survey results for a typical area of the Iron Age-cum-Roman settlement at Dragonby, Lincs. Weak normal (i.e. increase in magnetic field) and reverse (i.e. decrease in magnetic field) anomalies = 10^{-2} to 3×10^{-2} A m^{-1}, strong normal and reverse anomalies $> 3 \times 10^{-2}$ A m^{-1}.

lated) while the reverse anomalies were produced by roads (linear) or concentrations of building stone (isolated), the individual walls being too small for detection. It was thus possible to interpret the remainder of the survey results and so establish the road pattern for the settlement and define the major areas of occupation, without complete excavation of the site. In addition, help in selecting suitable and archaeologically distinct areas for excavation was provided. For example, a rectangular enclosure and an area parallel to one of the roads have so far been excavated while, for future excavation, a road junction or an area away from the roads, and containing only ditches and pits, could be selected. However, it must be emphasized that, with the exception of the roads which date from the Roman period, it was not possible on the basis of the survey to distinguish between the Iron Age features and the subsequent Roman occupation. Similarly, it was not easy to locate a specific type of isolated feature, such as pottery kilns, since their anomalies tended to be masked by the large number of linear anomalies associated with the roads and ditches. Finally, it should be noted that the success of the magnetic survey at Dragonby was due to the very high magnetic susceptibility of the soils on the site (100–900 × 10^{-8} SI/kg) and to the relatively shallow layer of topsoil (0·6 m above the subsoil and 0·3 m above the roads), conditions which do not necessarily exist on all village and town sites.

A second urban site for which the results of a large-scale magnetic survey have been published is that of the Etruscan town at Tarquinia, Italy (Linington, 1967a). Here the survey revealed a series of linear anomalies lying mainly on two perpendicular alignments. Although limited excavation is necessary for confirmation, it seems probable that these represent the main streets and larger buildings of the ancient town.

Geophysical prospecting has also been used to locate the defences of Roman towns. Excavation at Verulamium (St. Albans, Herts.) revealed a major ditch within the town walls which formed part of the first century AD defences. Using a proton magnetometer, it was possible to follow the line of this ditch for over a mile, to establish the position of two right-angled turns in its alignment and also to locate a break corresponding to the entrance into the town along Watling Street (Aitken, 1960). Because the ditch formed a continuous feature, its magnetic anomaly could be readily identified even though its intensity was normally only 10^{-2} A m^{-1}. In contrast at Bolonia (Cadiz, Spain), resistivity surveying was used to locate approximately 250 m of the town wall and establish the position of several towers incorporated into the wall (Linington, 1967b). Magnetic surveying was not possible at this site because the susceptibility of the topsoil was insufficient to produce a measurable reverse anomaly over the walls.

In the case of towns which have been continuously occupied up to the present day, geophysical prospecting is less useful since normally only small areas are free from modern buildings or roads and these can be completely excavated. In any case since the occupation typi-

cally spans more than a thousand years, detailed excavation would still
be necessary to establish the date of any features located by geophysical prospecting. Similarly, the role of geophysical techniques on deserted Mediaeval villages is somewhat limited since the plan of the
village can frequently be established from surface features, such as
the slight mounds associated with buildings or the shallow linear
depressions associated with streets.

Burial Sites

Although the megalithic tombs and long barrows of the Neolithic
period or the round barrows of the Bronze Age normally provide obvious surface features, in areas of intensive agriculture the barrow
mound has sometimes been ploughed flat. In these circumstances
the ditches are often revealed by aerial photography and their precise
position on the ground can then be established by means of geophysical prospecting techniques. At Stanton Harcourt, Oxon., magnetic surveying was used to locate several Bronze Age ring ditches
while secondary cremations inserted into the ditch were also located
because they produced a larger magnetic anomaly than that occurring
over the remainder of the ditch. In contrast, at Burton Fleming,
Yorks. (Clark, 1968), where the susceptibility of the soil was insufficient for magnetic surveying, the position of the rectangular ditched
enclosures of an Iron Age cemetery was established by resistivity
surveying (Fig. 21). Similarly the first application of resistivity surveying on archaeological sites was the location of the ditches of
Neolithic henge monuments at Dorchester, Oxon., which had been
revealed by aerial photography (Atkinson, 1952).

In Poland, magnetic surveying has been used to locate the iron
grave goods in the shallow cremation pits of an Iron Age cemetery
(Dabrowski and Linington, 1967). This type of application could of
course be extended to other Iron Age burials, including the chariot
burials of Yorkshire, as well as to Roman and Saxon cemeteries. In
addition, electromagnetic metal detectors could be used to supplement
the data obtained from magnetic surveying which, in any case, can
only locate iron grave goods. However, in the absence of metallic
grave goods, the burials pits, whether of the cremation or inhumation
type, are normally too shallow to be detected by either magnetic or
electromagnetic prospecting and consequently the techniques cannot
be reliably used to establish the overall plan and extent of a cemetery.

Probably the most important application of magnetic prospecting to burial sites has been the work done at the Etruscan necropolises at Tarquinia and Cerveteri in Italy (Linington, 1961). The tombs are typically in the form of chambers cut out of the rock and are reached by an entrance cut down from the old ground surface. Unless the roof of the chamber has collapsed, the chamber remains as an air space while the entrance passage is filled with soil. Because of the high density of tombs in the necropolises, the magnetic survey results are extremely complex and it is not normally possible to locate individual

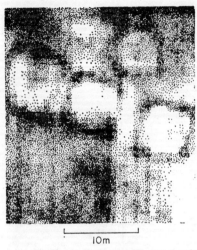

Figure 21. Resistivity survey results, in the form of a dot density diagram, for a typical area of the Iron Age cemetery at Burton Fleming, Yorkshire. High dot density is associated with regions of low resistivity such as are produced by the rectangular enclosure ditches, four of which are clearly evident in the diagram. (By permission of the Inspectorate of Ancient Monuments, Department of the Environment.)

tombs. However, from the results obtained for an area of the necropolis at Cerveteri, it is apparent that the magnetic anomalies do indicate the general distribution of the tombs (Fig. 22). A line of tombs produces an elongated region of low-magnetic field intensity (i.e. reverse anomaly) since the non-magnetic air spaces of the tomb chambers replace the strongly magnetic volcanic rock (tufa). The regions of high magnetic field (i.e. normal anomaly) between the lines of tombs are associated with the earth-filled necropolis roadways and also possibly the earth-filled entrance passages.

Industrial Sites

Magnetic surveying has been extensively used on industrial sites to locate pottery kilns and to a lesser extent, iron smelting and glass furnaces. In England, these sites are normally of Roman or post-Roman date since the "bonfire-type" firing of pottery during the prehistoric periods leaves insufficient quantities of fired clay for detection while iron smelting during the Iron Age was carried out only on a very limited scale.

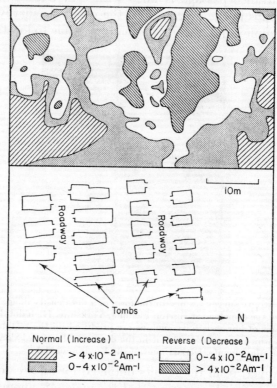

Figure 22. Magnetic survey results, in the form of a simplified contour diagram, for a typical area of the Etruscan cemetery at Cerveteri, Italy. The positions of the tombs and the roadways are shown on the lower diagram (after Linington, 1961).

The development of a portable magnetometer for archaeological work was stimulated in the first place by the desire to locate pottery kilns. In addition to their immediate archaeological significance in, for example, establishing the contemporaneity of different pottery types found in the same kiln, the location and excavation of pottery kilns is important because they provide the most satisfactory samples for magnetic dating (Chapter 5, p. 134). Since 1958, several hundred pottery kilns have been located using the proton magnetometer in

England as well as in most other European countries. The strength of the magnetic anomaly associated with a kiln varies considerably. Although frequently greater than 10^{-1} A m^{-1}, the anomalies can be as small as 2×10^{-2} A m^{-1} when the kiln is buried beneath 1 m of topsoil. In these latter circumstances the anomaly strength is not significantly different from that associated with a pit and it is often impossible to establish whether the anomaly is due to a kiln or a pit.

Roman industrial sites are of particular interest since very large quantities of pottery were manufactured at these sites and this pottery was subsequently distributed over a wide area. For example, Samian ware from Central and Southern Gaul was distributed throughout the Roman world and provides invaluable dating evidence for Roman sites. In England, the Nene valley around Peterborough was a major industrial centre during the second to fourth centuries AD and pottery manufactured at sites in this area was widely distributed in the Midlands and the North (Hartley, 1960). The potteries, together with iron smelting sites and substantial houses or villas, stretch along both banks of the river Nene and using a proton magnetometer, kilns have been located at Stibbington, Water Newton, Sibson and Castor. Other important Roman sites where groups of pottery kilns have been located include Hartshill and Mancetter in Warwickshire.

The location of the actual furnaces on iron smelting sites by means of magnetic surveying can be extremely difficult since the iron slag, filling pits or distributed over the site, produces strong magnetic anomalies which are often indistinguishable from those associated with the furnaces. At the extensive Roman iron smelting site near Bardown, Sussex, an extremely complex pattern of magnetic anomalies was observed. Excavation established that only one of these anomalies was associated with a furnace, the remainder being due to pits, roads and ditches containing, or constructed from, iron slag. In contrast, on the Nok culture site at Taruga, near Abuja in northern Nigeria, interference from iron slag was less pronounced and nine iron smelting furnaces were located (Tite, 1966).

Conclusions

The relative merits and limitations of the various geophysical prospecting techniques on archaeological sites and the relative importance to archaeology of the different applications are discussed below.

Prospecting Techniques

The location of buried features by magnetic and resistivity surveying, the two techniques most extensively used on archaeological sites, depend on quite different physical properties of the buried features and the two techniques are therefore complimentary. However, because of its greater operational speed and the greater ease in interpreting the results, magnetic surveying tends to be used in preference to resistivity surveying whenever the magnetic properties of the buried features are such as to produce detectable magnetic anomalies. Thus magnetic prospecting is of prime importance for the location of fired structures, such as pottery kilns, which exhibit a strong thermoremanent magnetism. The location of other features by magnetic surveying can be most readily achieved on sites which have been intensively occupied for a long period since this produces the enhanced soil susceptibility necessary for the features to produce strong magnetic anomalies.

Because of its relatively slow operation, resistivity surveying rarely provides a worthwhile substitute to magnetic surveying for the location of isolated features (e.g. pits) or for establishing the plan of a complex settlement, However, for the location of individual linear features, such as walls, roads and ditches, resistivity surveying provides an extremely valuable alternative. For example, a mortared wall foundation can have a lower water content than the loosely packed stone rubble lying beside it. Consequently, the wall produces a resistivity anomaly even when the contrast in magnetic susceptibility between the wall and rubble is insufficient to produce a magnetic anomaly. Similarly, even when a ditch is mainly filled with the material originally excavated in its construction, the packing and hence the water content can be different from that of the surrounding subsoil: again a resistivity anomaly can exist without any equivalent magnetic anomaly. In these situations, adequate operation speed can be achieved with resistivity surveying by employing a series of traverses across the supposed line of the feature.

In addition, the possibility of varying the electrode separation, and hence altering the penetration depth of the current, provides valuable flexibility in resistivity surveying which is absent from magnetic surveying. Thus a small electrode separation can be used to locate a road close to the surface while a large electrode separation can be used to locate a large ditch buried beneath several feet of topsoil. Finally, the possibility of using resistivity surveying close to buildings or iron fences, whose associated magnetic field gradient would render magnetic surveying impossible, should be emphasized.

Electromagnetic surveying, although not providing a satisfactory alternative to resistivity surveying, is useful for supplementing the results obtained from magnetic surveying especially with respect to defining areas of intense occupation and industrial activity. In contrast, induced polarization techniques can be used to supplement the results obtained from resistivity surveying.

Applications

The first role of geophysical prospecting techniques on archaeological sites is to establish the precise position of individual buried features for immediate excavation. This includes the location of kilns, whose existence is indicated by a concentration of pottery fragments on the surface, the location of pits within the ramparts of an Iron Age hill-fort and the location on the ground of ditches, walls and roads revealed by aerial photography. This application avoids the need for time-consuming and expensive trial trenching to locate features for excavation and has therefore already been extensively exploited. However, with the increasing use of mechanical excavators to remove the topsoil from large areas of a site, this first role has been modified: instead of the precise location of specific features, an indication of the range of features within a particular area is now often required.

The second major role of geophysical prospecting techniques is to provide an indication of the overall plan and extent of the site outside the area being excavated. This includes establishing the street pattern within a village or town, determining the arrangement and extent of the tombs in a cemetery and estimating the total number of pits in an Iron Age hill-fort. Although never providing a substitute for detailed excavation, this second role can significantly extend the information gained from excavations and is therefore being increasingly exploited. For example, in the time taken for a team of archaeologists to fully excavate a quarter of an acre, two people using a proton magnetometer can survey more than 20 acres. Since the results obtained are frequently extremely complex, analytical treatment of the survey data using computers must play an important part in the exploitation of this type of survey.

It is therefore anticipated that the development of analytical techniques to assist in the interpretation of survey results will be more important during the next decade than will be the development of new instruments for surveying.

References

Aitken, M. J. (1960). The magnetic survey. Appendix to S. S. Frere: Excavations at Verulamium 1959, 5th Interim Report. *Antiquary J.* **40**, 21–24.

Aitken, M. J. (1961). "Physics and Archaeology", pp. 1–78. Interscience, New York.

Aitken, M. J. and Tite, M.S. (1962a). A gradient magnetometer, using proton free-precession. *J. scient. Instrum.* **39**, 625–629.

Aitken, M. J. and Tite, M. S. (1962b). Proton magnetometer surveying on some British hill-forts. *Archaeometry* **5**, 126–134.

Aitken, M. J., Webster, G. and Rees, A. (1958). Magnetic prospecting. *Antiquity* **32**, 270–271.

Alcock, L. (1968). Excavations at South Cadbury Castle, 1967. *Antiquar. J.* **48**, 6–17.

Alldred, J. C. (1964). A fluxgate gradiometer for archaeological surveying. *Archaeometry* **7**, 14–19.

Aspinall, A. and Lynam, J. T. (1970). An induced polarisation instrument for the detection of near surface features. *Prospezioni Archeologiche* **5**, 67–75.

Atkinson, R. J. C. (1952). Méthodes électriques de prospection en archéologie. *In* "La Découverte du Passé" (Ed. A. Laming), pp. 59–70. Picard, Paris.

Bean, C. P., DeBlois, R. W. and Nesbitt, L. B. (1959). Eddy-current method for measuring the resistivity of metals. *J. appl. Phys.* **30**, 1976–1980.

Carson, H. H. (1962). A seismic survey at Harpers Ferry. *Archaeometry* **5**, 119–122.

Clark, A. J. (1968). A square array for resistivity surveying. *Prospezioni Archeologiche* **3**, 111–114.

Colani, C. (1966). A new type of locating device. I—the instrument. *Archaeometry* **9**, 3–8.

Colani, C. and Aitken, M. J. (1966). Utilization of magnetic viscosity effects in soils for archaeological prospection. *Nature* **212**, 1446.

Dabrowski, K. and Linington, R. E. (1967). Test use of a proton magnetometer near Kalisz, Poland. *Prospezioni Archeologiche* **2**, 29–42.

Foster, E. and Hackens, T. (1969). Decco metal detector survey on Delos. *Archaeometry* **11**, 165–172.

Hartley, B. R. (1960). Notes on the Roman pottery industry in the Nene valley. *Occasional Papers*, No. 2. Peterborough Museum Society.

Hesse, A. (1966). "Prospections Géophysiques à Faible Profondeur. Applications à l'Archéologie." Dunod, Paris.

Howell, M. (1966). A soil conductivity meter. *Archaeometry* **9**, 20–23.

Keller, G. V. and Frischknecht, F. C. (1966). "Electrical Methods in Geophysical Prospecting." Pergamon, Oxford.

Langan, L. (1966). Use of new atomic magnetometers in archaeology. *Prospezioni Archeologiche* **1**, 61–66.

Le Borgne, E. (1955). Susceptibilité magnétique anormale du sol superficiel. *Ann. Geophys.* **11**, 399–419.

Le Borgne, E. (1960). Influence du feu sur les propriétés magnétiques du sol. *Ann. Geophys.* **16**, 159–195.

Linington, R. E. (1961). "Quaderni di Geofisica Applicata, No. 22." Fondazione Lerici, Milan.

Linington, R. E. (1963). The application of geophysics to archaeology. *Am. Scient.* **51**, 48–70.

Linington, R. E. (1966). Étude de la résistivité des sols. Appendix to C. Burnez and H. Case: Les camps néolithiques des Matignons à Juillac-le-Coq. *Gallia Préhist.* **9**, 198–200.

Linington, R. E. (1967a). Magnetic survey at la Civita, Tarquinia, *Prospezioni Archeologiche*, **2**, 87–89.

Linington, R. E. (1967b). A short geophysical survey carried out at Bolonia, Cadiz. *Prospezioni Archeologiche*, **2**, 49–71.

May, J. (1970). Dragonby: an interim report on excavations on an Iron Age and Romano-British site near Scunthorpe, Lincolnshire, 1964–9. *Antiquar. J.* **50**, 222–245.

Musson, C. R. (1968). A geophysical survey at South Cadbury Castle, Somerset. *Prospezioni Archeologiche* **3**, 115–121.

Palmer, L. S. (1960). Geoelectrical surveying of archaeological sites. *Proc. prehist. Soc.* **26**, 64–75.

Parasnis, D. S. (1962). "Principles of Applied Geophysics." Methuen, London.

Ralph, E. K. (1964). Comparison of a proton and a rubidium magnetometer for archaeological prospecting. *Archaeometry*, **7**, 20–27.

Rees, A. I. and Wright, A. E. (1969). Resistivity surveys at Barnsley Park. *Prospezioni Archeologiche* **4**, 121–124.

Scollar, I. (1969). Some techniques for the evaluation of archaeological magnetometer surveys. *Wld Archaeol.* **1**, 77–89.

Scollar, I. (1970). Fourier transform methods for the evaluation of magnetic maps. *Prospezioni Archeologiche* **5**, 9–41.

Smellie, D. W. (1956). Elementary approximations in aeromagnetic interpretation. *Geophysics* **21**, 1021–1040.

Tite, M. S. (1966). Magnetic prospecting near to the geomagnetic equator. *Archaeometry*, **9**, 24–31.

Tite, M. S. (1967). The magnetic survey. Appendix to M. Avery, J. E. G. Sutton and J. W. Banks: Rainsborough, Northants, England—Excavations 1961–5. *Proc. prehist. Soc.* **33**, 296–300.

Tite, M. S. and Mullins, C. (1969). Electromagnetic prospecting: a preliminary investigation. *Prospezioni Archeologiche* **4**, 95–102.

Tite, M. S. and Mullins, C. (1970). Electromagnetic prospecting on archaeological sites using a soil conductivity meter. *Archaeometry* **12**, 97–104.

Tite, M. S. and Mullins, C. (1971). Enhancement of the magnetic susceptibility of soils on archaeological sites. *Archaeometry* **13**, 209–219.

Wailes, B. (1963). Excavations at Castle-an-Dinas, St. Columb Major: interim report. *Cornish Archaeol.* **2**, 51–55.

Wait, J. (Ed.) (1959). "Overvoltage Research and Geophysical Applications," Pergamon, Oxford.

Waters, G. S. and Francis, P. D. (1958). A nuclear magnetometer, *J. scient. Instrum.* **35**, 88–93.

3
Age Determination—Introduction

Since archaeology is concerned with reconstructing the development of human culture from its beginning with the first tool-makers approximately two million years ago up to the present day, the provision of a chronological framework is a basic necessity. The development of physical dating techniques (Aitken, 1970) has therefore had an immense impact on archaeology since many of these techniques provide essentially *absolute* dates which can be used to establish the temporal relationship between widely separated civilizations, and thus build up a world-wide chronology. In addition, absolute dates indicate the rate at which cultural and technological developments have occurred.

Prior to the advent of these methods, the archaeologist first established *relative* chronologies for particular areas based on sequences of artefacts, either found in a definite stratigraphic relationship to one another or exhibiting a definite typological development (Clark, 1960). Subsequently through the discovery of artefacts on widely separated sites which either exhibited a specific distinctive style or were associated with a particular environment (i.e. glacial or interglacial phases of the Pleistocene climatic fluctuations), these relative chronologies could be linked together. In some cases these relative chronologies could ultimately be linked to the absolute chronologies in areas for which approximate historical dates exist. However, historical dates exist for only a very small part of the period under consideration, the earliest being for Egypt and the Near East where they extend back to approximately 3000 BC. In addition the dates deduced by this method depend critically on the assumptions made concerning the rate of cultural diffusion and the extent of the time lag en route. Thus divergent high and low chronologies were obtained for the late Neolithic and Bronze Age in Europe when the dates were deduced from historical dates for the Near East. The high chronology resulted when a rapid cultural diffusion from the Near East was assumed while the low chronology resulted when a slow diffusion, with considerable time lags en route, was assumed.

Physical methods of age determination are based on the decay of radioactive isotopes (p. 59), the variations in the direction and intensity of the earth's magnetic field (p. 65) and the time-dependent chemical change occurring subsequent to burial (p. 66). In addition the annual recurrence of natural rhythmic processes (p. 68) and the sequence of floral and faunal development (p. 70), although not strictly physical methods of age determination, are important both in their own right and in providing material for checking, or calibrating, the physical methods. These methods of age determination are variously applied to the actual archaeological artefacts and structures, the floral and faunal remains and the geological strata with which the archaeological site is associated, their relative importance depending on the specific archaeological period (i.e. Palaeolithic, Mesolithic, Neolithic, etc.) under consideration (p. 73).

More detailed descriptions of the specifically physical methods of age determination are presented in Chapters 4 and 5 while the chronological framework provided by these methods is outlined in Chapter 6.

Radioactive Methods

Radioactive elements are unstable, the atomic nuclei decaying to a chemically different species with the emission of high energy radiation, typically alpha particles, beta particles and gamma rays. For example, the radioactive potassium isotope (^{40}K), referred to as the parent isotope, decays to argon (^{40}A), referred to as the stable daughter isotope, with the emission of a beta particle.

Radioactive decay is a spontaneous process which is unaffected by the external environment and thus provides an ideal basis for age determination. The rate of decay (i.e. the number of nuclei decaying in unit time, dN/dt) at any specified time is proportional to the number of nuclei (N) present at that time:

$$\frac{dN}{dt} = -\lambda N$$

where λ is the decay constant. Thus the number of parent nuclei decreases progressively with time and the number (N) present at time t is given by:

$$N = N_0 \exp(-\lambda t) \tag{3.1}$$

where N_0 is the initial number of parent nuclei at time $t = 0$. Similarly, the number of stable daughter nuclei increases progressively with time and assuming no daughter nuclei are present initially at time $t = 0$, the number (D) present at time t is given by:

$$D = N[\exp(\lambda t) - 1] \tag{3.2}$$

Alternatively, the radioactive decay process can be specified in terms of the half-life (τ) which is the time required for one half of a given initial number of the parent nuclei to decay to stable daughter nuclei. The half-life is related to the decay constant (λ) by the equation:

$$\tau = \frac{\ln 2}{\lambda} = \frac{0\cdot693}{\lambda}$$

and the decrease in the number of parent nuclei and the increase in the number of daughter nuclei with time, measured in unit of τ, is presented in Fig. 23.

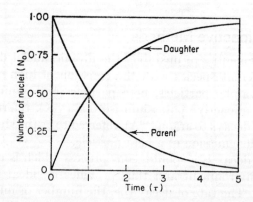

Figure 23. Radioactive decay (equation (3.1)). Curves showing the decrease in the number of parent nuclei (N) and the increase in the number of daughter nuclei ($D = N_0 - N$) with time. The number of nuclei is measured in units of N_0, the number of parent nuclei present at $t = 0$, and the time is measured in units of τ, the half-life. The number of parent nuclei has decreased to $N_0/2$, $N_0/4$, $N_0/8$, $N_0/16$ and $N_0/32$ after times of τ, 2τ, 3τ, 4τ and 5τ respectively.

Hence, if the decay constant or half-life is known, the time t, that has elapsed since the start of the radioactive decay, can be determined either by measurement of N together with a knowledge of N_0 (i.e. equation 3.1) or by measurement of the ratio D/N (equation 3.2). The radioactive isotopes which are relevant to the age determination of archaeological material are listed in Table 6, together with the values for their half-lives and an indication of their decay processes.

Radiocarbon Dating

Radioactive carbon (^{14}C), which decays to nitrogen with a half-life of 5730 years, is continually formed in the upper atmosphere due to cosmic ray bombardment of nitrogen atoms. It then becomes uniformly distributed throughout the atmosphere, the biosphere (i.e. animal and plant life) and the oceans, the ratio of radioactive ^{14}C atoms to the stable ^{12}C atoms being approximately 1 to 10^{12}. In dead material (e.g. dead wood and bone), the ^{14}C lost by radioactive decay is not replaced and therefore its concentration decreases slowly to zero according to equation (3.1). Hence the time that has elapsed since death can be determined from measurements of the ^{14}C content of the dead sample (N) and the ^{14}C content of living material (N_0). Because of small variations in the ^{14}C content of living material in the past, there is a significant deviation between the radiocarbon age, obtained from the above measurements, and the true calendar age. Therefore, in order to obtain a truly absolute chronology, corrections, provided by measurements on samples of known age (e.g. tree-rings), must be made to the radiocarbon ages. The most suitable types of sample for radiocarbon dating are charcoal and well-preserved wood, although leather, cloth, peat, shell and bone can also be used. Because of the comparatively short half-life of ^{14}C, radiocarbon dating is not applicable to samples with ages greater than approximately 50 000 years, the remaining ^{14}C concentration being too small for accurate measurement.

Geological Methods

For the age determination of archaeological material more than 50 000 years old, radioactive isotopes with half-lives longer than that for ^{14}C must be used and these normally involve the determination of the age of the geological strata with which the archaeological material is associated.

The radioactive isotopes which can be used for geological age determination (Table 6) were present in the earth's crust at its formation. They therefore exhibit extremely long half-lives since any radioactive isotopes with half-lives less than 10^7 to 10^8 years would have completely disappeared during the period that has elapsed since the formation of the earth, approximately $4\cdot6 \times 10^9$ years ago. The

Table 6. Radioactive isotopes used for age determination

Parent isotope	Decay mechanism	Stable daughter	Decay constant (year^{-1})	Half-life (years)
^{14}C	β emission	^{14}N	$1\cdot74 \times 10^{-4}$	5730
^{40}K	11% electron capture 89% β emission	^{40}A ^{40}Ca	$0\cdot58 \times 10^{-10}$ $4\cdot72 \times 10^{-10}$ }	$1\cdot31 \times 10^9$
^{238}U	(8α + 6β) series decay $4\cdot5 \times 10^{-5}$% spontaneous fission	^{206}Pb Various	$1\cdot54 \times 10^{-10}$ $6\cdot9 \times 10^{-17}$	$4\cdot51 \times 10^9$
^{235}U	(7α + 4β) series decay Neutron-induced fission	^{207}Pb Various	$9\cdot72 \times 10^{-10}$ —	$7\cdot13 \times 10^8$
^{232}Th	(6α + 4β) series decay	^{208}Pb	$4\cdot92 \times 10^{-11}$	$1\cdot41 \times 10^{10}$

associated age determination techniques are therefore more appropriate for dating rock formations older than 100 million years, rather than those of archaeological interest which are less than 2 million years old. However, by careful selection of samples and the use of sophisticated measurement techniques, both the potassium-argon and the spontaneous fission method can be applied to archaeologically revelant volcanic deposits. In addition various isotopes in the uranium decay series can be used for the age determination of deep sea sediments and bones.

When a volcanic rock is formed, its initial concentration of argon (^{40}A) is usually zero since any ^{40}A, which had accumulated prior to the volcanic eruption, will have been expelled when the rock was in a molten state. Subsequently the concentration of ^{40}A increases as a result of the decay of the radioactive potassium isotope, ^{40}K. Using a modified form of equation (3.2), the time that has elapsed since the formation of the volcanic deposit can be calculated from measurements of the concentration of ^{40}K (N) and ^{40}A (D). Because of the high abundance of potassium in the earth's crust (approximately 3 per cent) and the high sensitivity of the measurement techniques for argon, volcanic rocks formed as recently as 100 000 years ago can be dated by this method.

The spontaneous fission of the uranium isotope ^{238}U results in the formation of two heavy nuclei with very large kinetic energies. These energetic nuclei disrupt the crystal lattice of the minerals in which the ^{238}U occurs and produce damage tracks which are visible under a microscope after etching. Again, any damage tracks previously created are removed when the volcanic rock is molten so that the number of tracks present at the time of formation of a volcanic deposit is zero. Subsequently, tracks are created by spontaneous fission of ^{238}U and counting the number of tracks present in a rock sample provides a value for D, the concentration of the accumulated daughter product. The concentration of ^{238}U (N) is determined by counting the number of additional tracks produced by neutron-induced fission during a controlled neutron irradiation in a nuclear reactor. The age of the volcanic deposit can then be calculated using a modified form of equation (3.2), the method being referred to as fission track dating. The youngest volcanic deposits which can be dated by this method are typically 20 000 years old, this figure depending to a large extent on the uranium concentration in the rock. In addition, the method can be used to date man-made glasses which contain a high uranium concentration and obsidian artefacts which have been heated in antiquity while, by separating out specific minerals (e.g. zircons), the age determination of pottery is also possible.

In addition to radiocarbon dating, a number of other radioactive methods can be used to determine the age of deep sea sediments. These methods are based on the decay of intermediate radioactive isotopes in the ^{238}U and ^{235}U series which have half-lives in the range 10^4–10^5 years. For example, ionium (^{230}Th) is formed within the ^{238}U series and because of its chemical nature, it is precipitated in the sediment whereas the parent ^{238}U remains in the sea water in solution. Hence in the deposited sediment the ionium is no longer supported by its parent isotope and its concentration decreases according to equation (3.1) with a half-life of 75 200 years. Consequently, if it can be assumed that the concentration of ionium in freshly deposited sediment (N_0) has remained constant, the time that elapsed since the sediment at a given depth was deposited can be determined from measurement of its ionium content (N); age determination back to approximately 150 000 years being possible. Although no archaeological material is associated with the deep sea sediments, measurement of the ratio of the oxygen isotopes ^{18}O and ^{16}O in the calcium carbonate of the deposited fossil shells provides an estimate of the ocean temperature at the time of deposition. Hence the variations in the ocean temperature during the past 400 000 years can be determined and these fluctuations can be tentively correlated with the glacial and interglacial periods on the continents. Thus absolute dates are established for the glacial and interglacial deposits which contain the archaeological material.

The uranium decay series can also be used for the age determination of bone. In this case it is assumed that uranium, present in the ground water, is incorporated into the bone fairly soon after its burial but that no uranium decay products are incorporated. Hence the concentrations of ionium (^{230}Th) and protactinium (^{231}Pa), which is the radioactive decay product of ^{235}U and has a half-life of 32 500 years, increase from zero up to equilibrium concentrations which are proportional to their half-lives. Thus, measurement of the concentrations of these isotopes in bone provides a method of age determination. The results obtained by Hansen and Begg (1970) suggest that the underlying assumption is valid in wet conditions but that in dry situations the residence time of the uranium in the bone is less than the true age. In contrast, the results of Szabo et al. (1969) for bones from Mexico give ages which are unacceptably old from the archaeological point of view since they imply the presence of Homo sapiens more than 150 000 years before the accepted date for the Old World. An alternative approach involving the measurement of the amount of helium that has accumulated in the bones, as a result of the alpha particles produced during the decay of the uranium series, has been less successful; the results of Turekian et al. (1970) indicating that there is continuous loss of helium from the bone.

Thermoluminescent Dating

Unlike the methods outlined above, thermoluminescent dating of pottery does not depend on either the decreasing concentration of a parent radioactive isotope or the increasing concentration of a stable daughter isotope. Instead, the method is associated with the effect of the high energy radiation (i.e. alpha particles, beta particles and gamma rays) emitted as a result of the decay of the radioactive impurities in the pottery (i.e. a few parts per million of ^{238}U and ^{232}Th and a few hundred parts per million of ^{40}K). Because the half-lives of ^{238}U, ^{232}Th and ^{40}K are very long (Table 6), their concentrations in the pottery, and hence the radiation dose that they provide per year, have remained effectively constant.

A fraction of the energy associated with this radiation is permanently stored, in the form of trapped electrons, in the crystal lattice of the minerals present in the pottery. When the pottery is subsequently heated to 500°C, this stored energy is released in the form of visible light, referred to as thermoluminescence. Thus, when the raw clay is fired to produce the pottery, the stored energy acquired by the clay during geological times is removed. Subsequently the stored energy increases linearly from zero as a result of radiation from the radioactive impurities and the present-day amount, which is proportional to the time that has elapsed since firing, can be determined by measuring the thermoluminescence emitted when the pottery is heated. The age of the pottery can therefore be determined if, in addition to this so-called natural thermoluminescence, the thermoluminescence induced by a known radiation dose and the radiation dose received by the pottery per year are also measured.

Application of this method of age determination is obviously limited to those periods for which pottery or fired clay is available; that is, with a few exceptions, back to approximately 6000 BC. Although, in principle, the method should also be applicable to volcanic lavas, stone artefacts (e.g. flint and obsidian) which have been heated in antiquity and bones, a number of additional problems arise with these materials.

Magnetic Dating

When clay or rocks are fired to approximately 700°C and allowed to cool in the earth's magnetic field, they acquire a weak permanent magnetism, referred to as thermoremanent magnetism (see Chapter 2, p. 10). The direction of this magnetism is parallel to the Earth's magnetic field and therefore fired clay structures (e.g. pottery kilns, hearths) and rocks (e.g. volcanic lavas) found *in situ* provide a record of the direction of the Earth's magnetic field when they were last heated. Since the direction of the Earth's magnetic field, defined in terms of the angle of declination and the angle of dip, changes continuously with time, the measurement of thermoremanent magnetism provides the basis for a method of dating. Unfortunately, it is not possible to calculate the changes in direction that have occurred in the past and it is therefore necessary to first establish a reference curve using fired structures of known age. Furthermore, the reference curve thus obtained is only applicable to a region approximately 500 miles across. Consequently, in Britain the application of magnetic dating has been limited to the Roman and Mediaeval periods for which an adequate number of pottery kilns of known age are available for establishing the reference curve.

In addition to changes in direction, the intensity of the Earth's magnetic field also varies with time and the strength of the thermo-remanent magnetism is proportional to the magnetic field intensity when the material was last heated. The past magnetic field intensity can therefore be determined by comparing the strength of the thermo-remanent magnetism acquired in antiquity with that acquired as a result of reheating and cooling in a magnetic field of known intensity. In the case of intensity measurements the fired clay need not be found *in situ* and consequently pottery fragments can be used. A reference curve, showing the changes in intensity of the earth's magnetic field that have occurred in the past, must again be established and since the intensity changes more slowly than the direction, the possibility of using intensity variations as a basis for dating is somewhat remote. However, a knowledge of the past intensity of the earth's magnetic field is extremely important in explaining the difference between radiocarbon dates and true calendar dates.

Dating by Chemical Change

The progressive time-dependent chemical alteration of bone, obsidian, glass and parchment subsequent to burial in the ground provides a further approach to age determination. However, since the rate of chemical alteration depends on the environmental conditions, it is normally only possible to obtain relative dates for specimens found in the same environment; calibration with specimens of known age being necessary for each environment considered, if absolute dates are required.

The dating of bone depends on the accumulation or the deple-tion of specific chemical elements in the bone. For example, fluorine and uranium are gradually incorporated into the phosphatic material of the bone, the rate of acquisition depending principally upon the concentrations of these elements in the ground water percolating through the deposits. Similarly the nitrogen content of the bone decreases due to the gradual disappearance of protein, the rate of depletion depending on the temperature and moisture content of the deposits. Hence, by measurement of the concentrations of these elements in a series of bones found in a particular deposit, their relative ages can be determined. It is therefore possible to establish whether a specific bone is really of the age suggested by its position in the deposit or whether it was inserted at some later date, this information being particularly important in the case of the extremely rare human skeletal remains from the Palaeolithic period.

The dating of artefacts made from obsidian, which is a variety of volcanic glass, is possible because a fresh surface of obsidian, such as would be produced by the chipping and flaking employed in the manufacture of the artefacts, slowly absorbs water from its surroundings to form a hydration layer. The thickness of the layer is proportional to the square root of the time that has elapsed since the exposure of the fresh surface, the rate of growth depending on the temperature of the environment. The age of an obsidian artefact can therefore be determined from the measurement of the thickness of the hydration layer (typically a few microns) under a microscope, calibration with specimens of known age being necessary for each temperature zone considered. The method is applicable to obsidian artefacts ranging in age from 30 000 BC to 1500 AD. Unfortunately, the formation of a hydration layer appears to be restricted to obsidian and does not occur on other materials, such as flint, quartz and chert, which were also used for stone artefacts.

The surface of man-made glass can also be chemically altered during burial, the alkali in the glass being leached out and replaced by water to form a semi-opaque surface crust. Microscopic examination of the surface crusts has established that they consist of a series of very thin layers and it has been further suggested that, as a result of seasonal variations in temperature or availability of water, one layer is formed annually. With this assumption, it would be possible to determine the date at which the glass was buried by counting the number of layers in the crust. Unfortunately, the annual formation of a surface layer seems to only occur under exceptional, but ill-understood, environmental conditions and therefore the method has very limited application to the age determination of ancient glass.

The dating of parchment, which is made from unhaired animal

skins by drying under tension, is possible because of time-dependent degenerative changes occurring in the collagen fibres when the parchment is kept in a dry environment. The extent of these changes can be estimated by observing the temperature at which shrinkage of the collagen fibres occurs when they are heated at a constant rate after rehydration, the shrinkage temperature decreasing with increasing degeneration, and hence age, of the parchment. Burton *et al.* (1959) studied a wide selection of parchment-like materials ranging in age from 1300 BC to 1950 AD and including fragments from the Dead Sea scrolls. The shrinkage temperatures exhibited a general decrease from 55°C to 25°C with increasing age of the parchment and although no precise age determination was possible, the results confirmed the antiquity of the Dead Sea scrolls and indicated that the mediaeval date, suggested by some authorities, was unlikely.

Natural Rhythmic Processes

The annual recurrence of natural rhythmic processes, such as tree-ring formation and varve deposition, provide further methods of absolute dating.

Dendrochronology

Seasonal changes in the wood growth of trees produce annual rings, each ring starting with large cell-elements associated with spring growth and ending with small cell-elements associated with summer and autumn growth.

Dendrochronology (Bannister, 1969) involves the study of tree-rings for the purposes of dating, the age of a tree being determined by counting the number of rings. The thickness of the tree-rings is governed by environmental factors, such as rainfall and temperature. Thus in semi-arid climates, thick rings are associated with wet summers and thin rings with dry summers while in northern climates, temperature is the dominant factor, cold summers reducing the ring thickness. Hence a distinctive sequence of annual rainfalls or temperatures is reflected as a distinctive sequence in terms of the thickness of the annual rings. It is therefore possible to establish the sequence of tree-rings back through several generations of trees: starting with a living tree, a distinctive group of early rings is matched to a corresponding group in older wood from, for example, dead trees or building timbers (Fig. 24). Using the bristlecone pines from the White Mountains of California, which grow to ages of more than 4000 years and which are well preserved after death, a 7100 year chronology has been established by this technique, with expectation of eventual extension back to 9000 years (Ferguson, 1968).

Due to variations in climate, the tree-rings sequence must be established separately for each region or continent under consideration. In addition, detailed cross-checking between tree specimens from the chosen region is necessary in order to avoid error due to "missing rings" and "multiple rings". Having established the "mas-

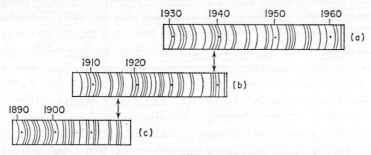

Figure 24. Idealized diagram representing the principles of dendrochronology. Series A represents a specimen taken from a living tree with a known outside date. A distinctive group of inner rings is matched to the corresponding group in a specimen from a dead tree (Series B) which can therefore be dated and can then be used to extend the tree-ring chronology back for a further twenty years. Similarly an older specimen of dead wood (Series C) extends the chronology further into the past.

ter" tree-ring sequence, then timber remains from archaeological sites can be dated by matching their ring patterns to the "master" sequence for the region. The classic example of this technique is provided by Douglass (1929) who was able to establish the prehistoric chronology of Indian dwelling sites in the south-western United States, showing that the earliest may have originated 1900 years ago. The work on Indian sites in the United States has now been considerably extended (Schulman, 1956) while the technique has also been applied to prehistoric and mediaeval timber from Europe (Huber and Giertz, 1970). In interpreting the results for archaeological material, the possibility that the timber originated from the centre of a large tree must be borne in mind since in this case the date obtained could precede the cutting of the tree, and hence its employment on the archaeological site, by several centuries.

Tree-ring studies are also extremely important because they provide reliably dated samples for establishing the relationship between the radiocarbon age and the true calendar age. Once an annual tree-ring has been formed, its constituent carbon atoms are no longer in equilibrium with the atmosphere and ^{14}C, lost by radioactive decay, is not replaced. Therefore, in the context of radiocarbon dating, the inner tree-rings can be regarded as dead, the radiocarbon age indicating the date of formation of the ring.

Varves

The annual layers of sediment formed on the bed of lakes at the edge of glaciers are in many ways analogous to tree-rings. During the summer melting of a glacier, gravel, sand and clay are delivered into the lake: the coarser gravel and sand are deposited during the summer season itself while during the winter, when melting of the glacier ceases, the finer clay particles gradually precipitate. Thus one year's sedimentation, known as a varve, consists of a coarse layer overlain by a fine layer. As in the case of tree-rings, the thickness of the varves is governed by climatic factors, a hot dry summer producing a thick varve while a cold wet summer produces a thin varve. Hence a distinctive climatic sequence is again reflected as a distinctive sequence in terms of the thickness of the annual varves. It is therefore possible to correlate the short series of varves formed at different points as the ice-sheet progressively withdrew across a considerable tract of country. By counting the varves in sections, as close together as possible, de Geer (1940) was able to establish a chronology for the retreat of the glacial ice-sheet across Scandinavia for the past 14 000 years, the varve sections studied being spread over several hundred kilometres.

Although, as in the case of deep-sea sediments, no archaeological material is associated with the varve deposits, it is possible by comparison of, for example, the pollen spectra (p. 71) to link the varve chronology to archaeological deposits in adjacent regions. However, the major importance of the varve sequences to archaeology is that they provide further dated samples for establishing the relationship between the radiocarbon and true calendar ages, especially for the period prior to 5000 BC when tree-ring specimens are not available.

Dating by Flora and Fauna

As with the earlier geological epochs, changes in the composition of the flora and fauna can be used as a means of relative dating in the Pleistocene and Postglacial periods (West, 1968). However during these periods, the rapid climatic changes (i.e. glacial and interglacial phases) are the main cause of the alteration in the distribution and abundance of the floral and faunal species, the evolutionary development of the species being less important than is the case in the study of the stratigraphy of older deposits.

Microscopic examination of tree, shrub and grass pollens which are retained in stratigraphic sequence in, for example, lake sediments and peat bogs, provides an almost complete record of the fluctuations in the composition of the flora during the Pleistocene and Postglacial

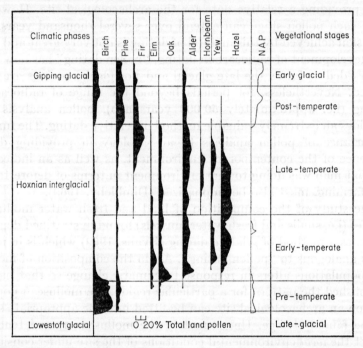

Figure 25. Simplified pollen diagram during the Hoxnian interglacial for which four major vegetational stages can be identified (see Table 13 for the climatic phases during the Pleistocene). During the pre-temperate stage, the pollen diagram is dominated by birch, pine and non-arboreal pollen (NAP—grass, herb, sedge); during the early-temperate stage, oak, alder, yew, and hazel dominate; during the late-temperate stage, fir and hornbeam pollen also become significant and during the post-temperate stage, birch, pine and non-arboreal pollen reappear (after West, 1968).

periods; the sequence of floral change being determined, at least prior to agriculture, principally by the climatic changes that occurred. Hence, during the glacial phases, trees are rare or absent and the pollen diagram is dominated by sedge and grass pollen. Towards the end of the glacial phase, birch and pine trees begin to appear while the subsequent interglacial phase is characterized by deciduous forests. The vegetational history of each interglacial can normally be divided into four major stages (Fig. 25) which differ in detail from those of the other interglacials. Similarly the end of the last glacial phase and the Postglacial period can be subdivided into nine major vegetational stages.

Therefore, having established the floral sequence of a particular region from pollen analysis, the pollen diagram associated with an archaeological site can be fitted into its appropriate pollen stage, thus providing a relative date for the archaeological site. However, since each pollen stage can extend over several thousand years, the precision achieved by this method of dating is not very great and with the development of radiocarbon dating, "pollen dating" has now been superseded as far as the late glacial and Postglacial periods are concerned. Nevertheless, for periods beyond the range of radiocarbon dating (i.e. approximately 50 000 years ago), pollen analysis still provides an extremely valuable method of relative dating. The further importance of pollen analysis to archaeology in providing direct evidence of the contemporary environment, as well as an indication of what man was doing to that environment in terms of deforestation and farming, must also be emphasized (Dimbleby, 1969).

The study of the composition of land and fresh water molluscan species (i.e. snails and fresh water mussels) found in stratified deposits provides a method of relative dating (Evans, 1969) which is in many ways analogous to "pollen dating". Again the composition of molluscan populations alters in response to climatic change so that having established the pattern for a particular region, the molluscan population on an archaeological site can be fitted into the appropriate stage in the faunal change. Unfortunately the molluscan record tends to reflect the *local* environmental conditions of the site under consideration to a far greater extent than does the pollen spectrum. This limitation is due to the fact that, because of their relatively large size and the immobility of the animals, molluscan shells are not transported over long distances by terrestrial and aerial agencies. The microscopic pollen grains are in contrast readily airborne and can be transported over distances as large as 100 km; thus strictly localized differences in the pollen spectra are averaged out. However it seems probable that, with further detailed study, the molluscan record could be valuable in supplementing "pollen dating", especially in the case of alkaline deposits in which the pollen is often not preserved.

Applications

It is apparent from the above discussion that the radioactive methods are of prime importance for obtaining a world-wide, absolute chronology and that, of these methods, radiocarbon dating has made the greatest impact on archaeology. Even though the radiocarbon age differs from the true calendar age, the necessary correction can be estimated and once obtained, it is applicable throughout the world. This contrasts with the situation for magnetic dating and for the methods based on chemical change when the calibration curve, necessary for absolute age determination, is only applicable to a specific geographical region.

For the Palaeolithic period, prior to approximately 50 000 BP, archaeological material is normally dated by means of the geological strata in which it is found. If volcanic in origin, the absolute age of the geological strata can be determined directly by the potassium–argon and fission track methods. Thus at Lake Rudolf in Kenya, a group of stone tools, found embedded in volcanic tuff, could be dated as not later than approximately 2·6 million years using the potassium–argon method. However most archaeological material is found in non-volcanic strata, such as glacial deposits and river terraces, and in this case the geological age determination techniques would merely provide a date for the original rock formations from which these later Pleistocene deposits were derived. Therefore non-volcanic strata, containing archaeological material, must be fitted into the sequence of glacial and interglacial phases for which a tentative absolute chronology is provided by the dating of related volcanic deposits and the study of the temperature fluctuations "recorded" in deep-sea sediments. With the exception of the fission track dating of obsidian which was heated in antiquity, no absolute dating methods are at present available for the direct age determination of the stone artefacts themselves, although it is possible that, with further developments, thermoluminescent dating might be used for the age determination of flint which was heated in antiquity. Similarly, the dating of bones by chemical change only provides relative dates, which can be used to confirm the ages suggested by their positions in the geological strata. However, it is again possible that with further developments both thermoluminescent dating and radioactive dating, based on the uranium decay series, might provide reliable absolute methods for the age determination of bone.

For the period subsequent to approximately 50 000 BP, radiocarbon dating has been extensively used to provide a world-wide and essentially absolute chronology. However care must be exercised in establishing the correct relationship between the archaeological artefacts or structures and the surviving organic material (e.g. wood, charcoal, bone) used for radiocarbon dating. Therefore the direct age determination of the artefacts or structures themselves is preferable whenever possible. With the development of man's material culture and technological competence during the Neolithic and subsequent periods, a greatly extended range of artefacts and structures is available for age determination by physical methods. In particular, thermoluminescent dating of pottery appears to be an extremely promising absolute method of age determination especially since pottery, because of its durability, is relatively abundant on most archaeological sites whereas suitable organic material for radiocarbon dating is frequently not available. In addition magnetic dating of pottery kilns can be valuable for recent periods (e.g. Roman and Mediaeval) when a more detailed chronology is required, its general application being limited by the need to establish calibration curves for each region under consideration. Although the volcanic glass, obsidian, can be dated by measurement of the thickness of the hydration layer on the surface, the age determination of man-made glass appears to be more difficult: dating by means of the equivalent chemical changes occurring at the surface of the glass is of uncertain validity while the fission track method is only applicable to glass with a high uranium content. Similarly, it should be noted that no generally applicable physical methods for the age determination of metal artefacts are at present available.

Finally, it must be emphasized that the physical methods of age determination are all liable to certain inherent errors, as indicated in the subsequent detailed descriptions. Therefore the dates, provided by these methods, must always be carefully considered in the context of the archaeological stratigraphy and the typology of the associated artefacts, together with the geological, floral and faunal environment.

References

Aitken, M. J. (1970). Physics applied to archaeology—I. Dating. *Rep. Prog. Phys.* **33**, 941–1000.
Bannister, B. (1969). Dendrochronology. *In* "Science in Archaeology," (Eds. D. Brothwell and E. Higgs), pp. 191–205. Thames and Hudson, London.

Burton, D., Poole, J. B. and Reed, R. (1959). A new approach to the dating of the Dead Sea scrolls. *Nature* **184**, 533–534.

Clark, J. G. D. (1960). "Archaeology and Society", pp. 132–138. Methuen, London.

Dimbleby, G. W. (1969). Pollen analysis. *In* "Science in Archaeology" (Eds. D. Brothwell and E. Higgs), pp. 167–177. Thames and Hudson, London.

Douglass, A. E. (1929). The secret of the south-west solved by talkative tree-rings. *Natn geogr. Mag.* **56**, 737–770.

Evans, J. G. (1969). Land and freshwater Mollusca in archaeology: chronological aspects. *Wld Archaeol.* **1**, 170–183.

Ferguson, C. W. (1968). Bristlecone pine: science and esthetics. *Science* **159**, 839–846.

Geer, G. de (1940). Geochronologia sueccia principles. *K. svenska Vetensk-Akad. Handl.* Ser. 3, **18**, No. 6.

Hansen, R. O. and Begg, E. L. (1970). Age of Quaternary sediments and soils in the Sacramento area, California by uranium and actinium series dating of vertebrate fossils. *Earth Planetary Sci. Lett.* **8**, 411–419.

Huber, B. and Giertz, V. (1970). Central European dendrochronology for the Middle Ages. *In* "Scientific methods in Medieval Archaeology" (Ed. R. Berger), pp. 201–212. University of California Press, Berkeley.

Schulman, E. (1956). "Dendroclimatic Changes in Semiarid America." University of Arizona Press, Tucson.

Szabo, B. J., Malde, H. E. and Irwin-Williams, C. (1969). Dilemma posed by uranium-series dates on archaeologically significant bones from Valsequillo, Pueblo, Mexico. *Earth Planetary Sci. Lett.* **6**, 237–244.

Turekian, K. K., Kharkar, D. P., Funkhouser, J. and Schaeffer, O. A. (1970). An evaluation of the uranium-helium method of dating fossil bones. *Earth Planetary Sci. Lett.* **7**, 420–424.

West, R. G. (1968). "Pleistocene Geology and Biology—with especial reference to the British Isles", pp. 110–134 and 292–355. Longmans, London.

4

Age Determination— Radioactive Methods

Of the available physical methods of dating, the methods based on radioactivity are of fundamental importance since they come nearest to providing the world-wide, absolute chronology required by archaeology.

The general principles of radioactive decay have been outlined in Chapter 3, (p. 59) where the time scales, for which the associated methods are applicable, have been indicated. In the present chapter, a detailed description of the principles, techniques and limitations of radiocarbon dating (p. 76), potassium-argon dating (p. 90), fission track dating (p. 99), the study of deep-sea sediments (p. 106) and thermoluminescent dating (p. 114) is presented. Typical age determination results are included for each of the methods, while the overall chronological framework provided for the different archaeological periods is presented in Chapter 6.

Radiocarbon Dating

The development of radiocarbon dating started when Libby (1946) predicted the formation of the radioactive carbon isotope, ^{14}C, in the course of a study of the effects of cosmic rays on the Earth's atmosphere. The early experiments were soon exploited (Arnold and Libby, 1949; Libby, 1955) and the value of the method, together with the theoretical perception behind it, was officially recognized in 1960 by the award to W. F. Libby of the Nobel Prize for Chemistry.

General Principles

When cosmic rays enter the Earth's atmosphere, slow or thermal neutrons are produced. These neutrons interact with atmospheric nitrogen (^{14}N) converting it to radioactive carbon (^{14}C). The chemical behaviour of ^{14}C is, except for isotopic fractionation, the same as that of ordinary carbon (^{12}C) and it is therefore rapidly oxidized to form heavy carbon dioxide which mixes with the ordinary carbon dioxide of the atmosphere. Plants grow by photosynthesis of atmospheric carbon dioxide while animals live off plants. Similarly, atmospheric carbon dioxide becomes dissolved in the oceans where it is taken up

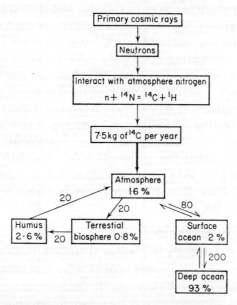

Figure 26. Production process for ^{14}C and the carbon exchange reservoir. The yearly transfer of natural carbon between the compartments of the reservoir is expressed in units of 10^9 tons. The percentages refer to the natural carbon in each compartment, the total natural carbon in the reservoir being 40×10^{12} tons.

by living organisms and enters into exchange reactions with dissolved carbonates and bicarbonates. Thus the ^{14}C formed by cosmic ray neutrons becomes uniformly distributed throughout the carbon exchange reservoir comprising the atmosphere, the biosphere (i.e. animals and plant life) and the oceans (Fig. 26); the time taken to achieve uniform distribution being short compared to the half-life for ^{14}C.

The estimated production rate for ^{14}C by cosmic ray neutrons is approximately 7·5 kg per year while ^{14}C disintegrates to ^{14}N, emitting a beta particle, with a half-life of 5730 years. Thus an equilibrium amount, approximately 62 tons, of ^{14}C exists in the exchange reservoir such that the loss by decay is just balanced by the creation in the atmosphere. Since the exchange reservoir contains approximately 40×10^{12} tons of carbon, the ratio of ^{14}C atoms to ^{12}C atoms is only 1 to $0·8 \times 10^{12}$.

Living plants and animals therefore contain the above equilibrium proportion of ^{14}C. However, once dead, the plant or animal is no longer taking in carbon dioxide from the atmosphere so that the ^{14}C lost by radioactive decay is not replaced and therefore its concentration slowly decreases—by approximately 1 per cent every 83 years. Consequently, by measuring the ^{14}C concentration in, for example, dead wood and comparing it with the concentration in modern living wood, the age of the dead wood can be calculated from equation (3.1), the half-life for ^{14}C being determined by laboratory measurements. The basic assumption on which this method of dating depends is that the ^{14}C concentration in living plants and animals has always been the same as it is today. Although recent measurements, to be discussed below, have shown that this assumption is not strictly justified, early confirmation of its approximate validity was obtained by measurements on wood from Egypt which could be dated by means of historical records (Libby, 1955).

Experimental Procedures

In living material the $^{14}C/^{12}C$ ratio is only 1 to $0·8 \times 10^{12}$ and in older samples it is less by a factor of two for each 5730 years (i.e. the half-life) that has elapsed since death. Measurement of this ratio by means of a mass spectrometer is therefore impossible and instead the radioactive decay of the ^{14}C must itself be employed. ^{14}C decays to the stable nitrogen isotope, ^{14}N, with the emission of a beta particle with a maximum energy of 160 keV. Hence, by measuring the number of beta particles emitted per sec by one gram (i.e. the specific activity) of ancient "dead" carbon (I) and comparing this with the number emitted by one gram of modern "living" carbon (I_0), the time (t years) that has elapsed since the death of the ancient carbon can be calculated using the relationship:

$$t = \frac{5730}{0·693} \ln \left(\frac{I_0}{I}\right) \qquad (4.1)$$

For modern carbon, only 15 beta particles are emitted per minute per gram of carbon while for ancient carbon the number emitted decreases progressively to approximately 1 per minute per gram for a 23 000-year-old sample (i.e. four half-lives). The counting equipment must therefore be shielded from cosmic rays otherwise the effect of beta particles from the sample itself will be insignificant. This necessitates a 20 cm thick shield of steel together with an anticoincidence shield which consists of a ring of Geiger counters surrounding the beta particle counter: with this shielding system the background cosmic ray count-rate can be reduced to less than 10 per cent of the count-rate for modern carbon. In addition, because of their low energy, the beta particles are weak in terms of penetrating power so that their intensity is roughly halved by a 2 cm thickness of air or a 10 μm thickness of aluminium. It is therefore essential that the sample is inserted inside the counter rather than being separated from it by a window.

The most commonly employed counting system involves the conversion of the carbon into a gas, such as carbon dioxide, methane or acetylene, which is then used as the counting gas of a proportional counter. Each beta particle emitted by the ^{14}C produces ionization in the gas which is recorded as an electrical pulse. Typically the counter volume is several litres and the gas pressure is 1–2 atmospheres; the sample size is approximately 1–2 g of carbon and the count-rate obtained with modern carbon is between 10 and 20 counts per minute. Alternatively, the carbon is converted into an organic liquid, such as methanol, benzene or toluene, which is then used as a solvent for a liquid scintillator. In this case the ionization produced by the beta particle results in the emission of "flash" of visible light which can be detected using a photomultiplier. Although the chemical conversion is more difficult, the liquid scintillator method has the advantage that, for the same weight of carbon, the active volume of the detector is much smaller than with the gas proportional counter: shielding against the cosmic ray background is therefore much easier.

Since radioactive decay is a spontaneous process, the observed rates of disintegration will vary about the average values specified by equation (4.1). Thus the total number of beta particles (n) counted for a carbon sample is subject to an inherent statistical error of $\pm \sqrt{n}$, the quantity $\sqrt{n}$ being referred to as the standard deviation. This means that there is a 68 per cent probability that the true average for the number of beta particles lies between $(n - \sqrt{n})$ and $(n + \sqrt{n})$.

The accuracy of the measurement of the specific activity (i.e. I and I_0), and thus the accuracy of the radiocarbon date, can therefore be increased by increasing the total number of beta particles counted. For an accuracy of 1 per cent in the specific activity, it is necessary to count 10 000 beta particles (i.e. $\sqrt{10\,000} = 100 = 1$ per cent of 10 000). Assuming a zero background count-rate, this accuracy would require a measurement time of 12 hours for one gram of modern carbon and 200 hours for one gram of 23 000-year-old carbon. However, because the background count-rate is approximately equal to the beta particle count-rate for a 23 000-year-old sample, the accuracy achieved, even after a 200 hour count, would be considerably less than 1 per cent and therefore the background count-rate sets a practical limit of approximately 50 000 years to the age that can be determined. This limit can, in principle, be extended to 70 000 years by means of isotopic enrichment in which the ^{14}C is artificially enriched with respect to the ^{12}C using a thermal diffusion column (Haring *et al.*, 1958). However problems of sample contamination then become formidable and in practice the limit remains at around 50 000 years.

A further measurement which is now normally undertaken is the evaluation of the isotopic fractionation that has occurred in the sample. Although ^{14}C is identical to ^{12}C in its chemical behaviour, its higher atomic weight does manifest itself in nature in terms of slight variations in $^{14}C/^{12}C$ ratio in different parts of the exchange reservoir. The exchange reaction between the atmospheric carbon dioxide and terrestrial plant life results in a lower (typically 2–4 per cent) ^{14}C concentration in the latter; conversely the exchange between atmospheric carbon dioxide and ocean carbonate favours a slightly higher (typically 1 per cent) ^{14}C concentration in the latter. The extent of this isotopic fractionation can be determined by comparing the ratio of ^{13}C to ^{12}C for the atmosphere with that for the carbon sample under consideration, using mass spectrometry measurements. ^{13}C, being a stable isotope which occurs in the ratio of approximately 1 to 100 with respect to ^{12}C, is unaffected by the age of the sample and its concentration therefore provides a true evaluation of the fractionation effect. The effect for ^{14}C is then obtained by doubling the percentage enrichment or deficiency found for ^{13}C and can be taken into account in age determination by suitable modification of equation (4.1).

Because of the elaborate chemical preparation of the carbon which is necessary to produce a suitable "counting" gas or liquid, together with the long counting times involved, it can be readily appreciated that radiocarbon dating is an expensive and time-consuming process.

Selection of Samples

The samples used for radiocarbon dating must once have been part of the carbon exchange reservoir, thus forming part of a living organism. It follows that the event dated is the death of the organism and therefore it is essential that after death the sample remains isolated from the exchange reservoir. Consequently, in selecting samples, it is essential to remove any extraneous contamination by modern carbon such as might arise from humic acids in the soil. This problem is particularly severe in the case of very old samples since for a 23 000-year-old sample (i.e. four half-lives), the addition of 1 per cent of modern carbon increases the specific activity by 16 per cent, corresponding to an under-estimation of its age by 1300 years. Conversely, the deposition of calcium carbonate may contaminate the sample with "old" carbon, thus leading to an over-estimation of its age. In most instances, contamination can be removed in the laboratory by treatment with alkali (for the humic acids) and acid (for the calcium carbonate) but clearly certain materials are more amenable to this treatment than others.

Charcoal, which is widely associated with human activity, and well-preserved wood provide the most reliable samples for radiocarbon dating. However there is always the possibility that the samples of charcoal or wood were derived from the inner rings of a slow growing tree and in this case the radiocarbon date could be earlier than the archaeological event of felling the tree by several hundred years. Peat, hair, skin, leather, textiles, antler and paper provide fairly reliable samples as long as care is taken to remove contaminants. Bone is not normally recommended because its carbon content is low and its porous structure facilitates the deposition of contaminants. However, recent work (Longin, 1971) has established that by extracting the collagen and confining measurements to this component, reliable ages can be obtained. Large, well-preserved marine shells provide reasonably reliable dates if allowance is made for the effect of isotopic fractionation between the atmospheric carbon dioxide and the ocean carbonate and the fact that, as a result of comparatively long mixing times, the $^{14}C/^{12}C$ ratio for deep ocean carbonate is lower than for atmospheric carbon dioxide. Attempts have also been made to date ancient iron (van der Merwe, 1969) using the carbon (typically less than 1 per cent) which is incorporated into the iron during smelting with charcoal.

The amount of sample required for radiocarbon dating varies both with the type of sample and the counting equipment. However it is normally desirable that the sample is sufficient to provide between one and two grams of carbon and therefore typical minimum sample weights range from 1 g for charcoal and wood to 10 g for shell, 50 g for uncharred bone and 500 g for iron.

Fossil Fuel Effect and Nuclear Weapon Tests

In addition to the natural fluctuations in the ^{14}C concentration of the exchange reservoir two recent effects associated with man's activities must be considered.

The combustion of coal and oil releases into the atmosphere large quantities of carbon dioxide from which the ^{14}C has long disappeared since the coal and oil were removed from the exchange reservoir millions of years ago. This "old" carbon dilutes the ^{14}C concentration in the atmosphere and therefore the specific activity of wood samples grown in 1950 (prior to hydrogen bomb testing) is in fact lower than that for samples grown in 1850 (prior to the industrial revolution), despite the decay that has occurred in the latter. The effect was first established by Suess (1955) and is referred to as the fossil-fuel effect. It is estimated that the "old" carbon released by the combustion of fossil-fuel between 1860 and 1954 amounts to 13 per cent of the existing carbon content of the atmosphere or 0·2 per cent of the carbon in the whole exchange reservoir. As a result of finite mixing times between the different components of the reservoir, the effective dilution of the ^{14}C in the atmosphere in 1954 was approximately 2 per cent.

The high neutron flux, associated with a nuclear bomb explosion, produces ^{14}C in the same way as do the naturally occurring neutrons produced by cosmic rays. As a result of nuclear weapon testing up to 1962, approximately 2 tons of ^{14}C have been added to the exchange reservoir (Walton et al., 1967) increasing its ^{14}C concentration by approximately 3 per cent and more than compensating for the dilution effect of fossil-fuel combustion. Again, as a result of finite mixing times within the reservoir, the atmospheric ^{14}C concentration, as determined from recently grown plants, is at present approximately double the level in the pre-bomb era.

As a result of the fossil-fuel effect and nuclear weapon testing, recently grown wood cannot be used to provide the standard for the specific activity of living material (I_0) in age determination measurements. Instead wood grown prior to the onset of the fossil-fuel effect in 1850 is used after correction for the decay of the ^{14}C: an oxalic acid standard, supplied by the National Bureau of Standards, Washington, U.S.A., then provides a universal reference against which individual laboratory wood standards may be checked.

Fluctuations in the ^{14}C Concentration of the Exchange Reservoir

Since radiocarbon dating involves comparing the specific activity of an *ancient* dead sample (I) with that of a *modern* living sample (I_0), the validity of the dates depends critically on the assumption that the atmospheric ^{14}C concentration, and hence the activity of the carbon in living material, has remained constant over past time. Although early measurements on known-age samples (Arnold and Libby, 1949) confirmed the validity of this assumption to within the accuracy then attainable, subsequent more precise measurements have conclusively established that significant natural fluctuations in the atmospheric ^{14}C concentration have occurred in the past. The quantitative evaluation of these fluctuations, together with the investigation of their geophysical causes, were the subject of a Nobel Symposium (No. XII: Radiocarbon Variations and Absolute Chronology) held in Uppsala in August 1969, the archaeologically relevant results being summarized by Neustupný (1970).

Tree-ring samples, dated by dendrochronology (Chapter 3, p. 68), provide a detailed sequence of known-age samples for investigating the past variations in the atmospheric ^{14}C concentration and hence the relationship between the radiocarbon age and the true calendar age. Evidence for short term fluctuations was first obtained by de Vries (1958) using European and American trees spanning the past 500 years while a more comprehensive evaluation of the variations, spanning the past 7000 years, has subsequently been achieved using the long-lived bristlecone pines from the White Mountains of California (Suess, 1970a). The results (Fig. 27a) indicate that the variations in the atmospheric ^{14}C concentration are of two types: first there is a gradual sinusoidal change, with a period of approximately 10 000 years, which produces the decrease in ^{14}C concentration from an excess of 9 per cent around 5000 BC to a deficit of 1 per cent by 500

AD and, second, there are the short-term fluctuations of a few per cent which are superimposed upon the sinusoidal change. Confirmation that these variations, derived from measurements on the bristle-cone pines from North America, are world-wide is provided by measurements on tree-rings from different latitudes in the northern and southern hemispheres (Lerman *et al.*, 1970) and by measurements

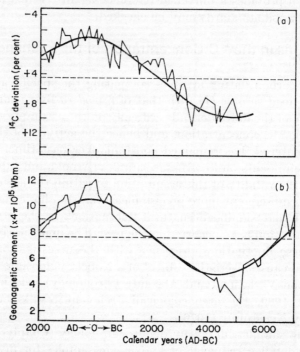

Figure 27. (a) Fluctuations in the ^{14}C concentration of the atmosphere over the past 7000 years, as determined from tree-ring data (after Suess, 1970b). The ^{14}C deviations are determined with respect to the standard atmospheric ^{14}C concentration prior to the industrial revolution and are calculated using the 5730 year half-life. The calendar years refer to dendrochronological tree-ring years. The best-fit sinusoidal change (period about 10 000 years) in the atmospheric ^{14}C concentration is also shown. (b) Fluctuations in the Earth's magnetic moment ($4\pi \times 10^{15}$ Wb m $= 10^{25}$ gauss cm^3) over the past 9000 years as determined from the thermoremanent magnetism measurements on fired clay from Europe, Central America and Japan (after Bucha, 1970). The best-fit sinusoidal change (period about 9000 years) in the geomagnetic moment is also shown and can be seen to exhibit a close inverse correlation with the deviations in the atmospheric ^{14}C concentration.

on Egyptian archaeological material (e.g. wood, reed and linen) which can be dated from historical records (Berger, 1970; Edwards, 1970). The fact that the variations in atmospheric ^{14}C concentration are the same throughout the world is of course to be expected since the atmosphere becomes thoroughly mixed within a time less than a decade.

Although it is anticipated that the "bristlecone pine" chronology will ultimately be extended back to 7000 BC, it is at present necessary to use the varve chronology (p. 70) in order to extend the investigation of the variation in the ^{14}C concentration beyond 5000 BC. Two extended varve sequences are currently available, one being the classic Swedish varve chronology of de Geer and the other being from the Lake of Clouds, Minnesota. The Minnesota sequence, which spans the period from the present day back to 8000 BC, contains sufficient

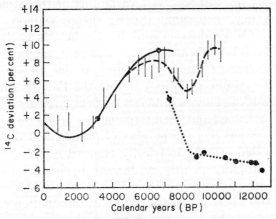

Figure 28. Fluctuations in the ^{14}C concentration of the atmosphere over the past 13 000 years (after Stuiver, 1970). Solid curve represents the simplified tree-ring data. Dashed curve and vertical lines represent the results from the Lake of Clouds varve sequence. Dotted curve and full circles represent the results from the Swedish varve sequence. The ^{14}C deviations are determined with respect to the standard atmospheric ^{14}C concentration prior to the industrial revolution and are calculated using the 5730 year half-life. The calendar years refer to dendrochronological tree-ring or varve-counting years.

organic material for direct radiocarbon dating. In contrast the Swedish sequence does not contain sufficient organic material for direct radiocarbon dating and therefore the pollen spectra associated with the varves must first be correlated with the spectra associated with nearby peat bogs from which satisfactory samples for radiocarbon dating can be obtained. The results for the deviations in atmospheric ^{14}C concentration provided by measurements on the Swedish (Tauber, 1970) and Minnesota (Stuiver, 1970) varve sequences are presented in Fig. 28, together with a simplified version of the tree-ring results.

Although the agreement between the tree-ring and the Minnesota varve sequence is excellent back to 5000 BC, there is a significant discrepancy between the two varve sequences prior to 5000 BC. The Minnesota sequence indicates that the atmospheric ^{14}C concentration remained at an excess of between 7 and 10 per cent back to 8000 BC, whereas the Swedish sequence indicates that between 10 000 BC and 6500 BC there was a 2 per cent deficiency in ^{14}C concentration after which a rapid increase in concentration occurred. Although as yet there is no satisfactory explanation for the discrepancy, current opinion tends to favour the results provided by the Minnesota varve sequence.

Explanations for the observed variations in the atmospheric ^{14}C concentration may be sought (Suess, 1970b; Damon, 1970) in (1) changes in the ^{14}C production rate due to changes in the cosmic ray flux entering the Earth's atmosphere and (2) changes in the size and the rate of exchange within the reservoir due to climatic effects. Changes in the cosmic ray flux entering the Earth's atmosphere can occur as a result of changes in magnetic field intensity. The magnetic field of the Earth itself and the interplanetary magnetic field associated with the solar wind (i.e. the patches of plasma sent out by the sun) both tend to deflect the electrically charged cosmic ray flux away from the Earth. Consequently, an *increase* in either of these magnetic fields would cause a *decrease* in the cosmic ray flux entering the Earth's atmosphere and hence a *decrease* in the ^{14}C production rate.

Information on the past variations in the Earth's magnetic field intensity can be obtained by measurement of the thermoremanent magnetism of fired clay specimens, such as pottery and kiln fragments (Chapter 5, p. 143). Bucha (1970) has combined the results of intensity measurements made for Europe, Central America and Japan in order to obtain average values for the Earth's magnetic moment during the past 9000 years. The results (Fig. 27b) show that, in addition to short term fluctuations in the magnetic field intensity, there is a gradual oscillatory change with a period of 9000 years and an amplitude amounting to an increase or decrease of approximately 30 per cent of the mean value. Comparison of the variations in the atmospheric ^{14}C concentration and the changes in the Earth's magnetic moment (Fig. 27) reveals a close inverse correlation with respect to the gradual sinusoidal changes in the two cases; that is a high ^{14}C concentration occurs when the cosmic ray flux reaching the Earth is high as a result of the low magnetic field intensity.

High solar wind intensity, and hence high interplanetary magnetic field intensities, are associated with sunspot maxima and therefore a low ^{14}C production rate is to be expected during periods of high sunspot activity (Lingenfelter, 1963). An estimate of the sunspot number per year during the past 1000 years can be obtained from historical records (Schove, 1955) and from comparison of this data with atmospheric ^{14}C concentrations (Fig. 29), it is apparent that a

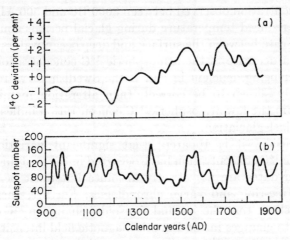

Figure 29. Comparison of (a) the fluctuations in the ^{14}C concentration of the atmosphere, as determined from tree-ring data (after Suess, 1970b) and (b) the sunspot number per year (after Schove, 1955) over the past 1000 years. Some correlation between low ^{14}C concentration and high sunspot activity can be seen. The ^{14}C deviations are determined with respect to the standard atmospheric ^{14}C concentration prior to the industrial revolution and are calculated using the 5730 year half-life.

reasonable correlation exists between low ^{14}C concentration and high sunspot activity. It therefore seems probable that variations in the interplanetary magnetic field are the cause of the observed short-term fluctuations in the atmospheric ^{14}C concentration. It also seems likely that the correlation between ^{14}C concentration fluctuations and climatic changes, suspected by de Vries (1958), arises because the state of the sun is responsible for both phenomena. Furthermore, the high value for the ^{14}C concentration at 8000 BC, indicated by the Minnesota varve sequence, could be a relic of the low sunspot activity during the cold climatic conditions associated with the last glacial period.

Consideration of the effect of climatic changes on the atmospheric ^{14}C concentration provides less conclusive correlations. The most obvious climatic effect is the lowering of sea levels during glacial periods: this produces a decrease in the size of the exchange reservoir since carbon that is "locked-up" in glaciers does not form part of the reservoir. Hence the reduction in reservoir size during the last glacial phase (terminating by 8000 BC) could explain the high atmospheric ^{14}C concentration indicated by the Minnesota varve results while the subsequent gradual melting of the glaciers, which introduces "old" carbon into the reservoir, could have caused a proportion of the decrease in ^{14}C concentration observed between 8000 BC and 500 AD. Alternatively, the reduced temperature during glacial periods could increase the mixing rate between the surface and deep ocean waters and therefore cause a decrease in the atmospheric ^{14}C concentration, the deep ocean water being deficient in ^{14}C. If the Swedish varve results were subsequently shown to be correct, then alteration in mixing rates could explain the low atmospheric ^{14}C concentration indicated for the end of the last glaciation.

In conclusion, it is apparent that significant variations in the atmospheric ^{14}C concentration have occurred in the past and therefore radiocarbon dates are not strictly absolute but must be calibrated using the tree-ring and varve chronologies. Further, there is good reason to believe that the gradual sinusoidal change in ^{14}C concentration is due to changes in the Earth's magnetic field intensity and that the short term fluctuations reflect solar activity: however it appears likely that climate also plays some part in both types of fluctuation.

Results

Several thousand radiocarbon dates, spanning the period from the present day back to approximately 50 000 BP, have now been determined using materials, such as charcoal, wood, peat, bone and marine shells. These dates are all published in the Radiocarbon Supplement to the *American Journal of Science*. For consistency, the dates are all calculated using the original Libby half-life of 5568 years rather than the more accurate value of 5730 years which is now available. The dates are expressed in the form $T \pm t$ BP (e.g. 5000 $\pm$ 200 BP), the present-day being taken, again for consistency, as 1950 AD.

The error, $\pm t$, involves only the statistical errors associated with determining the specific activity (i.e. counting the beta particles emitted) and takes no account of possible errors due to contamination of the sample or the discrepancy between radiocarbon and true calendar ages. A date of $T \pm t$ years implies a 68 per cent probability that the *radiocarbon date* lies between $(T - t)$ and $(T + t)$ years, a 95·4 per cent probability that it lies between $(T - 2t)$ and $(T + 2t)$ years and a 99·7 per cent probability that it lies between $(T - 3t)$ and $(T + 3t)$ years. Typical errors for samples up to 10 000 years old are in the range ± 50 to ± 250 years while for 50 000-year-old samples the error can, as a result of the low count-rate, be as large as ± 2000 years.

Using the data on the fluctuations in atmospheric ^{14}C concentration, derived from tree-ring and varve studies, it is possible to establish a tentative relationship between the radiocarbon age and the true calendar age; the correlation, obtained using the bristlecone pine results (Suess, 1970a) for the BC period, is presented in Fig. 30. For the AD

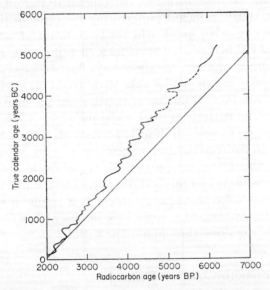

Figure 30. Relationship between the radiocarbon age (years BP calculated using the 5568 year half-life) of tree-ring dated wood and the true calendar tree-ring age (years BC), as determined from tree-ring studies on the bristlecone pines and other long-lived trees. The diagonal straight line represents the situation for coincidence of the radiocarbon and true calendar ages. The calibration curve is shown as a dashed line for these periods for which there is a scarcity of data (after Suess, 1970a).

period (not shown) and the first millennium BC, the differences between the radiocarbon age and the true calendar age are normally less than 200 years. However, beyond 1000 BC, the radiocarbon ages become progressively younger than the true calendar ages until during the period 5000 BC to 2500 BC, the discrepancy is between

600 and 800 years. Prior to 5000 BC, the Minnesota varve chronology suggests that the discrepancy is in the 600–800 year range back to 8000 BC while in contrast the Swedish varve chronology suggests that the radiocarbon and true calendar ages are approximately equal during the period 10 000–6500 BC. No detailed data are available for the period prior to 10 000 BC, although there is reason to believe that the discrepancy will not be greater than 1000 years.

Ultimately it is anticipated that a detailed table for the conversion between radiocarbon and true calendar age will become available, at least for the period (possibly back to 7000 BC) for which tree-ring samples can be obtained. However even with a detailed conversion table, a particular radiocarbon age could, as a result of the short-term fluctuations in ^{14}C concentration, correspond to more than one true calendar age, thus significantly increasing the error in the age determination. On the other hand, when a large beam of wood from the archaeological site being dated provides a "floating" tree-ring sequence of a hundred years or more, the short-term fluctuations can be utilized to provide a much more precise date than would otherwise be attainable. In this case the ^{14}C fluctuation pattern in the floating sequence is matched to the pattern in the bristlecone pine sequence and using this technique, Suess and Strahm (1970) have dated the Neolithic site of Auvernier in Switzerland to an accuracy of ±50 years.

Finally, it should be emphasized that, although not yet strictly absolute, the radiocarbon method does provide a world-wide chronological framework for archaeology since, as a result of rapid mixing within the atmosphere, any variations in the atmospheric ^{14}C concentration are the same throughout the world.

Potassium–Argon Dating

Subsequent to the discovery of radioactivity, the uranium and thorium decay series were soon used to provide an absolute geological chronology. During the past twenty years, all radioactive isotopes with long half-lives have been investigated with regard to their suitability for the absolute age determination of geological strata and the rubidium–strontium and potassium–argon methods have acquired increasing importance. Of these methods, the potassium–argon technique is especially valuable for dating recent rock strata by virtue of the high abundance of potassium and the high sensitivity of the measurement techniques for argon. In an archaeological context, the age determination is carried out on volcanic deposits which must subsequently be related to the archaeological material under consideration.

General Principles

Potassium, which is one of the most abundant elements in the Earth's crust (approximately 2·8 per cent by weight), is present in most rocks and minerals. Of the two principal potassium isotopes (^{39}K and ^{40}K), only ^{40}K is radioactive and this is present as a constant fraction (0·012 per cent) of the total potassium. ^{40}K decays by two entirely different processes, each with its own characteristic decay constant (λ). Approximately 89 per cent of the ^{40}K decays, with the emission of a beta particle, to the stable calcium isotope, ^{40}Ca. Because the majority of rock-forming minerals contain ^{40}Ca as a primary element, the radiogenic ^{40}Ca (i.e. ^{40}Ca formed by radioactive decay) cannot be estimated and therefore this decay process is not appropriate for age determination. The remaining 11 per cent of the ^{40}K decays by capture of an atomic electron to form the stable argon isotope, ^{40}Ar and it is this part of the "branching" decay which provides the basis for age determination.

Because argon is a gas, the melting associated with the formation of volcanic rocks results in the expulsion of any existing ^{40}Ar and therefore at the time of formation, the ^{40}Ar concentration in volcanic rocks is usually negligible. Subsequently the radiogenic ^{40}Ar concentration increases as a result of the decay of ^{40}K. From measurements of the concentration of ^{40}K (N) and radiogenic ^{40}Ar (D), the time (t) that has elapsed since the formation of the volcanic deposit can be calculated using the following modification of equation (3.2):

$$D = \frac{\lambda_{Ar}}{\lambda} N[\exp(\lambda t) - 1] \qquad (4.2)$$

where $\lambda_{Ar}(0·58 \times 10^{-10} \text{ yr}^{-1})$ is the decay constant for the ^{40}Ar process and $\lambda(5·30 \times 10^{-10} \text{ yr}^{-1})$ is the total decay constant for both processes.

In order to determine the concentration of radiogenic ^{40}Ar, the measured argon concentration must be corrected for the atmospheric ^{40}Ar which is absorbed by the rock. For young rocks, the radiogenic ^{40}Ar forms only a small fraction (less than 10 per cent) of the total ^{40}Ar (radiogenic plus atmospheric) in the rock and therefore accurate measurement of the radiogenic concentration becomes progressively more difficult with decreasing age of the rock: in normal circumstances, contamination by atmospheric argon limits the application of the method to rocks older than 100 000 years. In addition the following possible sources of error must always be considered: (1) at formation the rock contains radiogenic ^{40}Ar, (2) radiogenic ^{40}Ar is lost subsequent to formation and (3) the potassium concentration in the rock is altered subsequent to formation.

Experimental Procedures

In the conventional method of potassium–argon dating (Gentner and Lippolt, 1969), the potassium content of the rock is determined chemically by means of flame photometry and the ^{40}K concentration (N) is estimated by assuming that it always forms a constant fraction of the total potassium. In order to determine the argon content, the rock sample is melted in vacuum by heating to approximately 1800°C using, for example, an induction furnace. The argon, which is thus driven out of the rock, is mixed with a known quantity of the argon isotope ^{38}Ar, referred to as the "spike", and the ratio of the three argon isotopes, ^{40}Ar, ^{38}Ar and ^{36}Ar, in the resulting mixture is determined using a mass spectrometer. The ^{38}Ar "spike" provides a calibration of the mass spectrometer sensitivity and therefore an absolute value for the ^{40}Ar concentration in the sample. The ^{36}Ar, which exists in the atmosphere as a constant fraction (0·34 per cent) of the total argon but is not produced by radioactive decay, provides an estimate of the atmospheric ^{40}Ar absorbed by the sample. Therefore by subtracting this from the total ^{40}Ar concentration, the radiogenic ^{40}Ar concentration (D) can be determined.

In a conventional mass spectrometer (Fig. 31), the gas atoms are first ionized by a stream of low energy electrons from a hot filament. These ions are then accelerated by a potential difference (V volts) applied between the two slits adjacent to the source, thus producing a narrowly defined beam of monoenergetic ions. The beam enters the magnetic field (B tesla) which typically spans a 60 degree sector and which is applied perpendicular to the direction of motion. The ions are subjected to a force which is perpendicular to both the magnetic field and their direction of motion and therefore travel in a circular arc whose radius R (m) is given by:

$$R^2 = \frac{2VM}{B^2e}$$

where M (kg) is the mass and e (coulomb) is the electric charge of the ions. Hence the ions are separated by the magnetic field according to their mass. By varying the accelerating voltage, ions of different mass (i.e. ^{40}Ar, ^{38}Ar and ^{36}Ar) are collected at the detector and the ratio of their concentrations can be determined.

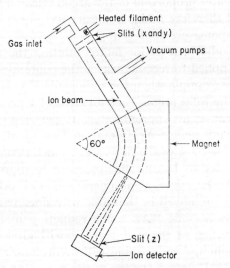

Figure 31. Block diagram of a mass spectrometer. Argon gas atoms are ionized by electrons from the heated filament and are accelerated by a potential difference (V volts) applied between the two slits (X and Y). The monoenergetic ion beam enters the magnetic field (B tesla applied perpendicular to the plane of the paper) in which the argon isotopes (^{40}Ar, ^{38}Ar and ^{36}Ar) are separated into three beams according to their mass. By varying either the potential difference or the magnetic field intensity, each beam can in turn be brought through the slit (Z) and onto the detector; the relative proportions of the three argon isotopes can thus be measured.

For measurement of the very low radiogenic ^{40}Ar content of recent rocks an improved mass spectrometer, which employs the cyclotron resonance principle and is referred to as the omegatron, has been developed (Grasty and Miller, 1965). The ionized gas is again injected into a magnetic field where the ions describe circular paths, the natural frequency of revolution (i.e. the cyclotron resonance frequency) of which is given by the relationship:

$$\nu = \frac{eB}{2\pi M}$$

In order to detect ions with a specific mass, and hence determine their concentration, a radio-frequency electric field is applied perpendicular to the magnetic field. Those ions whose cyclotron resonance frequency (ν) is equal to the frequency of the applied electric field are progressively accelerated and spiral outwards to be collected at a suitably placed detector: non-resonance ions continue to describe circular paths with pulsing radii and do not reach the detector. With this system a far greater proportion of the argon released from the sample is collected and therefore a higher sensitivity, greater reproducibility and a linear response are achieved.

As indicated above, a major factor limiting the accuracy of the method when applied to recent rocks is the contamination by atmospheric ^{40}Ar. For example when the radiogenic ^{40}Ar is present as only 10 per cent of the total argon, then an error of 1 per cent in the ^{40}Ar determination causes an approximately 10 per cent error in the estimation of the radiogenic ^{40}Ar. Contamination by atmospheric argon absorbed on the surface of the mass spectrometer components can be virtually eliminated by baking the apparatus to approximately 350°C after evacuation. However, atmospheric argon absorbed by the rock sample cannot be removed in the same way since baking also results in the loss of radiogenic ^{40}Ar. Some reduction in the atmospheric argon contamination of the rock sample, without loss of radiogenic argon, can be achieved by washing with hydrofluoric acid (Evernden and Curtis, 1965). However the use of the ^{40}Ar/^{39}Ar method provides a more satisfactory approach to the problem of atmospheric contamination since it has, at the same time, a number of other advantages.

$^{40}Ar/^{39}Ar$ Method (Mitchell, 1968). Irradiation of ^{39}K with fast neutrons produces the argon isotope ^{39}Ar, the concentration of ^{39}Ar being given by:

$$^{39}\mathrm{Ar} = {}^{39}\mathrm{K} \int \phi(E)\sigma(E)\mathrm{d}E$$

where $\phi(E)$ is the total neutron flux (i.e. neutrons per unit area) at energy E and $\sigma(E)$ is the cross-section for the conversion of ^{39}K by such neutrons. The integration is performed over all incident neutron energies.

Age determination by the ^{40}Ar/^{39}Ar method therefore involves the measurement of the ratio of the argon isotopes, ^{40}Ar, ^{39}Ar and ^{36}Ar, after having irradiated the rock sample with neutrons. As previously the ^{36}Ar provides an estimate of the atmospheric ^{40}Ar absorbed by the sample so that the radiogenic ^{40}Ar concentration (D) can be calculated. The ^{39}Ar provides a measure of the ^{39}K in the sample and hence its ^{40}K concentration (N), the integrated neutron flux *times* cross-section being determined by irradiating a standard known-age sample alongside the sample under consideration. Hence the mass spectrometer measurements provide a value for the ratio D/N required for age determination (equation (4.2)) without the necessity of a separate chemical determination of the potassium content. This represents a major advance over the conventional method described previously since (1) a precise knowledge of the sample weight is not required, (2) inhomogeneities in the distribution of potassium within the sample are of no consequence and (3) no calibration ^{38}Ar "spike" is required.

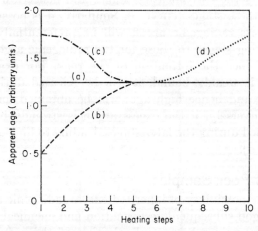

Figure 32. Hypothetical "age spectra" obtained with the ^{40}Ar/^{39}Ar method of potassium–argon dating, the ages associated with outgassing over a series of heating steps towards complete fusion (step 10) being determined. (a) The ideal sample for which there is no loss of radiogenic argon and which does not contain excess inherited radiogenic argon. (b) Sample for which argon loss has occurred. (c) Sample which contains weakly bound excess argon. (d) Sample which contains strongly bound excess argon. *N.B.* Where not drawn, the curves for samples (b)–(d) continue along that for sample (a).

In addition, the ^{40}Ar/^{39}Ar method can be extended in order to provide greater precision in the age determination of the young rock samples of interest to archaeology. This involves the repeated analysis of the isotopic composition of the argon being released from the irradiated rock sample over a series of heating steps towards complete fusion. By this means, the error associated with contamination by atmospheric argon is reduced since the atmospheric ^{40}Ar will be preferentially released during the early heating steps and therefore the proportion of radiogenic to atmospheric ^{40}Ar released during the later stages will be increased. Any loss of radiogenic ^{40}Ar during the early heating stages is now of no consequence since radiogenic ^{40}Ar and ^{39}Ar should be released in a constant ratio to one another. Furthermore, age determination at each heating stage is possible and the resulting "age spectrum" provides valuable information on the problems of inherited excess radiogenic ^{40}Ar (i.e. ^{40}Ar present at the time of formation of the rock) and ^{40}Ar loss subsequent to formation (Fig. 32). For an ideal sample, without excess argon or argon loss, the age should be the same at all heating steps (curve a). If argon loss has occurred, then this will be associated with weakly bound argon released during the early heating stages and hence low ages will be obtained for these stages (curve b). Similarly, it is possible that any inherited excess radiogenic argon will be preferentially released at different heating stages to those for the radiogenic argon which has accumulated since the formation of the rock. For example, if the excess argon is weakly bound, it will be released during the early heating steps and hence high ages will be obtained for these steps (curve c). Conversely, if the excess argon is strongly bound, it will only be released during the later stages, leading to high ages for these stages (curve d).

Selection of Rock Samples

Because of the possibility of inherited excess radiogenic argon, loss of radiogenic argon subsequent to formation and chemical alteration of the constituent minerals, careful selection of the rock samples for potassium–argon dating is essential if valid ages are to be obtained. In addition to the volcanic glass, pumice, suitable commonly occurring minerals include biotite, hornblende, muscovite and nepheline. High temperature forms of the potassium felspars (e.g. sanidine) and the sodium–calcium felspars (i.e. plagioclase) can also be used. In contrast, the most common potassium felspars, such as orthoclase and microline, are unsuitable because they can lose argon readily even at normal atmospheric temperatures.

Argon loss subsequent to the formation of the rock occurs as a result of diffusion of the argon through the crystal lattice, the argon eventually escaping into the atmosphere. The extent of the diffusion depends both on the type and grain size of the rock minerals. Thus biotite forms an effectively closed system to argon diffusion below 150–250°C while the corresponding "blocking" temperatures are

250–350°C for sanidine or muscovite and 400–500°C for hornblende. Furthermore, the basic laws of diffusion show that the larger the grain size of a particular mineral, the higher will be the effective "blocking" temperature. Thus, when possible, it is preferable to use separated mineral grains, of diameter greater than 1 mm, for potassium–argon dating, since whole rock samples are likely to include some mineral grains from which a significant quantity of argon has escaped.

Preliminary petrological examination (Chapter 8, p. 215) of the rock sample is invaluable. In addition to establishing the type and grain size of the minerals present, it can frequently reveal whether or not any chemical alteration of the rock, which could have changed its potassium content, has occurred subsequent to its formation. For example, recrystallization of potassium salts can occur, felspars can break down to kaolinite and other clay minerals or new minerals, such as calcite, can be deposited in the rock pores. Furthermore the presence of "old" minerals which did not lose their existing radiogenic argon at the time of formation, and thus contribute excess argon, can sometimes be detected: a possible source of such contamination is the wall rock of the lava vent. These inherent difficulties again emphasize the preference for age determination using selected separated mineral grains rather than the whole rock sample.

Results

By careful selection of rock samples and by means of detailed isotopic measurements, in particular the "age spectrum" possible with the $^{40}Ar/^{39}Ar$ method, it is apparent that many of the inherent difficulties associated with potassium–argon dating can be overcome and that valid ages for volcanic deposits can be obtained, at least for those older than 100 000 years. The ages obtained are typically accurate to between ± 10 per cent and ± 50 per cent depending on both the type of sample and the measurement technique employed.

Measurements undertaken on volcanic rock samples from the Lake Rudolf artefact site in Kenya (Fitch and Miller, 1970) provide an excellent case history, illustrating the difficulties and potential accuracy of the potassium–argon method. Preliminary measurements on the volcanic tuff, without any mineral separation, yielded a potassium–argon age of approximately 220 million years and thus confirmed that "old" minerals, contributing excess radiogenic argon, were present. Subsequently detailed measurements were undertaken on pumice lumps and felspar (i.e. sanidine) phenocrysts separated from the tuff.

In addition to the conventional method, involving the chemical determination of the potassium content, the $^{40}Ar/^{39}Ar$ method was employed: ages associated with total outgassing of the argon and "age spectra" associated with outgassing over a series of heating steps were determined.

Table 7. Potassium–argon results for Lake Rudolf artefact site

Method	Age (million years)	
	Felspar	Pumice
Conventional	$2 \cdot 37 \pm 0 \cdot 3$	$3 \cdot 02 \pm 1 \cdot 6$
$^{40}Ar/^{39}Ar$ (total outgassing)	$2 \cdot 64 \pm 0 \cdot 29$	$3 \cdot 45 \pm 1 \cdot 2$
$^{40}Ar/^{39}Ar$ (age spectrum plateau)	$2 \cdot 61 \pm 0 \cdot 26$	$2 \cdot 5 \pm 0 \cdot 5$

The results are tabulated in Table 7 and the "age spectrum" for the felspar phenocrysts is presented in Fig. 33.

The identical ages, within the experimental error, obtained for both the felspar phenocrysts and the pumice lumps with the three methods,

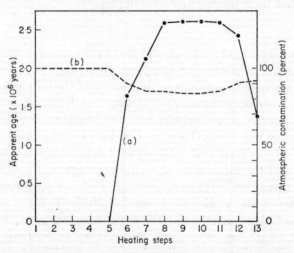

Figure 33. Results from $^{40}Ar/^{39}Ar$ method of potassium–argon dating for felspar phenocrysts from volcanic deposit at Lake Rudolf in Kenya. (a) Age spectrum obtained by outgassing over a series of heating steps towards complete fusion (step 13). (b) Contamination by atmospheric argon associated with each outgassing. These values should be compared with the 95 per cent contamination associated with total outgassing in a single heating (after Fitch and Miller, 1970).

strongly suggest that the minerals selected were all juvenile and that no "old" minerals were present. The lower ages provided by the early heating steps (5–7) in the felspar "age spectrum" suggest that some loss of radiogenic argon had occurred but the existence of an age "plateau" (heating steps 8–11) confirms that this age can be regarded as a very close estimate of the true age of crystallization. The much greater experimental errors for the pumice samples arise because of their low potassium content and the high atmospheric argon contamination (98 per cent). Although a complete age spectrum could not be determined for the pumice, preliminary low temperature heating removed a significant proportion of the weakly held atmospheric argon and subsequent measurements on the fused sample yielded a more accurate age (2·50 ± 0·5 million years). The lower value of this age further suggests that the preliminary heating also removed the weakly held excess radiogenic argon retained in the volcanic glass when solidification occurred. Consideration of these detailed measurements therefore provides an age of 2·61 ± 0·26 million years for the volcanic tuff which can be accepted with a considerable degree of certainty.

The major limitation to the use of the potassium–argon method for dating archaeological remains prior to 100 000 years ago is therefore the lack of occurrence of archaeological material in association with volcanic deposits. Only at Lake Rudolf in Kenya, quoted above, and at the Olduvia Gorge in Tanzania (Evernden and Curtis, 1965) has archaeological material been found in direct association with volcanic strata. In other instances, the archaeological deposits must be related, via the geological evidence for the glacial and interglacial phases, to distant volcanic strata dated by the potassium–argon method. In spite of this limitation, the potassium–argon method is invaluable for age determination in the Lower Palaeolithic period and was instrumental in establishing that man, the "tool-maker", evolved at least 2·5 million years ago rather than half a million years ago as previously assumed.

Fission Track Dating

The method of fission track dating has been developed over the past decade (Price and Walker, 1963; Fleischer and Price, 1964a) and shows considerable promise for archaeology since, by suitable selection of samples, dates over a time span extending from 20 years to

1000 million years ago can be obtained. The method is applicable to the age determination of volcanic deposits using, in particular, volcanic glass such as pumice and obsidian. In addition, some man-made glass and by the separation of suitable crystalline minerals, pottery can be dated.

General Principles

The uranium isotope ^{238}U, in addition to decaying via a series of daughter products to form the stable lead isotope ^{206}Pb, also undergoes spontaneous fission in which the uranium nucleus disintegrates to form two heavy nuclei with atomic weights in the range 70 to 160. Spontaneous fission is an extremely rare process, the ratio of the number of ^{238}U nuclei decaying by spontaneous fission to the number decaying via the normal series to ^{206}Pb being approximately 1 to $2 \cdot 2 \times 10^6$. However, the fission fragments are extremely energetic and cause substantial damage to the crystal lattice of the mineral in which the ^{238}U occurs. The fission damage tracks are submicroscopic but can be made visible, for counting under a microscope, by an etching process in which the damaged regions are preferentially dissolved.

The melting associated with the formation of volcanic rocks or the manufacture of glass and the firing involved in the production of pottery result in the removal of any existing tracks. Therefore no fission tracks are present at the time of formation or manufacture and subsequently they are formed as a result of the spontaneous fission of ^{238}U. The number of tracks (T) can be treated as the accumulating daughter product of radioactive decay and is given at a time t, after formation or manufacture, by the following modification of equation (3.2):

$$T = \frac{\lambda_F}{\lambda} N \left[\exp (\lambda t) - 1 \right]$$

where $\lambda_F (6 \cdot 9 \times 10^{-17} \text{ yr}^{-1})$ is the decay constant for spontaneous fission and $\lambda (1 \cdot 54 \times 10^{-10} \text{ yr}^{-1})$ is the decay constant for the normal radioactive decay process. Since only the surface of the sample is etched, it is not possible to count the total number of tracks formed and therefore T represents the number of tracks per unit area while N represents the number of ^{238}U nuclei per unit area.

The determination of N is achieved by counting the number of additional tracks per unit area (T_N) produced by neutron-induced fission of ^{235}U during a controlled irradiation with slow neutrons in a nuclear reactor. T_N is given by the relationship:

$$T_N = \phi \sigma N'$$

where ϕ is the total slow neutron flux, σ is the cross-section for ^{235}U fission and N' is the number of ^{235}U nuclei per unit area. The present-day ratio (R) of the concentration of ^{238}U to ^{235}U is a known constant in all geological material (approximately 138:1). Therefore, from measurement of the ratio of the number of spontaneous to neutron-induced fission tracks (T/T_N), the age of the sample (t) can be calculated using the relationship:

$$\frac{T}{T_N} = \frac{\lambda_F}{\lambda} \frac{R}{\phi\sigma} [\exp{(\lambda t)} - 1] \qquad (4.3)$$

The validity of the fission track method of age determination has been established by measurements on man-made glass, whose date of manufacture is either known or can be estimated on stylistic grounds, and on natural minerals, whose age can be independently determined by other radioactive methods such as potassium–argon dating (Fig. 34): these results, at the same time, provide a value for the decay constant λ_F.

A basic requirement in applying this method is that the particular mineral or glass under consideration must be able to retain the fission tracks over the long periods of time involved. Information on this problem can be obtained by heating in the laboratory and ascertaining the temperatures at which annealing occurs; that is at which the tracks disappear.These experiments (Fleischer, Price and Walker, 1965) indicate that, for the majority of minerals and glasses, the tracks are stable up to at least 500°C and therefore they should be retained at normal atmospheric temperatures over geological times. A further advantage of the fission track method is that, since fission tracks can only be formed in nature by the spontaneous fission of ^{238}U, the problem of contamination by a non-radiogenic daughter product, such as the absorption of atmospheric argon in the potassium–argon method, does not arise.

Experimental Procedures

In the case of man-made glass and obsidian, a small fragment (typically 100 mg) is cut from the specimen and one surface is polished to an optical finish. However, with many volcanic rocks, it is necessary to first crush the rock and then select suitable fragments of glass. Similarly, with pottery, zircon mineral fragments, which contain a relatively high concentration of uranium, are separated by standard heavy liquid techniques after crushing. In these latter cases, the glass or mineral fragments are mounted in a clear epoxy resin before polishing. The polished surface is then etched, the etch pits associated with the spontaneous fission tracks being approximately 4 μm in diameter (Plate 9). Glasses are normally etched with hydrofluoric acid at room temperature, the time required being typically a few seconds. For zircons, a more severe etching treatment is necessary, concentrated phosphorous pentoxide at 500°C for a few minutes or sodium hydroxide at 200°C for a few hours being normally employed. Typically the surface area of the sample made available for examination is approximately 0·5 cm².

The spontaneous fission track etch pits (T) are counted using an optical microscope at a magnification of approximately × 1000. In samples where the track density is very low, it may be necessary to repeatedly etch the surface and count the etch pits over a series of exposed surfaces in order to observe a sufficient number for accurate age determination. The sample is then irradiated with a known flux of thermal neutrons (ϕ), the surface is re-etched and the neutron-induced fission track etch pits (T_N) are counted. In using the ratio T/T_N for age determination, it is necessary to either examine equal areas in both cases or determine the sizes of the areas examined. Even when the same surface is employed for both counts, care must be taken to ensure that the area available for examination has not been changed by the re-etching following neutron irradiation. This problem is particularly severe when small glass or mineral fragments are employed.

Because of the very slow rate of spontaneous fission and the fact that most materials contain only a few parts per million of uranium, the spontaneous fission track density is normally very low. For example, a 1000 year-old sample having a uranium content of 1 ppm will have a track density of 500 per cm³: in scanning a surface for tracks, only those originating within a few microns of the surface are seen so that the number of tracks per cm² is approximately 0·3. If T spontaneous tracks are counted, the inherent statistical error (i.e. the standard deviation) is $\pm \sqrt{T}$. Therefore, for an accuracy of ± 10 per cent in the age determination, 100 spontaneous fission tracks must be counted ($\sqrt{100}/100 \times 100 = 10$ per cent): in comparison the statistical error associated with the neutron-induced fission tracks is negligible since the neutron irradiation typically produces at least 10^4 tracks per cm². Hence, for the 1000-year-old sample containing 1 ppm of uranium, approximately 300 cm² of surface must be scanned in order to achieve a 10 per cent accuracy in the age determination.

The time taken to count fission track etch pits depends very much on the quality of the specimen. For a typical sample, 1 hour of microscopic examination is required to scan a 1 cm² area although, when difficulties in distinguishing between fission track etch pits and those associated with dislocations or inclusions and bubbles in glass, the examination of the surface is necessarily somewhat slower. Hence, for young samples containing only a few ppm of uranium, an excessive counting time is necessary to achieve an accurate age determination and this effectively limits the application of fission track dating to either very old samples or those with a high uranium content. Data indicating the minimum sample age which can be determined with an accuracy of ± 10 per cent are presented in Table 8, 1 hour and 30 hours microscopic examination being considered.

Table 8. Fission track dating: minimum sample age

Uranium concentration	Minimum sample age[a] (years)	
	A	B
1 ppm	300 000	10 000
10 ppm	30 000	1000
100 ppm	3000	100
1000 ppm	300	10
1 per cent	30	1
10 per cent	3	0·1

[a] The minimum sample ages for the different uranium concentrations that can be determined with an accuracy of ±10 per cent after about 1 hour (column A) and 30 hours (column B) of microscopic examination.

Results

The potential applications of the fission track method of age determination to archaeology fall into three main categories—volcanic rocks, man-made glass and pottery.

In the age determination of volcanic deposits, the fission track method supplements, and provides a check for, the more widely used potassium–argon method. Again the method is principally of use for the Lower Palaeolithic period and it is normally necessary to correlate the relevant archaeological material with the volcanic deposits being dated. In this context, the fission track age determinations on the volcanic pumice from Bed I at the Olduvai Gorge, Tanzania (Fleischer *et al.*, 1965a) are of particular interest since early human skeletal remains and artefacts have been found in this volcanic deposit. The validity of the potassium–argon age of 1·75 ± 0·15 million years (Leakey *et al.*, 1961) has been queried by von Koenigswald *et al.* (1961) on the grounds that the sample might have been contaminated by excess radiogenic argon from inherited "old" minerals and by atmospheric argon. Fission track dating of Bed I was therefore of value since this method is unaffected by the argon contamination which could have produced too high a value for the age by the potassium–argon method. The fission track age was found to be 2·03 ± 0·28 million years and the agreement between the two ages, within the limits of experimental accuracy, therefore provided strong support for the validity of an age of approximately 2 million years for Bed I at Olduvai.

In addition to work on the volcanic strata themselves, fission track measurements on artefacts made from the volcanic glass, obsidian, can be of value. If, from its appearance, it is obvious that the obsidian artefact has been heated in antiquity, the date at which heating occurred can be determined since pre-existing fission tracks will have been removed by annealing (Fleischer *et al.*, 1965b). Alternatively with unheated obsidian artefacts, the age of the deposit from which the raw material was obtained and the uranium content of the obsidian can be determined by fission track measurements (Durrani *et al.*, 1971). By comparison with data for known obsidian sources, this information can be used to identify the source of the raw material for the particular group of obsidian artefacts under consideration (Chapter 10, p. 313).

The application of fission track dating to ancient man-made glasses is of limited value since their uranium contents are typically in the range 0·5–2 ppm (Fleischer and Price, 1964b). From consideration of the data presented in Table 8, it is apparent that excessively long periods of microscopic examination would be required in order to obtain an accurate age for glass 2000 years old. However, uranium has been added as a colorant to certain types of more recent glass, often in concentrations of a few per cent. Brill *et al.* (1964) have determined the fission track age for five such glass objects and good agreement with the known date of manufacture (1850–1943 AD) was achieved. In this case the results are principally of interest in providing a check on the validity of the fission track method (Fig. 34) and a value for the spontaneous fission decay constant (λ_F).

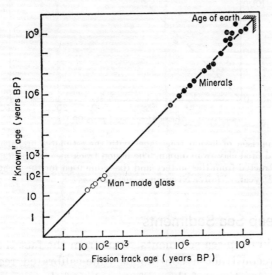

Figure 34. Comparison of the fission track ages with the known ages of the man-made glass and the ages determined by other radioactive methods (e.g. potassium–argon dating) in the case of the natural minerals (e.g. tektites, micas and obsidian). The value of the decay constant (λ_F) used in calculating the fission track age was $6\cdot9 \times 10^{-17}$ years^{-1} (after Fleischer and Price, 1964a).

Although the average uranium content of pottery is normally very low (a few ppm), uranium-rich mineral inclusions are frequently present. For example, zircon minerals typically have uranium contents in the range 1000 ppm to 1 per cent and therefore if zircon inclusions are separated out from the pottery, they can be used for age determination by the fission track method. Nishimura (1971) has thus obtained reasonably satisfactory fission track ages for a selection of pottery, tiles and baked clay from Japan which span the period from 1600 to 600 BP (Fig. 35). Extension of the method to other pottery samples containing a sufficient quantity of zircon therefore holds considerable promise for the future.

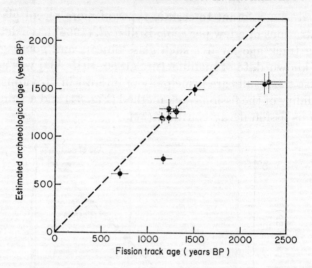

Figure 35. Comparison of fission track ages with the estimated archaeological ages of pottery, tiles and fired clay from Japan. The fission track measurements were made on zircon grains extracted from the pottery and the value used for the decay constant (λ_F) was $6 \cdot 85 \times 10^{-17}$ years^{-1} (after Nishimura, 1971).

Deep Sea Sediments

The interest in deep-sea sediments stems from the fact that they can be used to reconstruct a continuous time-calibrated record of the temperature variations of the surface water of the ocean during the Pleistocene period. The oceanic temperature curve can then, in principle, be correlated with the continental changes, the temperature minima and maxima corresponding to the glacial and interglacial phases respectively. It should therefore be possible to establish approximate ages for the glacial and interglacial geological deposits which contain the archaeological material.

Temperature Measurements

The ocean floor sediments, referred to as Globigerina-ooze, consist essentially of clay and a substantial amount (from 30 per cent to more than 90 per cent) of calcium carbonate. The clay component consists of the finest detritus brought to the ocean by rivers and winds while the carbonate component consists largely of shells of foraminifera which had lived in the ocean before being deposited. This clay and shell sediment accumulates at rates ranging from one to several centimetres per thousand years, depending on geographic location, depth of water and the local topography of the ocean floor. These sediments therefore contain continuous stratigraphic records ranging in time from the present to more than a million years ago and examination of the foraminifera, whose growth habitat was the surface waters of the oceans, can provide information on the temperature variations that occurred during the Pleistocene.

Using a piston corer, cylindrical sediment cores, 5 cm in diameter and up to 25 m in length, can be recovered from the ocean floor. For temperature measurements, only a small minority of the available cores are suitable since, in order to obtain a continuous temperature record, the sediments must be undisturbed. Cores containing sediment

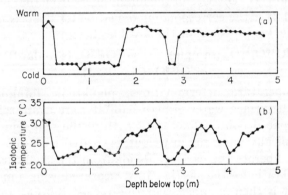

Figure 36. Palaeotemperature curves from deep-sea sediments: Caribbean core A179-4. (a) Curve based on the relative numbers of cold- and warm-water planktonic foraminifera species (after Ericson *et al.*, 1961). (b) Curve based on isotopic temperatures, determined from $^{18}O/^{16}O$ ratio measurements on planktonic foraminifera using equation (4.4) (after Emiliani, 1958).

layers introduced laterally by turbidity currents within the oceans or those from which layers have been removed by sudden disturbances, such as earthquake waves, are unsuitable.

Since different species of foraminifera have different temperature tolerances, estimation of the relative proportions of cold and warm water planktonic species (i.e. species with surface water habitat) at a series of points along the core (Fig. 36a) provide an indication of the sequence of cold and warm climatic phases that has occurred in the past (Ericson *et al.*, 1961).

An alternative approach, which in principle provides quantitative data on the past temperature variations, involves the measurement of the ratio of the concentrations of the two stable oxygen isotopes,

^{18}O and ^{16}O, in the calcium carbonate of the foraminiferal shells (Emiliani, 1955). Before being deposited on the ocean floor, the calcium carbonate in the shell is in exchange equilibrium with the sea water which contains both ^{18}O and ^{16}O, in the ratio of approximately 1 to 500. Because of isotopic fractionation effects, the ratio of ^{18}O to ^{16}O in the calcium carbonates depends on both the temperature and the oxygen isotopic ratio of the water. The water temperature ($T^\circ C$) at the death of the foraminifera can therefore be determined from the oxygen isotopic ratios using the relationship:

$$T = 16\cdot5 - 4\cdot3\,(\delta_s - \delta_w) + 0\cdot14\,(\delta_s - \delta_w)^2 \qquad (4.4)$$

where δ_s is the deviation, in parts per thousand, of the molecular oxygen ratio, $^{18}O^{16}O/^{16}O_2$, for the foraminifera from that of a standard sample and δ_w is the corresponding deviation for the ocean water, the mathematical expression for the δ-values being:

$$\delta = \frac{^{18}O^{16}O/^{16}O_2\,(\text{sample}) - \,^{18}O^{16}O/^{16}O_2\,(\text{standard})}{^{18}O^{16}O/^{16}O_2\,(\text{standard})} \times 1000$$

For temperature determinations, planktonic foraminifera (i.e. species with surface water growth habitats) are again selected from regularly spaced points along the length of the sediment core. Each sample, typically a few mg in weight, is treated with phosphoric acid in order to liberate the carbon dioxide from the shell carbonate and the $^{18}O/^{16}O$ ratio for the gas (i.e. δ_s) is measured using a mass spectrometer. If it is then assumed that the oxygen isotopic ratio for the water (δ_w) has remained constant, the surface ocean temperatures during the deposition of the sediments can be calculated using equation (4.4) (Fig. 36b).

A 1°C increase in the temperature of the ocean water produces a decrease in the oxygen isotopic ratio of the shell (δ_s) of approximately 0·2 parts per thousand. Therefore, using a typical mass spectrometer, the experimental error associated with the *isotopic* temperature, calculated from equation (4.4), is about $\pm0\cdot5$°C. However, due to uncertainties concerning the oxygen isotopic ratio of the ocean water (δ_w), the error for the *true*, as opposed to the *isotopic*, temperature is normally greater than 1°C. Furthermore, due to mixing by "animals" to a depth of several centimetres below the sediment surface, the time resolution from deep-sea sediments is generally not better than a few thousand years. Hence short-term variations in temperature (i.e. those of duration less than a few thousand years) are not recorded in the sediments.

In spite of their great bulk, the oxygen isotopic composition of the oceans (δ_w) has not remained strictly constant. The principal reason for the changes is that the extensive ice sheets, built up during the glacial phases of the Pleistocene, were composed of isotopically light snow (i.e. H_2O^{16} rather than H_2O^{18}): this in turn is due to the fact that water molecules containing ^{16}O evaporate more readily than those containing the heavier ^{18}O. Therefore the oceans, from which the snow originated, contained a higher $^{18}O/^{16}O$ ratio during glacial phases than during the interglacials. According to Emiliani (1955), the effect of this change in oxygen isotopic ratio of the ocean water is to lower the isotopic temperature maxima by approximately 1·3°C and increase the minima by about 1·7°C.

More recently, however, Shackleton (1967) has compared the oxygen isotopic ratios of planktonic foraminifera with those of benthonic foraminifera and has found that the variations in δ_s are similar for both types. The benthonic foraminifera effectively provide a record of the variations in the isotopic composition of the oceans (δ_w) since they live at the bottom of the ocean and consequently experience an almost constant temperature environment. The similarity between the δ_s variations for the two types therefore suggests that the variation in δ_s for the surface foraminifera reflects changes in the isotopic composition of the water, rather than changes in temperature. However since the changes in the isotopic composition of water are associated with glacial and interglacial phases, the data obtained from planktonic foraminifera are still valid. It is merely necessary to re-read the isotopic curves with "cold" (i.e. high δ_s) representing extensive continental glaciation and "warm" (i.e. low δ_s) representing a reduction in the extent of the glaciation. It is similarly possible that the changes in the relative proportions of different foraminifera species reflect changes in salinity, due to variations in the volume of the oceans between glacial and interglacial phases, rather than changes in temperature: if this is so then the faunal data can be re-read in the same way as the isotopic curves.

Age Determination

Having estimated the temperature variations that occurred during the deposition of the deep-sea sediments, it is then necessary to establish the absolute dates at which these variations occurred. Radiocarbon dating (p. 76), using the carbonate in the shells, is applicable for the upper levels in the core; that is the part of the sediment deposited during the past 50 000 years. Methods employing the short-lived isotopes in the uranium decay series provide absolute dates for the sediment back to approximately 150 000 years ago. The reversals in the direction of the Earth's magnetic field (i.e. through 180 degrees) which, from potassium–argon dating of volcanic deposits, are known to have occurred at about 0·7, 1·8 and 2·5 million years, provide additional absolute dates for specific layers within the sediment (Chapter 5, p. 140). In this case the remanent magnetism of the sediment layers, which provides a record of the direction of the Earth's magnetic field at deposition, is measured and therefore the layer at which the remanent magnetism reverses in direction can be dated. These absolute dates can then be used to estimate the rate of sedimentation and if this is assumed to have remained constant, tentative dates for the remainder of the sediment can be obtained by extrapolation.

The short-lived isotopes in the uranium decay series which are used for age determination are ionium (^{230}Th) and protactinium (^{231}Pa), either the ionium content or the protactinium to ionium ratio in the sediment being measured (Table 9). In the ionium method (Volchok

Table 9. Uranium decay series[a] used for dating deep-sea sediments

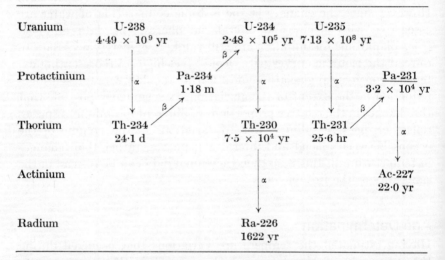

[a] The half-lives of the various isotopes are given in years (yr), days (d), hours (hr) and minutes (m). The high energy particles (i.e. alpha and beta particles) emitted as a result of the various decay processes are indicated. The isotopes used for age determination (i.e. ionium: Th-230 and protactinium: Pa-231) are underlined.

and Kulp, 1957), it is assumed that the ^{230}Th content of the ocean has remained constant, the loss of ^{230}Th by radioactive decay and absorption of the sediment being balanced by its formation from the parent uranium. Because of its chemical nature, the ^{230}Th is preferentially absorbed by the sediment whereas the parent uranium remains in the sea water in solution. Therefore in deposited sediment, the ^{230}Th is no longer supported by the uranium and its concentration decreases as a result of radioactive decay according to equation (3.1). Consequently, from measurement of the ^{230}Th concentration, which decreases progressively with increasing depth within the sediment, the time that has elapsed since the sediment at a given depth was deposited can be determined.

In ^{231}Pa/^{230}Th ratio method (Rolshot *et al.*, 1961), it is similarly assumed that the ratio of the ^{231}Pa and ^{230}Th concentrations in the ocean has remained constant. Both isotopes are preferentially absorbed by the sediment where they are again no longer supported by their parent uranium isotopes and where their concentrations decrease as a result of radioactive decay. Since the half-life ^{231}Pa (32 000 years) is less than that for ^{230}Th (75 000 years), the ratio of their concentrations (^{231}Pa/^{230}Th) decreases with increasing depth within the sediment. Therefore the time that has elapsed since deposition can be again determined from measurement of this ratio. In both methods the relevant isotopic concentrations are determined either using a mass spectrometer or by counting the alpha particles emitted as a result of their radioactive decay.

Errors in the ages obtained with the ionium method arise if the rate of sedimentation changes since this upsets the equilibrium between the formation and removal of ^{230}Th, and hence changes the ^{230}Th concentration of the ocean. Further errors are associated with changes in the capacity of the sediment to absorb ^{230}Th. These, and other errors, are to some extent reduced by using the ^{231}Pa/^{230}Th ratio method. Changes in the ^{231}PA/^{230}Th ratio for the oceans, due to variations in the rate of sedimentation, will be less than the changes in either of their individual concentrations: similarly variations in the absorption capacity of the sediment will tend to be the same for both isotopes.

Results

By correlating the data, similar to that presented in Fig. 36, for a large number of deep-sea sediments cores taken from the Atlantic,

Caribbean and Pacific oceans, it has been possible to produce generalized temperature curves for the majority of the Pleistocene period.

The temperature curve, based on measurement of the oxygen isotopic ratios (Emiliani, 1966), is shown in Fig. 37 together with the earlier tentative correlation (Emiliani, 1958) between the oceanic stages and the continental glacial and interglacial phases for N. America and Britain (see Table 13, p. 172 for the assumed relationship

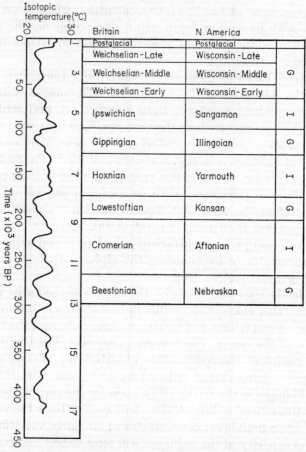

Britain	N. America	
Postglacial	Postglacial	
Weichselian-Late	Wisconsin-Late	
Weichselian-Middle	Wisconsin-Middle	G
Weichselian-Early	Wisconsin-Early	
Ipswichian	Sangamon	I
Gippingian	Illingoian	G
Hoxnian	Yarmouth	I
Lowestoftian	Kansan	G
Cromerian	Aftonian	I
Beestonian	Nebraskan	G

Figure 37. Generalized isotopic temperature curve for the surface water of the central Caribbean (after Emiliani, 1966), together with an earlier tentative correlation between the oceanic stages (numbered 1 to 17) and the continental glacial (G) and interglacial (I) phases for North America and Britain (after Emiliani, 1958). According to Shackleton (1967), the numerical values for the isotopic temperatures are not strictly valid and should be re-read with "cold" representing extensive continental glaciation and "warm" representing a reduction in the extent of the glaciation (i.e. an interglacial).

between the phases for Britain and those for the Alps and N. W. Europe). The absolute time scale is provided by radiocarbon and ^{231}Pa/^{230}Th ratio dating back to 150 000 years and by extrapolation, on the assumption of a constant sedimentation rate, beyond 150 000 years.

Radiocarbon dating of continental deposits has confirmed the correlation between the present Postglacial phase and oceanic stage 1 and between the Late, Middle and Early Weichselian glacial phases and the oceanic stages 2, 3 and 4 respectively. Further, it is reasonable to assume that oceanic stage 5 correlates with the Ipswichian interglacial while Shackleton and Turner (1967) have shown that the duration of the Hoxnian interglacial (30 000–50 000 years) is compatible with its correlation with oceanic stage 7. However the correlation between the earlier continental phases and oceanic stages 8–12, which was originally proposed on the basis of a shorter sequence of temperature variations (Emiliani, 1958), is no longer thought to be valid. Additional cold and warm oceanic stages have now been identified (Emiliani, 1966) while potassium–argon dates for the continental deposits suggest that the Beestonian glacial phase should be assigned to the period 340 000–420 000 years. It therefore appears that the simple scheme of four or five major continental glaciations will have to be abandoned in favour of a more complex pattern which includes interstadial phases (i.e. relatively short-term temperature increases within glacial phases) as well as interglacial phases. Consequently, the correlation between named continental phases and the oceanic stages can only be satisfactorily achieved with the aid of accurate absolute dates for the former.

The temperature curve, based on the relative abundance of selected foraminifera species (Ericson et al., 1964; Glass et al., 1967), is presented in Fig. 38 together with the tentative correlation between the oceanic stages and the continental phases for N. America. In addition to the radiocarbon and ^{231}Pa/^{230}Th ratio methods, the reversals in the direction of the Earth's magnetic field have been used to provide an absolute time scale back to 2·5 million years. In comparing the faunal temperature curve with the shorter isotopic temperature curve (Fig. 37), it can be seen that the faunal data suggests that a smaller number of temperature fluctuations between cold and warm have occurred. Furthermore, if the penultimate continental interglacial (i.e. Yarmouth = Hoxnian) is identified with either oceanic stage T (i.e. as shown in Fig. 38) or stage V (i.e. as alternative possibility), then the length of the oceanic stages (500 000 and 250 000 years respectively) is incompatible with

114   METHODS OF PHYSICAL EXAMINATION IN ARCHAEOLOGY

the known length (30 000–50 000 years) of this interglacial (Shackleton and Turner, 1967). It therefore seems clear that the faunal record, although providing a complete and reproducible sequence through the 2·5 million years of the Pleistocene, bears little relationship to the chronology of glacial events in Europe.

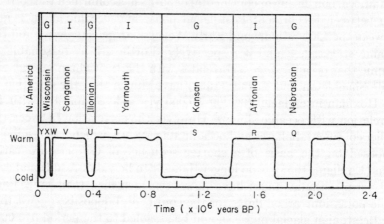

Figure 38. Generalized climatic curve based on the variations in the abundance of various temperature-sensitive planktonic foraminifera. A tentative correlation between the oceanic stages (lettered Q–Y) and the continental glacial (G) and interglacial (I) phases for North America is also shown (after Glass et al., 1967).

It is apparent that the oxygen isotopic data from deep-sea sediments provides a valid record of the climatic variations, and in particular the waxing and waning of the continental ice-sheets, during the past 450 000 years. It is therefore invaluable, in the context of archaeology, in that it provides information on the environmental conditions in Europe during the Palaeolithic period. However its use for the age determination of archaeological material is limited by the difficulties associated with correlating the continental glacial and interglacial phases with the oceanic stages: at present correlation, and this merely tentative, has only been achieved back to Hoxnian interglacial.

Thermoluminescent Dating

The phenomenon of thermoluminescence was first studied by Robert Boyle (1664) in the seventeenth century. He observed that visible light was emitted when a diamond was warmed by holding it in his hand, the glow being easily seen in a dark room. The present-day utilization of the effect in applied physics results from the work of Farrington Daniels at the University of Wisconsin (Daniels *et al.*, 1953).

The major application has been in radiation dosimetry (Attix, 1967), particularly in radiotherapy and health hazard control, where the thermoluminescence emitted by calcium fluoride and lithium fluoride crystals, for example, provides a measure of the radiation dose received since the crystal was last heated. Geological applications (McDougall, 1968), in particular the thermoluminescent dating of limestones, have met with only limited success but its application to the dating of ancient ceramics at several research centres (Aitken *et al.*, 1968; Ralph and Han, 1966; Ichikawa, 1965; Mejdahl, 1969) has shown that, in spite of many inherent difficulties, the method has considerable potential. In addition to pottery, the possibility of dating flints heated in antiquity, bones and shells by this method has also been investigated.

General Principles

When an inorganic non-conducting solid is subjected to ionizing radiation (e.g. alpha particles, beta particles and gamma rays), free electrons and holes are produced and some of these are trapped at defects (e.g. vacancies, interstitials, impurity atoms) in the crystal lattice (Fig. 39a). When the solid is subsequently heated, the electrons escape from their

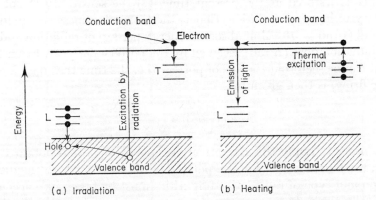

(a) Irradiation   (b) Heating

Figure 39. Electron energy levels for an inorganic non-conducting solid. The valence band, which is filled with electrons, is separated by an energy gap from the conduction band which is empty of electrons. The localized energy levels in the energy gap are due to lattice defects (i.e. vacancies, interstitials, impurity atoms): *L* refers to the luminescence centres and *T* refers to the electron traps. (a) Irradiation (i.e. alpha, beta and gamma particles) produces free electrons and holes, some of which are captured by the traps and luminescence centres respectively. (b) Heating releases the electrons from the traps and these electrons recombine with the holes at the luminescence centres with the emission of light—the thermoluminescence.

traps and if electron-hole recombination then occurs through a luminescent centre, light, referred to as *thermoluminescence*, is emitted (Fig. 39b). The intensity of this light provides a measure of the number of trapped electrons and hence a measure of the ionizing radiation dose which the solid received.

When raw clay is fired, at temperatures in the range 500–1200°C, to produce the pottery, the thermoluminescence acquired as a result of ionizing radiation during geological times is removed. Thus at the termination of firing, the number of trapped electrons, and hence the stored thermoluminescence in the pottery, is zero. Subsequently, as a result of ionizing radiation from the radioactive impurities in the pottery (i.e. a few ppm of uranium and thorium and a few per cent of potassium), the trapping of electrons begins again. Some of the electron traps are sufficiently deep for there to be negligible leakage from them at normally environmental temperature over many thousands of years. Furthermore, because of their very long half-lives (Table 6, p. 62), the radiation dose per year provided by the radioactive impurities remains constant over this period. Consequently, the trapped electron population, and hence the stored thermoluminescence in the pottery, should increase linearly with the age of the pottery. In order to determine the age it is therefore necessary to measure: (1) the natural thermoluminescence (L) stored at the present time, (2) the sensitivity (S) of the pottery to ionizing radiation, that is the thermoluminescence induced per rad (1 rad = 10^{-2}J of absorbed energy per kg) of radiation and (3) the radiation dose (R rad) received by the pottery per year. From Fig. 40, it can be seen that the age of pottery (i.e. the time that has elapsed since firing) is then given by:

$$\text{Age (years)} = \frac{L}{S \times R} \qquad (4.5)$$

In order to apply this deceptively simple formula and obtain valid ages, the inhomogeneity of the pottery fabric together with the distribution and type of radioactive impurities must be taken into account. Typically the pottery consists of a fine grained clay matrix in which mineral inclusions, ranging in diameter from less than 1 μm up to a few millimetres, are embedded. It has been shown that the majority of the thermoluminescence originates from the mineral inclusions, principally quartz. However, a major part of the radiation dose is due to alpha particles from the uranium and thorium (Fig. 41) and these impurities are carried predominantly by the clay matrix. Because of the short

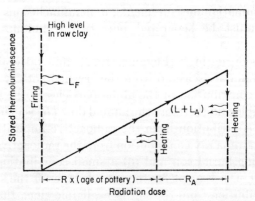

Figure 40. Thermoluminescent history of a clay sample. L_F is the thermoluminescence emitted during the firing of the raw clay. L is the natural thermoluminescence acquired since firing as a result of radiation (R rad per year) from the radioactive impurities in the pottery. L_A is the additional thermoluminescence emitted after exposure to a known radiation dose (R_A rad) using a calibrated source, the sensitivity (S) of the pottery to ionizing radiation being defined as L_A/R_A.

range of the alpha particles (20–50 μm), the alpha dose received by the mineral inclusions depends critically on their size and is practically negligible for inclusions greater than 100 μm in diameter. Consequently,

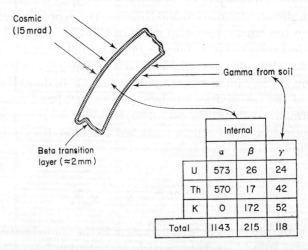

Figure 41. Annual radiation dose (mrads per year) received by a fragment of pottery with typical concentrations of radioactive impurities (uranium, U, 2 ppm; thorium, Th, 8 ppm; potassium, K, 2 per cent), buried in soil with the same radioactivity. Except for the surface layer (approximately 2 mm), the beta particle contribution from the soil is negligible; however, for gamma rays, the soil contribution is dominant (after Aitken *et al.*, 1968).

for age determination measurements, mineral inclusions within specific size ranges must be separated out, two techniques having been developed.

For "inclusion dating" (Fleming, 1970), mineral grains in the size range 90–105 μm are selected from the crushed pottery by sieving. In this case the contribution of the alpha particles to the total radiation dose is negligible and therefore the annual dose (R) is made up of (1) the beta particle contribution from the radioactive impurities in the pottery, (2) the gamma ray contribution from the radioactive impurities in the surrounding burial soil and (3) a small contribution from cosmic radiation (Fig. 41). Except for the surface layer of the sherd, the beta particle contribution from the soil is negligible since the range of the beta particles is approximately 2 mm; however, for gamma rays, with their much larger range, the soil contribution is dominant. Hence if, in addition to this annual radiation dose (R), the natural thermoluminescence (L) and the sensitivity (S) to beta radiation are measured for these mineral grains, the age of the pottery can be determined using equation (4.5).

For "fine-grain dating" (Zimmerman, 1971), both clay and mineral grains in the size range 1–5 μm are selected from the crushed pottery by a sedimentation technique. In these grains the alpha particles will have suffered negligible attenuation and therefore their contribution must be included in the annual radiation dose. In this case however, the sensitivity of the grains to both alpha and beta particles must be measured since a given alpha dose is typically an order of magnitude less effective in inducing thermoluminescence than the same beta dose. For pottery, the ratio of the sensitivities to alpha particles (S_α) and beta particles (S_β) is normally in the range 0·05–0·30, the sensitivity to gamma rays being identical to that for beta particles. Therefore the equation used for age determination must be modified to:

$$\text{Age (years)} = \frac{L}{S_\alpha R_\alpha + S_\beta R_\beta} \qquad (4.6)$$

where R_α is the alpha particle contribution to the annual radiation dose and R_β is the sum of the beta particle contribution from the pottery, the gamma ray contribution from the soil and the cosmic ray contribution.

Although a number of factors limit the accuracy of the method (p. 123), a series of test programmes using pottery of known age have established that the principles, on which both the "inclusion" and "fine-grain" approaches to thermoluminescent dating are based, are essentially valid.

Experimental Procedures

For "inclusion dating", the pottery sherd is crushed in an agate mortar and the mineral inclusions are extracted from the clay matrix using a magnetic separator. Mineral grains, typically in the 90–105 μm diameter range, are then obtained by sieving. Prior to the thermoluminescence measurements, this extract is treated with hydrofluoric acid. This treatment removes minerals, such as calcite and felspar, and therefore the age determination is restricted to the quartz inclusions. In addition, the surface layers (typically 6 μm thick) of the quartz grains themselves are removed. The consequences of this are to reduce the fraction of the grain that has received an alpha dose from the radioactive impurities in the clay matrix and to reduce contamination from impurities which have diffused into the quartz from the clay matrix.

For "fine-grain dating", the pottery sherd is crushed between the jaws of a vice to produce fragments ranging from 2 mm to less than 1 μm in diameter. Tests have established that, with this method of crushing, a negligible fraction of the large mineral inclusions are crushed down to the 1–5 μm size range used for dating. After crushing, grains in this size range are selected by means of their settling rate from a suspension in acetone and deposited onto thin 1 cm diameter aluminium discs. The amount of powder on each disc is typically about 1 mg, giving an average thickness of 4 μm. In this case the grains include both minerals, such as quartz, and the clay matrix.

All operations associated with the preparation, as well as the subsequent use, of the samples must be carried out in subdued light in order to avoid optical bleaching phenomena. Experiments have shown that exposure to sunlight, fluorescent and incandescent filament lighting, can either bleach (i.e. remove) or induce a significant amount of thermoluminescence. Exposure of the pottery to light before crushing is unimportant since only the surface layer, which can be easily removed, is affected.

In order to measure the thermoluminescence (Fig. 42), the appropriate separated sample (approximately 6 mg for "inclusion dating" and 1 mg deposited on an aluminium disc for "fine-grain dating") is heated to 500°C on a nichrome plate in approximately 25 sec. The light output is measured with a photomultiplier and is plotted against temperature, measured with a thermocouple attached to the nichrome plate, on an X–Y recorder; the resulting curve is referred to as the glow curve. After cooling, the sample is reheated to measure the thermal black-body radiation, the area between the two curves providing a measure of the thermoluminescence. By using suitable filters to reduce the black-body radiation, thermoluminescent measurements up to approximately 500°C are possible. The heating is always performed in an oxy-free nitrogen atmosphere in order to remove "spurious" thermo-

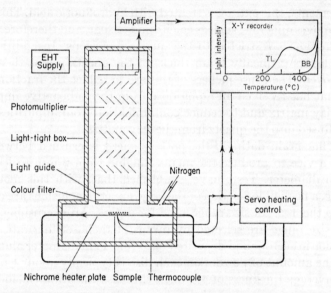

Figure 42. Block diagram of apparatus for thermoluminescence measurements. The heater current to the nichrome plate (about 100 A) is adjusted by means of the servo heating control to give a constant heating rate of 20°C/sec. The EHT voltage supplied to the photomultiplier is typically 1200 V. A pulse amplifier plus ratemeter can be used to count the number of photons emitted by the sample or alternatively a dc amplifier can be used to measure the integrated light output. A typical glow curve for ancient pottery is drawn on the X–Y recorder: curve TL represents the natural thermoluminescence plus thermal black-body radiation and curve BB represents the thermal radiation observed during a second heating after the removal of the natural thermoluminescence.

luminescence which has not been induced by ionizing radiation (Aitken *et al.*, 1968). Without this precaution, modern pottery could emit the same, apparently natural, thermoluminescence as pottery 8000 years old.

The thermoluminescence sensitivity (S) of the pottery to ionizing radiation may be changed by heating and therefore the sensitivity measurements cannot be carried out on the sample that has been used for the measurement of the natural thermoluminescence. The natural thermoluminescence (L) is therefore measured on one sample and the composite natural plus beta-induced thermoluminescence $(L + L_\beta)$ is measured on a second sample (Fig. 43a), the known beta dose being chosen to approximately double the natural thermoluminescence in the temperature range above 350°C. The beta sensitivity (S_β) is then calculated after subtraction of the natural thermoluminescence. In the "fine-grain method", the composite natural plus alpha-induced thermo-

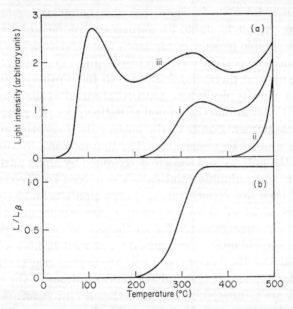

Figure 43. (a) Thermoluminescent glow curves for a typical specimen of ancient pottery: (i) natural thermoluminescence (L) plus thermal black-body radiation; (ii) thermal black-body radiation; (iii) thermoluminescence $(L + L_\beta)$ after exposure of a second unheated sample to a known dose of beta radiation, plus thermal black-body radiation. (b) "Plateau test". Ratio of the natural to the beta-induced thermoluminescence (L/L_β) plotted versus temperature. The constant "plateau" value for this ratio above 350°C indicates that negligible leakage from the associated traps has occurred since the pottery was fired in antiquity. Therefore, it is this "plateau" temperature region above 350°C that is used for age determination.

luminescence $(L + L_\alpha)$ is measured using a third sample, the alpha sensitivity (S_α) again being obtained after subtraction of the natural thermoluminescence. The known alpha and beta doses are provided by calibrated plaque-sources of polonium (^{210}Po) and strontium (^{90}Sr) respectively.

No natural thermoluminescence is observed below 200°C since, even at normal environmental temperatures (e.g. 20°C), thermally stimulated leakage of electrons from the traps responsible for the thermoluminescence below 200°C has occurred during antiquity. In contrast, the artificially induced thermoluminescence (L_α and L_β) is observed at all temperatures above approximately 50°C. The plot of the ratio of the natural to the artificially induced thermoluminescence (i.e. L/L_α or L/L_β) as a function of temperature therefore remains at zero until 200°C and then rises to a constant *plateau* value (Fig. 43b). The onset of this plateau is taken to indicate that the thermoluminescence in this temperature region is stable at normal environmental temperatures and that negligible leakage of electrons from the associated traps has occurred since the pottery was fired in antiquity. Consequently, it is the ratio of the natural thermoluminescence to the sensitivity (i.e. L/S) in the plateau region (typically 350–450°C) that is used for age determination.

In order to determine the annual radiation dose (R) received by the sample, measurements on both the pottery itself and the soil in which it was buried must be undertaken. The uranium and thorium concentrations in the pottery and soil are determined by alpha particle counting using a zinc sulphide scintillation counter (Turner *et al.*, 1958). Because of their low concentrations (a few ppm), only 10 to 30 counts per hour are obtained from a 5 cm diameter sample and therefore in order to achieve an accurate value for the annual radiation dose, counting on each sample must be continued for at least 12 hours. The potassium contents of the pottery and soil are determined chemically, by means of flame photometry, and the concentrations of the radioactive isotope ^{40}K are estimated by assuming that it always forms a constant fraction of the total potassium. From this data, it is possible to calculate the annual radiation doses (R_α and R_β) appropriate to both the "inclusion" and "fine-grain" methods. A superior technique for the evaluation of the gamma ray dose from the soil is direct on-site measurement using a thermoluminescent dosimetry phosphor, such as natural fluorite (Aitken, 1969). This involves placing a small capsule of the phosphor in as similar a burial position as possible to that from which the pottery fragment has been removed. The thermoluminescence induced in the phosphor by the gamma rays from the soil is easily measurable after a year's burial and can, after calibration of the phosphor, be used to determine the gamma ray dose.

Since the majority of the gamma ray dose originates from soil within a 30 cm radius of the pottery, it is important that the pottery was buried to a depth of at least 30 cm for the majority of its burial time and that the material lying within 30 cm of it was homogeneous. The ideal context is the middle of a pit or ditch, heterogeneous contexts, such as occupation layers and tombs, being less satisfactory. Because of the necessity to know the precise context in which the pottery was buried and to collect associated soil samples, the collection of pottery for age determination must be undertaken *during* the excavation of the archaeological site.

Complications

Although measurements on pottery of known age have established the essential validity of thermoluminescent dating, a number of complicating factors limit the accuracy that can ultimately be achieved with the method.

The basic assumption, associated with the use of equations (4.5) and (4.6) for age determination, is that the thermoluminescence increases linearly with radiation dose. Unfortunately, this assumption is not strictly justified since detailed measurements (Tite, 1966) have established that the initial increase in thermoluminescence with dose exhibits supralinearity (Fig. 44): that is, the slope of the growth curve initially increases progressively with dose before becoming constant. Normally the additional thermoluminescence (L_β), induced by the known beta radiation dose during sensitivity determinations, increases linearly. However, it is still probable that supralinear growth occurred during the acquisition of the natural thermoluminescence (L) and in these circumstances, the value estimated for the accumulated natural radiation dose $(T = R \times$ age) by extrapolation will be too low (Fig. 44—curve a): hence the estimated age will also be too low. An approximate correction for supralinearity can be obtained by first heating the samples to remove the natural thermoluminescence and then subjecting them to known beta radiation doses in order to obtain a second growth curve. In the ideal situation (Fig. 44—curve b), when the slopes of the linear portions of the two growth curves are equal, it is reasonable to assume that the intercept Δ provides a valid correction for supralinearity (i.e. accumulated natural radiation dose $= T + \Delta = R \times$ age). Unfortunately in many cases (Fig. 44—curve c), the slope of the linear portion is increased as a result of the heating and therefore the correction provided by the intercept Δ' is only approximate. Typically the effect of applying this correction for supralinearity is to increase the age estimated for the pottery by between 10 and 40 per cent.

A further deviation of the thermoluminescence growth curve from linearity can arise with pottery that has received a very large natural radiation dose (R × age) either because of its great age or because of the high concentration of radioactive impurities. In this case the natural thermoluminescence approaches a saturation value associated with the situation where all the traps are filled with electrons. The increase in thermoluminescence, when subjected to known radiation doses

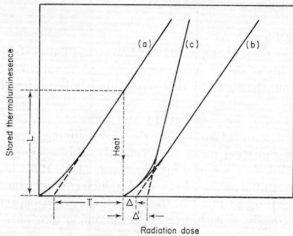

Radiation dose

Figure. 44. Supralinear growth of thermoluminescence with radiation dose. (a) Growth of the natural thermoluminescence (L) together with the additional thermoluminescence induced by a known beta dose: T represents the value for the accumulated natural radiation dose (R × age) estimated by extrapolation of the linear portion of the curve. (b) Ideal second growth curve after the removal of the natural thermoluminescence by heating to 500°C. The slopes of the linear portions of the two curves are the same so that Δ provides a valid correction for supralinearity (i.e. $T + Δ = R$ × age). (c) Second growth curve for which the slope of the linear portion differs from that for the initial growth curve (a). In this case Δ′ provides only an approximate correction for supralinearity.

during sensitivity measurements, will therefore be sublinear (i.e. the slope of the growth curve decreases with increasing dose) and age determination will not be possible.

Errors in the estimation of the annual radiation dose (R) received by the pottery further limit the accuracy of thermoluminescent dating. These arise principally from uncertainties in the water content of and the radon emanation from the pottery and soil. Ground water which permeates both the pottery and soil but which is, in comparison, low in radioactivity, absorbs radiation which would otherwise reach the mineral grains and induce thermoluminescence. The annual radiation dose is determined from measurements on dry pottery and soil and must therefore be corrected for the effect of the *in situ* water content; the reduction in the "effective" dose being related to the percentage weight of water. Although the present day *in situ* water content and the saturation water content (typically between 5 and 25 per cent by weight) can be determined, it is difficult to relate these values to the average wetness during burial because of uncertainties in the annual and long-term fluctuations. However, for wet sites (e.g. Britain), it is reasonable to assume that the pottery and soil have been three-quarters ± one-quarter saturated during the burial period and in this case the correction to the age is about 15 per cent with an associated error of about ± 5 per cent.

The gas radon (^{222}Rn) is formed about half-way through the uranium decay series and this gas can escape (i.e. emanate) from the pottery and the soil, thus again reducing the annual radiation dose received. With regard to the radiation dose from the soil, the effect of radon emanation will normally be small since, provided the soil is uniform for a sufficient distance, the flow of radon outwards will be compensated by the flow inwards. With regard to the radiation dose from the uranium in the pottery, radon escape can be more serious since the distances involved (i.e. the dimensions of the pottery sherd) are much smaller. However, movement of radon is reduced in a wet to saturated sherd and therefore the error in the age due to radon emanation is likely to be less than that due to uncertainties concerning the average water content of the pottery and soil.

Possible errors in the estimated radiation dose as a result of the distribution of uranium and thorium in the pottery have also been investigated. If, instead of being uniformly distributed in the clay matrix, these impurities were concentrated in inclusions, the associated alpha particles would not reach the fine grains in the clay matrix. They would, however, be counted with the zinc sulphide scintillation system and therefore the calculated radiation dose would be higher than that actually experienced by the thermoluminescent minerals. Fortunately, induced fission track studies have indicated that uranium-bearing inclusions are not normally present in significant numbers. Finally, the possibility of interchange (e.g. leaching) of uranium between the pottery and the soil has to be considered since this could have resulted in a change in the uranium concentration of the pottery during burial. Although no direct data on this problem are available, the satisfactory results obtained for pottery of known age suggest that the effect does not normally lead to serious errors.

Results

So far the majority of the effort in thermoluminescent dating of pottery has been devoted to establishing the validity and accuracy of the method and consequently pottery of known age has been studied. Zimmerman (1971) carried out detailed measurements on 14 pottery sherds from three sites which could be accurately dated from their archaeological context and established that the average deviation of the thermoluminescent age from the archaeological age for a single sherd was approximately 10 per cent. Since the spread in the thermoluminescent ages obtained from repeated measurements on a single sherd is only 5 per cent, it is clear that the observed 10 per cent deviation arises from errors in the corrections for supralinearity, water content and radon emanation. However, when the mean thermoluminescent age for a group of sherds from the same archaeological context was considered, the average deviation was reduced to 6 per cent. It is therefore reasonable to assume that if the thermoluminescent ages are determined for several sherds from the same context, the mean age will normally be accurate to between ± 5 and ± 10 per cent.

More recently thermoluminescent ages, using the "fine-grain" method, have been obtained for pottery for which there was no other dating evidence or for which it was thought desirable to check the associated radiocarbon age. In the first category, Zimmerman and Huxtable (1969) have studied pottery from Britain which could have been either of Iron Age (500 BC–50 AD) or Saxon (500–1000 AD) origin. In this case, because of the large difference in age for the two possibilities, the errors associated with thermoluminescent dating were less important and the measurements conclusively distinguished the Iron Age from the Saxon pottery.

In the second category, the measurements on fired clay fragments found with fired clay figurines on the Upper Palaeolithic site at Dolni Vestonice in Czechoslovakia are of particular interest (Zimmerman and Huxtable, 1971). The radiocarbon dates obtained for the deposits containing the figurines, which are among the earliest fired clay artefacts that have been found anywhere in the world, were around 28 500 BC (i.e. after adjustment to the 5730 year half-life). For the fired clay samples, the *plateau* test (p. 122) established that the traps responsible for the thermoluminescence above 400°C were stable at normal environmental temperatures even over this very long period since firing. Furthermore, the increase in thermoluminescence with beta radiation dose, supplied by the calibrated source during sensitivity measurements, was linear indicating that the natural thermoluminescence had not started to approach the saturation value (i.e. there was no sublinearity). It was therefore concluded that the mean thermoluminescent age of 31 000 BC (probable error = ± 3000 years) obtained for the fired clay fragments was valid. The result represents the first step towards correcting radiocarbon ages for the period in which neither tree-ring nor varve chronologies are available, measurements on additional fired clay samples being necessary before a reliable correction can be provided for this period.

A further comparison of radiocarbon and thermoluminescent ages is provided by the study of Linear Pottery (Bandkeramik) of the Central European Middle Neolithic (Zimmerman and Huxtable, 1970). The mean thermoluminescent ages for three groups of Bandkeramik sherds fall in the range 5350–4610 BC (probable error = ± 400 years) whereas the uncorrected radiocarbon dates for this period places the Bandkeramik at 4500–3900 BC. However, correction of the radiocarbon dates, using the tree-ring chronology, provides an age range of 5300–4700 BC which agrees more closely with the thermoluminescent ages. Because of the error associated with the thermoluminescent ages, these results do not conclusively establish the validity of the tree-ring correction. However, they do strongly support a "long" radiocarbon-based chronology rather than the previously favoured "short" historically based chronology which places the Bandkeramik at 3000–2500 BC (Quitta, 1967).

The above examples indicate that, in spite of its associated errors, thermoluminescence dating should be extremely valuable both in supplementing radiocarbon dating and in providing further data on the difference between the radiocarbon and true calendar ages. In comparing the thermoluminescent and radiocarbon methods, it should be noted that an important feature of the former method is that the event dated (i.e. the firing of the pottery) is well defined and archaeologically significant. In contrast, when dating wood or charcoal by the radiocarbon method, it is possible that the inner rings of a large tree are being dated and their age could precede man's involvement with the tree by several hundred years. Another advantage is that pottery is itself of direct archaeological interest whereas wood and charcoal are only circumstantially related to the artefacts, including pottery, which are the archaeologist's chief concern. Also because of their durability, pottery fragments are relatively abundant on most sites after approximately 5000 BC, whereas suitable material for radiocarbon dating is frequently not available.

Authenticity testing. A further important application of the thermoluminescent measurements is the identification of fakes. Many fired clay antiquities, including pottery, have considerable artistic merit and consequently command very high prices on the art market. Their "production" has therefore become a flourishing industry in some parts of the world and in many cases, the quality of these modern products is such as to deceive even the experienced museum curator. Since, for testing authenticity, it is usually a question of distinguishing between an age of less than 100 years and one of upwards of several hundred the problem of soil radiation dose can be neglected and measurements can be restricted to the museum specimens themselves. Thermoluminescent and approximate annual radiation dose measurements, made on an approximately 25 mg sample taken from an unobtrusive part of the object, can therefore be used to readily establish whether the object is of genuine antiquity or merely a modern copy.

Fleming *et al.* (1970) tested a selection of Chinese "Six Dynasties" figures and established that six out of the nine pieces were less than 200 years old whereas the period of manufacture for authentic terracotta figures of this type was between 222 and 618 AD. Similarly, Aitken *et al.* (1971) were able to show that 47 out of a group of 66 vessels and figurines, supposedly from the Neolithic site of Hacilar in Turkey and dating from the sixth millennium BC, were modern forgeries. In this case a subsidiary problem arose as a result of the persistent rumour that a number of these objects had originally been recovered in a waterlogged state and had therefore been refired in order to stabilize them before sale. This refiring would remove the thermoluminescence accumulated in antiquity and therefore invalidate the authenticity testing by the conventional thermoluminescent method. However, study of the "predose" effect (Fleming, 1971), which concerns the increased sensitivity to radiation of the 110°C thermoluminescence peak in quartz after preirradiation followed by heating, excluded the possibility of recent refiring for the majority of the objects designated as modern forgeries.

Extension to other materials. A basic requirement for thermoluminescent dating is that the stored thermoluminescence must be zero at the time of the event being dated. For pottery, this is achieved by the firing to above 500°C during its manufacture. The thermoluminescent "clock" will similarly have been set to zero in burnt stones (e.g. flints used as "pot-boilers") and glass, while for shell and bone, the stored thermoluminescence may also be zero on formation. Although, for a number of reasons, these materials appear to be less satisfactory than pottery, they could in principle be used for thermoluminescent dating.

Preliminary measurements on shell (Johnson and Blanchard, 1967) are fairly encouraging although more research is necessary before satisfactory thermoluminescent dates can be obtained. Both burnt flint and bone emit a "spurious" thermoluminescence which cannot be removed by heating in nitrogen and which tends to obscure the radiation-induced natural thermoluminescence measured for age determination. However, in the case of burnt flint (Gosku and Fremlin, 1972), the "spurious" thermoluminescence, which is associated with the surface absorption of water, can be virtually eliminated by reducing the effective surface area through the use of a thin slice rather than a powdered sample. As a result of the development of this thin slice technique, it should now be possible to obtain satisfactory thermoluminescent dates for those burnt flints whose natural thermoluminescence has not reached saturation. With bone, the "spurious" thermoluminescence is due to the combustion of the organic material (chemiluminescence) and the mechanical grinding of the material to produce a powder (triboluminescence). However, Christodoulides and Fremlin (1971) consider that for bone older than 100 000 years this "spurious" thermoluminescence should be negligible in comparison with the radiation-induced natural thermoluminescence while encouraging preliminary measurements have been reported by Jasinska and Niewiadomski (1970) for dinosaur bones from which the organic material has been removed by natural processes. In respect to glass, the major difficulties are associated with its transparency to light; optical bleaching of the stored thermoluminescence could occur or light-induced thermoluminescence could be acquired during the period prior to its burial in the ground.

References

Radiocarbon Dating

Arnold, J. R. and Libby, W. F. (1949). Age determination by radiocarbon content. Checks with samples of known age. *Science* **110**, 678–680.
Berger, R. (1970). Ancient Egyptian radiocarbon chronology. *Phil. Trans. R. Soc. Lond.* A**269** 23–36.

Bucha, V. (1970). Influence of the earth's magnetic field on radiocarbon dating. *In* "Radiocarbon Variations and Absolute Chronology". (Ed. I. U. Olsson), pp. 501–511. Almqvist and Wiksell, Stockholm.

Damon, P. E. (1970). Climatic versus magnetic perturbation of the atmospheric carbon-14 reservoir. *In* "Radiocarbon Variations and Absolute Chronology". (Ed. I. U. Olsson), pp. 571–593. Almqvist and Wiksell, Stockholm.

Edwards, I. E. S. (1970). Absolute dating from Egyptian records and comparison with carbon-14 dating. *Phil. Trans. R. Soc. Lond.* A269, 11–18.

Haring, A., Vries, A. E. de and Vries, H. de (1958). Radiocarbon dating up to 70 000 years by isotope enrichment. *Science* 128, 472–473.

Lerman, J. C., Mook, W. G. and Vogel, J. C. (1970). Carbon-14 in tree rings from different localities. *In* "Radiocarbon Variations and Absolute Chronology". (Ed. I. U. Olsson), pp. 275–301. Almqvist and Wiksell, Stockholm.

Libby, W. F. (1946). Atmospheric helium three and radiocarbon from cosmic radiation. *Phys. Rev.* 69, 671–672.

Libby, W. F. (1955). "Radiocarbon Dating." University of Chicago Press, Chicago.

Lingenfelter, R. E. (1963). Production of carbon-14 by cosmic ray neutrons. *Rev. Geophys.* 1, 35–55.

Longin, R. (1971). New method of collagen extraction for radiocarbon dating. *Nature* 230, 241–242.

Merwe, N. J. van der (1969). "The Carbon-14 Dating of Iron." University of Chicago Press, Chicago.

Neutstupný, E. (1970). A new epoch in radiocarbon dating. *Antiquity* 44, 38–45.

Schove, D. J. (1955). The sunspot cycle 649 BC to 2000 AD. *J. geophys. Res.* 60, 127–145.

Stuiver, M. (1970). Tree ring, varve and carbon-14 chronologies. *Nature* 228, 454–455.

Suess, H. E. (1955). Radiocarbon concentration in modern wood. *Science* 122, 415–417.

Suess, H. E. (1970a). Bristlecone pine calibration of the radiocarbon time-scale 5200 BC to the present. *In* "Radiocarbon Variations and Absolute Chronology". (Ed. I. U. Olsson), pp. 303–311. Almqvist and Wiksell, Stockholm.

Suess, H. E. (1970b). The three causes of the secular carbon-14 fluctuations, their amplitudes and time constants. *In* "Radiocarbon Variations and Absolute Chronology". (Ed. I. U. Olsson), pp. 595–605. Almqvist and Wiksell, Stockholm.

Suess, H. E. and Strahm, C. (1970). The Neolithic of Auvernier. *Antiquity* 44, 91–99.

Tauber, H. (1970). The Scandinavian varve chronology and carbon-14 dating. *In* "Radiocarbon Variations and Absolute Chronology". (Ed. I. U. Olsson), pp. 173–195. Almqvist and Wiksell, Stockholm.

Vries, H. de (1968). Variation in concentration of radiocarbon with time and location on earth, *Koninkl. Ned. Akad. Wetensch. Proc.*, Ser. B61, 1–9.

Walton, A., Baxter, M. S., Callow, W. J. and Baker, M. J. (1967). Carbon-14 concentrations in environmental materials and their temporal fluctuations. *In* "Radioactive Dating and Methods of Low-level Counting", pp. 41–47. International Atomic Energy Agency, Vienna.

Potassium-argon Dating

Evernden, J. F. and Curtis, G. H. (1965). The potassium–argon dating of Late Cenozoic rocks in East Africa and Italy. *Curr. Anthropol.* **6**, 343–385.

Fitch, F. J. and Miller, J. A. (1970). Radioisotopic age determinations of Lake Rudolf artefact site. *Nature* **226**, 226–228.

Gentner, W. and Lippolt, H. J. (1969). The potassium–argon dating of Upper Tertiary and Pleistocene deposits. *In* "Science in Archaeology". (Eds. D. Brothwell and E. Higgs), pp. 88–100. Thames and Hudson, London.

Grasty, R. L. and Miller, J. A. (1965). The Omegatron: a useful tool for argon isotope investigation. *Nature* **207**, 1146–1148.

Mitchell, J. G. (1968). The argon-40/argon-39 method for potassium–argon age determination. *Geochim. cosmochim. Acta* **32**, 781–790.

Fission Track Dating

Brill, R. H., Fleischer, R. L., Price, P. B. and Walker, R. M. (1964). The fission-track dating of man-made glasses: preliminary results. *J. Glass Stud.* **7**, 151–156.

Durrani, S. A., Khan, H. A., Taj, M. and Renfrew, C. (1971). Obsidian source identification by fission track analysis. *Nature* **233**, 242–245.

Fleischer, R. L. and Price, P. B. (1964a). Glass dating by fission fragment tracks. *J. geophys. Res.* **69**, 331–339.

Fleischer, R. L. and Price, P. B. (1964b). Uranium contents of ancient man-made glass. *Science* **144**, 841–842.

Fleischer, R. L., Price, P. B. and Walker, R. M. (1965). Effects of temperature, pressure and ionization on the formation and stability of fission tracks in minerals and glasses. *J. geophys. Res.* **70**, 1497–1502.

Fleischer, R. L., Price, P. B., Walker, R. M. and Leakey, L. S. B. (1965a). Fission-track dating of Bed I, Olduvai Gorge. *Science* **148**, 72–74.

Fleischer, R. L., Price, P. B., Walker, R. M. and Leakey, L. S. B. (1965b). Fission-track dating of a Mesolithic knife. *Nature* **205**, 1138.

Koenigswald, G. H. R. von, Gentner, W. and Lippolt, H. J. (1961). Age of the basalt flow at Olduvai, East Africa. *Nature* **192**, 720–721.

Leakey, L. S. B., Evernden, J. F. and Curtis, G. H. (1961). Age of Bed I, Olduvai Gorge, Tanganyika. *Nature* **191**, 478.

Nishimura, S. (1971). Fission track dating of archaeological materials from Japan. *Nature* **230**, 242–243.

Price, P. B. and Walker, R. M. (1963). Fossil tracks of charged particles in mica and the age of minerals. *J. geophys. Res.* **68**, 4847–4862.

Deep-sea Sediments

Emiliani, C. (1955). Pleistocene temperatures. *J. Geol.* **63**, 538–578.

Emiliani, C. (1958). Paleotemperature analysis of core 280 and Pleistocene correlations. *J. Geol.* **66**, 264–275.

Emiliani, C. (1966). Isotopic paleotemperatures. *Science* **154**, 851–857.

Ericson, D. B., Ewing, M., Wollin, G. and Heezen, B. C. (1961). Atlantic deep-sea sediment cores. *Bull. geol. Soc. Am.* **75**, 193–286.

Erison, D. B., Ewing, M. and Wollin, G. (1964). The Pleistocene epoch in deep-sea sediments. *Science* **146**, 723–732.

Glass, B., Ericson, D. B., Heezen, B. C., Opdyke, N. D. and Glass, J. A. (1967). Geomagnetic reversals and Pleistocene chronology. *Nature* 216, 437–442.

Rosholt, J. N., Emiliani, C., Geiss, J., Koczy, F. F. and Wangersky, P. J. (1961). Absolute dating of deep-sea cores by the $^{231}Pa/^{230}Th$ method. *J. Geol.* 69, 162–185.

Shackleton, N. J. (1967). Oxygen isotope analyses and Pleistocene temperatures reassessed. *Nature* 215, 15–17.

Shackleton, N. J. and Turner, C. (1967). Correlation of marine and terrestial Pleistocene successions. *Nature* 216, 1079–1082.

Volchok, H. L. and Kulp, J. L. (1957). The ionium method of age determination. *Geochim. cosmochim. Acta* 11, 219–246.

Thermoluminescent Dating

Aitken, M. J. (1969). Thermoluminescent dosimetry of environmental radiation on archaeological sites. *Archaeometry* 11, 109–114.

Aitken, M. J., Zimmerman, D. W. and Fleming, S. J. (1968). Thermoluminescent dating of pottery. *Nature* 219, 442–445.

Aitken, M. J., Fleming, S. J., Reid, J. and Tite, M. S. (1968). Elimination of spurious thermoluminescence. *In* "Thermoluminescence of Geological Materials". (Ed. D. J. McDougall), pp. 133–142. Academic Press, London and New York.

Aitken, M. J., Moorey, P. R. S. and Ucko, P. J. (1971). The authenticity of vessels and figurines in the Hacilar style. *Archaeometry* 13, 89–142.

Attix, F. H. (Ed.) (1967). "Luminescence Dosimetry." U.S. Atomic Energy Commission, Oak Ridge, Tennessee.

Boyle, R. (1664). "Experiments and Considerations upon Colours with Observations on a Diamond that shines in the Dark." H. Herringham, London.

Christodoulides, C. and Fremlin, J. H. (1971). Thermoluminescence of biological materials. *Nature* 232, 257–258.

Daniels, F., Boyd, C. A. and Saunders, D. F. (1953). Thermoluminescence as a research tool. *Science* 117, 343–349.

Fleming, S. J. (1970). Thermoluminescent dating: refinement of the quartz inclusion method. *Archaeometry* 12, 133–146.

Fleming, S. J. (1971). Thermoluminescent authenticity testing of ancient ceramics: the effects of sampling by drilling. *Archaeometry* 13, 59–70.

Fleming, S. J., Moss, H. M. and Joseph, A. (1970). Thermoluminescent authenticity testing of some "Six Dynasties" figures. *Archaeometry* 12, 57–66.

Goksu, H. Y. and Fremlin, J. H. (1972). Thermoluminescence from unirradiated flints: regeneration thermoluminescence. *Archaeometry* 14, 127–132.

Ichikawa, Y. (1965). Dating of ancient ceramics by thermoluminescence. *Bull. Inst. chem. Res. Kyoto Univ.* 43, 1–6.

Jasinska, M. and Niewiadomski, T. (1970). Thermoluminescence of biological materials. *Nature* 227, 1159–1160.

Johnson, N. M. and Blanchard, R. L. (1967). Radiation dosimetry from the natural thermoluminescence of fossil shells. *Am. Miner.* 52, 1297–1310.

McDougall, D. J. (Ed.) (1968). "Thermoluminescence of Geological Materials." Academic Press, London and New York.

Mejdahl, V. (1969). Thermoluminescence dating of ancient Danish ceramics. *Archaeometry* 11, 99–104.

Quitta, H. (1967). The C-14 chronology of the Central and S.E. European Neolithic. *Antiquity*, 41, 263-270.

Ralph, E. K. and Han. M. C. (1966). Dating of pottery by thermoluminescence. *Nature* 210, 245-247.

Tite, M. S. (1966). Thermoluminescent dating of ancient ceramics: a reassessment. *Archaeometry* 9, 155-169.

Turner, R. C., Radley, J. M. and Mayneord, W. V. (1958). The alpha-ray activity of human tissues. *Br. J. Radio.* 31, 397-406.

Zimmerman, D. W. (1971). Thermoluminescent dating using fine grains from pottery. *Archaeometry* 13, 29-52.

Zimmerman, D. W. and Huxtable, J. (1969). Recent applications and developments in thermoluminescent dating. *Archaeometry* 11, 105-108.

Zimmerman, D. W. and Huxtable, J. (1970). Some thermoluminescent dates for Linear Pottery. *Antiquity* 44, 304-305.

Zimmerman, D. W. and Huxtable, J. (1971). Thermoluminescent dating of Upper Palaeolithic fired clay from Dolni Vestonice. *Archaeometry* 13, 53-58.

5

Age Determination—
Non-Radioactive Methods

The physical methods of age determination described in this chapter are based on the variations in the direction and intensity of the Earth's magnetic field (p. 135) and the time-dependent chemical alteration of bone (p. 150), obsidian (p. 154) and glass (p. 161) that has occurred as a result of burial in the ground. In contrast to the radioactive methods described previously, these methods of dating do *not* provide a world-wide absolute chronology. Instead either relative dates for specimens taken from the same archaeological site are obtained or a calibration curve, using specimens of known age, must first be established for the specific geographical area under consideration. However, in spite of this limitation, these methods are frequently valuable in supplementing and refining the chronological framework provided by the radioactive age determination techniques.

Magnetic Dating

The thermoremanent magnetism acquired by fired clay whilst cooling in the Earth's magnetic field provides a record of the direction and intensity of the field at that time. Since the direction and intensity of the Earth's magnetic field change continuously with time, the measurement of the thermoremanent magnetism provides the basis for a method of dating, fired structures found *in situ* (e.g. kilns, hearths, furnaces) being normally required for direction studies. The study of the thermoremanent magnetism in fired clay of archaeological origin was pioneered at the end of the nineteenth century in Italy by Folgheraiter (1899) who measured the direction of thermoremanent magnetism in Etruscan vases and bricks. However it was Professor E. Thellier, working at L'Institut de Physique du Globe in Paris from 1933 onwards, who laid the foundations to the present day techniques and applications of archaeomagnetism (Thellier, 1938; Thellier and Thellier, 1959).

It should be appreciated that archaeomagnetism forms part of the much wider field of palaeomagnetism in which the "fossilized" magnetic record in rocks is used to give information about the past behaviour of the Earth's magnetic field on a geological time scale (Stacey, 1969).

Theory of Thermoremanent Magnetism

The thermoremanent magnetism of fired clay is associated with the few per cent of iron oxides which are present in most clays in the form of ferrimagnetic minerals, such as haematite (αFe_2O_3) and magnetite (Fe_3O_4), and which exist as small dispersed grains (Chapter 2, p. 9). In the case of haematite, each grain is a single magnetic domain which is spontaneously magnetized along a direction dictated by the shape and crystalline anisotropy of the grain. In contrast, magnetite, with its much stronger saturation magnetization (i.e. 1.2×10^{-4} Wb m/kg compared to 6×10^{-7} Wb m/kg for haematite), can only exist as single-domain grains when the grain size in less than 0.03 μm; the corresponding maximum grain size for haematite can be as large as 1 mm. Therefore in clay, a large proportion of the magnetite exists as multidomain grains for which adjacent regions within each grain are spontaneously magnetized in opposite directions. The theory for the thermoremanent magnetism of both single-domain and multidomain grains has been developed and reviewed by Néel (1955), Stacey (1963) and Dunlop and West (1969).

For single-domain grains of haematite the thermoremanent magnetism may be understood in comparatively simple terms. In the unfired clay, the directions of magnetization of the grains are randomly orientated so that the nett permanent magnetic moment of the clay is zero. When the temperature of the clay is increased, the direction of magnetization of the grain can reverse so that its component along the direction of the Earth's magnetic field can change from parallel to antiparallel and vice-versa. Reversal is possible when the thermal agitation energy is comparable with the potential energy of the constraints tending to maintain the magnetization along the preferred axis of the grain. The probability of reversal increases rapidly with temperature and for each grain it is possible to define a *blocking temperature*, T_B, above which there is a high probability of reversal in a few seconds and below which reversal is only likely to occur after a very long time. Magnetization with a component parallel, rather than antiparallel, to the Earth's magnetic field is energetically favourable. Consequently, when thermal agitation permits reversal of the direction of magnetization, there exists a fractional excess of grains with a component of magnetization parallel to the Earth's magnetic field direction. When the clay is subsequently cooled to below T_B, this fractional excess remains "frozen" in position and therefore the clay is left with a permanent magnetic moment, the thermoremanent magnetism, in the direction of the Earth's magnetic field.

The blocking temperature T_B increases with increasing grain volume and since there is a range of grain volumes in any clay, there exists a continuum of blocking temperatures from room temperature up to the Curie temperature (650°C for haematite) at which the grains lose their spontaneous magnetization and become paramagnetic. The magnitude of the thermoremanent magnetism therefore increases with increasing firing temperature, the blocking temperature for progressively larger grains being exceeded until the Curie temperature is reached (Fig. 45). The fractional excess of grains with a component of magnetization parallel to the magnetic field is directly proportional to the intensity of the magnetic field and therefore the magnitude of the thermoremanent magnetism in fired clay is proportional to the intensity of the Earth's magnetic field. In addition, the thermoremanent magnetism increases with increasing concentration of haematite in the clay, the precise relationship being somewhat complex since it also depends on the size and shape of the grains.

The thermoremanent magnetism due to haematite grains with blocking temperatures above 150°C is stable at normal environmental temperatures (i.e. 20°C) for many thousands of years. However, in the case of grains with lower blocking temperatures, the thermal agitation energy at 20°C is sufficient to cause reversal of the direction of magnetization. Therefore the thermoremanent magnetism associated with these grains tends to follow any changes in the direction of the earth's magnetic field rather than providing a record of the field direction during the original firing. This *viscous remanent magnetism* is typically less than 5 per cent of the total thermoremanent magnetism and can be readily eliminated by thermal demagnetization. If the sample is reheated to successively higher temperatures and cooled in zero magnetic field, it loses its thermoremanent magnetism, the demagnetization curve being the mirror image of the magnetization curve (Fig. 45). Therefore by reheating to 150°C and cooling in zero field, the viscous remanent magnetism is removed but the stable thermoremanent magnetism, due to grains with blocking temperatures above 150°C, is unchanged.

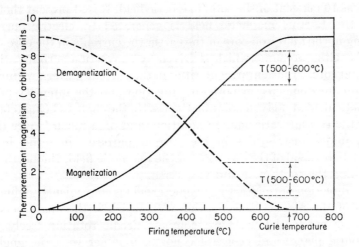

Figure 45. Idealized curves for the acquisition and removal of thermoremanent magnetism in fired clay. The solid curve shows the magnetism acquired by the sample on cooling in a magnetic field from the firing temperature indicated by the horizontal scale. The dashed curve shows the subsequent demagnetization of the sample which is achieved by reheating it to successively higher temperatures and cooling in zero magnetic field. Provided that there are no mineralogical changes during the reheating, the demagnetization curve is the mirror image of the magnetization curve: that is, the thermoremanent magnetism gained in a certain temperature interval (e.g. 500–600°C) is equal to that lost in the same temperature interval during demagnetization.

For multidomain grains of magnetite, the acquisition of thermoremanent magnetism is associated with the growth of those regions in the grain whose spontaneous magnetization is parallel to the magnetic field, at the expense of regions which are antiparallel. Although the actual physical processes are somewhat different and the theory is less straightforward, the thermoremanent magnetism of multidomain grains can still be discussed in terms of a continuum of blocking temperatures from 20°C up to the Curie temperature (580° C for magnetite) and exhibits the same pattern of behaviour as in the case of single-domain grains.

Principles of Age Determination

To a first approximation, the magnetic field of the Earth can be represented by the field due to a magnetic dipole (i.e. a small bar magnet) at the Earth's centre and inclined at a small angle to the axis of rotation (Stacey, 1969). Superimposed upon the dipole field are the so-called non-dipole components which in some regions contribute as much as 10 per cent of the total magnetic field. It is at present thought that the Earth's magnetic field is generated by electric currents flowing in the fluid iron core of the earth: the currents in the core form a self-exciting dynamo which is driven by convection currents within the fluid core. Transient irregularities in the current pattern within the core produce changes in both the direction and the intensity of the magnetic field at a given point on the Earth, the changes being referred to as the secular variation. In addition, and on a much longer time-scale, major instabilities in the current pattern can result in the complete reversal of the direction of the magnetic field, the north pole becoming the south pole and vice-versa.

The direction of the Earth's magnetic field is conveniently defined in terms of the magnetic declination (D), which is the angle between magnetic north (defined by a compass needle rotating freely in a horizontal plane) and geographic north, together with the angle of inclination or dip (I), which is the angle between the magnetic field direction and the horizontal plane. As a result of the magnetic dipole character of the Earth's magnetic field, the angle of dip is strongly latitude dependent, varying from 0 degrees at the magnetic equator to 90 degrees at the magnetic poles. Similarly the intensity of the magnetic field (H) changes with latitude, the value at the equator being half that at the poles. For London, the approximate present day values for the three parameters, representing the Earth's magnetic field, are $D = 5$ degrees, $I = 67$ degrees and $H = 38$ A m^{-1}.

The magnetic declination and the angle of dip change, in any given region, by a degree or two every 20 years and this secular variation in direction has been recorded in London over the past four hundred years from observations on suspended magnetized needles (Fig. 46). Since the thermoremanent magnetism associated with a fired archaeological structure is parallel to the Earth's magnetic field at the time of firing, the date of a structure which was last fired during this period can be determined if the structure is found *in situ* (e.g. kilns, hearths). For example, between 1600 and 1800 AD, the magnetic declination in

London changed from 10 degrees east of geographic north to 24 degrees west and therefore if the direction of the thermoremanent magnetism can be measured to within ± 2 degrees, the date of the last firing can be determined to within ± 12 years; an accuracy which is much greater than that possible with radiocarbon dating.

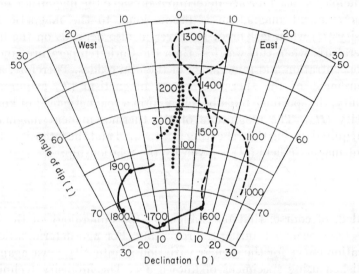

Figure 46. Secular variation of the declination (D) and the angle of dip (I) for London, the dates being shown in years AD. The data subsequent to 1540 AD (solid line) are based on recorded observations on suspended magnetized needles (Bauer, 1899) while the data for the Roman period (dotted line) and the Mediaeval period (dashed line) are based on measurements of the thermoremanent magnetism associated with fired archaeological structures found *in situ*. During the Roman period, the declination remained essentially constant while the magnetic direction was essentially the same during the twelfth and fourteenth/fifteenth centuries (from Aitken, 1970).

Unfortunately prior to 1540 AD, no records of the secular variation exist. Furthermore the secular variation is not the well-behaved cyclic phenomena that might be anticipated from the elliptical shape of the D versus I curve after 1540 AD and therefore the secular variation prior to 1540 AD cannot be determined by extrapolation. Instead an extended secular variation curve can only be obtained from thermo-remanent magnetism measurements on structures for which the date of the last firing is known from the archaeological evidence. The accuracy of the subsequent age determination of structures without archaeo-logical dating evidence then depends on the precision of this calibration curve for the secular variation. In addition, it must be appreciated that the calibration curve is only applicable to a region about 500 miles across since the secular variation depends on the geographical location and extrapolation between different locations is limited by the existence of the non-dipole contribution to the magnetic field.

The secular variation in the Earth's magnetic field intensity can also, in principle, be used for age determination since the magnitude of the thermoremanent magnetism is proportional to the magnetic field intensity (H) when last fired. However, it also depends on the firing temperature, when this was less than the Curie temperature, and on the concentration and mineralogy of the iron oxides. Therefore, after measurement of the thermoremanent magnetism (T) acquired in antiquity, the specimen must be reheated in a magnetic field of known intensity (H_0). The magnitude of the thermoremanent magnetism (T_0) acquired during this reheating is measured and the intensity of the ancient magnetic field (H) is given by the relationship:

$$\frac{H}{H_0} = \frac{T}{T_0} \tag{5.1}$$

provided, of course, that no changes in the mineralogy of the iron oxides have occurred during the reheating. For age determination a calibration curve for the secular variation in intensity must again be established using specimens of known age. The intensity technique has the advantage of not requiring *in situ* structures and so can be applied to the far more prolific pottery sherds. However, since the overall variation in intensity is about ± 50 per cent of the present value and since the precision of intensity measurements is only about ± 10 per cent, it is apparent that the errors in the age determination from intensity measurements will be very much greater than those associated with direction measurements.

The evidence from palaeomagnetism indicates that for certain periods of the geological past the Earth's magnetic field has been reversed with respect to its present direction (Cox, 1969). The present normal polarity epoch is termed the *Brunhes* and this was preceded by the *Matuyama* reversed epoch, the transition occurring around 0·7 million years ago. During an epoch there is the occasional occurrence of polarity events associated with reversals with respect to the primary direction of the epoch and lasting for between 5000 and 200 000 years. The polarity data for the past 2·5 million years, presented in Fig. 47, has been acquired principally from measurements of the direction of the thermoremanent magnetism of volcanic lavas, the age determination of the lavas being achieved using the potassium–argon method. These changes are synchronous throughout the world and therefore if any events were detected in the thermoremanent magnetism of fired archaeological structures (e.g. Palaeolithic hearths), they would provide approximate dates for these structures. Although no results for archaeological structures have been reported, the polarity data has

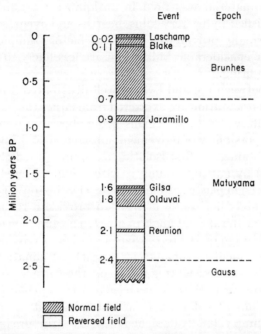

Figure 47. Changes in the polarity of the Earth's magnetic field during the past 2·5 million years. The epochs (i.e. Brunhes—normal present day polarity, Matuyama—reversed polarity, Gauss—normal polarity) refer to the long-term reversals in polarity while the events (i.e. Laschamp, Blake, etc.) refer to short-term reversals with respect to the primary polarity for the epoch.

been used for the age determination of deep-sea sediments (Chapter 4, p. 110). In this case it is the direction of the detrital or depositional remanent magnetism that is measured: the sediments include magnetic particles which inherit a remanence from their parent rocks and which tend to be aligned by the Earth's magnetic field as they settle (Harrison, 1966).

Experimental Procedures

The selection, extraction and treatment of samples differs according to whether measurements of the direction or the intensity of the Earth's magnetic field are being undertaken. However, in both cases similar magnetometers are used for the measurement of the thermoremanent magnetism.

Direction measurements. In order to determine the direction of the ancient magnetic field (i.e. *D* and *I*), it is essential to know the position in which the material was fired in antiquity; a condition which is obviously satisfied by pottery kilns, hearths and ovens. Pottery kilns, (Plate 10) normally provide the most satisfactory samples since, as a result of their considerable bulk, they are less likely to have moved subsequent to firing.

Typically between ten and twenty well-distributed samples of fired clay of known orientation are extracted from either the kiln floor or the base of the kiln walls, these regions being chosen in order to further minimize the possibility of movement subsequent to firing. Orientated samples are obtained by first isolating a stump of fired clay (about 10 cm by 10 cm) by cutting around it with a knife. The stump is then partially encased in plaster of Paris (Plate 11), the top surface of which is made accurately horizontal in order to provide a reference for the measurement of the ancient angle of dip, *I*. The direction of geographic north is also marked on the top surface in order to provide a reference for the measurement of the ancient magnetic declination, *D*. This is effectively achieved by sighting a line on the surface from a nearby theodolite whose azimuth scale has been related to geographic north by shooting the sun at a known time and using suitable astronomical tables. The stump is finally detached from the structure by cutting underneath and the plaster of Paris case is extended to enclose the entire sample.

The direction of the thermoremanent magnetism in each sample is measured in the laboratory using either an astatic or spinning magnetometer and from this the magnetic declination and the angle of dip at the time of the last firing can be determined. A necessary preliminary to this measurement is the removal of the viscous remanent magnetism by refiring to 150°C and cooling in zero magnetic field.

Although the precision of the direction measurements is better than 1 degree, the scatter in the values for *D* and *I* obtained for a group of samples from a single structure can be between 5 and 20 degrees (Fig. 48). The most obvious cause of this scatter is that irregular subsidence of the structure has taken place but there is also evidence that it can be due to distortion of the Earth's magnetic field by the magnetism of the structure itself (Weaver, 1962; Aitken and Hawley, 1971). In either case it is essential to take at least ten well-distributed samples from each structure and to determine the mean values for D and I. The resulting precision varies greatly from structure to structure. In general, the well-fired flat floors associated with mediaeval kilns give good results (standard error of the mean better than ± 1

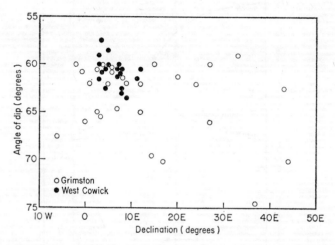

Figure 48. Scatter in the values of the declination (D) and the angle of dip (I) for groups of samples taken from mediaeval kilns at Grimston, Norfolk and West Cowick, Yorkshire. The West Cowick samples were taken from the kiln floor and exhibited closely grouped values for D and I (mean $D = 5\cdot7°$E, mean $I = 60\cdot6°$) while the Grimston samples were taken from the base of the kiln walls and exhibited widely scattered values for D and I (mean $D = 12\cdot6°$E, mean $I = 63\cdot8°$).

degree in I and ± 2 degrees in D), while for the circular walls of Romano-British kilns, the results are often poor (standard error of the mean worse than ± 3 degrees in I and ± 6 degrees in D).

Intensity measurements. For intensity measurements, somewhat smaller samples of fired clay, typically 2 cm cubes, are used. Again samples can be obtained from structures, such as pottery kilns, but since it is not necessary to know the orientation of the samples during firing, pottery fragments and bricks can also be used.

The most satisfactory technique for determining the ancient magnetic field intensity (H) is the double-heating method developed by Thellier and Thellier (1959) and subsequently used extensively by Bucha (1967). The samples are successively heated to each of a set of increasing temperatures (e.g. 100°C, 200°C, 300°C, etc.) and cooled in the present-day laboratory field which is of known intensity, H_0. By this means the thermoremanent magnetism associated with the ancient magnetic field is progressively replaced by that associated

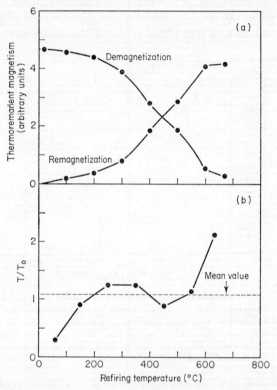

Figure 49. Typical results obtained using the double-heating method for determining the ancient magnetic field intensity. (a) The demagnetization curve for the fired clay sample represents the progressive removal during refiring of the thermoremanent magnetism (T) associated with the ancient magnetic field (H). Conversely, the remagnetization curve represents the progressive acquisition during refiring of the thermoremanent magnetism (T_0) associated with the present-day laboratory field (H_0). (b) The ratios of the ancient to the new thermoremanent magnetism (T/T_0) for each refiring temperature interval: the values for T/T_0 are plotted at the midpoint of the appropriate temperature interval. The ancient magnetic field intensity (H) can be calculated (equation (5.1)) using the mean value of the ratios for the refiring temperature intervals between 100 and 600°C (horizontal dashed line). The low ratio for the 20–100°C interval is due to interference from viscous remanent magnetism while the high value for the 600–670°C interval is probable due to mineralogical changes occurring during the refiring (after Bucha, 1967).

with the present-day laboratory field (Fig. 49a). Two separate heatings at each temperature are employed and after each, the resultant thermoremanent magnetism (T_1 and T_2) is measured. In the first heating, the ancient thermoremanent magnetism is effectively parallel to the present-day field while in the second it is effectively antiparallel. Therefore the magnitudes of the ancient and the new thermoremanent magnetism (i.e. T and T_0 respectively), corresponding to each temperature interval, can be evaluated from the sum and the difference of the measured resultant thermoremanent magnetisms respectively (i.e. $T_1 + T_2$ and $T_1 - T_2$). The ancient magnetic field intensity can then be calculated from the ratios of T and T_0 for each temperature interval (Fig. 49b) using equation (5.1).

A fundamental difficulty associated with this technique is the possibility that mineralogical changes occur during the laboratory reheating. Since the magnitude of the thermoremanent magnetism depends on the oxidation state of the iron oxide (e.g. haematite or magnetite), these changes would be reflected in variations in the ratio of the ancient to the new thermoremanent magnetism (T/T_0) for different temperature intervals and would render invalid the values calculated for the ancient field intensity. In particular, with grey to black coloured specimens, in which the iron oxide exists in the reduced state, magnetite (Fe_3O_4), oxidation to haematite (αFe_2O_3) can start at comparatively low temperatures (e.g. 200°C) during the laboratory refiring. Since haematite has a much lower saturation magnetization than magnetite, the ratio T/T_0 would become progressively larger as the oxidation proceeded during reheating at the higher temperatures. With red to brown coloured specimens, in which the iron oxides already exist in the oxidized state, these problems are less severe. However, mineralogical changes can still occur at high temperatures (e.g. above 500°C), thus rendering invalid the associated T/T_0 ratios.

In addition, the ratio T/T_0 for the 20–100°C temperature interval cannot normally be used because of interference from viscous remanent magnetism. Conversely, the ratios for the high temperature intervals may be invalid if the sample was not uniformly heated to above the Curie temperature (i.e. approximately 650°C) in antiquity. In this case low ratios will be observed above the original firing temperature since demagnetization (i.e. removal of the ancient thermoremanent magnetism) is complete but remagnetization (i.e. acquisition of the new thermoremanent magnetism) continues up to the Curie temperature.

In spite of these inherent difficulties, satisfactory data on the ancient magnetic field intensity can be obtained if samples exhibiting mineralogical instability during reheating are rigorously excluded. In general, the mean value for the ancient field intensity is accurate to between ±5 and ±15 per cent if several samples, which are red coloured (i.e. oxidized) and which have been homogeneously fired to above 600°C, are selected from the same archaeological context.

Magnetometers. The simplest instrument for measuring the thermo-remanent magnetism of fired clay is the astatic magnetometer (Fig. 50). This consists of two bar magnets of identical strength fixed rigidly

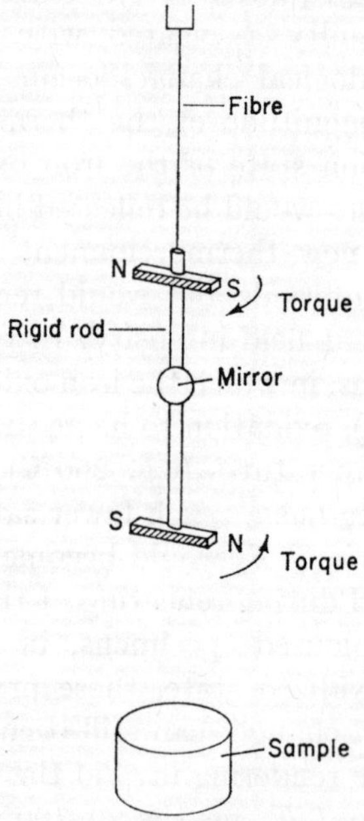

Figure 50. Astatic magnetometer. Two antiparallel magnets of equal strength are employed in order to eliminate the torque due to the Earth's magnetic field. However there is a resultant torque due to the magnetic sample since it is closer to the lower magnet. The resulting rotation of the pair of magnets is typically measured in terms of the deflection of a light beam reflected from the mirror.

at either end of a rod about 10 cm long and suspended by a fine fibre of phosphor bronze or quartz. The two magnets are mounted antiparallel so that the torques on each magnet due to the Earth's magnetic field are equal and opposite. However, when a magnetic sample is held close to the lower magnet, the torque on this magnet is greater than that on the upper magnet and therefore the system rotates. By measuring the rotation for various orientations of the sample, the direction and magnitude of the thermoremanent magnetism can be determined.

An alternative instrument is the "spinner" magnetometer (Aitken et al., 1967) in which the sample is rotated at 5 revolutions per second within a large coil system (Plate 12). By measuring the phase and magnitude of the small alternating voltage, which is induced in the coil by the rotating magnetic moment associated with the sample, the direction and magnitude of the thermoremanent magnetism can again be determined.

Although both magnetometers are sufficiently sensitive for the measurement of archaeological specimens, the more complex "spinner" magnetometer has the advantage of being more flexible. By varying the size of the coil system, it can be used to measure both the large and small samples normally employed for direction and intensity studies respectively. In contrast, the astatic magnetometer has the disadvantage that, except for the small samples employed in intensity studies, irregular shape and non-uniform magnetization can reduce the accuracy of the thermoremanent magnetism measurement. In addition, although both instruments are affected, the astatic magnetometer is more sensitive to external magnetic and vibratory disturbances.

Results

For England, the majority of the magnetic field direction measurements have been carried out by the Research Laboratory for Archaeology at Oxford and results from nearly one hundred archaeological structures, mainly pottery kilns, have been obtained (Aitken and Weaver, 1962; Aitken and Hawley, 1967). Reliable data for the pre-Roman period back to 2000 BC are still too sparse to provide a satisfactory secular variation curve, although the results are of interest in showing that the magnetic field directions were not dramatically different from those for the more recent past. For the Roman period (50–350 AD) and the late Saxon to Mediaeval period (1000–1540 AD), an adequate number of archaeologically dated kilns have become available and therefore the secular variation in magnetic direction (i.e. D and I) has been established with reasonable precision (Fig. 46).

Unfortunately, during the Roman period, the magnetic declination (D) remained essentially unchanged while the angle of dip (I) executed only a small oscillation. In view of this, together with the fact that the chronology of pottery types is already reasonably well established, the potential application of magnetic dating to the Roman period is somewhat limited. However, for the six centuries following 1000 AD, the changes in the magnetic direction are somewhat larger and in addition the chronology of pottery types is, perhaps surprisingly, less precise. There is consequently plenty of scope for the application of magnetic dating to this period (Hurst, 1966). Nevertheless, this application calls for close cooperation and mutual understanding between the scientist and the archaeologist since the absence of closely dated structures makes the provision of the basic secular variation curve rather more difficult than during the Roman period. In addition, the fact that the magnetic directions are essentially the same during the twelfth and the fourteenth/fifteenth centuries can lead to ambiguities in age determination. Subsequent to 1540 AD, when a directly recorded secular variation curve is available, magnetic dating is at its prime and a structure exhibiting only a small scatter in magnetic directions can be dated to within a span of 25 years.

Data on the secular variation in both D and I has also been obtained, using fired archaeological structures, for various other parts of the world, notably France (Thellier, 1966) and Japan (Kawai et al., 1965). In addition, the secular variation in the angle of dip, I, has been determined from measurements on bricks (Burlatskaya et al., 1970) and pottery (Aitken, 1958), rather than on structures found in situ. In the case of bricks, a regular way of stacking during firing can normally be assumed while for pottery, the method is only applicable when heavy glazing suggests that it must have been fired standing on its base on a horizontal surface.

Thermoremanent magnetism measurements on fired clay from archaeological sites have provided data on the secular variation in the Earth's magnetic field intensity for Europe back to 7000 BC (Bucha, 1967), for Central America back to 2000 BC (Bucha et al., 1970) and for Japan back to 3000 BC (Nagata et al., 1963; Sasajima, 1965). For Europe (Fig. 51a), it is evident that the Earth's magnetic field intensity attained a maximum value of approximately twice the present-day value at around 400 BC and a minimum occurred around 5000 BC when the intensity decreased to less than half the present-day value. Similar variations in the ancient magnetic intensity are also observed for central America (Fig. 51b) and Japan (Fig. 51c), the major difference being that the maxima and minima are displaced along the time axis. Since these three geographical regions are equally spaced, in terms of longitude, around the world (i.e. Europe 15°E, Japan 135°E,

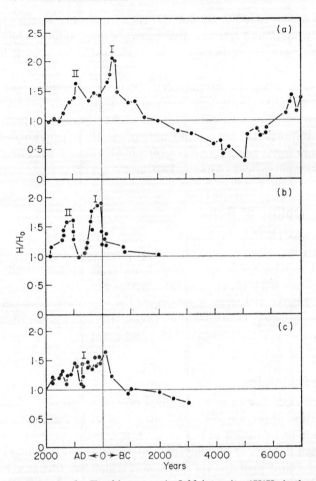

Figure 51. Variation in the Earth's magnetic field intensity (H/H_0 is the ratio of the ancient field intensity to the present-day intensity) for (a) Europe (i.e. Czechoslovakia, Hungary, Poland and Turkey), (b) central America (i.e. Mexico and Arizona) and (c) Japan. The time displacement of the intensity maxima, I and II, for the three regions can be explained in terms of a westward drift of the non-dipole component of the Earth's magnetic field (after Bucha, 1970).

central America 105°W), the time displacement can be explained in terms of a westward drift of the non-dipole component of the Earth's magnetic field.

These data for the secular variation in intensity are at present insufficiently precise to provide a basis for age determination. However, Bucha (1970) has combined the data from the three regions and obtained an averaged curve for the variation in the Earth's magnetic moment which has been valuable in explaining some of the observed differences between radiocarbon and true calendar ages (Chapter 4, p. 86).

Finally, it must be emphasized that the detailed data for the secular variation in both direction and intensity, obtained for the past few millennia from measurements on archaeological material, are of obvious importance to geophysics since they provide additional information for developing and confirming theories for the origin of the Earth's magnetic field (Aitken, 1970).

Dating of Bone

The progressive time-dependent chemical alteration of bone, subsequent to its burial in the ground, provides a valuable method for establishing whether a particular bone (e.g. human skull) is contemporaneous with other skeletal remains found in the same deposit (Oakley, 1969). Although, in contrast to radiocarbon dating, these techniques do *not* provide absolute dates, they are applicable to bones of far greater age than those that can be dated by the radiocarbon method.

General Principles

The chemical dating of bone depends on the progressive depletion or accumulation of certain elements, either native or foreign to the bone, subsequent to its burial in the ground.

The organic content of bone is mainly fats which disappear rapidly after burial and proteins (i.e. collagen) which are lost at a relatively slow, uniformly declining rate. The most useful index for the amount of protein present in a bone is its nitrogen content which for modern fresh bone is approximately 4 per cent. The rate at which the nitrogen content of bone declines depends on the temperature, as well as the water, chemical and bacteriological content of the environment in which it is buried. Typically the nitrogen content is less than 0·1 per cent after about 10 000 years but under frozen conditions or when air and bacteria are excluded (e.g. burial in clay), the protein may persist indefinitely.

The inorganic content of bone is a phosphatic mineral, hydroxy-apatite, which is made up of calcium, phosphate and hydroxyl ions. This phosphatic mineral is altered during burial through the progressive substitution of fluorine and uranium ions, which are in solution in the percolating ground-water, for the hydroxyl and calcium ions respectively. Therefore the fluorine and uranium content of the bone increases with time, the rate of accumulation being determined principally by the concentration of fluorine and uranium in the ground water. However, the hydrological conditions and the nature of the burial medium are also important. For example, the rate of accumulation is more rapid in sands and gravels than in limestones where the percolation of fluorine and uranium ions is inhibited.

Hence the depletion of nitrogen and the accumulation of fluorine and uranium provide criteria for estimating the relative ages of a series of bones which have experienced the same environmental conditions. Whenever possible the concentrations of all three elements should be determined and comparison should be made between bones of similar type and texture (e.g. compact bone or spongy bone) since these factors also affect the rate of depletion or accumulation.

Experimental Procedures

The nitrogen and fluorine contents of the bone are normally determined by chemical analysis, typically between 25 and 100 mg of bone being required for each determination. Alternatively for the fluorine determination, X-ray powder diffraction techniques (Chapter 9, p. 286) can be employed. The replacement of the hydroxyl ion by a fluorine ion changes the dimensions of the unit crystal cell which, in turn, causes a shift in the position of specific lines in the X-ray diffraction pattern, the extent of this shift being related to the concentration of the fluorine in the bone. Although less precise than chemical analysis, this method has the advantage of only requiring a few milligrams of bone.

The uranium content of the bone can be estimated by measuring its radioactivity: the beta particles emitted as a result of the decay of the uranium series are counted with a Geiger counter. This measurement has the advantage over the nitrogen and fluorine determinations in that it is essentially non-destructive, the beta emission from the surface of the bone being measured directly.

Results

An early application of these techniques for the relative dating of bone involved the study of the Galley Hill skeleton and the Swanscombe skull (Oakley and Montagu, 1949). The Galley Hill skeleton, which is of the modern *Homo sapiens* type, was found in river terrace gravels near Swanscombe, which also contained hand-axes and fossil animal bones, dating from before the time of Neanderthal man. The Swanscombe skull was found in the same gravels at a much greater depth. The results of the fluorine and nitrogen determinations (Table 10) confirmed the antiquity of the Swanscombe skull since it contained high fluorine and negligible nitrogen contents, similar to those for the fossil

Table 10. Fluorine, nitrogen and uranium contents of bones from Europe and North Africa (after Oakley, 1969)

Description of bone	Fluorine (per cent)	Nitrogen (per cent)	Uranium (ppm)
Modern fresh bone	0·03	4·0	0
Swanscombe skull	1·7	trace	27
Fossil animal bones from			
Swanscombe gravels	1·5	trace	—
Galley Hill skeleton	0·5	1·6	—
Piltdown jawbone	< 0·03	3·9	0
Piltdown skull	0·1	1·4	1
Piltdown hippopotamus molar	< 0·1	< 0·1	3
Malta hippopotamus molar	0·1	< 0·1	7
Piltdown elephant molar	2·7	nil	610
Ichkeul elephant molar	2·7	trace	580

animal bones. In contrast, the lower fluorine and higher nitrogen contents of the Galley Hill skeleton indicated that this was an intrusive burial considerably later than the gravels in which it lay. These results did not of course provide absolute dates for the bones, although subsequent radiocarbon dating of the Galley Hill skeleton provided a date of 3310 ± 150 BP (5568 year half-life).

A more widely publicized application of these techniques was their use in establishing that the "Piltdown Man" was a fake (Oakley and Weiner, 1955; Weiner *et al.*, 1955). In 1912, a jawbone and a fragment of a human braincase, together with several fossil mammalian specimens, were found in a gravel pit near to the village of Piltdown in Sussex. The jawbone and fragment of braincase were originally thought to belong to the same human skull, subsequently referred to as the "Piltdown Man". However, in comparison with human fossil remains of Pleistocene date from Java and China, the braincase appeared to be more human and the jawbone more ape-like and therefore several experts did not believe that they were part of the same skull. These suspicions were dramatically confirmed by fluorine and nitrogen analyses together with subsequent uranium determinations (Table 10).

The jawbone contained negligible fluorine and uranium but had a high nitrogen content, thus establishing conclusively that it was modern bone, which had been artificially stained in order that it appear ancient. The braincase fragment contained higher fluorine and lower nitrogen contents than the jawbone, indicating that it was of some antiquity although not from the late Pleistocene, as had originally been suggested. The negligible nitrogen content of the Piltdown hippopotamus molar indicates that it was of considerable antiquity. In this specimen, the low fluorine content suggests that it originated from a limestone deposit since limestone inhibits the passage of fluorine ions whereas the depletion of protein (i.e. nitrogen) continues at a normal rate: a Mediterranean origin, such as Malta, is therefore suggested. The very high fluorine content and negligible nitrogen content of the Piltdown elephant molar is consistent with its undoubted Early Pleistocene origin. However, its uranium content is very much higher than that of any equivalent fossil animal bone found in Britain: the only comparable uranium content is that found for an elephant molar of similar age from Ichkeul in Tunisia. Hence these analyses conclusively established that the Piltdown group of fossil bones were of diffuse geographical and temporal origin and were fraudulently introduced into a Sussex gravel pit.

Although the fluorine analyses of bone have been used primarily for determining relative dates, Richter (1958) has attempted to establish a calibration curve for fluorine content versus age for western Germany and thus use the method to provide absolute dates. The X-ray diffraction technique was used to determine the fluorine content of the bone, that is the extent to which fluorine ions have replaced hydroxyl ions in the apatite mineral. Absolute ages were obtained by the radiocarbon method for the period from 50 000 BP to the present day and by the uranium–lead method (see Table 6) for the period prior to about 10 million years ago. A calibration curve for the intervening period was then achieved by extrapolation and absolute dates for fossil bones from the Pleistocene period were obtained. From the geological context in which the bones were found, it was further possible to suggest tentative absolute dates for various interglacial phases within the Pleistocene period (Fig. 52).

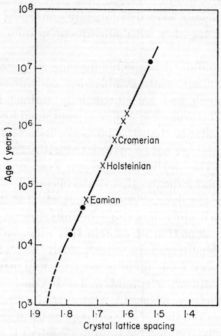

Figure 52. Fluorine dating results for bones from western Germany (after Richter, 1958). The fluorine concentrations were measured in terms of the crystal lattice spacing of the apatite minerals using X-ray diffraction techniques: the crystal lattice spacing, which is presented in units of the angular separation of specific lines on the X-ray film, decreases with increasing fluorine concentration. The solid dots represent calibration points obtained from bones whose age was independently determined by either the radiocarbon method (less than 50 000 years) or the uranium–lead method (greater 10 million years). On the basis of the resulting calibration curve, the ages of bones (indicated by the crosses) associated the Eamian, Holsteinian and Cromerian interglacials (see Table 13) could be estimated from their fluorine contents (i.e. their crystal lattice spacings).

Obsidian Dating

The method of dating obsidian artefacts by measurement of the thickness of the hydration layer found on surface has been developed over the past decade (Friedman and Smith, 1960). In spite of the necessity for calibration using obsidian artefacts of known age, the method shows considerable promise, satisfactory results being obtained for specimens ranging in age from 30 000 BC to 1500 AD.

General Principles

Water is absorbed at the surface of obsidian and diffuses into the material to form a hydration layer which contains approximately 3 per cent water and which is visible under a microscope. Therefore for an archaeological artefact, hydration begins as soon as the surface is exposed by chipping or flaking in the manufacture of the artefact. Subsequently, hydration continues at an essentially constant rate and the present-day thickness of the hydration layer provides a measure of the time that has elapsed since manufacture.

The rate of penetration of the water is determined by the standard diffusion equations, so that the thickness of the hydration layer (D) after the surface has been exposed for a time t is given by:

$$D^2 = kt \qquad (5.2)$$

where the constant, k, depends on the temperature of the environment during hydration and the chemical composition of the obsidian. The relative humidity of the environment does not affect the hydration rate since, in any natural environment, there is sufficient water to maintain a saturated film at the surface of the obsidian and it is the slow diffusion of this water into the body of the material which is the time-dependent process.

As with all diffusion processes, the rate of hydration increases with increasing temperature. From measurements on obsidian artefacts whose age is known from, for example, the radiocarbon dating of associated organic material, calibration curves for the increase in the thickness of the hydration layer with time can be obtained for the different climatic zones (Fig. 53). Typically the rate of hydration (i.e. the constant k) for obsidian buried in equatorial regions (30°C) is more than ten times the rate for obsidian buried in Arctic regions (1°C). From these calibration data, together with the results obtained from hydration experiments at 100°C in the laboratory (Friedman et al., 1966), the temperature dependence of the constant k in the hydration equation (equation (5.2)) has now been established.

The influence of chemical composition on the hydration rate in obsidian is more difficult to quantify. Obviously gross differences in composition, such as exist between rhyolitic and trachytic obsidian, cause a major change in the hydration rate, the constants (k) for the two types of obsidian from Egypt differing by a factor of almost 2. However, the effect of minor differences in composition, such as can exist between obsidian outcrops within a specific geographical region, is not as yet fully understood. For example, the different hydration layer thicknesses observed for green and grey obsidian artefacts could, in some instances, be due to the difference in chemical composition and in other instances to a genuine difference in age.

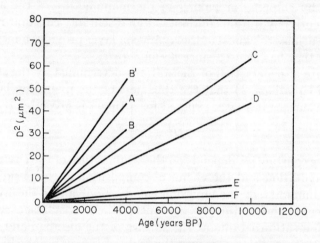

Figure 53. Variation in the thickness of the hydration layer (D) for obsidian artefacts of known age under different climatic conditions. Group B′ artefacts were made from trachytic obsidian while groups A–F were made from rhyolitic obsidian (after Friedman *et al.*, 1966).

	Effective environmental temperature (°C)	Hydration rate constant, k ($\mu m^2/10^3$ years)
A Coastal Ecuador	30	11
B Egypt	28	8·1
B′ Egypt	28	14
C Temperate No. 1	25	6·5
D Temperate No. 2	20	4·5
E Sub-Arctic	5	0·9
F Arctic	1	0·4

Therefore, from measurement of the hydration layer thickness, the age of an obsidian artefact can be determined using equation (5.2), provided that the environmental temperature subsequent to manufacture is known and that a calibration curve for obsidian of similar composition is available.

Experimental Procedures

In order to measure the thickness of the hydration layer, a thin slice is cut from the obsidian artefact perpendicular to the surface to be examined. The slice is mounted on a glass slide, ground down to a thickness of about 0·05 mm and then examined under an optical microscope at a magnification of approximately × 500. Because hydrated obsidian has a higher refractive index than does the non-hydrated obsidian, the division between the two regions is seen under the microscope as a relatively sharp line (Plate 13). In addition, the mechanical strain associated with the absorption of water causes the hydrated layer to appear as a bright band (i.e. strain birefringence) when viewed between crossed polarizers (p. 219). Measurement of the thickness of the hydration layer, which can vary from less than 1 μm to as much as 20 μm, is achieved using a filar micrometer eyepiece. This type of eyepiece contains a movable scale or hair line, the movement of which can be read on a drum attached to the side of the eyepiece. Typically the time taken for the preparation and measurement is about half an hour per obsidian sample and the measurement of the thickness of the hydration layer is accurate to within ± 0·2 μm.

In selecting obsidian artefacts for age determination studies, it is obviously essential to avoid those artefacts whose hydration layer has been altered by either physical or chemical processes. For example, an artefact which has been exposed to running water or wind-blown sand for any length of time may have lost part or all of its hydration layer through abrasion. Similarly, certain chemical environments, such as those in the vicinity of hot springs, can effectively dissolve away part of the hydration layer. In addition, since the mechanical strain increases as the hydration layer becomes thicker, it is possible that, with very old artefacts, an initial hydration layer has fallen off in places and hydration has begun again on the new surface thus created. Although artefacts suffering from the above faults can normally be rejected on the basis of careful microscopic examination, it is advisable whenever possible to make measurements on at least six artefacts from the archaeological context under consideration.

Since the hydration rate for obsidian depends on the environmental temperature, the soil temperature at the depth at which the artefact was buried should be determined. However, this information does not necessarily provide an accurate estimate for the effective environmental temperature during burial since it is possible either that a significant period elapsed between manufacture and burial or that climatic changes have occurred during the burial period.

Results

The majority of the effort, so far devoted to obsidian hydration dating, has been concerned with establishing the validity of the technique and with determining the hydration rates (i.e. the constant, k) for different environmental temperatures and types of obsidian. In addition to the data for artefacts from America and the Near East (Friedman and Smith, 1960) which is shown in Fig. 53, Katsui and Kondo (1965) have determined the hydration rates for northern Japan over the past 15 000 years. Obsidian artefacts from six archaeological sites, which were dated by the radiocarbon method, were studied and from the results (Fig. 54), it was apparent that a change in the hydration rate

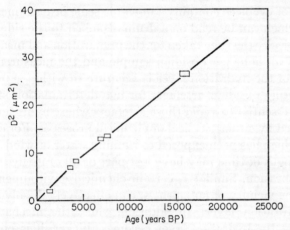

Figure 54. Variation in the thickness of the hydration layer (D) for obsidian artefacts from Japan whose age is known from radiocarbon dating. It can be seen that prior to 4000 BP the hydration rate constant (k) was $1 \cdot 6 \ \mu m^2/10^3$ years compared to the present-day value of $2 \cdot 0 \ \mu m^2/10^3$ years. This lower value is probably due to the colder climate prior to 4000 BP (after Katsui and Kondo, 1965).

occurred about 4000 years ago. The 25 per cent higher hydration rate for the past 4000 years is probably related to the warmer climate during this period as compared to the Late Pleistocene climate in Japan.

Although, on the basis of currently available hydration rate data, the technique could be used to provide absolute dates for obsidian artefacts from different parts of the world, its most important archaeological application is probably to the study of artefacts from a particular site or region (Michels, 1967). In these circumstances, the hydration rate is the same for all the artefacts and the cheapness of the technique, in comparison with radiocarbon dating, means that a large number of obsidian artefacts can be studied. Typically for the cost of one commercially processed radiocarbon date, the archaeologist can obtain 80 obsidian dates. These relative dating applications include (1) the study of the typological development of artefacts with time, (2) the testing of the stratigraphy deduced for a site, (3) the separation of artefacts from a poorly stratified site into chronological groups and (4) the identification of the horizontal stratigraphy across large areas on a site with shallow deposits. A significant factor in interpreting the relative dating results is the extensive re-use of old obsidian artefacts during later periods. On well-stratified sites, the re-used artefacts can be distinguished from the indigenous group for a particular stratum because of the greater thickness of their hydration layer. Alternatively, when the obsidian was reworked during the later period, it is often possible to distinguish two hydration layers of different thickness on the same artefact. In either case, the percentages of re-used artefacts in the total artefactual assemblage for a particular period can be of cultural significance.

The results obtained by Evans and Meggers (1960) for obsidian artefacts from the Chorrera site on the coast of Ecuador provide an illustration of the relative dating application of obsidian hydration measurements, together with the type of problems encountered. The site consists of habitat refuse deposits to a depth of approximately 4 m which, on the basis of the change in pottery types, were subdivided into three periods (Milagro, Tejar and Chorrera). About 60 obsidian artefacts from the deposits were studied and on the basis of the thicknesses of the hydration layers, the artefacts were divided into four main groups as shown in Fig. 55. The first group (hydration layer less than 2 µm) was classified as "modern" and is probably associated with cultivation of the site subsequent to the Milagro period. The second and third groups (hydration layers from 2·9 to 3·9 µm and from 3·9 to 4·9 µm respectively) are both found throughout the deposits associated with the Milagro and Tejar periods. The fourth group (hydration layers greater than 5 µm) was found throughout the entire deposits but represents the *only* group occurring in the lower deposits associated with the Chorrera period. It is therefore reasonable to assume that this fourth group represents artefacts which were made during the

Chorrera period and which can be used to provide absolute dates for this period, provided the hydration rate constant (k) for this temperature environment is known. The appearance of this group throughout the subsequent periods can be interpreted in terms of the re-use of old obsidian artefacts. Unfortunately, there is no equivalent clear demarcation between the artefacts made during the Milagro and Tejar periods. However, it is suggested that the third group of artefacts (hydration layers from 3·9 to 4·9 μm) were made during the Tejar period and that their appearance in the Milagro deposits again represents the re-use of old artefacts. Similarly, the second group of artefacts (hydration layers from 2·9 to 3·9 μm) could have been made during the Milagro period and their appearance in the earlier Tejar deposits could be due to mechanical mixing, either during the occupation of the site or as a result of subsequent burrowing by small animals. Tentative absolute dates for the individual artefacts, and therefore for the three periods defined by the pottery sequence, can also be obtained since for this temperature zone there is sufficient data from known-age specimens to provide a value for the hydration rate constant: these absolute dates are also included in Fig. 55.

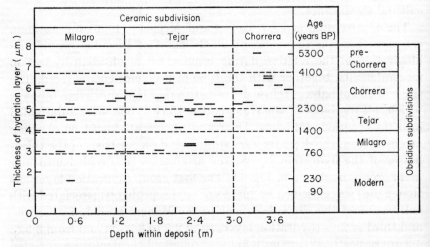

Figure 55. Thickness of the hydration layers of obsidian artefacts from various depths within the refuse deposits at the Chorrera site on the coast of Ecuador. The cultural divisions derived from the pottery classification together with the depth at which they subdivide are shown at the top. The subdivisions suggested by the differences in the thickness of the hydration layers of the obsidian artefacts are shown on the right together with tentative absolute dates calculated from equation (5.2), using the hydration rate constant (k) of 11 μm²/10³ years for group A in Fig. 53 (after Evans and Meggers, 1960).

Glass Layer Counting

The possibility of dating ancient man-made glass by counting the number of layers present in the surface crust (Plate 14) was first suggested by Brill and Hood (1961) who obtained excellent results for the specimens which they investigated. However, subsequent studies, summarized by Newton (1971), suggest either that the method is invalid, any agreement between the number of layers and the age of the glass being fortuitous, or even with the most optimistic interpretation, that it has only very limited application.

General Principles

Glass having soda–lime–silica or potash–lime–silica compositions is subject to a slow chemical deterioration in the presence of water. The chemical attack involves the selective leaching of the more soluble components, principally the alkali metal oxides (i.e. soda—Na_2O and potash—K_2O), to leave a hydrated residue with a high silica content. For ancient glass, this weathering occurs during burial and appears typically in the form of a surface crust of hydrated material. Brewster (1863) first examined the crust under an optical microscope and noted that, in cross-section, it could often be resolved into a fine laminar structure. The individual layers in the crust range in thickness from 0·3 to about 20 μm and are responsible, through optical interference phenomena, for the colourful iridescence exhibited by some ancient glass.

A possible explanation for the layered structure of the surface crust on ancient glass is that it reflects some periodic or cyclic changes in the environment during burial. If annual seasonal variations in temperature or rainfall were responsible, then the number of individual layers would depend only on the number of annual seasonal cycles experienced, even though the total extent of weathering must, in addition have a complicated dependence on the composition of the glass and the burial conditions (e.g. mean temperature, acidity of the soil). If this were true, ancient glass might be directly dated by counting the number of layers in the weathered crust, the method being analogous to the counting of tree-rings in dendrochronology. The technique would, of course, produce the date at which burial occurred and the weathering process began, rather than the date of manufacture of the glass.

Results

In order to test the hypothesis cf "annual growth" of layers in weathered glass, Brill and Hood (1961) carried out measurements on glass objects which had been either buried in soil or submerged under water for known periods of time ranging from 150 to 1600 years. In order to count the number of layers, the samples were mounted in plastic, polished and observed in cross-section under an optical microscope at a magnification of about × 350 (Plate 15 upper). The results, presented in Table eleven, indicated that for the Colonial glass, the agreement between the dates estimated by counting the layers and those known from the archaeological evidence was excellent. In addition, the results obtained for the much older samples from Nishapur and Sardis were reasonable in view of the far less precise archaeological dating evidence. These results therefore seemed to provide support for the hypothesis of "annual growth" and indicated the possible value of this method of dating ancient glass.

Obviously, in order to apply the technique, it would be essential that the chemical composition of the glass and the environmental conditions are such that a sufficiently thick weathered crust with laminar structure is formed. Furthermore, the crust must be sufficiently robust for it to be preserved intact. These conditions alone would immediately limit the application of the technique to only a small fraction of the ancient glass that has been excavated (Brill, 1969). Thus the most suitable glass for age determination appears to be that dating from the early eighteenth century back through the Mediaeval period. Roman and Byzantine glass is in general too resistant to chemical attack to form a weathered crust while, because of the arid environment, Egyptian glass also does not suffer from weathering. In contrast, Mesopotamian glass is often so heavily weathered that the fragments are too fragile to handle without destroying some of the layers.

Application of the dating technique to this somewhat limited range of ancient glass would still be of value to the archaeologist were it not for the fact that recent research (Newton, 1971) has thrown considerable doubt on the original hypothesis of the "annual growth" of weathered layers. This uncertainty arises because, for some glass fragments, the weathering does not proceed uniformly over the entire surface but occurs sporadically from randomly located centres to form cone-shaped intrusions or "plugs" into the body of the glass. These "plugs" have a laminar structure but do not all contain the same

Table 11. Results for layer counting on ancient glass (after Brill and Hood, 1961)

Sample	Description of glass	Date based on archaeological evidence	Excavation date	Layers counted	Date calculated for onset of weathering
J-5	English wine bottle York River, Virginia	Submerged 1781	1935	150-156-170	1765-1779-1785
J-4	Window glass Jamestown, Virginia	Buried 1639-1670	1935	256-266-273	1662-1669-1679
J-6	English wine bottle Jamestown, Virginia	Buried c. 1660-1675	1935	261-271-286	1649-1664-1674
J-2	Dutch gin bottle Jamestown, Virginia	Submerged c. 1600-1640	1956	295-310-320	1636-1646-1661
P1-1	Medicine bottle Kingston, Massachusetts	Buried 1676 or later	1959	259-269-289	1670-1690-1700
PR-5	Wine bottle Port Royal, Jamaica	Submerged 1692	1959	258-268-274	1685-1691-1701
SA-2	Bottle Shipwreck off Bermuda	Submerged 1621	1959	319-334-349	1610-1625-1640
N-4	Islamic glass Nishapur, Iran	Manufactured 8th-10th century AD	c. 1950	930 ± 30	1020 ± 30 AD
N-9	Islamic Glass Nishapur, Iran	Manufactured 9th-13th century AD	c. 1950	775 ± 20	1175 ± 20 AD
N-11	Islamic Glass Nishapur, Iran	Manufactured 9th-13th century AD	c. 1950	810 ± 25	1140 ± 25 AD
S-1b	Lump of glass Sardis, Turkey	Buried late 3rd-early 7th century AD	1960	1582 ± 10	378 ± 10 AD

number of layers (Plate 15, lower). For example, Newton (1966) examined in detail two pieces of window glass from England which had been buried for 288 years and found that, over the majority of the surface, the number of layers was considerably less than 288. The largest number of layers observed was 285 and this was associated with only *one* of the many "plugs" growing into the body of the glass. This type of result, together with the fact that layered crusts can also be produced in accelerated weathering experiments under unvarying conditions (i.e. constant temperature and humidity) in an autoclave, suggests that the formation of layers is not necessarily related to annual seasonal variations in the environment.

Newton (1971) therefore suggests that layers are produced at a fairly constant rate which is generally rather less than one per year. The mechanism that gives rise to the layers is not fully understood but it seems possible that they result from internal strains set up by chemical change in which there is an associated expansion or contraction. Consequently until the mechanism for layer formation has been elucidated, the age determination results obtained for glass by layer-counting should be treated with caution.

References

Magnetic Dating

Aitken, M. J. (1958). Magnetic dating. *Archaeometry* 1, 16–20.

Aitken, M. J. (1970). Physics applied to archaeology—I. Dating. *Rep. Prog. Phys.* 33, 941–1000.

Aitken, M. J. and Hawley, H. N. (1967). Archaeomagnetic measurements in Britain, IV. *Archaeometry* 10, 129–135.

Aitken, M. J. and Hawley, H. N. (1971). Archaeomagnetism: evidence for magnetic refraction in kiln structures. *Archaeometry* 13, 83–85.

Aitken, M. J. and Weaver, G. H. (1962). Magnetic dating: some archaeomagnetic measurements in Britain. *Archaeometry* 5, 4–22.

Aitken, M. J., Harold, M. R., Weaver, G. H. and Young, S. A. (1967). A "big-sample" spinner magnetometer. *In* "Methods in Palaeomagnetism", (Eds. D. W. Collinson, K. M. Creer and S. K. Runcorn), pp. 301–305. Elsevier, Amsterdam.

Bauer, L. A. (1899). On the secular variation of a free magnetic needle. *Phys. Rev.* 3, 34–38.

Bucha, V. (1967). Intensity of the earth's magnetic field during archaeological times in Czechoslovakia. *Archaeometry* 10, 12–22.

Bucha, V. (1970). Influence of the earth's magnetic field on radiocarbon dating. *In* "Radiocarbon Variations and Absolute Chronology", (Ed. I. U. Olsson), pp. 501–512. Almqvist and Wiksell, Stockholm.

Bucha, V., Taylor, R. E., Berger, R. and Haury, E. W. (1970). Geomagnetic intensity: changes during the past 3000 years in the Western Hemisphere. *Science* **168**, 111–114.

Burlatskaya, S. P., Nachasova, I. E., Nechaeva, T. B., Rusakov, O. M., Zagniv, G. F., Tarhov, E. N. and Tchelidze, Z. A. (1970). Archaeomagnetic research in the U.S.S.R.: recent results and spectral analysis. *Archaeometry* **12**, 78–88.

Cox, A. (1969). Geomagnetic reversals. *Science* **163**, 237–245.

Dunlop, D. J. and West, S. (1969). An experimental evaluation of single domain theories. *Rev. Geophys.* **7**, 709–755.

Folgheraiter, G. (1899). Sur les variations séculaire de l'inclinaison magnétique dans antiquité. *Archs Sci. phys. nat.* **8**, 5–16.

Harrison, C. G. A. (1966). The paleomagnetism of deep sea sediments. *J. Geophys. Res.* **71**, 3033–3043.

Hurst, J. G. (1966). Post-Roman archaeological dating and its correlation with archaeomagnetic results. *Archaeometry* **9**, 198–199.

Kawai, N., Hirooka, K., Sasajima, S., Yashawa, K., Ito, H. and Kume, S. (1965). Archaeomagnetic studies in southwestern Japan. *Ann. Géophys.* **21**, 574–578.

Nagata, T., Arai, Y. and Momose, K. (1963). Secular variation of the geomagnetic total force during the last 5000 years. *J. Geophys. Res.* **68**, 5277–5281.

Néel, L. (1955). Some theoretical aspects of rock magnetism. *Adv. Phys.* **4**, 191–243.

Sasajima, S. (1965). Geomagnetic secular variation revealed in the baked earths in West Japan. *J. Geomagn. Geoelect., Kyoto* **17**, 413–416.

Stacey, F. D. (1963). The physical theory of rock magnetism. *Adv. Phys.* **12**, 45–133.

Stacey, F. D. (1969). "Physics of the Earth", pp. 125–191. Wiley, New York.

Thellier, E. (1938). Sur l'aimantation des terres cuites et ses applications géophysiques. *Annls Inst. Phys. Globe* **16**, 157–302.

Thellier, E. (1966). Le champ magnétique terrestre fossile. *Nucleus* **7**, 1–35.

Thellier, E. and Thellier, O. (1959). Sur l'intensité du champ magnétique terrestre dans le passé historique et géologique. *Ann. Géophys.* **15**, 285–376.

Weaver, G. H. (1962). Archaeomagnetic measurements on the second Boston experimental kiln. *Archaeometry* **5**, 93–107.

Bone, Obsidian and Glass Dating

Brewster, D. (1863). On the structure and optical phenomena of ancient decomposed glass. *Trans. R. Soc. Edin.* **23**, 193–204.

Brill, R. H. (1969). The scientific investigation of ancient glasses. *Proc. 8th Int. Cong. Glass.* pp. 47–68.

Brill, R. H. and Hood, H. P. (1961). A new method for dating ancient glass. *Nature* **189**, 12–14.

Evans, C. and Meggers, B. J. (1960). A new dating method using obsidian: Part II, An archaeological evaluation of the method. *Am. Antiq.* **25**, 523–537.

Friedman, I. I. and Smith, R. L. (1960). A new dating method using obsidian: Part I, The development of the method. *Am. Antiq.* **25**, 476–522.

Friedman, I. I., Smith, R. L. and Long, W. D. (1966). Hydration of natural glass and formation of perlite. *Geol. Soc. Am. Bull.* **77**, 323–328.

Katsui, Y. and Kondo, Y. (1965). Dating of stone implements by using hydration layer of obsidian. *Jap. J. Geol. Geogr.* **36**, 45–60.

Michels, J. W. (1967). Archaeology and dating by hydration of obsidian. *Science* 158, 211–214.

Newton, R. G. (1966). Some problems in the dating of ancient glass by counting the layers in the weathering crust. *Glass Technol.* 7, 22–25.

Newton, R. G. (1971). The enigma of the layered crusts on some weathered glasses, a chronological account of the investigations. *Archaeometry* 13, 1–9.

Oakley, K. P. (1969). Analytical methods of dating bones. *In* "Science in Archaeology", (Eds. D. Brothwell and E. Higgs), pp. 35–45. Thames and Hudson, London.

Oakley, K. P. and Montagu, M. F. A. (1949). A re-consideration of the Galley Hill skeleton. *Bull. Br. Mus. (Nat. Hist.)* 1, 25–48.

Oakley, K. P. and Weiner, J. S. (1955). Piltdown Man. *Am. Scient.* 43, 573–583.

Richter, K. (1958). Fluorteste quartarer Knochen in ihrer Bedeutung fur die absolute Chronologie des Pleistozans. *Eiszeitalter Gegenw.* 9, 18–27.

Weiner, J. S., Le Gros Clark, W. E., Oakley, K. P., Claringbull, G. F., Hey, M. H., Edmunds, F. H., Bowie, S. H. U., Davidson, C. F., Fryd, C. F. M., Baynes-Cope, A. D., Werner, A. E. A. and Plesters, R. J. (1955). Further contributions to the solution of the Piltdown problem. *Bull. Br. Mus. (Nat. Hist.)* 2, 225–288.

6

Age Determination— Archaeological Results

In the north temperate zone, the geological division between the Pliocene and Pleistocene periods was marked by a pronounced climatic deterioration during which the warm-preferring flora and fauna of the Pliocene period were partially replaced by cold-tolerant genera and species which included the mammalian fauna referred to as Villafranchian. The subsequent Pleistocene era witnessed a succession of climatic fluctuations, that is the glacial and interglacial phases. Although in a broad sense the Pleistocene period continues down to the present day, it is convenient to designate the time since the last major climatic fluctuation (i.e. the last glacial phase) by a distinct term: the Postglacial or Neothermal phase (i.e. in geological terminology, the Holocene or Recent period).

Over the tropical and subtropical zones the boundary between the Pliocene and Pleistocene periods is less well defined, the Villafranchian fauna, for example, possibly spanning both periods. However, during the Pleistocene period, significant climatic changes did occur in the form of pronounced and prolonged periods of heavier rainfall, referred to as the pluvial phases, which were interrupted by interpluvial phases with lower rainfall. The extent to which these pluvial and interpluvial phases were synchronous throughout, for example, Africa, as well as their correlation with the glacials and interglacials of northern Europe, is not, however, fully understood. Similarly, less information is available on the climatic changes in the tropical and subtropical zones during the period coinciding with the Postglacial or Neothermal phase in the north temperate zone.

In terms of the archaeological nomenclature, the Lower and Upper Palaeolithic cultures occupy the Pleistocene period while the Mesolithic, Neolithic, Bronze Age and Iron Age cultures occupy the subsequent Postglacial or Neothermal phase extending up to the present day.

The *radiocarbon dates*, which are extensively quoted in this chapter, have all been calculated using the 5568 year half-life and are uncorrected for fluctuations in the atmospheric ^{14}C concentration: years BP and years BC are employed for the Pleistocene and Postglacial periods respectively. The *true calendar dates* refer to the dates which have been obtained by correcting the radiocarbon dates for fluctuations in the atmospheric ^{14}C concentration, using the tree-ring data (Fig. 30). In making this correction only the gradual long-term deviation between the radiocarbon and true calendar ages has been considered and the short-term fluctuations have been ignored since their validity remains somewhat uncertain. The errors associated with these tentative true calendar dates are therefore somewhat greater than those associated with the radiocarbon dates. The *historical dates* refer to the dates which have been inferred from the historical calendars available for Egypt and Mesopotamia back to about 3000 BC.

Pleistocene

For the majority of the Pleistocene period, potassium–argon dating of volcanic deposits provides the primary means of establishing an absolute world-wide chronology, radiocarbon dating being applicable only during the late Pleistocene from about 50 000 BP onwards. The potassium–argon results are supplemented by fission track dating on volcanic deposits and the data obtained from the study of deep-sea sediments. In addition, as a result of recent developments, it should be possible, in the future, to use thermoluminescent dating for the absolute age determination of stone artefacts (e.g. flint) which have been heated in antiquity. Similarly, radioactive dating, based on the uranium decay series, might be further developed to provide reliable absolute ages for bone.

The boundary between the Pliocene and Pleistocene was formalized by a committee of the 18th International Geological Congress in 1948 who defined it as being the base of the Callabrian stage in a sequence of marine sediments in Italy. Although direct age determination of the Callabrian stage has not been possible, Glass *et al.* (1967) have suggested an age of about 2 million years for the Pliocene–Pleistocene boundary, on the basis of the appearance of particular foraminifera species and the magnetic field polarity-reversal chronology in deep-sea sediments (Chapter 4, p. 110). Alternatively, if the first evidence for climatic deterioration (i.e. glaciation) is used to define the boundary, then it probably occurred about 2·5 million years ago.

The chronology for the evolution of human cultures during the Pleistocene period varies radically in different parts of the world (Coles and Higgs, 1969). The tentative absolute chronologies provided by the physical methods of age determination in East Africa, Western Europe and the New World are therefore considered separately, these areas being chosen to illustrate both the value and the limitations of the currently available methods.

East Africa

The earliest *dated* evidence of human culture in East Africa, or in fact anywhere in the world, is provided by a group of artificially struck flakes and tools found in the Koobi Fora area, east of Lake Rudolf in Kenya (Leakey, 1970). A few of the flakes were found *in situ* in a volcanic tuff while the majority lay on the surface close to the *in situ* flakes and distributed in such a manner as to suggest that they had originally been embedded in the tuff and had weathered out during comparatively recent times. In view of this close association, together with the fact that the *in situ* and surface specimens are mineralogically indistinguishable, it seems reasonable to assume that the entire group was in fact derived from the tuff. The potassium–argon date of 2·61 ± 0·26 million years obtained for the volcanic tuff (see Chapter 4, p. 97) is therefore also applicable, with a reasonable degree of certainty, to the tool assemblage itself. The result consequently provides direct evidence that man, the skilled tool-maker, existed in East Africa during the late Pliocene or early Pleistocene period, the appropriate terminology depending on one's definition of the Pliocene–Pleistocene boundary.

The subsequent development of early human cultures in East Africa has been recently surveyed by Isaac (1969). In this context the evidence from the Olduvai Gorge in Tanzania occupies a central place (Leakey, 1961; Bishop and Clark, 1967) since the sediments exposed in the gorge represent a quasi-continuous sequence spanning a period of about 2 million years. The sediments contain a vast wealth of stone artefacts, as well as fossil hominid and animal bones, and interstratified with this material are a number of volcanic deposits which have been dated using the potassium–argon method.

A concordant sequence of potassium–argon dates (Table 12) ranging from approximately 1·6 to 1·9 million years have been obtained for the volcanic horizons in Bed I at Olduvai (Evernden and Curtis, 1965). The series of dates for the strata between Marker Bed A and the Zinjanthropus floor suggest an age of about 1·75 million years for the deposits containing the skeletal remains of *Zinjanthropus* (i.e. Olduvai man) and *Homo habilis*. Confirmation of this potassium–argon age has since been obtained by fission track dating of related volcanic

Table 12. Potassium–argon dates for Bed I at the Olduvai Gorge, Tanzania (after Evernden and Curtis, 1965)

Strata	Age (million years)
Marker Bed A	{ 1·57 { 1·66
	1·86
	1·64
	1·65
	1·79
	1·86
	1·78
ZINJANTHROPUS FLOOR	
	1·85
Basalt	1·92
Below basalt	{ 1·85 { 1·91

deposits (Chapter 4, p. 104) and by independent potassium–argon dating of the magnetic field polarity reversal recorded in Bed I (i.e. the Olduvai event in the Matuyama reversed epoch) in other parts of the world (Chapter 5, p. 140). The earlier dates (1·85, 1·92, 1·85 and 1·91 million years) are associated with strata below the lowest known occurrence of tool and fossil hominid remains (i.e. the Zinjanthropus floor). Unfortunately, except for a potassium–argon date of 0·50 million years for a volcanic deposit of uncertain position in the upper part of Bed II, no suitable material for age determination has been obtained from the more recent strata at Olduvai. However, it is clear that human occupation continued at Olduvai from about 1·75 million years ago at least until sometime in the Middle Pleistocene which ended approximately 100 000 years ago.

Western Europe

The basic chronological framework for the European Pleistocene is provided by the study of the sequence of glacial and interglacial phases which affected the entire region (West, 1968).

Geological evidence for these phases in glaciated areas exists in the form of boulder clay deposits (i.e. a fine-grained deposit which does not necessarily contain either boulders or clay) laid down beneath the ice and terminal moraines which are deposits of debris carried in front of the advancing ice and laid down at the point of maximum advance of the ice sheet. In the periglacial zone immediately beyond the margin of the ice sheets, great sheets of loess (i.e. a fine dust blown out of exposed frost soils by winds issuing from glaciated territories) blanketed the ground during glacial phases. During the subsequent interglacial, the loess-covered surfaces weathered to leave a clear record of the climatic fluctuations. In addition, glacial phases produced, on a worldwide scale, a lowering of the sea level as a result of the locking-up of water in the ice sheets. Study of these geological phenomena provided the initial basis for identifying the various glacial and interglacial phases, of particular note being the classic study of the Alpine succession where in 1909 four Pleistocene glaciations (Gunz, Mindel, Riss and Wurm) were distinguished.

More recently increased use has been made of the palaeobotanical data, especially that derived from pollen analysis. Study of the pollen diagrams (Chapter 3, p. 71) again indicates a series of alternating cold (i.e. glacial) and temperate (i.e. interglacial) phases, the boundary between them being placed where the vegetation changes from an open sub-arctic park landscape to a wooded landscape with temperate forests, and vice-versa.

From examination of the geological and palaeobotanical evidence, it has been possible to establish the Pleistocene climatic sequence back to the Pliocene–Pleistocene boundary and correlate, to some extent, the various phases in different parts of Europe. A tentative correlation between the glacial and interglacial phases for the Alps, N.W. Europe and Britain during the later stages of the Pleistocene, which are of interest to archaeology, is presented in Table 13, together with currently available proposals for the absolute chronology of this climatic sequence.

Radiocarbon dating has established absolute dates for the final glaciation (Weichselian–Wurm) as well as dating a number of minor

Table 13. Stages and absolute chronology for the European Pleistocene

Climate[a]	Stage			Absolute chronology[b] (thousand years BP)			
	Britain	N.W. Europe	Alps	(a)	(b)	(c)	(d)
Upper Pleistocene							
G	Weichselian	Weichselian	Wurm	10–60			
I	Ipswichian	Eamian	Wurm/Riss	60–100			60
G	Gippingian	Saalian	Riss	100–130			
I	Hoxnian	Holsteinian	Riss/Mindel	130–180	140–150	270	240
Middle Pleistocene							
G	Lowestoftian	Elsterian	Mindel		220–300	430	
I	Cromerian	Cromerian	Mindel/Gunz		320		
G	Beestonian	Menapian	Gunz		340–420		640
Lower Pleistocene							

[a] G refers to glacial phase and I refers to interglacial phase.
[b] Column (a): Radiocarbon dates (Weichselian–Wurm glacial) and dates obtained from the temperature fluctuations inferred from oxygen isotopic measurements on deep-sea sediments.
Column (b): Potassium–argon dates for volcanic deposits in the Eifel (after Frechen and Lippolt, 1965).
Column (c): Potassium–argon dates for volcanic deposits in Italy (after Evernden and Curtis, 1965).
Column (d): Fluorine dates for bones from western Germany (after Richter, 1958).

temperate phases (i.e. interstadials) occurring during this final glacial phase. These radiocarbon dates have been confirmed by the absolute chronology for the world-wide oceanic temperature fluctuations which are inferred from oxygen isotopic measurements on deep-sea sediments. Correlation between these oceanic temperature fluctuations and the continental climatic phases also provides tentative absolute dates for the Ipswichian–Eamian–Wurm/Riss interglacial, the Gippingian–Saalian–Riss glacial and the Hoxnian–Holsteinian–Riss/Mindel interglacial (Chapter 4, p. 112).

Where volcanic deposits formed during the Pleistocene can be correlated with the geology of the glacial and interglacial phases, the potassium–argon method can be used to provide further absolute dates. Of particular importance is the sequence of potassium–argon dates obtained for the volcanic deposits of the Laacher-See area in the Eifel (Frechen and Lippolt, 1965). These volcanic deposits can be correlated chronologically with the formation of terraces by the River Rhine and these terraces can in turn be tentatively related to the glacial and interglacial phases: a tentative absolute chronology back to the Beestonian–Menapian–Gunz glacial can thus be established. This chronology is however in disagreement with the dates proposed by Evernden and Curtis (1965) for the Hoxnian–Holsteinian–Riss/Mindel interglacial and the Lowestoftian–Elsterian–Mindel glacial on the basis of potassium–argon dating of volcanic deposits in Italy. There is similarly disagreement between the Frechen–Lippolt chronology and the dates proposed by Richter (1958) for the Hoxnian–Holsteinian–Riss/Mindel and Cromerian–Mindel/Gunz interglacials on the basis of the fluorine dating of bone (Chapter 5, p. 153). Therefore, although on the present evidence the chronology provided by the study of deep-sea sediments and the Frechen–Lippolt potassium–argon dates show the greatest consistency, it is obvious that no really satisfactory absolute chronology for the glacial and interglacial phases of the European Pleistocene is, as yet, available.

Prior to the period to which radiocarbon dating is applicable, the relative dating of man-made tools and fossil hominid remains from the European Pleistocene is achieved by relating these archaeological assemblages to the glacial and interglacial sequence on the basis of the geology and the pollen diagrams of the strata in which they were found. Tentative absolute dates can then be provided on the basis of overall absolute chronology summarized in Table 13. The stone eoliths found within the Lower Pleistocene Crags of East Anglia are now not normally thought to have been of human manufacture. Therefore, the earliest undoubted evidence for the presence of man in Western Europe is provided by the human jaw found near Heidelberg where the associated flora and fauna indicated that it dated from the Cromerian interglacial. In addition various unspecialized flake and pebble industries can be associated with the Cromerian interglacial and possibly the preceding glacial phase. The development of the subsequent specialized stone industries (i.e. Clactonian, Abbevillian, Acheulian, etc.), which provide the basis of the archaeological subdivision of the Lower Palaeolithic in Europe, can also be related to the glacial and interglacial sequence as shown in Table 14.

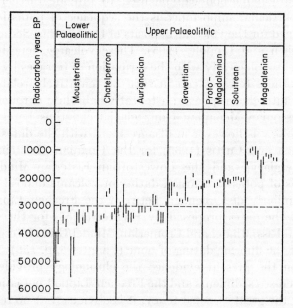

Figure 56. Radiocarbon dates (5568 year half-life) for the Palaeolithic period in France: each date is shown with a range of three standard deviations. The suggested termination of the Mousterian culture is indicated by the horizontal dashed line (after Coles and Higgs, 1969).

In particular, the Mousterian industry, which is associated with Neanderthal man, appears first at the end of the Ipswichian interglacial and continues through into the early Weichselian glacial when the direct absolute age determination of the archaeological deposits is possible using radiocarbon dating. From the radiocarbon dates for sites in France (Fig. 56), it can be seen that during the Weichselian glacial, a considerable overlap in time existed between the Mousterian culture of the Lower Palaeolithic and those of the Upper Palaeolithic (i.e. Chatelperron and Aurignacian) which, being associated with *Homo sapiens*, ultimately became dominant. Although radiocarbon dating provides the basic method for establishing a world-wide absolute

Table 14. Archaeological sequence during the European Pleistocene

Climatic stage[a]	Industry/ artefact type[b]	Human Species	Archaeological stage
Weichselian-Late Weichselian- Middle	Magdalenian Solutrean Aurignacian	*Homo sapiens*	Upper Palaeolithic
Weichselian-Early Ipswichian	Mousterian	Neanderthal man	Lower Palaeolithic
Gippingian	Levalloisian		
Hoxnian	Acheulian Clactonian	Swanscombe man	
Lowestoftian	Abbevillian		
Cromerian	Unspecialized industries	Heidelberg man	

[a] The climatic stages are specified in terms of the glacial and interglacial phases in Britain.
[b] The assignment of the various artefact industries to specific climatic stages is only approximate and does not mean that they are wholly confined to the climatic stage indicated.

chronology during the Upper Palaeolithic, thermoluminescent dating of fired clay fragments (Chapter 4, p. 126), associated with fired clay figurines, can be useful in supplementing and confirming the radiocarbon results.

New World

The advent of human cultures in the New World (i.e. America, Australia and New Zealand) fortunately falls within the period to which radiocarbon dating can be applied.

In America, the earliest stone industries to have been dated by the radiocarbon method occur at about 11 000 BP. However, in spite of the lack of any precise chronological evidence, some authorities believe that man arrived on the continent some 20 000 to 40 000 years ago. Since man would have crossed from Asia to Alaska, a first consideration is to establish the periods at which this would have been possible. Migration requires both a land-bridge, which exists during a glacial phase as a result of the associated lowering of the sea-level, and the absence of an extensive ice-sheet barrier which would prevent free passage at either end of the land-bridge. Therefore the crossing must have taken place either before or after the glacial maximum and radiocarbon dating suggests two possible periods. The first is 26 000–20 000 BP while the second, 12 000–11 000 BP, effectively coincides with the earliest dated stone industries.

In Australia, the earliest radiocarbon dates associated with man-made artefacts range from 22 000 to 16 000 BP and indicate that the arrival of man on that continent was far earlier than had been anticipated prior to the development of the radiocarbon method. In this case migration from south-east Asia must have occurred using boats since, even when the sea-levels were at their lowest during glacial phases, no land bridge could have been formed across the ocean-bed depression (i.e. the Wallace Divide) between Borneo and the Celebes.

In contrast to Australia, man did not migrate to New Zealand during the Pleistocene period, radiocarbon dates of about 1000 BP being obtained for the earliest settlements round the coastline. Migration is generally assumed to have been from Polynesia, a distance of about two thousand miles, rather than from the closest neighbouring land-mass of Australia which is more than one thousand miles to the west.

Postglacial

For the Postglacial phase, which begins at about 8000 BC in Europe and during which the Mesolithic, Neolithic, Bronze Age and Iron Age cultures developed, radiocarbon dating at present provides the primary means of establishing an absolute world-wide chronology. For the Near East and Europe, radiocarbon dating is mainly appropriate for the period prior to 600 BC since after this date historical records normally provide a more accurate chronology than can be obtained from radiocarbon dating. However, within the historical period, radiocarbon dating has been of considerable value in the study of the development of European mediaeval architecture (Horn, 1970; Fletcher, 1970), radiocarbon measurements being undertaken on the timbers from either the roof or the framework of a wide range of buildings. In addition radiocarbon dating continues to be of prime importance up to the period of European colonization in parts of the world, such as Mexico (Johnson and Willis, 1970) and Nigeria (Shaw, 1969), in which indigenous literate societies maintaining historical records did not exist.

Although radiocarbon dating will probably retain its supremacy for absolute age determination, it seems likely that other physical methods, which can be applied to the greatly extended range of artefacts employed during this period, will in the future assume increasing importance. In particular, thermoluminescent dating of pottery appears to be an extremely promising absolute method of age determination, especially considering the comparative abundance of pottery on most archaeological sites dating from the latter half of the Postglacial period. Over a rather more limited geographical area, the dating of obsidian from measurement of the thickness of the surface hydration layer could be useful, while magnetic dating of pottery kilns could provide a more detailed chronology for the later periods and in particular mediaeval Europe. The major advantage of these methods over radiocarbon dating is that they provide a *direct* age for the archaeological artefacts and structures themselves. The need to establish the correct stratigraphical relationship between the artefacts or structures and the surviving organic material used for radiocarbon dating is therefore avoided.

It is obviously neither appropriate nor possible in this volume to discuss all the currently available radiocarbon dates which are directly relevant to archaeology (Thomas, 1967). Therefore two topics, the development of agriculture during the Neolithic period and the development of metallurgy during the Copper and Bronze Ages in the Near East and Europe, have been chosen in order to illustrate the impact that radiocarbon dating has made on the chronological framework used by archaeologists. From the beginning, the availability of radiocarbon dates indicated that the tentative absolute chronology for the Neolithic, which had been inferred from the historical dates existing for Egypt and Mesopotamia, was too short and had to be considerably expanded. However, at this stage, much of the Bronze Age chronology, which had also been inferred from the historical dates, appeared to be essentially in agreement with the radiocarbon dates and the possible necessity for further modification was only appreciated more recently when the discrepancy between the radiocarbon age and the true calendar age was established by means of tree-ring studies.

Neolithic

The evolution from the Palaeolithic to the Neolithic way of life is of fundamental importance in man's advance towards civilization, since in general terms it can be regarded as the phase during which man ceased to be a hunter and food-gatherer and started to produce food. The development of a farming economy, which involved both the cultivation of cereals and the domestication of animals, led to a more static existence in which permanent village communities tended to replace nomadic groups occupying seasonal camps in, for example, caves. Associated with this change in the basic economy were a series of technological advances including the use of sun-dried mud bricks for building, an extended range of stone artefacts and perhaps most important, the production of pottery. This Neolithic "revolution" therefore provided the basis for the subsequent social and technological developments such as urban settlements, complex social hierarchies, literary and metallurgy.

Although it was generally assumed that a farming economy was first developed in the Near East and that it subsequently spread westwards across Europe, the chronology for this development was extremely ill-defined prior to the advent of radiocarbon dating. Milojčić (1949) provided a tentative chronology based on supposed synchronisms between the Late Neolithic at Vinca in Yugoslavia and the early Bronze Age at Troy (Fig. 57): an absolute date of about 2700 BC for Troy was inferred on basis of contacts with Egypt and Mesopotamia for which historical chronologies back to about 3000 BC are available. This system of dating was, however, subject to massive uncertainty even for Europe where it was thought that the spread of a farming economy occurred after 3000 BC: for the Near East where farming developed prior to the earliest historical dates, the situation was even more uncertain. The early radiocarbon dates for the appearance of agriculture and a Neolithic way of life immediately suggested that the historically based chronology was too short and with the large number of radiocarbon dates now available, a more satisfactory absolute chronology for the expansion of a farming economy can be established.

Clark (1965) has summarized the radiocarbon dates for early farming settlements in Europe and the Near East and has shown that the radiocarbon dates for the earliest pottery Neolithic can precede the historically based dates by as much as 2000 years (Fig. 57). In addition, this difference is greater for some territories than for others: for instance there is a notable greater difference for Iran, Iraq and Anatolia than for Egypt. Consequently, the previously accepted pattern of relationships for the spread of agriculture between the several

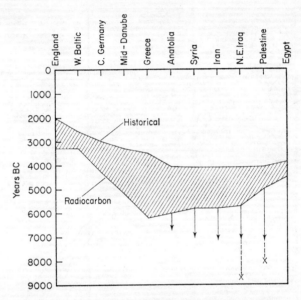

Figure 57. Graph showing the difference between the historically derived dates and the radiocarbon dates (5568 year half-life) for the beginning of the pottery Neolithic in different parts of Europe and the Near East. The vertical arrows and the crosses mark the radiocarbon dates for the appearance, in the Near East, of a pre-pottery and incipient Neolithic respectively (after Clark, 1965).

territories had to be modified. From the map of the earliest known farming settlements shown in Fig. 58, it can be seen that down to about 5200 BC, agricultural communities were confined to a ten degrees of latitude zone between Greece and Iran. The main expansion of this farming economy during the subsequent period from 5200 to 4000 BC was north of the Mediterranean through the Balkans and central Europe up to the margins of the north European plain, with a side branch westwards to central Italy and Iberia. In contrast the expansion south of the Mediterranean into Africa was relatively weak during this period, being confined to the coastal zone and the lower Nile. This new economy then spread to Scandinavia, the British Isles, France, the Alpine zone and the Ukraine during the period 4000–2800 BC, while a similar further expansion down the Nile and across the Sahara occurred in the region south of the Mediterranean. In presenting this general picture for the expansion of agriculture, it must be emphasized that the blank areas on the map (e.g. Poland) do not necessarily mean that no farming communities had been established

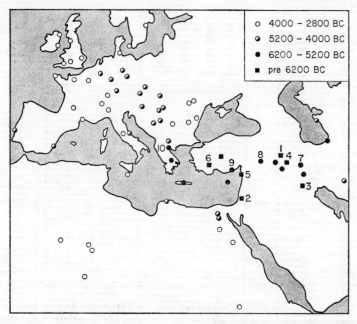

Figure 58. Sketch map of Europe and the Near East showing the earliest known agricultural settlements, as determined by radiocarbon dating (5568 year half-life). The sites dated to before 6200 BC are either incipient Neolithic (sites 1–2) or pre-pottery Neolithic (sites 2–6) settlements, while those dated to after 6200 BC are pottery Neolithic settlements. In most cases the pre-pottery Neolithic settlement is replaced by a pottery Neolithic settlement. The numbered sites (1–10) are referred to in the text (after Clark, 1965).

by 2800 BC but rather that no radiocarbon dates are available for the earliest farming communities in these regions.

In addition to providing a much earlier date for the beginnings of a farming economy and modifying the pattern for the expansion of this economy across Europe, radiocarbon dating has effectively increased the time range for the Neolithic period. This enlargement of the time range, together with the possibility of pin-pointing specific stages of development, has necessarily had drastic effects on the interpretation of Neolithic prehistory in certain territories, of which England provides a typical example. Prior to the availability of radiocarbon dates, Piggott (1954) assumed that the Neolithic phase in England was confined to the period from 2000 BC to about 1500 BC. On the basis of this short time-scale, he divided the Neolithic cultures into two separate but essentially contemporary groups, the Primary and Secondary Neolithic groups. The Primary Neolithic people, who arrived from Europe, introduced a farming economy to England together with causewayed enclosures, such as Windmill Hill, earthen long-barrows and flint-mines. In contrast the Secondary Neolithic people represented the indigenous Mesolithic population whose way of life had been modified through contact with the "invading" Primary Neolithic farmers. However, this short time-scale was seen to be erroneous as a result of the radiocarbon dating results which indicated that the Neolithic phase in England started prior to 3000 BC. With this greatly expanded time-scale, the hypothesis of a Secondary Neolithic people, contemporary with the "invading" Primary Neolithic farmers, is no longer necessary and a new pattern for the development of the Neolithic in England has now emerged.

Godwin (1970) has recently summarized the radiocarbon dates for the Neolithic period in England and from this data, some of which is presented in Fig. 59, the various subdivisions of the Neolithic period can be identified. The Early Neolithic (3400–2500 BC) is characterized by the introduction of causewayed enclosures, earthen long-barrows and flint mining: that is the main components of the previously defined Primary Neolithic. However, the Windmill Hill causewayed camp (2580 BC) is more recent than originally anticipated and is considerably pre-dated by the Hembury camp (3240 BC). For the Middle Neolithic (2500–2000 BC), there is a comparative dearth of radiocarbon dates, although this does not necessarily imply an absence of settlements. Indeed, many of the numerous wooden trackways found in the Somerset Levels date from this phase, while there is evidence from pollen studies that temporary forest clearance continued throughout the Neolithic. The Late Neolithic (2000–1500 BC) includes those pottery groups which were previously assigned to the Secondary Neolithic. Contemporary with the Late Neolithic cultures is the Beaker culture which again represents an "invasion" from Europe and which was responsible for the introduction of metallurgy to Britain. The construction of phases I (2180 and 1850 BC) and II at Stonehenge also

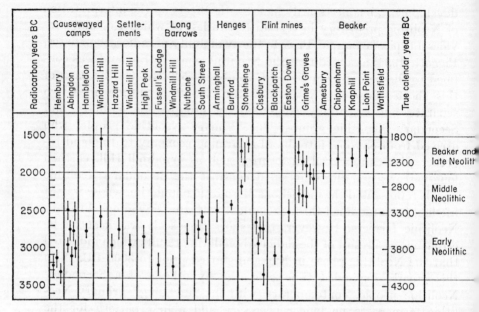

Figure 59. Radiocatbon dates (5568 year half-life) for the Neolithic period in southern England: each date is shown with a range of one standard deviation. The approximate true calendar dates, based on tree-ring data, are also indicated (after Godwin, 1970).

dates from this period and presumably represent a development of the less elaborate henge monuments (e.g. Arminghall and Burford) built during the previous phase. The construction of phase IIIa at Stonehenge is thought to be associated with the Wessex culture (Early Bronze Age), the radiocarbon dates for the II/IIIa transition being 1720 and 1620 BC.

Although radiocarbon dating has been instrumental in elucidating many aspects of the Neolithic, the initial stages, prior to 6000 BC, in the development of a farming economy within the primary zone between Greece and Iran are still not fully understood (Braidwood, 1970). An incipient Neolithic, in which a predominantly hunting-based diet is supplemented by harvested grain, has been supposedly identified in the Near East at Shanidar cave and Zawi Chemi Shanidar village (Site 1 on Fig. 58: radiocarbon dates—8650 and 8850 BC) in Iraq (Solecki, 1963) and in the Natufian basal levels at Jericho (Site 2: 7950 and 7900 BC) in Palestine (Kenyon, 1959). At these sites, the presence of large grinding stones, mortars and knives, consisting of flint blades attached to bone handles, are regarded as evidence for the harvesting of grain which was probably growing wild rather than having been specifically cultivated as a source of food. In addition, the earliest known pre-pottery Neolithic settlements, whose economy was undoubtedly strongly dependent on the harvesting of grain and the herding of sheep and goats, have also been located in the Near East. These settlements include Ali Kosh (Site 3: Bus Mordeh and Ali Kosh phases—8000–5800 BC) in Iran (Hole and Flannery, 1967), Jarmo (Site 4: Lower Level—7100–6100 BC) in Iraq, Ras Shamra (Site 5: Level VC—7100–6200 BC) in Syria, Jericho (Site 2: pre-pottery Neolithic B—7100–5900 BC) in Palestine and Hacilar (Site 6: 6800 BC) in Anatolia. However, by about 6000 BC, there were farming settlements at which pottery was being produced throughout the primary agricultural zone. Typical early pottery Neolithic settlements include Tepe Serab (Site 7: 5700 BC) in Iran, Tell Halaf (Site 8: 5700 BC) in Iraq, Ras Shamra (Site 5: Level VB—5800 BC) in Syria, Mersin (Site 9: 6000 BC) in Anatolia and Nea Nikomedeia (Site 10: 6200 BC) in Greece.

Therefore on the basis of the evidence at present available, it seems probable that the beginnings of agriculture occurred in the Near East. However, future excavation and radiocarbon dating might well indicate alternative or additional early centres, such as Anatolia, for the domestication of plants and animals. Similarly on the present evidence, the dates at which the domestication of typical cereals (e.g. emmer, wheat, barley) and animals (e.g. sheep, goats, pigs, cattle) occurred remain somewhat imprecise although it is clear that agriculture formed a significant part of the economy in the primary zone between Greece and Iran by about 6000 BC. Again, future excavations should provide additional information on the beginnings of agriculture during the period from 10 000 to 6000 BC. However, Higgs and Jarman (1969) have emphasized that, in considering these early developments, the term domestication must be used with caution since it tends to obscure the gradation from one plant or animal form to another and draws a classifactory line which may not correspond with nature. Instead they suggest that the emergence of an agricultural economy should be considered in terms of the development of the symbiotic man/animal/plant relationship as a result of environmental changes. With this hypothesis, the search for the beginnings of agriculture in a particular region is no longer realistic since it does not imply an "invention" or a series of "inventions".

Finally, it should be emphasized that the conversion of the radiocarbon dates to true calendar dates is unlikely to necessitate any major changes in the interpretation of the beginnings of the Neolithic period. From consideration of the tree ring and varve data (Chapter 4, p. 83; Fig. 30), it seems probable that throughout the period from 2500 to 8000 BC, the radiocarbon ages are less than the true calendar ages by about 800 years (i.e. radiocarbon dates of 2500 and 8000 BC convert to true calendar dates of about 3300 and 8800 BC respectively). Therefore, although the beginnings of agriculture occurred about 800 years earlier than anticipated from the radiocarbon dates, the time scale and pattern of relationships for its spread from the primary zone into Europe and Africa remains essentially unchanged. However, as discussed in more detail on p. 186, the corrections to the radiocarbon dates after 3000 BC do upset some of the previously suggested relationships between Europe and the Aegean (e.g. the spread of megalithic tombs). In addition, since a radiocarbon age of 1500 BC is less than the true calendar age by only 300 years, the duration of the Neolithic phase in certain territories is effectively increased. For example, in Britain the Neolithic spans the radiocarbon period from 3400 to 1500 BC (i.e. a duration of about 1900 years) whereas in terms of true calendar dates, it extends from 4200 to 1800 BC (i.e. a duration of about 2400 years).

Copper and Bronze Ages

The Copper (i.e. Chalcolithic) and Bronze Ages refer to those periods during which the introduction and development of metallurgy took place. It is generally accepted that the first stage in this development is associated with use of native copper (i.e. metallic copper found among copper ores) which was hammered into the required shape. Subsequently, metallic copper was obtained by smelting copper ores and artefacts were made by casting the molten copper. The next stage was, typically, the addition of a small quantity of tin ore to the copper ore during smelting. The resulting copper–tin alloy (about 10 per cent tin), known as bronze, was significantly harder than pure copper and therefore provided a more useful metal. In addition, the casting of artefacts was made easier by the fact that bronze has a lower melting point than copper.

As in the case of agriculture, the first use of copper occurred in the Near East. Prior to the advent of radiocarbon dating, the chronology for the development of metallurgy in this region was based on the fact that bronze was being used during the Early Dynastic phase of the

Sumerian civilization which could be dated to about 3000 BC by means of historical records. Further, it could be shown that metallurgy had spread to the Aegean during the first half of the third millennium BC and it was assumed that the technology subsequently diffused westwards and northwards into Europe.

Childe (1957) suggested two main routes whereby a chronological link could be established between Europe and the Aegean. The first involved the supposed similarity between the megalithic tombs of the Copper Age in the Iberian peninsular (i.e. Los Millares culture) and the round tombs of the Bronze Age in Crete. These latter can be dated to about 2500 BC on the basis of contacts with Egypt for which historical dates are available. It was therefore assumed that megalithic architecture, together with metallurgy, had diffused from the Aegean to Spain and Portugal by about 2500 BC. The second route involved the supposed synchronism between the Late Neolithic at Vinca in Yugoslavia and the Early Bronze Age at Troy. Since Early Bronze Age Troy can be dated to about 2700 BC, it was assumed that the Balkan Copper Age, which succeeds the Neolithic, arose around 2500 BC as a result of contacts with Troy. These links were then extended across Europe to provide a chronology for both the spread of a Neolithic way of life, including the diffusion of megalithic tombs from Iberia to France, Britain and Scandinavia, and the spread of a copper and bronze metallurgy. A further fixed date for Europe was provided by the Wessex culture in southern England which was dated to between 1600 and 1400 BC on the basis of its supposed similarities with the Mycenaean civilization, for which historical dates are again available.

The advent of radiocarbon dating provided, in the first place, a chronology for the development of metallurgy in the Near East. Thus native copper was being used to make small ornaments by about 5500 BC, the smelting of ores and the casting of copper artefacts had begun by about 4500 BC and a bronze metallurgy had been developed by about 3500 BC. Although the precise area within the Near East in which these developments occurred is not known, in all probability they were made near to the copper and tin ore sources (e.g. mountainous regions of east Turkey and north Syria, Zagros Mountains of Iran) rather than in Mesopotamia where the Sumerian civilization, with its sophisticated bronze technology, finally flourished.

In addition, the radiocarbon results indicated that the late Neolithic at Vinca must be dated to before 4000 BC and therefore the

Balkan Copper Age preceeded the Early Bronze Age at Troy by more than 1000 years. Similarly, the radiocarbon dates of around 3000 BC for megalithic tombs in Brittany contradicted the hypothesis that megalithic architecture had diffused from the Aegean, via Iberia, after 2500 BC. However, much of the later historically based Bronze Age chronology for Europe was not changed by the radiocarbon dates until, as a result of the tree-ring data, it became clear that the radiocarbon ages were less than the true calendar ages by several hundred years. Application of this correction to the radiocarbon dates resulted in the appearance of further errors in the historically based chronology since only the radiocarbon dates for Europe were altered, the historical dates for Egypt and Mesopotamia obviously remaining unchanged. Indeed, the corrected radiocarbon dates for Egyptian material agree far better with the historical chronology for this area than did the uncorrected radiocarbon dates.

The effect of the correction to the radiocarbon dates can be expressed in terms of a chronological "fault line" extending across the Mediterranean and southern Europe. This "fault line" separates those areas for which valid historical dates are available (i.e. Egypt, the Near East and the Aegean) from the rest of Europe where the historically based chronology was achieved merely on the basis of a diffusion hypothesis. On each side of the "fault line" the relationships and the successions of cultures remains unaltered but the two sides have shifted *en bloc* in relation to each other, as would the geological strata on the two sides of a geological fault.

As a consequence of the radiocarbon dating results, both uncorrected and corrected, the pattern of relationships for the spread of metallurgy across Europe must be modified and the possibility of its independent invention in Europe must be considered. In order to illustrate this changed pattern of relationships, the Balkan Copper Age, the Iberian Copper Age together with the spread of megalithic tombs and the Wessex culture are discussed below in more detail.

Renfrew (1969 and 1971) has recently reconsidered the Balkan Copper Age both in the context of its chronology and the origin of the metallurgical techniques employed. A selection of the radiocarbon dates associated with Aegean and Balkan sites during the period from the later Neolithic through to the Early Bronze Age is presented in Fig. 60. The results from the *tell* site at Sitagroi are of particular importance since its location in north Greece means that this site lies in a key position between the Balkans and the Aegean. The radiocarbon results clearly indicate that the Balkan Copper Age (Karanova V–VI and Vinca C–D) was contemporary with the later Neolithic of the Aegean (Sitagroi III, Dhimini and the later phases at Knossos and Saliagos) and preceded the Aegean Early Bronze Age (Sitagroi IV–V,

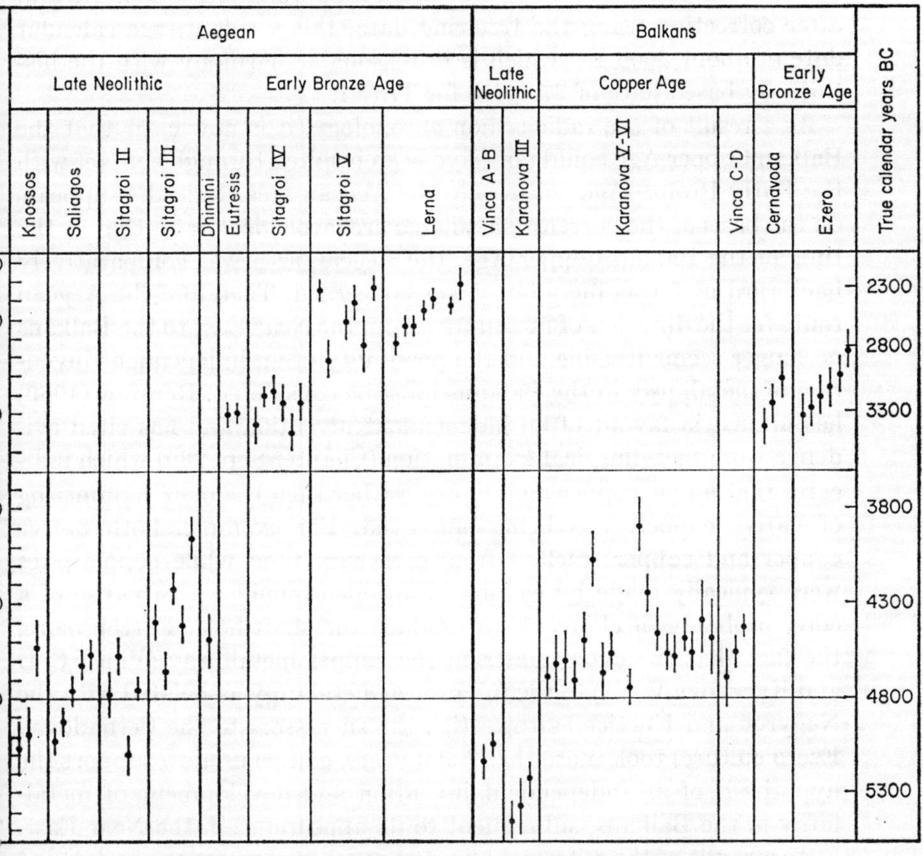

Figure 60. Radiocarbon dates (5568 year half-life) for the Aegean and the Balkans from the Late Neolithic through to the Early Bronze Age: each date is shown with a range of one standard deviation. The approximate true calendar dates, based on tree-ring data, are also indicated (after Renfrew, 1969 and 1971).

Eutresis and Lerna) by about a thousand years. Furthermore, these later Neolithic Aegean cultures were rather lacking in invention compared to the Balkan Copper Age cultures since, except in Thessaly and north Greece (i.e. Sitagroi III and Dhimini), there is an absence of elaborately decorated pottery and metallurgy. Similarly it can be seen that the Balkan Early Bronze Age (Cernavoda and Ezero) was contemporary with the first phase of the Aegean Early Bronze Age (Sitagroi IV and Eutresis). Although no radiocarbon dates are available for the Early Bronze Age at Troy (phase I), it seems likely that Troy I coincides with the transition from Sitagroi IV to Sitagroi V. The radiocarbon date for this transition is approximately 2300 BC and after correction using the tree-ring data, this yields a true calendar date of about 3000 BC which is in reasonable harmony with the historically based date of 2700 BC for Troy I.

As a result of the radiocarbon chronology, it is now clear that the Balkan Copper Age could not have been inspired through contact with the Early Bronze Age cultures in the Aegean area. Indeed, it appears on the basis of the currently available archaeological data, that at the time of the Balkan Copper Age, the Aegean area was comparatively backward as far as metallurgy was concerned. Therefore the Aegean route for the diffusion of metallurgy from the Near East to the Balkans no longer seems feasible and the possibility of an independent invention of metallurgy in the Balkans must be considered. Renfrew (1969) has argued in favour of an independent invention and has cited evidence from metallurgical examination (Chapter 8, p. 230) which indicates that a true copper metallurgy, rather than the mere hammering of native copper, was being employed. For example, both native copper and copper smelted from ores were used while copper axes were typically made by casting in an open mould with the use of a core, probably of charcoal, to produce the shaft-hole. Furthermore, the fact that the evolution from the copper metallurgy (Vinca C–D and Karanova V–VI) to the full bronze metallurgy associated with the Nagyrev and Unetice cultures (i.e. the successors to the Cernadova–Ezero culture) took more than 1500 years, can be used to support the hypothesis of an independent invention and development of metallurgy in the Balkans, subsequent to its appearance in the Near East.

As a result of the extremely limited number of radiocarbon dates at present available, the development of metallurgy in the Iberian peninsular and the relationship of this area to the spread of megalithic tombs (i.e. Gallery and Passage Graves) are still not fully understood (Renfrew, 1967). However, it is already clear that the previously assumed links between the Aegean and Iberia must be severely modified. In the first place the radiocarbon date for the walls and tombs at Los Millares (i.e. Copper Age) in Spain is about 2350 BC and after correction this yields a true calendar date of about 3000 BC which preceeds the historically based date (2500 BC) for the supposed prototypes in the Aegean (i.e. the round tombs of Bronze Age Crete) by several centuries. Furthermore, the Breton Passage Graves, which are closely comparable with those of Iberia, have yielded radiocarbon dates between 3250 and 2800 BC (i.e. true calendar dates between 4050 and 3600 BC). Therefore although the present evidence is insufficient to establish the origin and pattern for the spread of megalithic tombs within Europe, it is clear that Passage Graves were being built in Brittany more than a millennium before the appearance of monumental funerary architecture in the Aegean and the pyramids in Egypt. On the basis of the available radiocarbon dates (2350 BC), the Spanish Copper Age (i.e. Los Millares culture) was contemporary with the Aegean Early Bronze Age (Fig. 60) and therefore the development of metallurgy in Iberia could have been inspired through contacts with the Aegean. However, since the diffusion of megalithic tombs from the Aegean to Iberia is no longer acceptable and since the metal artefact typology for the two regions is different, an Aegean origin for the Iberian metallurgy seems unlikely. Therefore, the independent invention of metallurgy in Iberia, as well as the Balkans, represents a feasible alternative hypothesis.

The Wessex culture, which refers principally to a group of rich Early Bronze Age burials in southern Britain, was first defined by Piggott (1938). On the basis of the bronze artefacts, the goldwork, the faience beads and the amber ornaments found in these Wessex culture graves links with the Mycenaean world were suggested. This hypothesis was re-enforced by the dagger carved on a sarsen at Stonehenge which was supposedly of Mycenaean type and it was further suggested that the sarsen circle and sarsen trilithons at Stonehenge (phase IIIa) were the work of skilled craftsmen or architects who had come to Britain from Mycenaean Greece. Synchronisms between the Aegean Late Bronze Age and Egypt, for which there is an historical calendar, suggest that the first phase of the Mycenaean culture begins at about 1600 BC and therefore the Wessex culture was dated to the period between 1600 and 1400 BC.

Although there are as yet no radiocarbon dates for the early Wessex culture (phase I: Bush Barrow), Renfrew (1968) has assembled a series of radiocarbon dates for British and European archaeological sites which can be related to the early Wessex culture. The later Beaker culture in Britain and the early Unetice culture (Reinecke's phase A1/2) can be regarded as preceeding or overlapping with Wessex phase I. The Early Bronze Age in Brittany and the Netherlands to-

190   METHODS OF PHYSICAL EXAMINATION IN ARCHAEOLOGY

gether with the Stonehenge II/IIIa transition are essentially contemporary with Wessex phase I. With regard to the later Wessex culture (phase II—Camerton–Snowshill), radiocarbon dates for actual Wessex culture material are now available. Therefore the radiocarbon dates, presented in Fig. 61, suggest that the Wessex culture falls somewhere within the period 1700–1200 BC which is in reasonable agreement with the "historical" dates inferred from assumed links with

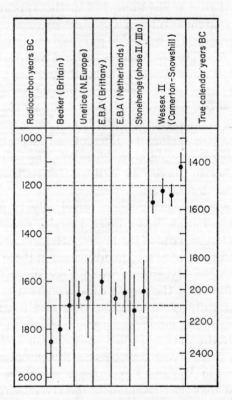

Figure 61. Radiocarbon dates (5568 year half-life) for archaeological material related to the Wessex culture: each date is shown with a range of one standard deviation. The approximate true calendar dates, based on tree-ring data, are also indicated. The suggested period for the Wessex culture falls within the two horizontal dashed lines.

Mycenae. However, after correction of the radiocarbon dates, the true calendar dates indicated for the Wessex culture are approximately 2100–1500 BC. Since the historically based date of 1600 BC for the beginnings of the Mycenaean culture obviously remains unchanged by the correction of the radiocarbon dates, these results suggest that the early Wessex culture precedes Mycenae by several centuries. Since there are no radiocarbon dates for actual early Wessex culture material and since the errors associated with the radiocarbon dates and especially their conversion to true calendar dates are quite large, this new chronology for the Wessex culture must at present be regarded only as a hypothesis. However, Renfrew (1968) has reconsidered the basis for the supposed chronological links between Wessex and Mycenae and has come to the conclusion that these links are less impressive than previously assumed and that it is acceptable to regard the development of the Wessex culture as having occurred prior to and independently of Mycenae.

Conclusions

The results discussed above indicate that the essentially absolute dates provided by the physical methods of age determination during the past decade have necessitated a radical change in the archaeological chronology which had previously been built up. Furthermore, it is reasonable to assume that these physical methods will in the future provide the archaeologist with an increasingly more precise and reliable world-wide absolute chronology; especially for the period subsequent to about 7000 BC during which the radiocarbon dates can be converted to true calendar dates using the tree-ring data. As this absolute chronology is progressively established, it is clear, although perhaps paradoxical, that chronological considerations will become less important and less interesting to archaeologists since the detailed seriations, typologies and cross-datings of artefacts will no longer be necessary.

Already the available absolute chronology has led to a reconsideration of the concepts and procedures employed in archaeology and to a change in emphasis as far as the basic aims of archaeology are concerned (Renfrew, 1970). For example, the radiocarbon dates have established that it is no longer legitimate to explain all the changes taking place in Europe in terms of the diffusion or influence of innovations originating in the Near East and Aegean and that the originality and creativity of the inhabitants of prehistoric Europe have been undervalued. Equally a reversal of roles, in which it would be suggested that innovations diffused from Europe to the Near East and the Aegean, is not acceptable. Instead, in considering how innovations are communicated between cultures, the meaning of the concepts of diffusion, influence and migration, which arose in part as a result of the need to establish a chronological framework, must be re-examined. Thus, although it is obvious that one culture frequently did influence another and that migration sometimes did take place, merely to state the existence of an influence or migration is insufficient. The mechanism for the influence or diffusion must be elucidated and its effects analysed in detail. Similarly, if a migration of people occurred, then the reasons why they came and the effects of their arrival must be understood.

In addition, it is becoming increasingly obvious that the concept of the diffusion of innovations has been somewhat over-employed by archaeologists in the past. Instead, the possibility of the independent invention of a new technology, such as metallurgy, in different parts of the world must be considered. Similarly, the subsequent innovations and cultural changes may on occasions be more readily explained in terms of the interaction of the technical, economic and social processes at work within the culture rather than in terms of further diffusion or influence from outside. For example, the characteristics of the Wessex culture (e.g. metallurgy, increased wealth, exotic goods, improved weapons, social hierarchy) are in many ways analogous to the developments that occurred in other areas (e.g. Balkans, Aegean, Iberia) at the time when metallurgy really got under way. However, although the Wessex culture metallurgy was presumably initiated as a result of the earlier migration of Beaker people from Europe, its other features need not necessarily be explained in terms of the further diffusion of ideas from Europe. Instead, it is possible that the similarities between the Wessex culture and other Early Bronze Age cultures are due to the fact that increased wealth, the appearance of exotic goods, the improvement in weapons and social differentiation are themselves a direct consequence of the development of metallurgy. In other words, the development of metallurgy could represent an enlargement of the cultural environment which itself independently generates similar cultural changes in each area.

Therefore probably the most important consequence of the absolute chronology, provided by the physical methods of age determination, is that it has encouraged archaeologists to re-examine their underlying philosophy. As a result of this re-examination, the main emphasis in archaeological interpretation is now being placed on the explanation of the sequence of events in prehistory rather than merely the *reconstruction of the timetable* for this sequence.

Plate 1. Experimental earthwork constructed at Overton Down, Wiltshire in 1960. Upper: immediately after completion. Lower: four years later, by which time considerable silting of the ditch and erosion of the rampart had occurred. (By permission of the Research Committee on Archaeological Field Experiments of the British Association for the Advancement of Science.)

Plate 2. The experimental firing of a pottery kiln of Romano-British type at Boston, Lincs. in 1962.

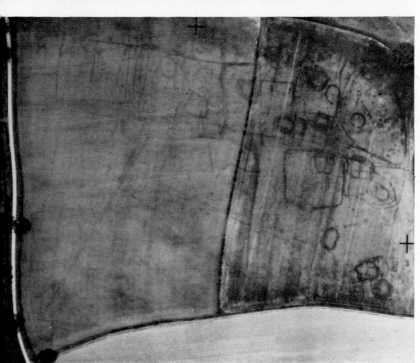

Plate 8. Aerial photographs. Left: crop-marks associated with huts, enclosures and ditches of a pre-Roman or Roman Iron Age settlement near to Lockington, Leics. Right: differences in relief (i.e. shadow-marks) associated with the houses and streets of the deserted mediaeval village at Argam, Yorks. (By permission of the Committee for Aerial Photography, University of Cambridge. Copyright reserved. Ph.: J. K. St Joseph.)

Plate 4. The proton magnetometer in operation with one person moving the detector bottle and the second person reading the instrument. (Photo courtesy of Thomas-Photos, Oxford.)

Plate 5 (left). The square array resistivity probe system in operation. A single person can both move the probe system and subsequently read the instrument. (Photo courtesy of A. Clark.)

Plate 6 (right). Typical electromagnetic surveying instrument in operation. A single person can both carry the coil system and read the instrument.

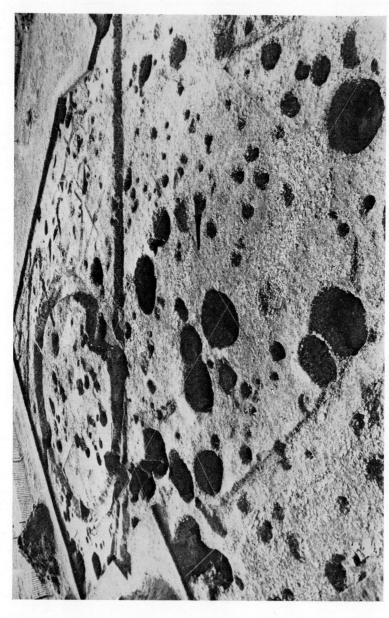

Plate 7. Excavated area at Cadbury Castle, Somerset showing the pits, the circular wall trench or drainage gulley of an Iron Age hut, the Mediaeval boundary ditch and the foundation trenches of the cruciform building (see Fig. 18 for the associated magnetic and electromagnetic survey results). (By permission of the Camelot Research Committee and the Society of Antiquaries of London.)

Plate 8. Excavated area at the Iron Age-cum-Roman settlement at Dragonby, Lincs. showing the remains of the road (foreground) and the soil fillings of various pits and ditches which appear dark in contrast to the light-coloured sand sub-soil.

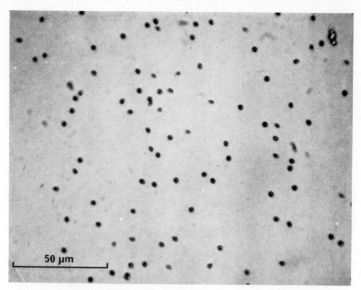

Plate 9. Photomicrograph of a polished etched surface of a modern glass showing the etch pits developed from artificially-induced fission tracks.

Plate 10. Typical pottery kiln (Romano-British type: Dragonby, Lincs.) used to provide samples for magnetic dating. (By permission of the Society of Antiquaries of London.)

Plate 11. Magnetic dating samples showing both an isolated stump of fired clay and several completed samples which have been encased in plaster of Paris and are ready for detachment.

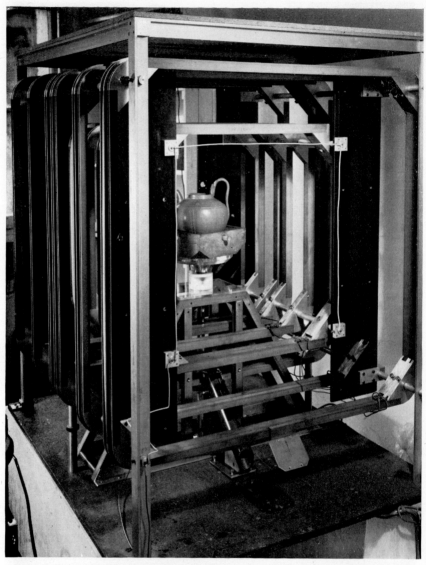

Plate 12. Spinner magnetometer coil system showing a pottery vessel in position on the table which is rotated at 5 revolutions per sec. (Photo courtesy of Thomas-Photos, Oxford.)

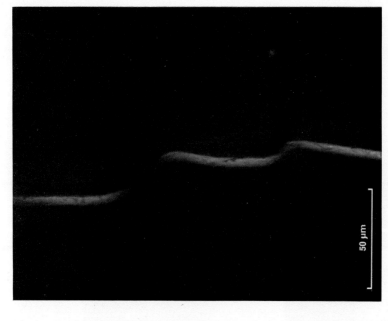

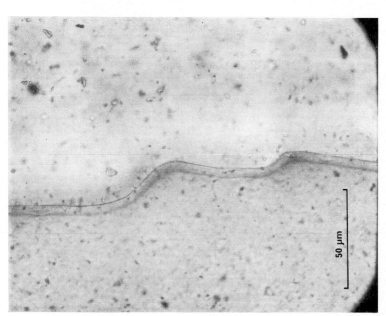

Plate 13. Photomicrographs of a thin section of an obsidian artefact showing the hydration layer, (left) as viewed in ordinary light and (right) as viewed between crossed polarizers. (Photo courtesy of I. Friedman.)

Plate 14. Weathering crust which has formed on the surface of a fragment of a glass wine bottle recovered at Port Royal, Jamaica. (By permission of the Corning Museum of Glass.)

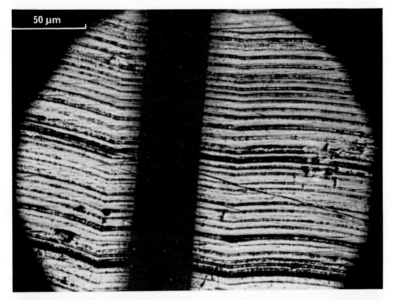

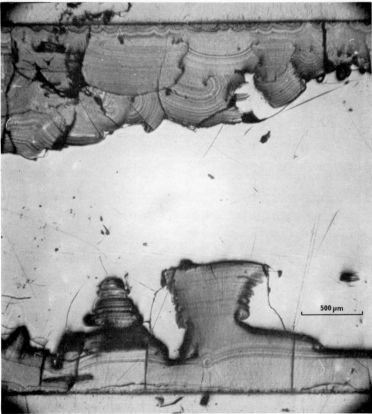

Plate 15. Photomicrographs of sections through the weathering crusts of ancient glass samples showing their fine laminar structure. Upper: uniform laminar structure with a human hair (dark central band) placed across the layers to illustrate the magnification. Lower: non-uniform weathering with randomly located intrusions or "plugs", each containing a different number of layers. (Upper by permission of the Corning Museum of Glass; lower by permission of the Society of Glass Technology. Ph.: R. G. Newton.)

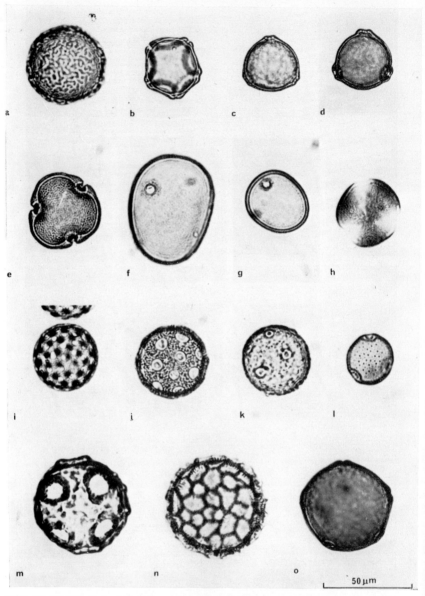

Plate 16. Photomicrographs of a selection of pollen grains. (a) Elm. (b) Alder. (c) Hazel. (d) Birch. (e) Lime. (f) Rye. (g) Wave hairgrass. (h) Field maple. (i) Fat hen. (j) Ragged robin. (k) Ribwort plantain. (l) Sheep's-bit. (m) Common fumitory. (n) Persicaria. (o) Hornbeam. (Photo courtesy of G. W. Dimbleby.)

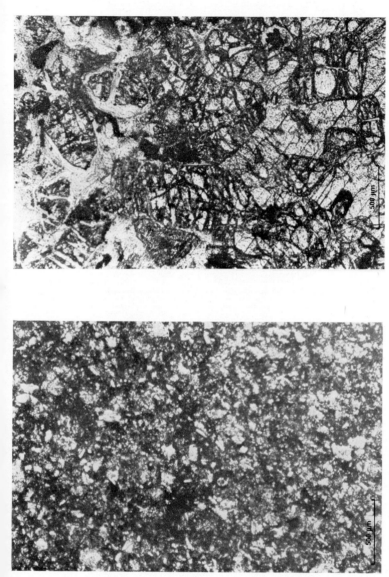

500 μm

500 μm

Plate 17. Photomicrographs of thin sections of stone axes viewed between crossed polarizers. Left: Group VI (Great Langdale): dark isotropic matrix embedded with small angular shattered fragments which are largely felspathic. Right: Group XII (Montgomeryshire): intergrowth of large crystals of olivine, pyroxene and felspar. (Photo courtesy of F. W. Shotton.)

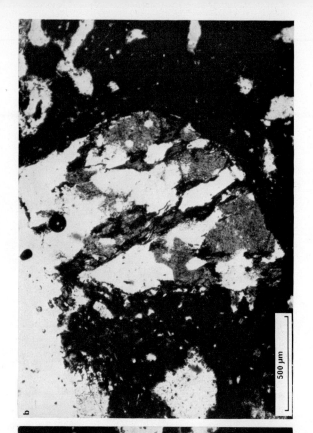

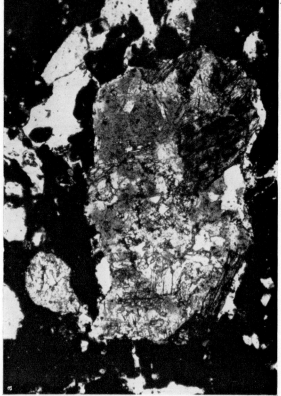

500 µm

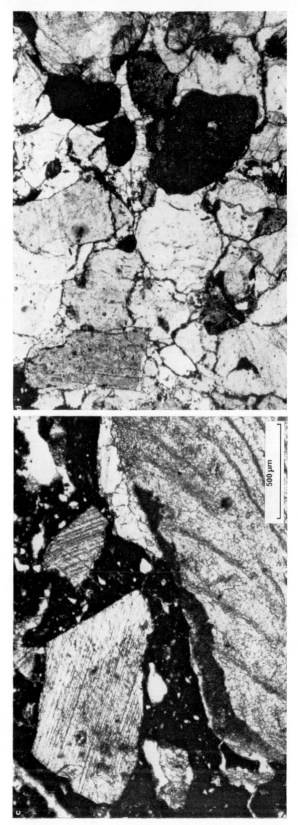

Plate 18. Photomicrographs of thin sections, viewed between crossed polarizers, of Iron Age pottery showing the different types of temper added to the clay (dark isotropic matrix). Facing page (a) Fragment of quartz diorite. (b) Fragment of metamorphic rock. This page (c) Fragments of limestone. (d) Single large fragment of sandstone (no clay matrix visible). (Photo courtesy of D. P. S. Peacock.)

500 μm

Plate 19. Photomicrograph of a polished etched section of the head of a rivet from a Minoan dagger showing the silver–copper eutectic layer (b) which provides the bonding between the copper rivet (c) and the silver capping (a). The deformed grains of the cold-worked copper in the rivet and the primary silver dendrites growing into the eutectic layer from the interface with the silver are also visible. (Photo courtesy of J. A. Charles and Antiquity Publications Ltd.)

Plate 20. Photomicrograph of a polished etched section of a wrought iron specimen showing the ferrite grains and fibrous inclusions of slag (dark streaks). (Photo courtesy of H. Cleere.)

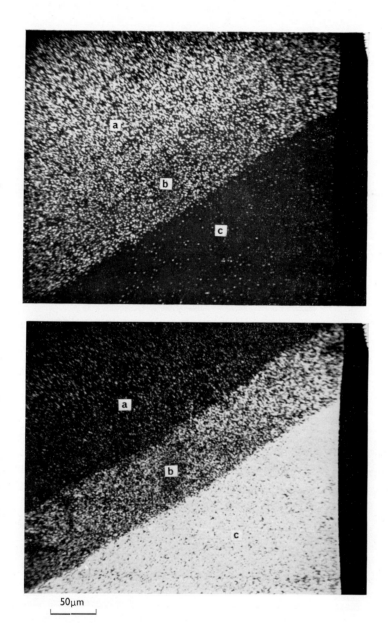

50μm

Plate 21. Scanning fluorescent X-ray images, obtained using the electron probe microanalyser, for (upper) silver and (lower) copper across a section through the head of a
rivet from a Minoan dagger. (a) Silver capping; (b) eutectic layer; (c) copper rivet.
Photo courtesy of J. A. Charles and Antiquity Publications Ltd.)

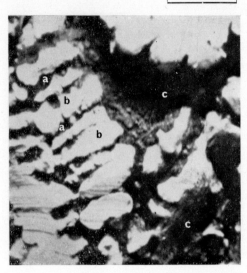

Plate 22. Backscattered electron image, obtained using the scanning electron microscope, for a Greek electrum coin showing the gold-rich dendrites. (a) Gold deficient areas; (b) gold-rich dendrites; (c) "valleys" filled with dirt. (By permission of Macmillan Journals Ltd. *Nature.*)

Plate 23. Radiograph of the hilt end of a pattern-welded iron sword dating from the third century AD and found at South Shields showing the bronze inlay of Mars (on one side) and an eagle with palm branches (on the other side). (By permission of South Shields Corporation.)

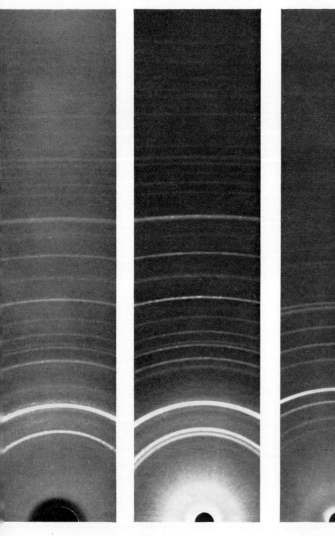

Plate 24. X-ray diffraction patterns (power method) for typical pottery samples, the bright lines on the print corresponding to the dark lines on the original photographic film. The principal minerals which can be identified from these diffraction patterns are: (upper) quartz, (middle) quartz and mica and (lower) quartz and calcite.

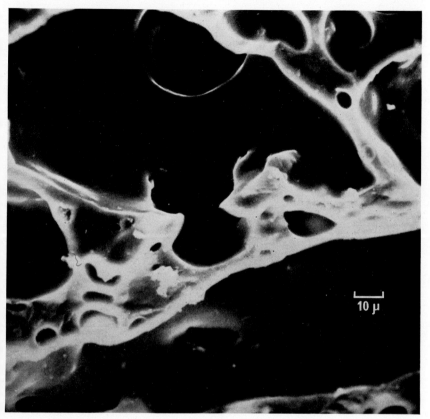

Plate 25. Photomicrographs of the surface topography of unfired and fired clay specimens obtained using the scanning electron microscope (backscattered/secondary electron
image). Facing page (upper) Carboniferous shale: unfired. Facing page (lower) Carboniferous shale: fired at 875°C. Above: London Clay: fired at 1025°C. (By permission of the
Director of the Building Research Establishment and the Controller of Her Majesty's
Stationery Office. Crown copyright.)

References

Bishop, W. W. and Clark, J. G. D. (Eds.) (1967). "Background to Evolution in Africa." University of Chicago Press, Chicago.

Braidwood, R. J. (1970). Prehistory in the Near East. In "Radiocarbon Variations and Absolute Chronology", (Ed. I. U. Olsson), pp. 81–91. Almqvist and Wiksell, Stockholm.

Childe, V. G. (1957). "The Dawn of European Civilisation", Routledge and Kegan Paul, London.

Clark, J. G. D. (1965). Radiocarbon dating and the expansion of farming culture from the Near East over Europe. Proc. prehist. Soc. 31, 58–73.

Coles, J. M. and Higgs, E. S. (1969). "The Archaeology of Early Man", Faber and Faber, London.

Evernden, J. F. and Curtis, G. H. (1965). The potassium-dating of Late Cenozoic rocks in East Africa and Italy. Curr. Anthropol. 6, 343–385.

Fletcher, J. M. (1970). Radiocarbon dating of medieval timber-framed cruck cottages. In "Scientific Methods in Medieval Archaeology", (Ed. R. Berger), pp. 141–157. University of California Press, Los Angeles.

Frechen, J. and Lippolt, H. J. (1965). Kalium-argon-daten zum alter des Laacher vulkanismus der Rheinterrassen und der Eiszeiten. Eiszeitalter Gegenw. 16, 5–30.

Glass, B., Ericson, D. B., Heezen, B. C., Opdyke, N. D. and Glass, J. A. (1967). Geomagnetic reversals and Pleistocene chronology. Nature 216, 437–442.

Godwin, H. (1970). The contribution of radiocarbon dating to archaeology in Britain. Phil. Trans. R. Soc. Lond. A269, 57–75.

Higgs, E. S. and Jarman, M. R. (1959). The origins of agriculture: a reconsideration, Antiquity, 43, 31–41.

Hole, F. and Flannery, K. V. (1967). The prehistory of south-western Iran: a preliminary report. Proc. prehist. Soc. 33, 147–206.

Horn, W. (1970). The potential and limitations of radiocarbon dating in the Middle Ages: the art historian's view. In "Scientific Methods in Medieval Archaeology", (Ed. R. Berger), pp. 23–87. University of California Press, Los Angeles.

Isaac, G. Ll. (1969). Studies of early culture in East Africa. Wld Archaeol. 1, 1–28.

Johnson, F. and Willis, E. H. (1970). Reconciliation of radiocarbon and sidereal years in Meso-American chronology. In "Radiocarbon Variations and Absolute Chronology", (Ed. I. U. Olsson), pp. 93–104. Almqvist and Wiksell, Stockholm.

Kenyon, K. M. (1959). Earliest Jericho. Antiquity 33, 5–9.

Leakey, L. S. B. (1961). "The Progress and Evolution of Man in Africa", Oxford University Press, Oxford.

Leakey, M. D. (1970). Early artefacts from the Koobi Fora area. Nature 226, 228–230.

Milojčić, V. (1949). "Chronologie der Jüngeren Steinzeit Mittel- und Südoosteuropas", Deutsches Archaeologisches Institut, Berlin.

Piggott, S. (1938). The Early Bronze Age in Wessex. Proc. prehist. Soc. 4, 52–106.

Piggott, S. (1954). "The Neolithic Cultures of the British Isles", Cambridge University Press, London.

Renfrew, C. (1967). Colonialism and megalithismus. Antiquity 41, 276–288.

Renfrew, C. (1968). Wessex without Mycenae. *Ann. Br. Schl Archaeol.*, *Athens* 63, 277–285.

Renfrew, C. (1969). The autonomy of the south-east European Copper Age. *Proc. prehist. Soc.* 35, 12–47.

Renfrew, C. (1970). New configurations in Old World archaeology. *Wld Archaeol.* 2, 199–211.

Renfrew, C. (1971). Sitagroi, radiocarbon and the prehistory of south-east Europe. *Antiquity* 45, 275–282.

Richter, K. (1958). Fluorteste quartarer knochen in ihrer bedeutung fur die absolute chronologie des Pleistozans. *Eiszeitalter Gegenw.* 9, 18–27.

Shaw, T. (1969). Archaeology in Nigeria. *Antiquity* 43, 187–199.

Solecki, R. S. (1963). Prehistory in Shanidar Valley, northern Iraq. *Science* 139, 179–193.

Thomas, H. L. (1967). Near Eastern, Mediterranean and European chronology. *Stud. Meditern Archaeol.* 17, 175 pp., 65 charts..

West, R. G. (1968). "Pleistocene Geology and Biology with especial reference to the British Isles", Longmans, London.

7
Physical Examination of Artefacts and Biological Material—Introduction

The material remains obtained from archaeological sites are extremely wide ranging. In the first place there are the artefacts, such as tools, weapons, domestic utensils, clothing, jewellery and coinage, and structures, such as houses, henge monuments, burial chambers and pottery kilns. These can be made from either inorganic materials, such as stone, metal, pottery and glass, or organic biological material, such as wood, vegetable and animal fibres, skins and bones. Secondly, there is the surviving biological material which is not specifically associated with man's material culture (i.e. his artefacts and structures). This includes vegetable remains, such as wood, charcoal, pollen, fruit and seeds; animal remains, such as bones and shells, as well as human bones and coprolites.

Survival of this wide range of material on an archaeological site varies according to the nature of the material and the climatic conditions prevailing on the site. Thus inorganic materials (e.g. stone, metal, pottery) survive under most conditions whereas many organic materials (e.g. wood, fibres, skins) normally survive only in either very dry or permanently waterlogged conditions.

Since the archaeologist's reconstruction of the past development of human cultures is based primarily on the study of the surviving artefacts, structures and biological materials, it is obviously essential to extract the maximum possible amount of information from the available material. The starting point for the study of the surviving material is of course direct visual examination. However, having exhausted the possibilities of identification and classification in terms of visual characteristics, examination using a wide range of physical techniques provides essential additional information.

The techniques of physical examination can be conveniently divided into two main groups. The first group effectively provides a natural extension to direct visual examination and involves examination either at a high magnification (e.g. optical and electron microscopy) or with radiation having a greater penetration than visible light (e.g. X-ray radiography). The additional data, which is obtained using these techniques, is essentially descriptive and qualitative. The second group, which in contrast typically provides quantitative data, is principally concerned with obtaining information on all aspects of the composition of the material. It includes physical methods for determining the chemical composition (i.e. the concentrations of major, minor and trace elements), for identifying the chemical compounds and mineral phases present and for determining the isotopic composition of selected elements.

In the study of artefacts, microscopy, radiography and the full range of analytical techniques are all employed to assist in establishing the identity and geographical source of the raw materials used and to obtain information on the techniques of manufacture. In contrast, in the study of biological material, the primary aims are the identification of the animal and plant species involved and the acquisition of additional information on the biological aspects of man himself from the examination of his skeletal remains. Consequently microscopy and radiography are extensively employed whereas the physical methods of analysis are less relevant.

The techniques of physical examination (p. 197) together with the results obtained for *both* artefacts (p. 206) and biological materials (p. 211) are summarized below. However, the detailed descriptions, provided in the subsequent chapters, are for the most part restricted to the physical examination of artefacts. This follows the traditional emphasis of archaeology in which human cultures were defined in terms of the artefacts or artefactual assemblages that they employed (e.g. Stone Age, Bronze Age and Iron Age). However, in spite of this emphasis on artefacts, the considerable, and perhaps primary, importance of the information gained from the study of biological material must be appreciated. The omission of any detailed description of the physical examination of biological material is justified, in the present context, on the grounds that the study of this material remains the province of the biological sciences, even though many of the techniques now employed derive from the physical sciences. Publications relevant to the study of biological material are included in the bibliography provided at the end of this chapter.

Techniques

A common factor linking many of the techniques of physical examination is that they involve either the interaction of electromagnetic radiation with the material being examined or the emission of characteristic electromagnetic radiation from this material. Electromagnetic radiation, which includes visible light, can be considered either as a wave motion with an associated wavelength and frequency or as a particle (i.e. the photon) with an associated energy. The relationship between the frequency (ν), measured in Hertz (i.e. cycles per second), and the wavelength (λ), measured in metres, is given by:

$$\nu = \frac{c}{\lambda} = \frac{3 \times 10^8}{\lambda} \qquad (7.1)$$

where c (m s^{-1}) is the velocity of light in vacuo. The relationship between the wavelength, measured in metres, and energy of the photon (E), measured in electron-volts (eV), is given by:

$$\lambda = \frac{hc}{1 \cdot 6 \times 10^{-19} E} = \frac{1 \cdot 24 \times 10^{-6}}{E} \qquad (7.2)$$

where h (J s) is Planck's constant.

The spectrum of electromagnetic radiation extends from the short wavelength, high energy gamma rays to the long wavelength, low energy radiowaves and is presented in Fig. 62. From this it can be seen that visible light forms only a minute fraction of the total electromagnetic spectrum.

Because of their equivalent particle-wave duality, the interaction between electrons and matter is in many ways similar to that of electromagnetic radiation and thus provides the basis for further techniques of physical examination. For electrons, the corresponding relationship between the wavelength, measured in metres, and the energy, measured in electron-volts, is, provided relativistic effects can be neglected, given by:

$$\lambda = \frac{h}{(3 \cdot 2 \times 10^{-19} mE)^{1/2}} = \frac{1 \cdot 23 \times 10^{-9}}{E^{1/2}} \qquad (7.3)$$

where m (kg) is the mass of the electron. Therefore 100 keV electrons have an associated wavelength of approximately $3{\cdot}9 \times 10^{-12}$ m

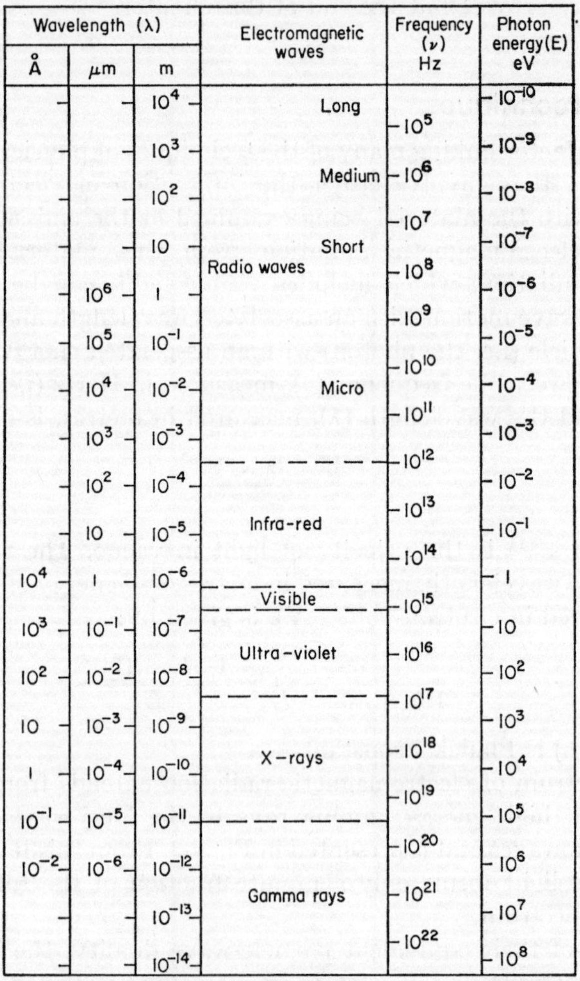

Wavelength (λ) Å	μm	m	Electromagnetic waves	Frequency (ν) Hz	Photon energy(E) eV
		10^4	Long		10^{-10}
				10^5	
		10^3			10^{-9}
			Medium	10^6	
		10^2			10^{-8}
				10^7	
		10	Short		10^{-7}
			Radio waves	10^8	
	10^6	1			10^{-6}
				10^9	
	10^5	10^{-1}			10^{-5}
				10^{10}	
	10^4	10^{-2}	Micro		10^{-4}
				10^{11}	
	10^3	10^{-3}			10^{-3}
				10^{12}	
	10^2	10^{-4}			10^{-2}
				10^{13}	
	10	10^{-5}	Infra-red		10^{-1}
				10^{14}	
10^4	1	10^{-6}			1
			Visible	10^{15}	
10^3	10^{-1}	10^{-7}			10
			Ultra-violet	10^{16}	
10^2	10^{-2}	10^{-8}			10^2
				10^{17}	
10	10^{-3}	10^{-9}			10^3
				10^{18}	
1	10^{-4}	10^{-10}	X-rays		10^4
				10^{19}	
10^{-1}	10^{-5}	10^{-11}			10^5
				10^{20}	
10^{-2}	10^{-6}	10^{-12}			10^6
			Gamma rays	10^{21}	
		10^{-13}			10^7
				10^{22}	
		10^{-14}			10^8

Figure 62. Spectrum of electromagnetic radiation.

which is five orders of magnitude smaller than the wavelength range associated with visible light.

Microscopy and Radiography

The most obvious extension to direct visual examination is the use of the low-power binoncular microscope. Having typically a magnification of up to × 20, this microscope provides a reasonable depth of focus and hence three-dimensional vision. It is invaluable for studying surface markings, such as tool marks on stone and metal artefacts, and for examining the mineral grains in pottery. However, this simple technique should be regarded essentially as a preliminary stage to higher-power optical microscopic examination employing specialized techniques; the details of which depend on the type of material being considered.

For stone and pottery artefacts, a thin section of the material is normally prepared and this is examined in transmitted light using a petrological microscope. The size, shape and arrangement of the mineral grains is thus revealed and identification of the mineral phases present is possible. This data can sometimes be used to establish the source of the raw materials (i.e. rock, clay, tempering material added to the clay), as well as providing, in the case of pottery, information on the techniques of manufacture. For metal artefacts, a polished etched surface is prepared and is examined in reflected light using a metallurgical microscope. This metallographic examination reveals the internal crystal structure of the metal, thus providing information on the methods employed in the fabrication of the artefact.

Biological material is again normally examined in thin section using transmitted light although reflected light is employed in the case of materials exhibiting heavy pigmentation. The thin sections are normally stained with appropriate organic dyes in order to reveal details of the cell structure which is otherwise frequently transparent and colourless. Alternatively phase contrast microscopy can be employed. With this technique, cell structure is revealed as a result of the differential modification of the phase of the light rather than through the differential absorption achieved after staining. The phase contrast results from appreciable optical path differences in different parts of the specimen, the optical path differences being due to differences in refractive index (i.e. optical path length = actual path length × refractive index). The details of the cell structure, revealed by either of these microscopic techniques, is invaluable for the identification of the plant or animal species from which the specimen is derived.

As a result of radiation diffraction effects, the limit of resolution (d metres) of specimen detail for any microscope is given by the relationship:

$$d = 0.61 \frac{\lambda}{n \sin \alpha} \tag{7.4}$$

where λ (m) is the wavelength of the radiation, n is the refractive index of the immersion medium (e.g. $n = 1$ for air) and α is half the angular aperture of the objective lens: $n\sin\alpha$ is described as the "numerical aperture" of the lens. For a typical optical microscope employing visible light of wavelength 0·4 μm (i.e. 4000 Å), the limit of resolution is approximately 0·5 μm and the maximum usable magnification is about × 1000. If a significantly higher resolution is required then it is obvious from equation (7·4) that radiation of much shorter wavelength must be employed. In the electron microscope, high resolution is consequently achieved through the use of high energy electrons (e.g. 100 keV) with wavelengths less than 10^{-5} μm (equation 7·3) rather than electromagnetic radiation.

The transmission electron microscope can be used to provide information on the surface and internal structure of a wide range of artefacts and biological material. Typically the limit of resolution is approximately 5×10^{-4} μm (i.e. 5 Å) and the maximum usable magnification is greater than × 100 000: thus the structural information acquired is far more detailed than that acquired with the optical microscope. However the use of this instrument requires fairly elaborate techniques of specimen preparation, either replicas of the surface or thin sections, less than 0·2 μm in thickness, being employed. The more recent development of the scanning electron microscope is therefore of considerable importance. This instrument, which is in many ways equivalent to the reflected light optical microscope, uses a fine probe of electrons to directly examine the surface microtopography of solid bulk specimens. Thus, although having a lower resolution (about 2×10^{-2} μm, i.e. 200 Å) than the transmission electron microscope, it does not require such elaborate specimen preparation while its large depth of focus (several microns) permits the detailed examination of the rough surfaces frequently associated with archaeological material.

Radiography, in which high energy electromagnetic radiation, such as X-rays and gamma rays, is used to examine the specimen, provides a further extension to direct visual examination. Because of the greater penetration of these types of radiation, as compared to that of visible light, radiographic examination can reveal details of structure and composition invisible to the naked eye. Thus silver and copper inlays to iron artefacts are revealed beneath a conglomeration of corrosion products while, following the example set by modern medicine, palaeo-pathological information can be obtained from the radiographic examination of human and animal bones.

A detailed description of the above techniques together with examples of their application to the study of archaeological artefacts is presented in Chapter 8.

Physical Methods of Analysis

Physical methods of analysis are primarily employed in the study of artefacts and involve the determination of the chemical composition (i.e. chemical analysis), the identification of the chemical compounds and minerals present and the isotopic analysis of selected elements.

The chemical analysis of archaeological artefacts typically involves the determination of the concentrations of selected major elements (greater than 2 per cent), minor elements (2 to 0·01 per cent) and trace elements (less than 0·01 per cent). The major elements normally affect the general character of the artefacts and changes in their concentrations can reflect technological developments. In contrast the pattern of minor and trace element concentrations tends to "characterize" the raw materials used in the manufacture of the artefact and can therefore, in principle, be used to identify the geographical source of these raw materials.

Physical methods of chemical analysis are normally employed in the study of archaeological artefacts since, in comparison with the standard wet chemical methods, they are rapid and essentially non-destructive. The principal physical methods involve the measurement of electromagnetic radiation whose constituent wavelengths can be used to identify the elements present in the specimen and whose intensity at these wavelengths provides an estimate of the concentrations of the associated elements. In optical emission spectrometry and atomic absorption spectrometry, the outer electrons of the constituent atoms are excited and characteristic visible light is emitted and absorbed respectively. In X-ray fluorescence spectrometry, the inner electrons are excited and characteristic X-rays are emitted while in neutron activation analysis, the atomic nuclei are excited and characteristic gamma rays are emitted. For quantitative analysis, a series of standard specimens, whose chemical composition is known and which resemble the composition of the archaeological artefacts as closely as possible, is required. The selection of the most appropriate method is governed by the concentrations and range of elements chosen for analysis which in turn varies according to the type of artefact under investigation. However, it should be emphasized that, in combination, these physical methods can be used to analyse an extremely wide range of elements present at concentrations extending from 100 per cent to less than 0·1 part per million.

In addition to the above methods of chemical analysis, which have fairly general application, a number of more specialized techniques are available. Firstly there is the electron probe microanalyser which effectively combines chemical analysis with microscopic examination. In this instrument, the surface of the specimen is scanned with a fine beam of electrons which excite the inner electrons of the constituent atoms so that characteristic X-rays are emitted. By measuring the intensity of these X-rays, the distribution of selected elements across the surface of the specimen can be determined on a microscopic scale (resolution about 1 μm). The technique is therefore used in the examination of inclusions in metals and glass as well as in the study of paint pigments. Secondly, specific gravity and beta ray back-scattering measurements can be used to provide an indication of the chemical composition when only a very limited number of elements are present. The former technique is employed in the study of silver and gold coins while the latter is used for the determination of the lead concentration in glass and glaze.

The identification of the mineral phases and chemical compounds, both inorganic and organic, present in an artefact again provides information on the nature and source of the raw materials and in the case of pottery, on the techniques used in manufacture. In X-ray diffraction, the sample is bombarded with monochromatic X-rays which are diffracted at different angles depending on the crystal lattice structure. Therefore study of the resulting diffraction pattern permits the identification of the mineral phases present in the sample. In infra-red absorption spectrometry, identification is possible because the spectrum of infra-red radiation absorbed by the specimen is determined by the pattern of vibrations executed by the constituent atoms and is therefore characteristic of the chemical compounds and mineral phases present. Both these techniques can be used to identify a wide range of chemical compounds. In contrast, Mössbauer spectroscopy is limited to the study of iron compounds, principally in pottery. The technique involves the measurement of the gamma rays absorbed by the iron nuclei and information on the oxidation state of the iron is obtained since the wavelength of the absorbed gamma rays is characteristic of the local crystallographic symmetry around the iron atoms. Related to these techniques are the various methods of thermal analysis which involve the investigation of the physical and chemical changes occurring when a specimen is heated from room temperature to approximately 1000°C. Thermal analysis is again employed principally in the study of pottery in order to obtain information on the firing conditions used in its manufacture.

Isotopic analysis of archaeological artefacts, using mass spectrometry techniques, is normally confined to the elements, lead and oxygen. The relative abundance of the four lead isotopes (^{204}Pb, ^{206}Pb, ^{207}Pb and ^{208}Pb) varies significantly between different ore sources, depending in part on their age of formation. Consequently, measurement of their relative abundance in lead-containing specimens (e.g. metal, glass, glaze, pigment) is useful for identifying the source of the ore from which the lead was smelted. The ratio of the oxygen isotopes, ^{18}O and ^{16}O, also varies significantly according to the material in which the oxygen is found. Since oxygen is the most abundant element in glass, oxygen isotopic ratio measurements provide an index for classifying ancient glass and possibly an indication of the source of the raw materials. In addition, the oxygen isotopic analysis of marine mollusc shells found on archaeological sites provides information on the aquatic environment in which the molluscs grew.

A detailed description of the above techniques is provided in Chapter 9, while examples of their application to the study of archaeological artefacts are discussed in Chapter 10.

Chromatography

Chromatography is the name given to a family of analytical techniques which involve the separation of a mixture of substances as a result of their different rates of movement along a column of solid or liquid. The term chromatography stems from the fact that the method was originally used for the separation of coloured substances. However, the method is nowadays more often applied to mixtures of colourless substances, including gases, and in conjunction with infrared absorption spectrometry, it is of prime importance for the identification of the organic compounds encountered in archaeological artefacts.

In paper chromatography, a drop of a solution, containing the mixture of organic substances to be separated, is placed at one end of a strip of filter paper. This end of the filter paper is then immersed in a specially selected solvent which percolates through the fibres of the paper by capillary action and moves the components of the mixture to different extents in the direction of flow. The components are thus separated into distinct zones or spots along the strip of filter paper and can be detected by applying a suitable reagent which reacts to give coloured zones or spots. The position along the strip of a particular substance depends on its solubility in the cellulose-bound water associated with the filter paper compared to that in the moving solvent: if the substance has a high solubility in the water, it moves only a short distance whereas if it has a high solubility in the solvent, it moves almost as far as the solvent itself. Therefore the substance associated with each zone or spot can be identified on the basis of its position relative to the position reached by the solvent, typically through comparison with the positions of the spots associated with known reference substances (Fig. 63).

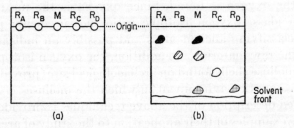

(a)   (b)

Figure 63. Paper chromatography. (a) Starting situation with a drop of solution (M), containing the mixture of organic substances to be analysed, placed at one end of a filter paper, together with drops of known reference solutions (R_A, R_B, R_C and R_D). (b) Final situation after solvent has percolated through the filter paper and separated the components of the mixture (M). Comparison of the positions of the spots associated with the mixture with those associated with the reference substances provides the basis for identification. In this example, the mixture (M) contains the reference substances, R_A, R_B and R_D but not R_C.

Gas chromatography is used for the separation of mixtures of gases and volatile liquids. The mixture is introduced at one end of a column which is filled with a porous material coated with an organic liquid. The components of the mixture are then carried through the column at different rates by a stream of pure gas, such as nitrogen or argon. The various components are thus separated and emerge from the column at different time intervals after the introduction of the mixture, a plot of the quantity of gas emerging *versus* time being obtained using a suitable gas detector (Fig. 64). The length of time taken for a particular component to travel through the column depends on its "solubility" (i.e. partition coefficient) in the organic liquid in the column compared to that in the carrier gas. Therefore the substance associated with each peak on the detector record can be identified on the basis of the time taken to emerge from the column, comparison with the peaks associated with known reference mixtures again being possible. The column can be maintained at a constant temperature between 20 and 400°C, the choice of temperature being governed by the volatility of the substances under consideration. Alternatively, if the mixture contains substances with a wide range of volatilities, the temperature of the column can be raised progressively as separation proceeds.

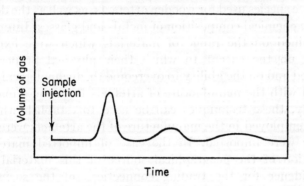

Figure 64. Gas chromatography record showing the volume of sample gas emerging from the liquid column *versus* time, zero signal being obtained from the gas detector when pure carrier gas is passing through it. Each peak represents the emergence of a particular component of the sample mixture. The various components in the mixture are identified on the basis of the time intervals (typically several minutes) between the sample injection and their emergence from the column.

In addition to the above methods of chromatography, which involve partition between a stationary liquid phase and a mobile liquid or gas phase (i.e. paper/liquid–liquid and gas–liquid chromatography respectively), there are two other basic physical systems. These involve a stationary solid phase, separation being achieved through the differential absorption between this solid phase and a mobile liquid or gas phase (i.e. liquid–solid and gas–solid chromatography respectively). Furthermore, there are many modifications of the experimental arrangement which can be employed with each of the four basic methods. For example, a column of liquid supported on a solid matrix can be employed for liquid–liquid chromatography instead of using a filter paper while either a column or a thin layer of powder, coated on a glass slide, can be employed for liquid–solid chromatography.

Artefacts

In the study of archaeological artefacts, both microscopy and the full range of analytical techniques provide important information. Firstly, these techniques assist in the identification of the materials from which the artefacts were made. This includes the identification of the rock type used for stone artefacts, the minerals used for paint pigments and the tree species used for wooden artefacts, as well as the determination of the chemical composition of metals and glasses. Information is thus obtained on the range of materials which were exploited in antiquity, on the extent to which their physical properties were appreciated and on the ability to overcome the technological problems associated with the manufacture of artefacts from these materials.

Secondly, these techniques can be used to establish whether the materials employed in the manufacture of the artefacts were obtained locally or were imported. In the case of imported materials, the identification of the geographical source of this material provides direct evidence for the trading connections of the society under consideration and by inference, information on its social and economic organization. In using the term "trade" it must be emphasized that this does not necessarily imply the existence of full-time professional traders since this concept is probably inappropriate to most prehistoric communities. Furthermore, it is not always possible to decide with complete certainty whether it was the raw material itself or the artefact manufactured from it that was imported. Therefore the term "trade" is employed in the widest possible sense to describe any transfer of raw materials or artefacts away from some central source.

Finally, physical examination of artefacts provides information on the techniques used in their fabrication. These data, together with that obtained from the identification of the materials employed in their manufacture, provide an indication of the technological capabilities and the stage of technological development of the society under consideration.

As summarized in Table 15, the relative importance of these three principal areas of investigation, as well as the most appropriate techniques for physical examination, varies according to the material and type of artefact under consideration.

Table 15. Principal techniques appropriate to the physical examination of archaeological artefacts

Artefact type	Area of investigation			
	Identification of raw materials	Geographical source of raw materials	Techniques of fabrication	
Stone artefacts	Petrological examination X-ray diffraction	Petrological examination Chemical analysis (mn–tr)[a]	—	
Pottery	Petrological examination	Petrological examination Chemical analysis (mn–tr)	Petrological examination X-ray diffraction Mössbauer spectroscopy Thermal analysis	
Metal artefacts	Chemical analysis (mj–mn) Specific gravity	Chemical analysis (mn–tr) Isotopic analysis (Pb)	Metallographic examination	
Glass, glaze, faience	Chemical analysis (mj–mn) Isotopic analysis (O)	—	—	
Colorants, pigments	Chemical analysis (mj–mn) X-ray diffraction Infra-red spectrometry	Chemical analysis (mn–tr)		
Biological—wood, bone, skins, fibres, shell, amber	Optical microscopy	Isotopic analysis (shell: O and C) Infra-red spectrometry (amber) Chromatography (amber)	—	
Biological—adhesives, varnishes, etc.	Infra-red spectrometry Chromatography	—		

[a] Chemical analysis refers to the generally applicable methods (i.e. optical emission spectrometry, atomic absorption spectrometry, X-ray fluorescence spectrometry and neutron activation analysis) described on pp. 260–278; mj, mn and tr refer to the analysis of the major, minor and trace elements respectively.

Stone Artefacts

Direct visual examination is frequently sufficient for the identification of the general type of rock (e.g. granite, volcanic tuff, sandstone, flint, obsidian) used for stone artefacts. However, in order to identify the precise source of the rock, a fuller determination of the mineral composition and texture of the rock by means of petrological examination in thin section is necessary, the identification being based on the comparison of the artefact with samples of possible source material. When diagnostic differences between the same rock type from different deposits exist, as is the case for many igneous rocks, the geographical source of the material used to make the artefacts can be established with considerable precision.

Unfortunately fine textured rocks and glasses, such as flint and obsidian, are not amenable to petrological examination. However, since different deposits of the same rock type can often be distinguished by their chemical composition, it is possible to group together artefacts made from rock from a particular deposit on the basis of the pattern of concentrations of the minor and trace elements: similarly it is possible to differentiate between artefacts made from rock from different deposits. Subsequently, it is sometimes possible, through the comparison of the concentration patterns of the artefacts with those of samples from known deposits, to identify the actual geographical source of the material used to make the artefacts. However, due to variations in the concentrations of minor and trace elements within a particular deposit and also similarities in the concentrations for different deposits, this identification of the source is often less clear-cut than that which can be achieved for rock types amenable to petrological examination.

Pottery

Petrological examination of pottery in thin section is used, in the first instance, to establish whether any coarse material (i.e. temper) has been added to the clay in order to facilitate firing. In addition, the minerals and rock fragments used as temper, as well as those occurring naturally in the raw clay, can be readily identified. Therefore, if they are sufficiently distinctive, the geographical source of the tempering material or the clay can be satisfactorily established as in the case of the rock used to make stone artefacts. However, for fine textured pottery or pottery containing only quartz sand inclusions, chemical analysis for the minor and trace elements again provides the only method of grouping together pottery made from the same clay and ultimately identifying the clay source.

Petrological examination is also invaluable for establishing the method of forming the pottery (e.g. wheel-thrown, coil-built) and the conditions prevailing during firing. More precise data on the firing temperatures employed and the atmospheric conditions during firing can be obtained using the various methods of thermal analysis, X-ray diffraction or Mössbauer spectroscopy.

Metals

The determination of the concentrations of the major and minor elements is of considerable importance in the study of metal artefacts, since changes in the composition of the copper alloys or the iron, used by the ancient metal-workers, are indicative of technological developments. In addition, changes in the composition of silver and gold coins can provide information on the debasement of the currency and hence evidence for the economic difficulties encountered by early societies.

Although it should, in principle, be possible to group together metal artefacts made from the same ore on the basis of the concentrations of minor and trace elements, the results obtained are less reliable than in the case of stone artefacts and pottery. A major problem in using analytical data to identify metal ore sources is the fact that the concentrations of minor and trace elements in the finished artefact also depend on the method of smelting employed. In addition, since scrap metal was frequently re-used, metals from widely differing sources may well become mixed in the same artefact. An important feature of the use of isotopic analysis for the identification of lead sources is the fact that the relative abundance of the lead isotopes, unlike the concentrations of the impurities, does not depend on the method of smelting.

Metallographic examination of polished etched surfaces is the principal technique for studying the methods used in the fabrication of metal artefacts. Information is obtained on the method of casting employed as well as on the subsequent mechanical and thermal treatment to which the artefact was subjected.

Glass, Glaze and Faience

In the study of glass, glaze and faience, which are produced by sintering or fusing finely ground quartz (e.g. sand) with various modifying oxides (e.g. soda, potash, lime), the determination of the concentrations of selected major and minor elements is of prime importance in establishing their general character.

For glass, the variations in the concentrations of, for example, potassium, magnesium, lead, antimony and manganese reflect the different glass-making traditions in different parts of the world at different periods in time. Further information on the different glass-making traditions is provided by measurement of the relative abundance of the oxygen isotopes. Similarly from the chemical analysis of glazes, the different types of glaze (e.g. lead, soda–lime and potash–lime glazes) which were commonly employed can be identified.

Colorants and Pigments

Chemical analysis is used to identify the elements (e.g. copper, cobalt, iron) present in the colorants used in glass, glaze and faience, as well as those in the pigments employed for paintings. In addition, X-ray diffraction and infra-red absorption spectroscopy are used to identify the actual chemical compounds employed as paint pigments as well as those formed in glass. Again this information can be used to establish the different types of colorant used by different cultural groups, while, in some instances, the different geographical sources for the raw materials can be distinguished.

The electron probe microanalyser is also of considerable importance in the study of colorants and pigments since, with this instrument, adjacent areas of different colour or superimposed layers of pigment can be resolved and therefore analysed separately.

Artefacts derived from Biological Material

In the case of artefacts made from biological materials, such as wood, bone, skin and animal or vegetable fibres, the principal aim of physical examination is to assist in the identification of the species of plant or animal involved, the appropriate microscopy techniques being discussed on p. 212. In addition, physical methods of analysis can, in specific instances, be used to establish the geographical source of the biological material employed in the making of artefacts. For example, the ocean or sea in which mollusc shells, used as ornaments (e.g. beads), originated can sometimes be identified by means of oxygen isotopic analysis. Similarly infra-red absorption spectrometry and gas chromatography have been employed in an attempt to distinguish the various sources of the fossilized tree resin, amber, used extensively for making beads and other personal ornaments.

Infra-red absorption spectrometry and the various methods of chromatography are also used to identify the minor organic components, such as adhesives, varnishes and binding media, employed in the fabrication of artefacts. With these techniques it is normally possible to distinguish between the main types of organic material which include animal waxes; animal fats and oils; gelatinous protein material (e.g. animal glues and egg-yolk); gums and resins derived from plant material and bitumen. However, further identification of the precise animal and plant origins of the different materials within these main groups is rather more difficult, even when the materials have not changed chemically as a result of exposure to the atmosphere.

Biological Materials

The physical examination of the biological material found on archaeological sites is concerned principally with the reconstruction of the floral and faunal environment through the identification of the plant and animal species, together with the anatomical and pathological study of human bones. Although much of the required information can be obtained by direct visual examination, a number of physical techniques must be employed in order to extract the maximum amount of information from the available material. Optical microscopy and radiography are of particular importance in this context while it seems probable that, in the future, scanning electron microscopy will provide valuable additional information.

Plants and Animals

Since human life is intimately related to and dependent upon the environment, the reconstruction of the floral and faunal environment in the past is of fundamental importance to archaeology. In the first place, a knowledge of the prevailing plant and animal species permits the reconstruction of the past climatic conditions. Secondly, the available plant and animal life provides the basis for man's subsistence in terms of food, shelter and clothing. Thirdly, the effect of man on his environment is revealed through the examination of the plant and animal record. Of particular relevance, with regard to food and the modification of the environment, is the development of cultivated cereals and domesticated animals from the "wild" species, together with the associated deforestation of the landscape.

Analysis of the tree, shrub and grass pollens, which are retained in stratigraphic sequence in, for example, lake sediments and peat bogs, provides the main source of information on the past floral environment. After extraction of the pollen grains from the soil deposit, the various types of pollen in the sample can be identified and enumerated by examination under the optical microscope (Plate 16). The resulting pollen diagram (p. 71) provides a clear indication of the vegetational pattern that existed at the time of deposition. Further information on the floral environment, as well as man's employment of its products, is provided through the identification of seeds, cereal grains, fruit, vegetable fibres (e.g. cotton and bast fibres) and wood fragments. In the case of wood and fibres, the identification of the plant species is achieved through the examination of the cell structure, cell arrangement and cell size in thin section under an optical microscope.

Information on the past faunal environment is obtained chiefly through the study and identification of animal bones. Further data concerning the animals in contact with man are obtained from the microscopic examination of surviving skins and animal fibres. The species of animals from which the skin was obtained can often be identified on the basis of the form and arrangement of the hair roots (i.e. follicles). Similarly the pattern of scales on the surface of animal fibres and the form of the central medulla provide diagnostic features for identifying the animals species involved and in the case of sheep, for distinguishing between the different varieties.

Coprolites (i.e. fossil faecal remains) provide an extremely valuable source of floral and faunal material and at the same time provide direct information on the diet of ancient man. Seed-cases, the wing-cases of small beetles and fragments of shell and bone, for example, can be extracted from the coprolites for identification while microscopic examination can reveal traces of animal and plant tissue.

Man

Information on the biological aspects of man in the past is obtained primarily from the study of his skeletal remains. In addition to providing the basis for studying the evolution of *Homo sapiens*, the physical stature, sex and age at death, together with information on injuries and diseases suffered, can all be inferred from the examination of skeletal remains. Palaeopathological studies are of particular interest since, in addition to revealing healed fractures and traumatic injuries leading to death, bones also contain a record of a wide range of "diseases". These include tuberculosis, syphilis, leprosy, arthritis and poliomyelitis as well as diseases, such as rickets, associated with dietary deficiencies; endocrine disorders, such as dwarfism (i.e. hypopituitarism), and congenital disorders, such as those associated with skull formation (e.g. hydrocephaly and microcephaly).

Although much of this information can be obtained by direct visual examination, it is supplemented by the data provided by X-ray radiography. For example, dental radiography is important in estimating the exact age of non-adult skulls and also facilitates the detection of any unerupted teeth. Similarly radiography of bones can assist in confirming the diagnosis of injuries and diseases, distinguishing, for example, between bone swellings associated with healed fractures and those associated with tuberculous abscesses.

In addition to its importance in the examination of individual bones, X-ray radiography is extremely valuable in the study of Egyptian and Peruvian mummies. In the first place, it is possible to establish whether or not a skeleton exists within the wrappings and also whether any jewellery is incorporated within the wrappings. Secondly, if a skeleton exists, the determination of its physical stature, sex and age at death, together with the identification of any pathological features, can be achieved directly without entailing the laborious task of unwrapping the mummy.

Select Bibliography

General

Brothwell, D. and Higgs, E. S. (Eds.) (1969). "Science in Archaeology", Thames and Hudson, London.
Goodyear, F. H. (1971). "Archaeological Site Science", Heinemann, London.

Techniques

Stock, R. and Rice, C. B. F. (1963). "Chromatographic Methods", Chapman and Hall, London.
Zussman, J. (Ed.) (1967). "Physical Methods in Determinative Mineralogy", Academic Press, London.

Artefacts

Aitchison, L. (1960). "A History of Metals", Macdonald and Evans, London.
Hodges, H. W. M. (1964). "Artifacts", John Baker, London.

Hodges, H. (1970). "Technology in the Ancient World", Penguin Press, London.
Lucas, A. (1962). "Ancient Egyptian Materials and Industries", Edward Arnold, London.
Rosenfeld, A. (1965). "The Inorganic Raw Materials of Antiquity", Weidenfeld and Nicolson, London.
Shepard, A. O. (1968). "Ceramics for the Archaeologist", Carnegie Inst., Washington.
Tylecote, R. F. (1962). "Metallurgy in Archaeology", Edward Arnold, London.

Biological Materials

Brothwell, D. (Ed.) (1968). "The Skeletal Biology of Earlier Human Populations", Pergamon, Oxford.
Chaplin, R. E. (1971). "The Study of Animal Bones from Archaeological Sites", Seminar Press, London.
Dimbleby, G. W. (1967). "Plants and Archaeology", John Baker, London.
Janssens, P. A. (1970). "Palaeopathology—Diseases and Injuries of Prehistoric Man", John Baker, London.
Ucko, P. J. and Dimbleby, G. W. (Eds.) (1969). "The Domestication and Exploitation of Plants and Animals", Duckworth, London.

8
Microscopy and Radiography

Microscopy and radiography represent a natural extension to direct visual examination and provide additional data on archaeological material which is essentially of a descriptive and qualitative nature. The principles and techniques of petrological microscopy (p. 215), metallographic microscopy (p. 230), electron microscopy (p. 242), and radiography (p. 252) are described below together with examples of the application of these techniques to the study of artefacts.

Petrological Microscopy

In an archaeological context, petrological examination (Hartshorne and Stuart, 1970) is primarily employed for the identification of the rocks used for stone artefacts and the minerals or rock fragments found in the clay matrix of pottery. This identification is achieved by examining a thin section, cut from the artefact, in transmitted light using a petrological (i.e. polarizing) microscope and the ultimate aim is normally to establish the precise geographical source of the raw materials used. In addition, in the study of pottery, microscopic examination in thin section can provide valuable information on the techniques employed in its manufacture.

Experimental Procedures

In order to obtain a thin section for microscopic examination a slice, approximately 1 mm in thickness and 2 cm^2 in area, is first cut from the artefact. In the case of highly porous, friable pottery, impregnation with a plastic may be necessary in order to prevent disintegration during the subsequent polishing. One side of the slice is polished with progressively finer grades of abrasive until perfectly flat and mirror smooth. The polished face is then stuck onto a glass slide using a suitable adhesive and the other face is gradually abraded away until the slice is approximately 30 μm thick.

The majority of the minerals present are transparent at this thickness (Plates 17 and 18) and the thin section can be examined in transmitted light using a petrological microscope (Fig. 65). This microscope

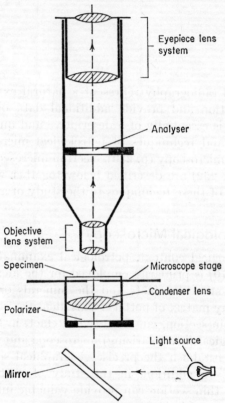

Figure 65. Schematic diagram showing the principal components of a petrological (i.e. polarizing) microscope.

differs from the normal optical microscope through the addition of a polarizer and analyser. Light from a suitable source is reflected by a mirror through the polarizer and is focussed onto the thin section by means of the condenser lens. Magnification, typically in the range × 20 to × 200, is achieved through the objective and eyepiece lens systems, between which is placed the analyser. Both the stage on which the thin section is mounted and the polarizer can be rotated and are graduated in degrees.

The light emitted by ordinary sources, such as the sun and filament lamps, is unpolarized since the associated vibrations (i.e. the oscillating electromagnetic field) occur in all possible directions perpendicular to the direction of propagation of the light wave. The action of the polarizer and analyser, which are typically Nicol prisms or Polaroid filters, is to transmit light vibrating in one direction only, the light then being referred to as plane polarized. The polarizer and analyser are normally arranged so that the vibration directions which they transmit are perpendicular (i.e. crossed polars). Therefore, in the absence of a thin section, light from the polarizer is not transmitted through the analyser. However, as discussed below, many minerals can effectively rotate the direction of vibration so that some light is then transmitted through the analyser.

Principles of Mineral and Rock Identification

Minerals are clearly defined substances in which the constituent atoms are arranged in an orderly manner to form a regular three-dimensional lattice structure. Although the chemical composition of a mineral phase can vary to a certain extent, the regular lattice structure of minerals provides a precise characteristic which can be used in their identification. Rocks, which are made up of a close aggregate of mineral grains, are first grouped into igneous, metamorphic and sedimentary types depending on their mode of formation and are subsequently classified according to the mineral phases present and the size, shape and arrangement of the mineral grains. A detailed survey of the minerals and rocks relevant to archaeology, together with a description of those macroscopic properties which can assist in their identification, is provided by Rosenfeld (1965).

The principal rock-forming minerals, which need to be identified, can be broadly classified as follows:

(i) quartz (crystalline silica—SiO_2);

(ii) silicate minerals, such as felspars, micas, pyroxenes, amphiboles and olivines, which are complex compounds of metallic elements (e.g. potassium, sodium, calcium, aluminium, magnesium, iron) with silicon and oxygen;

(iii) hydrous silicates, such as the clay minerals (e.g. kaolinite, montmorillonite, illite), serpentine and talc, which are formed by the action of water on existing silicates;

(iv) soluble products of chemical weathering such as calcite (calcium carbonate), dolomite (calcium–magnesium carbonate), gypsum (hydrated calcium sulphate) and flint (cryptocrystalline silica);

(v) metal ores such as malachite (hydrated copper carbonate), cassiterite (tin oxide), galena (lead sulphide), pyrite (iron sulphide), siderite (iron carbonate) and limonite (hydrated iron oxide).

In the identification of minerals in thin section using the petrological microscope, the principal diagnostic features considered are crystal shape, cleavage planes (i.e. planes of weakness along which the crystal is liable to fracture or cleave) and the optical properties in plane polarized light. Identification through shape is only of limited use because, in rocks, the minerals can rarely grow into well-formed crystals. In addition, the shape actually observed depends on the crystal plane cut by the thin section and is thus somewhat arbitrary. However, since there is an intimate connection between cleavage and

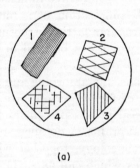

(a)   (b)

Figure 66. Identification of minerals in thin section. (a) Cleavage lines observed in ordinary light for (1) mica, (2) calcite, (3) pyroxene (augite) and (4) amphibole (hornblende). Viewed at different crystal orientations, the hornblende would exhibit cleavage at 120 degrees and the augite would exhibit parallel cleavage.
(b) Twinning, observed between crossed polars, for (1) plagioclase felspar (albite), (2) pyroxene (diopside) and (3) gypsum. The dark and bright regions in the minerals are associated with differences in crystallographic orientation.

crystal form, the cleavage lines, which appear in thin sections as striae crossing the crystal, do provide a valuable diagnostic feature. For example, the flaky plate-like character of mica produces clear cleavage lines in one direction only whereas calcite fractures along three crystal planes and exhibits a characteristic rhombohedral cleavage pattern (Fig. 66a).

When considering the transmission of plane polarized light through minerals, the fundamental difference between the properties of iso-topic and anisotropic minerals must first be understood. The velocity of light in isotropic media is independent of the direction of propaga-tion and therefore no change in the vibration direction of the polarized light occurs when it passes through an isotropic material. In contrast the velocity of light in anisotropic media varies with the direction of propagation and as a consequence, the phenomenon of double refrac-tion or birefringence is normally observed when light passes through an anisotropic mineral. A ray of light entering such a mineral is divided into two rays which travel through the mineral with different velocities and which are plane polarized such that their vibration directions are perpendicular to one another. In using these optical phenomena as the basis for mineral identification, it should be noted that glasses and minerals belonging to the cubic crystal system are isotropic while all non-cubic minerals (i.e. the tetragonal, trigonal, hexagonal, orthorhombic, monoclinic and triclinic crystal systems) are anisotropic.

By examining the thin section in plane polarized light with the analyser removed, some anisotropic minerals can be identified as a result of their characteristic pleochroism. Pleochroism refers to the different degrees of absorption suffered by the two polarized compon-ents into which a ray of light is resolved on entering an anisotropic mineral and produces a change in the colour of the mineral when it is rotated on the microscope stage. Isotropic minerals do not exhibit pleochroism since their absorption is independent of the vibration direction of the polarized light.

Isotropic and anisotropic minerals can be distinguished and many anisotropic minerals can be identified by examining the thin section in plane polarized light between crossed polars. The vibration direction of the light from the polarizer is unaltered as a result of passing through isotropic minerals and is not therefore transmitted by the analyser (Fig. 67a): isotropic minerals consequently appear dark or extinct for all positions of the microscope stage. In contrast, the light from the polarizer is, in anisotropic minerals, resolved into two com-ponents with vibration directions perpendicular to one another (Fig. 67b). Since these two components travel with different velocities, they emerge from the mineral with a phase difference or relative retardation and therefore produce a resultant component with a vibration direction parallel to the analyser direction: an anisotropic mineral consequently appears bright and coloured. If the mineral is now rotated on the microscope stage, it becomes dark or extinct in four positions at intervals of 90 degrees, extinction occurring when the vibration directions of the two components in the mineral are parallel to

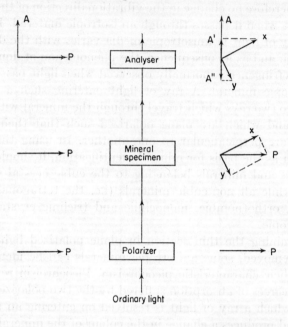

(a) Isotropic mineral   (b) Anisotropic mineral

Figure 67. Examination of minerals in thin section between crossed polars. The heavy arrows indicate the polarization directions of the light, the length of the arrows representing the amplitude of the light vibrations. (a) Isotropic mineral. The direction of the polarization of the light (P) is unchanged by the mineral so that there is no component parallel to the analyser direction (A). Therefore no light is transmitted by the analyser and the mineral appears dark.

(b) Anisotropic mineral. The polarized light (P) is resolved into two components (X and Y) in the mineral so that there are two components (A' and A") parallel to the analyser direction (A). As a result of the different velocities of the X and Y components in the mineral, there is a phase difference between the A' and A" components. Therefore, even though these components have the same amplitudes, they do not cancel to zero. Consequently light is transmitted by the analyser and the mineral appears bright.

those of the polarizer and analyser directions. The colours exhibited between these extinction positions are known as interference colours. They arise because the light transmitted through the analyser reaches its maximum intensity for those wavelengths (λ) of the incident white light for which the relative retardation of the two components equals $\lambda/2, 3\lambda/2, 5\lambda/2$, etc. The interference colour observed therefore depends on the thickness of the mineral (d) and the difference in the refractive indices (refractive index = velocity in vacuo/velocity in medium) of the two components, the relative retardation (R) being given by:

$$R = d(n_1 - n_2)$$

where n_1 and n_2 are the two refractive indices.

Although the theory for the above phenomena is rather complex, it is possible to identify anisotropic minerals by studying the interference colours produced, together with the interference figures which are observed when the thin sections are examined in convergent, rather than parallel, light. A further phenomena which assists in the identification of anisotropic minerals, when examined between crossed polars, is the presence of twinned crystals. Twinned crystals are groups of two or more crystals in which the individual crystals grow together symmetrically so that they share a common plane, while being orientated differently. As a result of this difference in orientation, twinned crystals appear as parallel bands which alternately become bright and extinct as the microscope stage is rotated (Fig. 66b).

The identification of the constituent minerals is, of course, only the first step towards the classification of a rock or rock fragment and the relative proportions, size, shape and arrangement of the different mineral grains observed in the thin section must also be considered. Igneous rocks (Table 16), in which the principal minerals are quartz and silicates, are first classified on the basis of the amount of silica present. Quartz and alkali felspars predominate in acid rocks, which are rich in silica, while plagioclase felspars and the mafic silicates (i.e. micas, amphiboles, pyroxenes and olivines) predominate in basic rocks, which are poor in silica. Within each category in the acid-basic sequence, igneous rocks are further subdivided according to their texture (i.e. grain size and shape). The mineralogical compositions of metamorphic rocks obviously depend on the parent rocks from which they originated but again quartz and silicates together with hydrous silicates, formed as a result of the metamorphism, are the predominant minerals. The subdivision of metamorphic rocks into gneisses and schists is based on their textural characteristics which are related to the shear stresses, and consequent folding, associated with metamorphism. Gneisses exhibit a coarsely banded structure whereas schists exhibit a much more distinct banding and alignment of the minerals. The mineralogical compositions of sedimentary rocks again vary widely depending on the parent rock or rocks. Sedimentary rocks formed from the insoluble products of weathering are classified into conglomerates, sandstones, shales and mudstones on the basis of their particle size distribution: the predominant minerals being quartz, felspars, micas and clay minerals. In contrast, the calcareous rocks (e.g. limestone, chalk) contain mainly calcite, although varying amounts of sand and clay are also present.

Table 16. Simplified classification of igneous rocks

	Acid	Intermediate[a]		Basic
Coarse	Granite	Syenite	Diorite	Gabbro
Medium	Microgranite	Microsyenite	Microdiorite	Diabase
				Dolerite
Fine	Rhyolite	Trachyte	Andesite	Basalt

[a] The two groups of intermediate rocks can be distinguished on the basis of the types of felspar that they contain: the first group (i.e. syenite, etc.) contains predominantly alkali felspars while the second group (i.e. diorite, etc.) contains predominantly plagioclase felspars, together with a higher concentration of mafic minerals.

Stone Artefacts

The primary aim, in the petrological examination of thin sections cut from stone artefacts, is to identify the geographical source of the rock used and thus obtain information on the extent to which stone artefacts were traded and transported away from the source of the raw material.

Identification of the rock source involves the comparison of thin sections cut from the stone artefact with those from possible source material. Artefacts made from igneous and metamorphic rocks are particularly suitable since these rocks possess a large number of diagnostic features which enable the source to be defined within very close limits; provided, of course, that detailed information on the geology of the region under consideration is available. In contrast, artefacts made from sedimentary rocks, such as pure limestones and sandstones, present more difficulty since these rocks can outcrop over a wide area or in several localities. The different outcrops may have the same mineralogy and consequently the possible sources of the rock used in the artefact remain numerous. This problem is also particularly severe in the case of artefacts made from fine-textured or homogeneous rock, such as flint and obsidian. The numerous sources of these materials cannot be distinguished by petrological examination and therefore chemical analysis for the minor and trace elements provides the most appropriate method for characterizing flint and obsidian sources (Chapter 10, p. 307).

A further difficulty, which is relevant to the classic application of petrological examination to the "bluestones" erected at Stonehenge, arises as a result of the presence of rock erratics which have been transported over large distances by glaciation. Because of the presence of characteristic irregularly spaced white and pink felspar in the otherwise undistinctive dolerite, Thomas (1923) was able to establish that the bluestones at Stonehenge came from the Prescelly Mountains of Pembrokeshire. Furthermore, Thomas rejected the possibility of glacial transport and it has therefore become accepted that the bluestones were transported, the 150 miles from Pembrokeshire to Wiltshire, by boat or raft either via the Severn estuary and Bristol Avon or around Land's End, an operation requiring considerable nautical skill and social organization. However, Kellaway (1971) has recently re-examined the geological evidence for glaciation in south-western Britain and has come to the conclusion that ice-sheets, carrying rock erratics from South Wales, extended into Wiltshire during the Lowestoftian–Elsterian glacial phase. He has therefore suggested that the bluestones, as well as the other non-indigenous stones (i.e. Old Red Sandstone, quartzite, greywacke, rhyolite, volcanic ash) at Stonehenge, were transported to the Salisbury Plain as a result of this glaciation and existed in the Stonehenge region as glacial erratics during the Neolithic period.

A major project during the past thirty years has been the petrological examination of more than one thousand stone axes found in Britain and dating from the Neolithic period and Early Bronze Age (Keiller et al., 1941; Evens et al., 1962). On the basis of their mineralogical composition and texture (Plate 17), it has been possible to group together artefacts made from the same rock type. More than twenty such groups have been identified to date and in several instances, the precise location of the rock source has been established. For example, it was found that the rock used for one group (Group VI: Great Langdale Group) belonged geologically to the bedded tuffs of the Borrowdale Volcanic Series since the thin sections exhibited the characteristic matrix of isotropic material embedded with grains of epidote felspar, cryptocrystalline silica and quartz. Subsequent support for this petrological identification was, in this case, provided by the discovery of several working floors, covered with unfinished axes and rough-outs, in the region of Great Langdale. The distribution of the Great Langdale axes covers a wide area, including southern Scotland, Antrim, the Isle of Man, the Lake District, Wessex, South Wales, the Midlands and East Anglia. The location of the rock source has not been established with such precision, nor has confirmatory archaeological evidence been obtained, for all the groups identified. However, the project has been of considerable value in establishing the various "trade routes" that operated in Britain during the Neolithic and Early Bronze Age.

The related study of the jade axes found in Britain has produced less conclusive results (Campbell Smith, 1963). In this case petrological examination was supplemented by X-ray diffraction, density and refractive index measurements and chemical analysis. It was shown that the vast majority of the axes found in Britain was made from jadeite (a pyroxene mineral) rather than nephrite (an amphibole mineral). Since there are no sources of jadeite in Britain, it has been assumed that the axes were imported in a finished condition from Europe, where jade axes are known from Brittany and other parts of France and from north-west Europe and Switzerland. Petrological examination has established a mineralogical similarity between some of the jade axes found in Britain and those from Brittany. However, petrological examination of rocks found in Brittany and other parts of Europe, which were considered to be possible sources of the jadeite, has established that these rocks differ mineralogically from the jadeite axes. Therefore, the sources of the jadeite used to make the western European and British axes have yet to be located.

Pottery

The minerals and rock fragments, which either occur naturally in the raw clay or have been added as temper, can be identified by means of petrological examination of thin sections cut from the pottery. Consequently, as in the case of stone artefacts, the geographical source of the raw materials used to make the pottery can sometimes be established. In addition, since clays have been radically altered by man in the manufacture of pottery, the examination of thin sections is invaluable for research into ancient ceramic technology.

Source of raw materials. Many applications of petrological examination to the identification of the raw materials used in the manufacture of pottery have been reported. The classic example, which first established the importance of this technique in archaeology, is the study of the Rio Grande Glaze-Paint pottery of New Mexico (Shepard, 1942). Because of the varied geology, it was possible to distinguish the products of different regions on the basis of the rock temper; materials such as andesite, basalt, tuff and sandstone having been added to the clay according to their local availability. It was thus possible to relate the ceramic sequence to cultural innovations at specific localities and to changes in trade patterns.

Peacock (1968 and 1969) has recently studied the petrology of prehistoric pottery from southern and south-western Britain and has obtained valuable information on the organization of pottery production and the extent to which pottery was traded across the region. Due to the presence of relatively large angular grains of felspar and amphibole in the clay matrix of the pottery and the comparative scarcity of quartz, Peacock (1969) has suggested that the clay used to make the fine "Hembury" ware of the Neolithic period was obtained from above the gabbro outcrop on the Lizard peninsula in Cornwall. It is therefore probable that the fine "Hembury" ware was manufactured in Cornwall and subsequently distributed through south-western and southern Britain (Fig. 68). In addition, the similarity between its distribution and that of two of the earlier stone axe groups (e.g. XVI and XVII), originating from Cornwall, suggests that the same trade routes could have been used in both cases.

Similarly, a petrological study of Iron Age pottery from the Severn Valley and the Welsh Borderlands (Peacock, 1968) established that the pottery had been tempered with igneous and metamorphic rocks, which can only be obtained from the Malvern Hills, or with limestone or sandstone, for which sources in the Malvern region again seem probable (Plate 18). In this case, no definite clay sources have been identified although it is probable that these were also in the Malvern region. These results again suggest that the pottery was being produced by specialized potters at some centre or centres in the Malvern area and that it was then traded over a wide area, up to 100 miles away from the production centre. The possibility of the transportation of raw materials, rather than the finished pottery, seems unlikely in this instance since each of the three groups, defined on the basis of the temper (i.e. igneous/metamorphic, limestone and sandstone), is accompanied by a characteristic range of stylistic tracts. The concept of specialized potters trading their wares throughout the region has important implications for the interpretation of pottery finds on settlement sites (e.g. hill-forts). It was previously assumed that the pottery found on Iron Age sites was made locally and that its characteristic stylistic traits could therefore be used to define cultural groups. However, it now seems probable that the distribution of the different styles represents, at least in part, the marketing areas of the different potters and that these areas could easily include more than one cultural group.

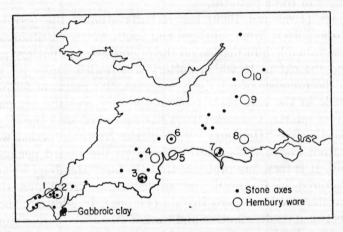

Figure 68. Sketch map of south-western Britain, showing the distribution of stone axes originating from Cornwall (Groups XVI and XVII) and the fine "Hembury" ware made from the gabbroic clay on the Lizard peninsula. The sites at which fine "Hembury" ware has been found, together with the percentages (in brackets) of the Neolithic pottery at these sites made from the gabbroic clay, are as follows: (1) Gwithian (100), (2) Carn Brea (100), (3) Hazard Hill (30), (4) Haldon (25), (5) High Peak (4), (6) Hembury (10), (7) Maiden Castle (9), (8) Corfe Mullen (13), (9) Robin Hood's Ball (1·3) and (10) Windmill Hill (0·2). (After Evens *et al.*, 1962 and Peacock, 1969.)

Petrological examination can only be used to identify the source of the raw materials when distinctive minerals or rock fragments, and especially igneous or metamorphic rock fragments, are present. It is therefore usually impossible to say very much about the provenance of such commonplace materials as quartz sand, which is the only inclusion present in a very large quantity of pottery. In such cases heavy mineral analysis is a useful approach although, being excessively laborious and time-consuming, it is not suitable for routine examination. In this technique about 20–30 g of the potsherd are crushed and floated on a liquid (e.g. bromoform) with a specific gravity of 2·9. The quartz sand and clay float while the heavy minerals (e.g. zircon, garnet, tourmaline) sink, enabling them to be separated and mounted on a microscope slide for identification and counting. A corpus of information on the distribution of heavy minerals throughout the geological system is available for some parts of the world, such as Britain. Consequently by comparing the assemblage of heavy minerals obtained from the pottery with published data, it is possible to determine the geological formation to which the sand temper is most closely related. From the distribution of rocks of that type, it is then

Table 17. Heavy mineral analysis of Romano-British black-burnished
pottery (after Peacock, 1967)

Non-opaque heavy minerals	Percentage of total non-opaque heavy minerals[a]	
	Category 1 pottery	Category 2 pottery
Zircon	5·6	76·0
Tourmaline	87·4	2·8
Rutile	1·6	13·4
Kyanite	—	3·1
Andalusite	4·1	1·0
Staurolite	—	0·4
Garnet	0·5	1·4
Epidote	—	0·5
Apatite	0·5	0·4
Sphene	0·1	—
Anatase	0·1	1·0

[a] A total of approximately 800 grains were counted for each pottery sample and the percentage yield of heavy minerals was 0·09 for category 1 and 0·26 for category 2 pottery.

sometimes possible to establish the source of the sand in the pottery. Peacock (1967), using this technique, has been able to distinguish two distinct categories of the black-burnished ware which is found on Roman sites throughout Britain. Data on the percentage of non-opaque heavy minerals in typical sherds from each category is given in Table 17. The predominance of tourmaline in category 1 pottery suggests that the quartz sand was derived from the granites of Devon and Cornwall. Similarly, the appreciable amounts of kyanite in category 2 pottery suggest the post-Triassic sedimentary rocks which outcrop in the eastern half of England. Again the results indicate wide-scale trading of pottery from a central "factory" or a number of "factory" sites, the discovery of which is still awaited.

An alternative possible approach to the ubiquitous sand-tempered ware would be to first group the pottery on the basis of its granulometric characteristics. This would involve studying the ratio of sand grains to clay matrix, the grain size distribution and the grain shape. Heavy mineral analysis could then be applied to one or two sherds from each group in order to establish the origin of the sand. Because the texture of a sand-tempered sherd is extremely complex, subjective comparison would not be adequate. Instead each attribute (e.g. grain size and shape) would have to be isolated, measured and expressed in terms of mathematical parameters. Research into this technique is currently in progress (Peacock, 1970).

It must be further emphasized that petrological examination also has only limited application in the case of very fine-textured pottery wares. The situation is analogous to that for homogeneous rocks, such as flint and obsidian, and again characterization of the raw materials is best achieved by chemical analysis (p. 314).

Technology. Information on the methods employed in preparing and shaping the clay, as well as on the conditions prevailing during the firing, can be obtained from the study of thin sections cut from the pottery (Hodges, 1963). This information provides an indication of the technological competence of the ancient potters and, when innovations in technique occur, can suggest direct contact between different groups of potters.

Non-plastic temper, such as sand, rock fragments, grog (i.e. crushed pottery) and chopped vegetable matter, was frequently added to the raw clay in order to improve its working qualities. The general type of temper employed can be identified by microscopic examination and in the case of sand inclusions, it is frequently possible to establish, on the basis of the grain size and shape, whether the sand occurred naturally in the clay or was added deliberately. Even when the geographical source of the temper cannot be identified, the data obtained can have archaeological significance. For example, Hodges (1966) observed that the bulk of Neolithic Fengate and Mortlake pottery was tempered with crushed calcined flint whereas the later Bronze Age collared urns were almost invariably tempered with grog. He therefore suggested that this widespread technological change was due to the influence of the Beaker invaders whose pottery was also normally tempered with grog.

The method of building the vessel can sometimes be determined by examining the orientation of the mineral inclusions and air spaces in the pottery; the individual clay particles, themselves, being too small to see under normal magnification. As a general rule the inclusions in wheel-thrown pottery tend to become orientated with their long axes parallel to the plane of the wheel-head while in coil- or ring-built pottery the orientation is far more haphazard. In addition, the nature of the surface finish applied to pottery can be studied in thin section. For example, a slip, unlike a wet-hand finish, invariably shows a distinct line of demarcation from the body.

The study of thin sections also provides information on the maximum temperature attained and the atmospheric conditions prevailing during firing. The optically anisotropic clay minerals break down to form an amorphous phase in the temperature range 700–850°C. Consequently, in pottery fired to these temperatures and above, the clay matrix is isotropic and appears extinct when viewed between crossed polars. At even higher temperatures (1100–1600°C), partial fusion between the clay and the mineral inclusions occurs. However, the presence of partial fusion in pottery rarely provides a precise guide to the firing temperature since the temperature, at which it occurs, depends critically on the "fluxing" impurities present in the clay. Other minerals that are altered by heat can also provide an indication of the firing temperature. These include calcite which decomposes to calcium oxide, with the emission of carbon dioxide, in the temperature range 750–850°C.

The quantity and distribution of residual carbon seen in the thin section provides some indication of the atmosphere present in the kiln during firing. Under oxidizing conditions (i.e. a fire with a clear flame and adequate oxygen supply), the organic matter in the clay is converted first to carbon which, provided the firing is continued for long enough, is subsequently burnt out; residual carbon is therefore absent from the sherd. In contrast under reducing conditions (i.e. a fire with a sooty flame and an inadequate supply of oxygen), the carbon is not burnt out and is normally distributed throughout the sherd. Under semi-reducing conditions, the carbon is only burnt out

relatively slowly and appears as a central core to the sherd. In practice, precise statements about the atmospheric conditions which
prevailed during firing are not possible since the distribution of carbon
also depends on the porosity of the fabric, the maximum temperature
reached and the duration of the firing.

Metallographic Microscopy

In an archaeological context, metallographic examination (Shrager,
1961) is used primarily for studying the techniques employed in the
fabrication of metal artefacts. A polished etched surface of a section,
cut from the artefact, is examined in reflected light using a metallurgical microscope. This examination reveals the internal structure
of the metal which, in turn, provides information on the thermal and
mechanical treatments to which the metal has been subjected. Metallographic examination does not normally provide precise data on the
composition of an alloy nor does it assist in identifying the geographical source of the raw materials, information on both these topics being
obtained from the chemical analysis of the metal artefact (p. 328).

Non-ferrous metals and alloys (e.g. copper, gold, silver and bronze)
are considered separately from iron and steel since these two groups
involve different techniques for the fabrication of artefacts and
provide distinctive metallurgical data.

Experimental Procedures

The nature of the specimen used for metallographic examination is
governed both by the type of artefact under consideration and by the
amount of damage to the artefact which is permitted. Ideally a thin
slice providing a cross-section through the artefact would be used but
in practice, a small core through the body of the artefact or a tapered
slice cut from the edge of the artefact is normally adequate. One
surface of the specimen is then polished to produce a mirror smooth
surface, using progressively finer grades of emery paper and finally
a diamond or alumina paste. The polished surface is then etched in
order to dissolve away part of the metal and thus reveal its internal
structure. Typical etching reagents are a solution of ferric chloride,
acidified with hydrochloric acid, for non-ferrous metals and alloys
and a solution of nitric acid in alcohol for iron and steel.

The polished, etched surface is examined under reflected light using a metallurgical microscope (Fig. 69). Light from an intense source is reflected by a glass plate and is concentrated by the objective lens

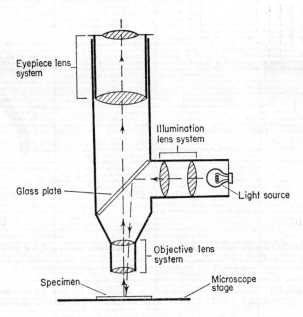

Figure 69. Schematic diagram showing the principal components of a metallurgical (i.e. reflecting) microscope.

onto the surface of the specimen. After reflection from the specimen, the light passes back through the objective lens and up the microscope tube to the eyepiece lens system, some light being lost through reflection by the glass plate. The overall magnification employed is typically in the range × 40 to × 400.

Details of the internal structure of the metals, such as grains, grain boundaries, cracks and precipitates, can be distinguished under the microscope (Plates 19 and 20) because they reflect different amounts of light into the microscope objective and therefore exhibit different degrees of contrast (i.e. brightness). These differences in contrast are caused principally by variations in the surface topography occurring as a result of the etching: an uneven surface, which scatters light, appears dark whereas a smooth surface, which reflects light, appears bright.

232   METHODS OF PHYSICAL EXAMINATION IN ARCHAEOLOGY

For example, grain boundaries appear as a network of dark lines since the metal is more readily etched at these points and a minor "indentation" is produced (Fig. 70a). In some cases, grains with the same com-

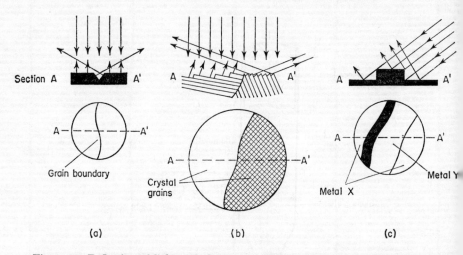

(a)   (b)   (c)

Figure 70. Reflection of light and the contrast pattern observed for polished etched metal surfaces. (a) Grain boundary appears as a dark line as a result of the associated minor "indentation" produced by etching. (b) Crystal grains of the same metal appear either bright or dark according to the orientation of the lattice planes which are preferentially etched. (c) Boundaries between two metal phases (X and Y) appear dark under oblique illumination as a result of the steps produced by differential etching.

position can appear bright or dark depending on the orientation, with respect to the incident light, of those crystallographic lattice planes which are preferentially attacked by the etchant (Fig. 70b). Similarly, the various constituents of a non-homogeneous metal can be distinguished because of differences in the extent to which they are attached by the etchant, the resulting stepped boundary between the two phases producing a shadow effect under oblique illumination (Fig. 70c).

Non-ferrous Metals and Alloys

Except when native copper or gold was used, artefacts made from non-ferrous metals and alloys in antiquity were cast from the molten metal using various types of mould. As cast, the metals and alloys are reasonably soft and can be hammered or drawn at room temperature (i.e. cold-working) with comparative ease. The effect of cold-working is to distort the internal structure of the metal so that it becomes increasingly hard and brittle. Ultimately, if this treatment is continued, the metal will crack and therefore before reaching this point, it must be annealed by reheating it and allowing it to cool. Annealing results in the formation of a fresh internal structure, which is different from the as-cast structure, and leaves the metal soft, malleable and ductile again. When much cold-working is necessary to shape the artefact, the annealing process must be repeated several times, while, in making many tools and weapons, the metal would be left unannealed after the final cold-working in order to provide a suitably hard cutting edge.

As a *pure* molten metal cools, small crystals begin to form from nuclei throughout the liquid. These crystals grow radially outwards, the first branches putting out smaller secondary arms so that each nucleus of crystallization results in a tree-like growth in three dimensions, known as a dendrite. As solidification progresses, the dendrites grow until they come into contact with one another and at this point, the liquid metal remaining between the branches of the dendrites solidifies to fill the spaces. Thus the dendritic structure disappears and is replaced by a pattern of polyhedral crystals with their surfaces in contact, these crystals being referred to as grains.

When a molten alloy of two or more metals cools, the situation is more complicated. Although most metals are miscible in the molten liquid state, on solidification several processes can occur depending mainly on the sizes of the different metal atoms and their crystal habit. Those metals, which remain in solution in each other on solidification and produce alloys of the *solid solution* type (i.e. atoms of one metal replace atoms in the crystal of the second metal in a completely random fashion), are of primary importance since the resulting alloys are harder than the constituent metals but retain sufficient ductility for cold-working. For example, gold can contain any proportion of silver in solid solution. In contrast, some alloys can only form solid solutions within a limited range of compositions. Thus a copper–silver alloy forms two types of solid solution; the α phase in which copper atoms replace atoms in the silver lattice and the β phase in which silver atoms replace atoms in the copper lattice. Similarly, copper–tin alloys (i.e. bronzes) form a solid solution of tin in copper (α phase) up to a 13·2 per cent concentration of tin: at higher tin concentrations, intermetallic compounds of tin and copper are formed. Finally, some alloys, such as copper–lead, do not form solid solutions and on solidification separate into their constituent metals.

Normally when alloys which form solid solutions cool from the molten state, the first branches of the dendrites contain a higher proportion of the metal with the higher melting point than is present in the molten liquid. Consequently as the dendrites grow, the proportion of the lower melting point metal in the remaining molten material increases so that the final infilling around the dendrites is richer in the low melting point metal. In the case of alloys forming solid solutions of any composition (e.g. gold–silver), the same phase exists throughout, although variations in composition occur. However, when the solid solution can have only a limited range of compositions (e.g. copper–silver, copper–tin), it is possible that the composition available for the infilling is such that the phase deposited within the dendrites cannot still be formed. In this case the infilling around the dendrites solidifies to produce a eutectic which is an intimate mechanical mixture of two phases (i.e. α and β phases for a copper–silver alloy or α phase and an intermetallic compound for a copper–tin alloy). Provided the cooling is sufficiently rapid, these variations in composition within the alloy are retained. Therefore, in contrast to pure metals, the "cored" structure of the dendrites, with centres rich in one metal and infilling rich in the other, is readily observable in an etched section from an alloy (Fig. 71a).

The size, shape and orientation of the dendrites, or the grains formed when the dendritic structure disappears in a pure metal, provide some indication of the rate of cooling and hence the method of casting. Rapid cooling, as in a metal mould which quickly conducts away the heat, produces small dendrites or grains whereas slower cooling, as in a clay or sand mould, produces a coarse dendrite or grain structure. Similarly if the cooling is uneven, as when the molten metal is poured into a cold mould, nuclei first appear near to the mould face and elongated dendrites or grains, with their long axes perpendicular to the mould face, are formed.

Subsequent mechanical and thermal treatment radically affect the dendrite or grain structure formed during casting. For example, on annealing an alloy, the dendrite structure gradually disappears, as differences in composition are removed by diffusion, and a homogeneous structure of polyhedral grains (Fig. 71b), similar to that in pure cast metals, is eventually formed. Cold-working distorts and elongates the grains (Fig. 71c) or dendrites and in addition, the grains become crossed with numerous lines, referred to as slip-bands. Subsequent annealing results in the formation of a fresh grain structure in which the grains are no longer elongated. Such cold-worked and annealed metal is also characterized by the presence of twinned grains (Fig. 71d), in which the crystal lattice structure of adjacent regions within a grain develop as mirror images of each other. If a metal containing twinned grains is again cold-worked, the twinning

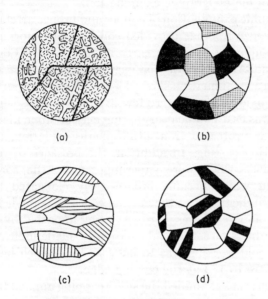

Figure 71. Polished etched surfaces of a non-ferrous alloy (e.g. bronze) observed under reflected light using a metallurgical microscope. (a) Cored structure of dendrites present in the alloy after casting. (b) Polyhedral grains formed when the cast alloy is annealed. (c) Distorted grains (crossed by slip-bands) produced by cold-working. (d) Twinned polyhedral grains formed when the cold-worked alloy is annealed.

is not eliminated but the originally straight twin boundaries become bent and irregular. Further repetition of the annealing and cold-working cycle results in the reformation of the microstructures already described and consequently it is not normally possible to establish the number of cycles to which an artefact has been subjected. Similarly if a metal is worked at a high temperature, an undistorted twinned structure, identical to that associated with cold-working followed by annealing, is obtained.

The relationship between the microstructure of non-ferrous metals and alloys and the thermal and mechanical treatment to which they have been subjected is summarized in Table 18.

Applications. Details of the microstructure of non-ferrous metals (i.e. dendrites, grains, twinning, alloy phases) are revealed by examining polished etched sections under reflected light. Consequently considerable information on the techniques employed in the fabrication of non-ferrous metal artefacts (i.e. casting, cold-working, annealing) is obtained from metallographic examination.

Metallographic examination of copper and bronze artefacts from the European Bronze Age has provided considerable information on the techniques employed by these early metal-workers (Coghlan, 1951; Penniman and Allen, 1960). For example, in the case of a typical bronze halberd, examination showed a coarse cored dendrite structure in which tin oxide crystals were few in number. This suggested that the halberd was cast in a heat insulating clay or stone mould and that the metal was protected from atmospheric oxidation, probably by charcoal, during casting. In addition, the presence of recrystallized twinned grains, which were superimposed on the cored dendrite structure and which became progressively elongated towards the cutting edge, indicated that the cutting edges were made by alternate cold-working and annealing; hardness being imparted by a final cold-working. Hardness measurements across the blade indicated that the effect of the cold-working was to increase the Brinell hardness from 65 at the centre to 133 at the cutting edge.

Charles (1968) has examined the silver capping applied to the copper rivets which were used to attach the handle, presumably made from wood, bone or horn, to a Minoan bronze dagger and has shown that bonding was achieved through the formation of a layer of silver–copper eutectic at the interface (Plate 19). Metallographic examination was supplemented by studying the interface between the copper and the silver with an electron probe microanalyser (p. 278). This latter technique clearly revealed a layer with both copper and silver present (i.e. the eutectic) and confirmed that possible solders (e.g. lead, tin) were absent (Plate 20). The use of this method of bonding approximately 3500 years ago is especially interesting since it greatly pre-dates the discovery of "Sheffield Plate", which is normally attributed to Bolsover of Sheffield in 1743 AD. In order to form the eutectic bonding layer (i.e. an intimate mixture of the α and β phases of the silver–copper alloy), molten eutectic, which subsequently solidifies when the source of heat is removed, must be formed at the interface without melting the silver. This requires a temperature in excess of $779\,^\circ$C (melting point of the eutectic) but less than $960\,^\circ$C (melting point of

Table 18. The development of the microstructure in non-ferrous metals and alloys

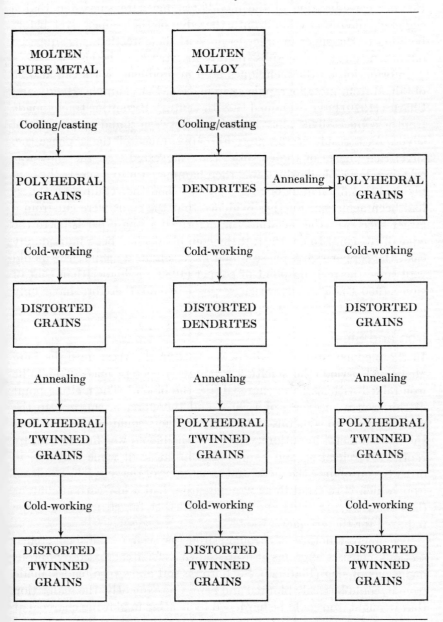

silver) and the achievement in providing this controlled heating indicates the high technical skills of the Minoan metal-workers. Further consideration of the metallographic data suggested that a slight chamfer was ground onto the edge of the copper rivet before bonding to the silver in order to prevent the eutectic being squeezed out when the rivet was subsequently inserted into the handle.

Information on the techniques used in producing coins can also be obtained from metallographic examination. For example, Hendy and Charles (1970) have examined twelfth-century Byzantine trachy made from a copper–silver alloy containing between 2 and 10 per cent of silver. As a result of the plate-like appearance of the α phase (i.e. silver-rich phase) of the eutectic, they suggested that the alloy was cast in a large block which was then hammered into a sheet; the coin blanks being finally cut out for striking when the required thickness had been achieved. Further evidence that the coins were cut from a larger sheet was the fact that the deformed α phase persisted to the edge of the coin. In contrast, if the coin blanks had been individually cast, the copper-rich β phase would have solidified against the mould wall since the melting point of copper (1083°) is higher than that of silver (960°C). The silver-rich α phase would therefore have only appeared away from the edge of the coin.

Iron and Steel

In the bloomery process, which was used in the West until the Late Mediaeval period, the smelting produces a spongy mass of metallic iron mixed with slag and charcoal (i.e. the bloom). The melting point of this iron is in excess of 1500°C and therefore, in contrast to the case of non-ferrous metals and alloys, artefacts could not be cast from the molten metal in antiquity. Instead the bloom was first forged, by repeatedly reheating and hammering on an anvil while still hot, in order to consolidate the metal and expel some of the slag. The resulting iron, which is referred to as wrought iron, had a low carbon content (less than 0·5 per cent) and could be further forged into the shape required for the artefact.

The microstructure of wrought iron, as seen in polished etched sections, consists of grains of iron, known as ferrite, crossed by fibrous inclusions of slag (Plate 20). Such iron is soft and sword blades, made from it, could be easily blunted and bent. Consequently, the realization that wrought iron could be hardened by heating in glowing charcoal at temperatures above 900°C represented a major advance in the production of artefacts. This process, known variously as carburization or cementation, converts the wrought iron into steel by allowing it to absorb carbon, the concentration of carbon in the iron–carbon alloy (i.e. the steel) being in the range 0·5 to 2 per cent. The carbon combines chemically with some of the iron to form cementite (i.e. iron carbide—Fe_3C) and the resulting microstructure consists initially of a mixture of ferrite and pearlite grains, the latter being a eutectic mixture of cementite laminae in a ferrite matrix. With increasing concentrations of carbon (i.e. greater than 0·85 per cent), the microstructure converts to a pearlite and cementite mixture.

The steel produced by carburization possesses an additional important property in that it can be hardened still further by heating to a temperature above 750 °C in a reducing atmosphere and then quenching rapidly in, for example, cold water. This process eliminates the pearlitic structure and in its place a new phase, martensite, which is a supersaturated solution of carbon in iron and has a needle-like structure, is formed. The quenched steel, although very hard, is distinctly brittle and liable to fracture. However, the brittleness can be reduced, with some loss of hardness, by reheating to a lower temperature. This process, referred to as tempering, converts the martensite into a new phase, sorbite, which is a fine dispersion of cementite in ferrite.

The relationship between the microstructure of iron and steel and the heat treatments to which the metal has been subjected is summarized in Table 19.

Applications. Identification of the various phases in iron–carbon alloys (i.e. ferrite, cementite, pearlite, martensite, sorbite) is possible through the examination of polished etched sections under reflected light. Consequently the processes (i.e. carburization, quenching, tempering) used in the manufacture of iron and steel artefacts can be ascertained and the progressive evolution of iron metallurgy can be established (Coghlan, 1956).

In the case of Europe, it has been shown that the carburization of wrought iron, to produce the harder steel, was employed during the Iron Age (i.e. Hallstatt and La Tène). Furthermore, since it was only possible to carburize a thin surface layer, the technique of forgewelding together a number of thin strips of carburized iron, to produce a "piled" or laminated structure, was also developed during the Iron Age. The resulting artefact (e.g. sword) was effectively carburized

Table 19. The development of the microstructure in iron and steel

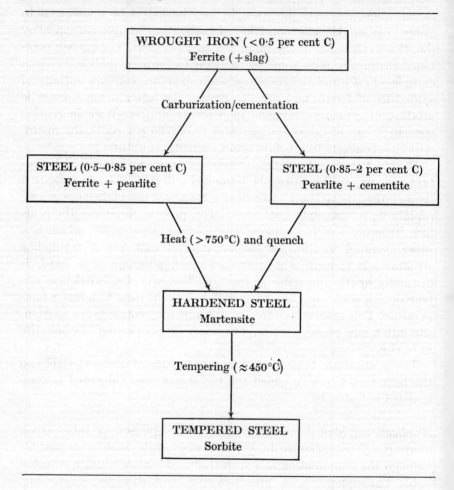

throughout and was therefore considerably stronger than a wrought iron artefact which had been carburized after forging into shape. From the examination of artefacts from the Roman period, evidence for the further hardening of the steel by quenching, together with some rudimentary tempering, has been found.

The detailed examination of Merovingian and Viking swords has elucidated the somewhat laborious technique referred to as "pattern-welding" which was employed throughout this period and which was effectively a development from the earlier piled structure. According to Maryon (1960), several thin strips of wrought iron and steel, arranged alternately, were bound together and twisted to form a composite rod of spiral structure. After twisting, the strips, making up the rods, were forge-welded together and the resulting flat ribbons were either attached to or were used as the spine of the sword blade: separate strips of steel were then fitted on each side to form the cutting edges of the sword (Fig. 72). As a result of the alternating areas of low

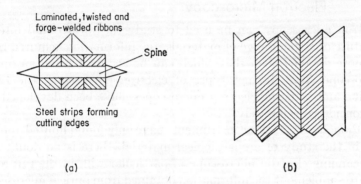

(a)   (b)

Figure 72. Schematic representation of (a) the structure and (b) the surface appearance of a typical "pattern-welded" sword.

and high carbon content, associated with the original wrought iron and steel laminations, subsequent etching produced the characteristic wavy-lined pattern on the surface. The precise details of this pattern, which are extremely diverse, obviously depend on the structure and mechanical treatment of the original laminations.

A further technique for producing sword-blades with a wavy-lined or "watered silk" surface pattern was developed in Syria, Persia and India during the first millennium AD. This is referred to as the dama-scene process and has also been investigated using metallographic techniques (Maryon, 1960). Damascening differs fundamentally from pattern welding in that the surface pattern is effectively developed, before the sword-blade is forged, by employing specialized techniques in the preparation of the steel. In the Indian process, a high carbon steel (1–2 per cent carbon), known as wootz, is produced by first firing wrought iron with wood or charcoal in a sealed clay crucible and then reheating the resulting cast iron in a current of air in order to remove excess carbon. The wootz consists of light-coloured, globular cementite grains distributed in a darker pearlite matrix and it is this micro-structure which produces the characteristic watered silk pattern when the metal is forged into a sword and subsequently etched. In addition to its considerable beauty, damascene steel had significant practical advantages in that it was extremely strong and possessed a high elastic limit.

Electron Microscopy

Electron microscopy can be used to study the surface and internal structure of a wide range of materials, the information acquired being far more detailed than that which can be acquired using an optical microscope. Two distinct types of electron microscope, the trans-mission and scanning electron microscopes, have been developed and are considered separately.

Although, as yet, these instruments have only found limited applica-tion in the study of archaeological material, there is no doubt that the scanning electron microscope in particular will, in the future, be used to supplement the information obtained from optical microscopy.

Transmission Electron Microscope

The main components of a transmission electron microscope (Heiden-reich, 1964), which are maintained under high vacuum conditions, are shown schematically in Fig. 73, from which it is obvious that the lay-out is similar to that used in an optical microscope. Electrons are generated by a heated filament and are accelerated through, typically, 100 kV in order to provide a high energy electron beam. The beam is then focussed onto the specimen by means of the condenser lens system so that the area illuminated is a few microns in diameter. After transmission of the electron beam through the specimen, an appro-priate magnified image of the specimen is formed by the objective lens and further magnification is achieved with the intermediate lens. Finally, the projector lens throws a magnified view (greater than × 100 000) of the specimen area irradiated by the electron beam onto a fluorescent screen, below which is located a photographic plate for recording the image. Magnetic lenses, consisting of massive iron cores which are energized by current-carrying coils, are normally employed throughout the instrument.

At an accelerating voltage of 100 kV, the wavelength associated with the electrons is approximately 4×10^{-6} μm (equation 7.3). Since this wavelength is much smaller than the spacing between atoms in a crystal lattice, resolution of sub-atomic detail in the specimen examined would be possible with a perfect imaging system. However,

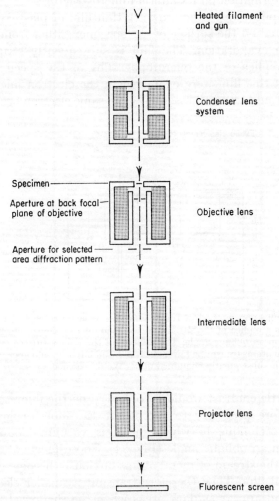

Figure 73. Block diagram showing the principal components of a transmission electron microscope.

lens-aberration effects severely limit the useful aperture of a magnetic lens and therefore the practical limit of resolution of specimen detail, as defined by equation (7.4), is approximately 5×10^{-4} μm (i.e. 5 Å).

The transmission electron microscope can be used either to examine replicas of the specimen surface or the actual specimen itself. The replication method provides information on the microtopography of the specimen surface while the direct observation of the specimen provides information on its internal microstructure.

In the replication method, a very thin film of plastic or carbon is first deposited on the surface of the specimen either from solution or by vacuum evaporation. The film is subsequently stripped off to provide a replica of the microtopography of the specimen surface. However, if this film were examined in the electron microscope, all parts of it would transmit essentially the same electron beam intensity

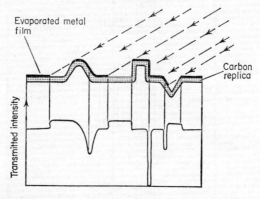

Figure 74. Replication method of transmission electron microscopy. The carbon film, which provides a replica of the surface microtopography of the specimen, is shadowed with metal from an oblique angle. Those facets of the replica surface which faced the stream of metal atoms transmit a lower electron beam intensity and appear as dark areas when the film is subsequently examined under the microscope.

and very little contrast would be observed on the fluorescent screen. It is therefore necessary to accentuate the film topography by a shadowing technique in which metal is vacuum-deposited on its surface from an oblique angle (Fig. 74). Those facets of the surface which face the stream of metal atoms obviously become coated with a thin metal film. They therefore transmit a smaller electron beam intensity and appear as dark areas when the shadowed film is subsequently examined in the electron microscope. The strong contrast, which is now observed on the fluorescent screen, therefore provides a representation of the surface microtopography of the original specimen, the limit of resolution of surface detail being approximately 50×10^{-4} μm (i.e. 50 Å).

For direct observation in the electron microscope, the specimen thickness must be less than about 0·2 μm (i.e. 2000 Å) otherwise the specimen is completely opaque to electrons. This can be readily achieved by using finely ground material which is typically deposited from suspension onto a supporting carbon film. However, in order to examine bulk specimens, specialized techniques for preparing the necessary thin foils must be employed. The electropolishing techniques, which are used in preparing thin metal foils, are well established but it is only with the more recent development of ion-thinning techniques that it has been possible to prepare satisfactory non-metallic foils (e.g. minerals, rocks, ceramics). In the direct examination of a specimen, as opposed to the examination of a replica, the differential absorption of the electron beam by different parts of the specimen is comparatively unimportant. Instead, electron diffraction phenomena normally provide the basis for obtaining information on the crystalline structure of the specimen.

Electron diffraction arises as a result of the elastic scattering of the electrons in the incident beam by the three-dimensional *periodic* array of lattice atoms associated with crystalline materials, the effect being analogous to X-ray diffraction (p. 285). Diffraction patterns, associated with the various crystalline phases in the specimen, are formed at the back focal plane of the objective lens. In the case of weakly diffracting crystals, the majority of the electron beam intensity transmitted by the crystal is concentrated in the direct beam (i.e. zero order of the diffraction pattern) while for strongly diffracting crystals, the majority of the intensity is diverted into the diffracted beam (i.e. non-zero orders of the diffraction pattern). Therefore if an aperture, which only permits the passage of the direct beam (i.e. bright field operation), is inserted at the back focal plane of the objective lens, weakly diffracting crystals will appear as bright areas on the fluorescent screen while strongly diffracting crystals will appear as dark areas. Contrast that arises in this way is described as electron-diffraction contrast. The phenomenon provides the basis for resolving the microstructure of the specimens and for studying defects (e.g. dislocations) in the crystal lattice structure, the limit of resolution being approximately 5×10^{-4} μm (i.e. 5 Å).

In addition to the electron-diffraction contrast effects, the actual diffraction patterns formed at the back focal plane of the objective lens can also be studied. By using appropriate apertures and defocussing the intermediate lens, the diffraction pattern associated with a particular area of the specimen can be selected and observed on the fluorescent screen. Examination of this diffraction pattern can assist in the identification of the crystal phase present at the selected area and in the determination of its crystallographic orientation.

Scanning Electron Microscope

In the scanning electron microscope (Thornton, 1968), a high energy electron beam is passed through a series of magnetic lenses which serve to demagnify the beam diameter so that the illuminated area of the specimen is approximately $2\cdot5 \times 10^{-2}$ μm (i.e. 250 Å) in diameter. Incorporated in the final lens assembly are two sets of

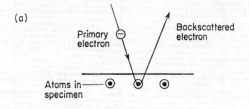

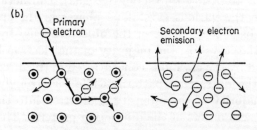

Figure 75. Schematic representation of the interaction between the primary electron beam and the specimen in a scanning electron microscope. (a) Backscattered electrons produced by elastic collisions with the constituent atomic nuclei. (b) Cascade of secondary electrons produced by impact ionisation of the constituent atoms (i.e. inelastic collisions). Some of these electrons diffuse to and escape from the surface to provide the secondary electron emission.

magnetic scanning coils which cause the beam to be deflected in a raster-like pattern over the specimen surface, in much the same manner as in a television tube. The entire assembly is again maintained under high vacuum conditions.

The primary electron beam interacts with the specimen to give a backscattered electron current and secondary electron emission, both of which provide information on the surface microtopography of the specimen. The backscattered electrons are primary electrons which are deflected (i.e. elastically scattered) out of the specimen as a result of their interaction with the electric charge carried by the nuclei of the atoms at the surface of the specimen (Fig. 75a). The secondary electrons are electrons ejected from the atoms of the specimen as a result of inelastic collisions between the primary electrons and these atoms. A cascade of secondary electrons is thus produced in the specimen and some of these electrons diffuse to the surface, from which they then escape to provide the secondary electron emission (Fig. 75b). The backscattered electrons have energies comparable to those of the primary electrons (i.e. up to about 100 keV) while the secondary electrons emitted from the surface have energies up to about 50 eV.

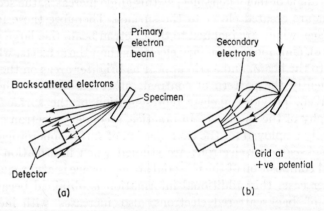

Figure 76. Detection systems for (a) the backscattered and (b) the secondary electrons in the scanning electron microscope.

The backscattered and secondary electrons are detected using either a scintillation or semiconductor counter. In the case of the high energy backscattered electrons, only those which are scattered into the solid angle subtended by the counter are detected (Fig. 76a). In contrast, the low energy secondary electrons emitted from the surface are effectively pulled towards the counter by means of a positively charged wire mesh (Fig. 76b). The electrical signal from the counter is used to control the brightness of the spot on the screen of a cathode ray tube. This spot scans the cathode ray tube screen in synchronism with the scanning of the specimen surface by the primary electron beam. An enlarged picture (up to about × 50 000) of the distribution of the backscattered electron current or the secondary electron emission over the specimen surface is therefore displayed on the screen.

The dominant factor determining the yield of backscattered and secondary electrons is the angle of incidence (θ) of the primary electron beam on that facet of the surface being examined. The most probable angle of emergence of backscattered electrons is that corresponding to specular reflection (i.e. angle of incidence equals angle of reflection). Therefore those facets of the surface, for which the angle of specular reflection lies within the solid angle subtended by the counter, produce the greatest number of *detected* backscattered electrons and appear as bright areas on the cathode ray tube screen. Similarly the number of secondary electrons emerging from the surface increases with increasing angle of incidence since, as this angle increases, the secondary electrons are created closer to the surface. Therefore those facets of the surface, which are inclined to the electron beam (i.e. large angle of incidence), emit more secondary electrons than those facets, which are normal to the beam, and again appear as brighter areas on the screen. Consequently the pattern of contrast, observed on the cathode ray tube screen, provides a clear representation of the surface micro-topography of the specimen. In practice, secondary electron emission is normally employed for the examination of surface microtopography while backscattered electrons are studied when information on the chemical composition of the material at the surface is also required. In the latter case, this additional information is obtained because the number of backscattered electrons also increases with increasing atomic number of the element on which the primary electrons are incident (p. 281).

With the scanning electron microscope, the limit of resolution of surface detail is determined principally by the diameter of the primary electron beam and is therefore typically in the range $1 \cdot 5 \times 10^{-2}$ to 5×10^{-2} μm (i.e. 150–500 Å). Although higher resolution can be achieved using replicas in conjunction with the transmission electron microscope, the depth of focus provided by the scanning electron microscope is several microns, even at a high magnification, and is therefore far greater than that achieved with the transmission micro-scope. Furthermore, bulk specimens, several millimetres in thickness, can be employed in the scanning microscope and the only specimen preparation required is the coating of the surface with a thin conduc-ting film (e.g. carbon). It is therefore clear that the scanning electron microscope provides an extremely powerful tool for obtaining information about the surface microtopography of specimens.

Two further aspects of the scanning electron microscope are also relevant in the present context. These depend on particular electrons being ejected from the constituent atoms by the incident primary electron beam. If electrons are ejected from luminescent centres (p. 115), light referred to as cathodoluminescence (i.e. luminescence excited by electrons or cathode rays), is emitted when electron-hole recombination subsequently occurs at these centres. Alternatively, if electrons are ejected from inner electrons orbits of the atoms, the resulting vacant energy levels are immediately filled by electrons from the outer orbits and X-rays, whose wavelengths are characteristic of the particular chemical elements involved, are emitted. A photomultiplier for detecting the cathodoluminescence is sometimes incorporated into the scanning electron microscope. In this case, an enlarged picture of the distribution of the cathodoluminescence from the specimen can be displayed on a cathode ray tube screen, as with the backscattered electron current and the secondary electron emission. The observation of the cathodoluminescence from minerals is of interest since it provides information on the distribution of specific trace impurities, such as manganese and the rare earths. Similarly, the detection of the characteristic X-rays can provide a picture of the distribution of the various chemical elements across the surface of the specimen. However, in this case, a separate instrument, referred to as the electron probe microanalyser and described on p. 278, is normally employed.

Applications

In using electron microscopy for the examination of archaeological material, the information that can be obtained from the study of the surface microtopography is probably of primary importance, the interpretation of this information obviously depending on the type of material under examination. Although the examination of surface replicas with the transmission electron microscope has been employed in the past, it seems likely that the scanning electron microscope, with its much larger depth of focus, will normally be employed in the future. Furthermore, with the increasing availability of these instruments, it is clear that the study of surface microtopography will become an important aspect of the physical examination of a wide range of archaeological material.

Hofmann (1962) has shown that the study of replicas of the surface of Greek (i.e. Attic) black and red figured pottery and Roman Samian pottery (i.e. *terra sigillata*) is of considerable value in elucidating the techniques employed in their manufacture. It is now generally accepted that, in order to produce the black coloured "paint" on Attic pottery, a thin surface coating (i.e. a slip) of an illitic clay (i.e. hydrous mica) was first applied to the appropriate areas of the vessel. The pottery was then fired at about 850°C in a reducing atmosphere before continuing the firing at higher temperatures under oxidizing conditions. At the end of the reducing stage, the entire surface of pottery would have been black since the iron oxide in the clay would have been reduced to either wustite (FeO) or magnetite (Fe_3O_4). However, during the subsequent oxidizing stage, those areas which had been coated with the illitic clay remained a black colour while the remainder of the surface become red, as a result of the re-oxidation of the iron oxide to haematite ($\alpha\ Fe_2O_3$). An explanation for this differential re-oxidation was obtained by studying replicas of the surface of the pottery. These showed that the red surfaces were comparatively rough and had remained porous during the firing whereas the black surfaces were fine-grained and had, as a result of the coating of illitic clay, sintered to form a more impervious layer. Consequently during the oxidizing stage, oxygen could penetrate through the pores of the ultimately red surfaces and re-oxidize the iron oxide whereas oxygen could not penetrate the impervious black surfaces, which therefore withstood re-oxidation and remained black.

In the case of Samian pottery, the red gloss is thought to have been produced by applying a slip of illitic clay to the entire surface and then firing the pottery to about 950°C with oxidizing conditions being maintained throughout. Examination of replicas of the surface of Samian pottery showed that the illitic clay slip had sintered during the firing to form an impervious layer which was similar to that of the black surface areas on the Attic pottery. The higher firing temperature (950°C) required to produce an impervious sintered layer in an oxidizing atmosphere, as opposed to a reducing atmosphere (850°C), is due to the fact that the fluxing properties of Fe^{3+} ions (oxidized state) are inferior to those of Fe^{2+} ions (reduced state).

Freeman and Rayment (1968) have used the scanning electron microscope to study the changes in microstructure that occur when a clay is fired (Plate 25), the surfaces of freshly broken flakes of unfired and fired clay being examined. In the case of a Carboniferous (Coal

Measure) Shale, they found that the external flaky appearance of the clay minerals was essentially unaltered after firing at 875°C, even though dehydroxylation (i.e. removal of the chemically combined water from the clay minerals) had occurred. However, after firing at 1025°C, there had been extensive sintering together of clay aggregates while the particulate character of the unfired material had been completely obliterated after firing at 1100°C. In contrast, with London Clay, extensive glass formation had occurred and large vesicular pores had developed after firing at 1025°C. These results clearly indicate that the study of the microtopography of freshly broken pottery surfaces, using the scanning electron microscope, would provide data on the state of the original clay minerals, the development of a glassy phase and the pore structure. Therefore, if the technique was applied to archaeological pottery, it would be possible to obtain some indication of the firing temperature and atmospheric conditions (i.e. reducing or oxidizing) employed in its manufacture.

The scanning electron microscope is also useful for examining the microstructure of metals in situations where the damage caused by preparing polished etched sections for optical examination is not permissible. For example, Darling and Healy (1971) have used the backscattered electrons in order to study the microstructure of a fourth century Greek coin (hekte) made from the gold–silver–copper alloy, electrum (Plate 22). In this case, the dendritic structure was clearly apparent since the dendrite cores, being the first regions to solidify from the melt, were rich in gold whereas the region between the dendrites, which solidified last, were deficient in gold. The dendrite cores therefore appeared as bright areas on the cathode ray tube screen since, having a higher effective atomic number, they backscattered a higher proportion of the incident primary electron beam. This interpretation was confirmed by means of electron microprobe analysis which established that the concentration of gold at the centre of the dendrites was about 60 per cent whereas at the edges it was only about 50 per cent. On the basis of this data and other physical properties, Darling and Healy suggested that the coin was struck, with a considerable amount of cold-working, from a bead of cast electrum.

Other potential applications of the scanning electron microscope to the study of archaeological material (Brothwell, 1969) include the examination of scratch patterns on stone artefacts, attritional marks on teeth and the cellular structure of biological material.

Radiography

Radiography refers to the examination of specimens using high energy electromagnetic radiation (Fig. 62), which, because of its high penetration, can reveal details of composition and structure invisible to the naked eye. X-rays, produced by a high-voltage X-ray tube, are normally employed. The object to be examined is placed in the X-ray beam and the X-rays which penetrate the object impinge on a suitably sensitized photographic film. Variations in composition within the object are revealed as a result of their differential absorption of X-rays and therefore appear as variations in contrast (i.e. bright and dark areas) on the film. The absorption of X-rays increases with increasing density and atomic number so that those parts of the object containing high density, high atomic number components appear as dark areas (i.e. underexposed) on the film. Obviously in interpreting X-ray radiographs, variations in the thickness of the object must be considered since the degree of absorption by a thick layer of low density material is similar to that associated with a thin layer of high density material.

A further difficulty encountered in interpreting radiographs is associated with the fact that a three-dimensional structure is being examined in terms of the shadow projected onto a two-dimensional surface. The radiograph therefore provides no indication of the depth, within the object, at which any specific feature lies. This difficulty can, however, normally be overcome by making two separate exposures, at left and right oblique incidence respectively, and by studying them simultaneously through a stereoviewer.

Radioactive isotopes, emitting gamma radiation, can sometimes be used as an alternative to a high-voltage X-ray tube. The compactness of these gamma ray sources means that they can be used in confined situations where it would be difficult to position a conventional X-ray tube. However, they do not normally compare in intensity with X-ray tubes and therefore, in order to obtain satisfactory gamma ray radiographs, very much longer exposure times are required.

Considering the overall range of available archaeological material (i.e. artefacts and biological material), the radiographic examination of human and animal bones is undoubtedly of primary importance (Brothwell et al., 1969). In this context, the recent study of the remains of Tutankhamun (Harrison and Abdalla, 1972) indicates the wide range of information that can be gained using this technique. Firstly, the X-ray radiographs assisted in the precise measurement of the dimensions of the skull and bones of the skeleton and revealed remarkable similarities with the dimensions previously obtained from the remains of Smenkhkare. Taken in conjunction with the fact that analysis of the tissues has indicated that both pharaohs possessed the same blood groups, the skeletal similarities suggest close kinship between Tutankhamun and Smenkhkare, in fact it is possible that they were brothers. Secondly, the radiographs revealed the stage reached in the eruption of the teeth and the growth of the humeri and from this information, it was inferred that, at death, Tutankhamun's age was in the range from 18 to 20 years. Thirdly, the fact that all the vertebrae, including the epiphysical plates, were seen to be intact suggested that Tutankhamun did not die from tuberculosis, as has previously been proposed by some authorities. Finally, the radiographs provided considerable information on the procedures employed in mummification.

In the context of artefacts, the most important application of radiography is probably in the examination of iron objects (Plate 23). For example, non-ferrous metal inlays (e.g. copper, silver) are revealed beneath a conglomeration of corrosion products since they have a higher density than the corrosion products and therefore absorb a greater proportion of the incident X-rays. Similarly, welded surfaces can often be detected because of the associated low density oxidation products and included slag.

Microradiography

In addition to the macroscopic radiographic examination described above, microradiographic techniques, which can resolve details of the specimen microstructure to better than 1 μm, have been developed. In this case flat, parallel-sided specimens are normally required, in order to avoid variations in X-ray absorption due to variations in specimen thickness. For dense metals, such as copper and iron, the specimen thickness should be less than 0·1 mm while for the less dense organic materials (e.g. bone, wood), the thickness of the specimen can be a few millimetres.

Two distinct microradiographic techniques are currently employed. With the contact method, the specimen is placed directly on the photographic film, as for normal macroscopic examination, and enlargement of the resulting radiographic image is achieved by examining the film using an optical microscope. In this case the resolution of specimen detail is limited by the grain size of the photographic emulsion. With the projection method, which is sometimes referred to as X-ray microscopy, the specimen is separated from the film and a specially designed, ultrafine focus X-ray tube (focal spot diameter approximately 1 μm) is employed. The magnified radiographic image of the specimen is thus directly projected onto the photographic film, the magnification being given by the ratio of the distance between the X-ray source and the film to that between the source and the specimen.

It seems probable that, in the future, microradiography will prove to be valuable for certain bio-archaeological investigations, such as the study of bone changes and plant tissue morphology. In addition, the technique could supplement metallographic examination since it effectively integrates over the entire thickness of a metal specimen (i.e. about 0·1 mm) whereas metallography only provides information to the depth of etching (i.e. typically 0·1 μm).

References

Brothwell, D. (1969). The study of archaeological materials by means of the scanning electron microscope: an important new field. In "Science in Archaeology" (Eds. D. Brothwell and E. Higgs), pp. 564–566, Thames and Hudson, London.

Brothwell, D., Molleson, T., Harcourt, R. and Gray, P. H. K. (1969). The application of X-rays to the study of archaeological material. In "Science in Archaeology" (Eds. D. Brothwell and E. Higgs), pp. 513–525, Thames and Hudson, London.

Campbell Smith, W. (1963). Jade axes from sites in the British Isles. *Proc. prehist. Soc.* **29**, 133–155.

Charles, J. A. (1968). The first Sheffield Plate. *Antiquity* **42**, 278–285.

Coghlan, H. H. (1951). "Notes on the Prehistoric Metallurgy of Copper and Bronze in the Old World", Pitt Rivers Museum, Oxford.

Coghlan, H. H. (1956). "Notes on the Prehistoric and Early Iron in the Old World", Pitt Rivers Museum, Oxford.

Darling, A. S. and Healy, J. F. (1971). Micro-probe analysis and the study of Greek gold–silver–copper alloys. *Nature*, **231**, 443–444.

Evens, E. D., Grinsell, L. V., Piggott, S. and Wallis, F. S. (1962). Fourth report of the sub-committee of the South-western Group of Museums and Art Galleries on the petrological identification of stone axes. *Proc. prehist. Soc.* **28**, 209–266.

Freeman, I. L. and Rayment, D. L. (1968). Scanning electron micrographs of some structural ceramic materials. *Trans. Br. ceram. Soc.*, **67**, 611–618.

Harrison, R. G. and Abdalla, A. B. (1972). The remains of Tutankhamun. *Antiquity* **46**, 8–14.

Hartshorne, N. H. and Stuart, A. (1970). "Crystals and the Polarizing Microscope", Edward Arnold, London.

Heidenreich, R. D. (1964). "Fundamentals of Transmission Electron Microscopy", Interscience, New York.

Hendy, M. F. and Charles, J. A. (1970). The production techniques, silver content and circulation history of twelfth-century Byzantine trachy. *Archaeometry* 12, 13–22.

Hodges, H. W. M. (1963). The examination of ceramic materials in thin section. In "The Scientist and Archaeology" (Ed. E. Pyddoke), pp. 101–110, Phoenix House, London.

Hodges, H. W. M. (1966). Aspects of pottery in temperate Europe before the Roman Empire. In "Ceramics and Man" (Ed. F. R. Matson), pp. 114–123, Methuen, London.

Hofmann, U. (1962). The chemical basis of ancient Greek vase painting. *Angewandte Chemie* 1, 341–350.

Keiller, A., Piggott, S. and Wallis, F. S. (1941). First report of the sub-committee of the South-western Group of Museums and Art Galleries on the petrological identification of stone axes. *Proc. prehist. Soc.* 7, 50–72.

Kellaway, G. A. (1971). Glaciation and the stones of Stonehenge. *Nature* 233, 30–35.

Maryon, H. (1960). Pattern-welding and damascening of sword blades. *Stud. Conserv.* 5, 25–37 and 52–60.

Peacock, D. P. S. (1967). The heavy mineral analysis of pottery: a preliminary report. *Archaeometry* 10, 97–100.

Peacock, D. P. S. (1968). A petrological study of certain Iron Age pottery from Western England. *Proc. prehist. Soc.* 34, 414–427.

Peacock, D. P. S. (1969). Neolithic pottery production in Cornwall. *Antiquity* 43, 145–149.

Peacock, D. P. S. (1970). The scientific analysis of ancient ceramics: a review. *Wld Archaeol.* 1, 375–389.

Penniman, T. K. and Allen, I. M. (1960). A metallurgical study of four Irish Early Bronze Age ribbed halberds in the Pitt Rivers Museum, Oxford. *Man* 60, 85–89.

Rosenfeld, A. (1965). "The Inorganic Raw Materials in Antiquity", pp. 1–156, Weidenfeld and Nicolson, London.

Shepard, A. O. (1942). "Rio Grande Paint Ware, a Study Illustrating the Place of Ceramic Technological Analysis in Archaeological Research", Carnegie Institute, Washington.

Shrager, A. M. (1961). "Elementary Metallurgy and Metallography", Dover Publications, New York.

Thomas, H. H. (1923). Source of the stones of Stonehenge. *Antiquar. J.* 3, 239–260.

Thornton, P. R. (1968). "Scanning Electron Microscopy", Chapman and Hall, London.

9

Physical Methods of Analysis— Techniques

An extremely wide range of physical methods of analysis, involving the determination of the chemical composition, the identification of mineral phases and the isotopic analysis of selected elements, are currently being used in the study of archaeological artefacts. The extensive use of physical methods arises principally because, in comparison with the standard wet chemical methods, they are rapid in operation and essentially non-destructive. Furthermore, they can provide information on the mineralogical and isotopic composition which cannot be obtained using the standard chemical methods.

The criteria, involved in the selection of the most appropriate method for determining the chemical composition of archaeological artefacts (i.e. the concentrations of major, minor and trace elements), are discussed on p. 257. Detailed descriptions of those physical methods of chemical analysis (i.e. optical emission spectrometry, atomic absorption spectrometry, X-ray fluorescence spectrometry and neutron activation analysis) which have general application are presented on pp. 260–278 while the more specialized techniques (i.e. electron probe microanalysis, beta ray backscattering and specific gravity determination) are described on pp. 278–285. The methods used for the identification of the chemical compounds and mineral phases present in artefacts (i.e. X-ray diffraction, infra-red absorption spectrometry, Mössbauer spectroscopy and thermal analysis) are described on pp. 285–301 while the techniques and range of elements appropriate for isotopic analysis are discussed on p. 301.

Some indication of the *relative* merits and limitations of these various physical methods, together with a brief summary of the types of artefact to which they are applicable, is also included in this chapter. However, the factors governing the choice of the most appropriate method for the examination of each type of artefact (i.e. stone artefacts, pottery, metal artefacts, glass, etc.) are further discussed in Chapter 10, where examples of the application of these techniques to the study of archaeological material are presented.

A more detailed discussion of many of the physical methods described in this chapter is presented in "Physical Methods in Determinative Mineralogy" (Zussman, 1967). The majority of the remaining references are to papers in which the application of the methods specifically to archaeological artefacts are discussed: further technical details in this context can be found in the references included in Chapter 10.

Chemical Analysis: General Discussion

An important difference between chemical analysis in, for example, an industrial context and the analysis of archaeological artefacts is the fact that, in the latter case, either no damage to the artefact is permissible or only a very small sample can be removed. With coins, for example, a method which leaves absolutely no mark after analysis must normally be employed. Alternatively, with bronze artefacts, only a small drilling which in no way detracts from their appearance can be taken. The amount of permissible damage is therefore often of primary importance in selecting the method used for the analysis of archaeological artefacts. Furthermore, where no damage is allowed, the artefact must be accommodated in the equipment used for analysis and its size and shape (e.g. a long sword or a large pottery vessel) may then present difficulties, necessitating the modification of standard commercial equipment.

A second important consideration is whether analysis of the surface of the artefact or its interior is required. Thus, in the case of glazed pottery, the analysis of either the glaze or the clay body may be of interest and the appropriate technique must accordingly be chosen. However, where an originally homogeneous metal object has become corroded during burial, a method which analyses only the surface would provide misleading information concerning its original composition. In addition, the need to analyse a particular part of the surface, such as an area of pigment used in colouring a glaze or a piece of inlay on a sword, may further limit the choice of technique.

Depending on the type of artefact under consideration, it may be necessary to determine the concentrations of the major elements (greater than 2 per cent). Alternatively, these may not be particularly relevant and the concentrations of selected minor elements (2 to 0·1 per cent) and trace elements (less than 0·1 per cent) must instead be determined. A range of concentrations from less than 1 part per million (ppm) up to 100 per cent must therefore, on occasions, be estimated and not surprisingly, no one method of analysis will operate over such a wide range for all the elements in the periodic table. Consequently, the selection of the method of analysis is further influenced by the particular elements chosen for analysis, together with their anticipated concentration range.

The selection of the elements for analysis and the experimental accuracy required obviously depends on the use to which the analytical data are to be put. For example, artefacts which have been made from raw materials obtained from a particular geographical region can sometimes be grouped together on the basis of their chemical composition. There is, however, an inherent spread in the chemical compositions of such a group due to minor variations in the composition of the raw materials and to changes in composition which occur as a result of the manufacturing processes. Consequently, the analysis of a single artefact rarely provides useful results and instead it is essential to analyse a large group of similar artefacts in order to define, as precisely as possible, the range of compositions which are characteristic of the group. A highly accurate quantitative analysis for all the detectable elements would obviously be an extremely time-consuming and expensive process and only on rare occasions would the results justify the effort expended. Therefore, the number of elements should be kept to the minimum, consistent with defining and differentiating between groups of artefacts, and the appropriate elements should be selected on the basis of a well-considered pilot programme, undertaken before embarking on the analysis of hundreds of artefacts. Similarly, the experimental accuracy required is largely determined by the inherent spread in compositions observed for a group of similar artefacts. Highly accurate analysis is obviously of limited relevance when the spread in compositions is large and for the majority of archaeological artefacts, it is sufficient to determine the concentrations of the chosen elements to an accuracy of between ± 5 and ± 10 per cent.

From the above discussion, it is clear that, in the study of archaeological artefacts, the essentially non-destructive analysis for several elements in a large number of artefacts is normally necessary. Methods of chemical analysis which are rapid in operation, and hence have low "running costs", are thus required. Consequently whenever possible physical methods are employed in preference to the standard wet chemical methods, even though they require a large capital outlay in order to purchase the necessary equipment. A summary of the characteristics which are relevant to making a choice between the four generally applicable physical methods of chemical analysis is presented in Table 20, together with a list of the principal types of artefact

Table 20. Comparison of the physical methods of chemical analysis

	Optical emission spectrometry	Atomic absorption spectrometry	X-ray fluorescence spectrometry	Neutron activation analysis
Damage to artefact	Slight (5–100 mg)	Slight (10–100 mg)	Non-destructive or slight (100 mg–2 g)	Non-destructive or slight (50–100 mg)
Analysis of surface or body	Body	Body	Surface	Body
Concentration range	100 ppm– 10 per cent	10 ppm–10 per cent	50 ppm–100 per cent	1 ppm–100 per cent
Elements analysed	30–40 elements (mainly metal elements)	30–40 elements (mainly metal elements)	Elements with $Z > 22$ (air) or $Z > 12$ (vacuum)	40–50 elements
Accuracy	± 10 per cent	± 2 per cent	± 2 to ± 5 per cent	± 2 to ± 5 per cent
Speed of operation	Manual (photographic recording)	Manual (individual elements)	Automatic recording and sample changing	Automatic recording and sample changing
Applications	Obsidian Pottery Bronzes Glass	Flint Bronzes	Obsidian Pottery Coins (milliprobe) Glass, glaze, faience Pigments (milliprobe)	Obsidian and flint Pottery Coins Glass and faience

to which these techniques have been applied. It must, however, be emphasized that, in practice, the choice of the physical method for the analysis of archaeological artefacts is often governed mainly by the availability of the necessary equipment.

Although the description of the multifarious chemical methods lies outside the scope of this book, their continuing importance in supplementing the data obtained from physical methods must be appreciated. Firstly, chemical methods provide values for the concentrations of the elements present directly, whereas physical methods required calibration with a series of standard specimens whose composition has previously been determined by chemical methods. Secondly, chemical methods provide the only means by which the concentrations of certain major elements (e.g. silicon, carbon) can be determined with high accuracy, while the minor element concentrations can also normally be determined with an accuracy greater than that attainable with physical methods. Furthermore, with the development of microchemical methods, the analysis requires only a small sample, comparable in size to that required for some physical methods, such as optical emission and atomic absorption spectrometry. Finally, the replacement of the classical gravimetric methods by various instrumental methods can provide a considerable saving in time in the investigation of a large number of samples with similar compositions. The currently available instrumental methods, which are employed after preliminary chemical reactions, include colorimetry, potentiometric titration, ultraviolet and visible spectrophotometry.

Optical Emission Spectrometry

Optical emission spectrometry involves the excitation of the outer electrons of the atoms in the sample under analysis. The energy released when these electrons return to their unexcited ground state appears as near ultraviolet and visible light (Fig. 62). This light consists of a number of sharply-defined wavelengths or spectral lines which are characteristic of the particular element excited. Consequently, the determination of the constituent wavelengths in the light emitted by the sample provides the basis for identifying the elements present in the sample while the intensity of the light, at a particular wavelength, provides an estimate of the concentration of the associated element.

Excitation is achieved by means of an electric discharge between two electrodes or a laser beam. The resulting light is separated into its constituent wavelengths using a prism or a diffraction grating and is then detected by means of a photographic plate or a photomultiplier.

Experimental Procedures

For the analysis of metal artefacts, excitation is normally achieved using a high frequency, high voltage a.c. spark discharge. Typically a 10 mg sample, taken from the artefact, is dissolved in a suitable acid (e.g. acqua regia). This solution is placed in a hollow graphite cup which forms the upper electrode and which has been made porous by previously heating in a flame. The solution therefore slowly creeps through the bottom whereupon it is completely volatilized, and its constituent atoms excited, by the a.c. spark discharge which is struck between the lower electrode, also of graphite, and the bottom of the cup.

In the case of non-metallic materials (e.g. pottery, glass, obsidian), it is more difficult to prepare a suitable solution and in addition, the a.c. spark discharge is not hot enough to volatilize many of the elements present. Therefore a low voltage, d.c. arc source is normally used for excitation. Typically a 10 mg sample is ground to a fine powder, mixed with graphite powder and then placed in a graphite cup (non-porous), which forms the lower electrode. A d.c. arc is struck between this electrode and an upper graphite electrode, thus completely volatilizing the sample and exciting its constituent atoms.

A more recent development has been the use of a ruby laser as the excitation source. In this case, the artefact can, in principle, be analysed directly without the prior removal of a small sample. The laser beam is directed onto a suitable area of the artefact, approximately 100 μm in diameter, and the brief burst of intense light, emitted when the laser is "fired", is sufficient to vaporize a few micrograms of material. The constituent atoms of this vapour are then excited by an auxiliary a.c. spark discharge. Although this method has the advantage of being both less destructive and less time-consuming, its reproducibility is, at present, such that it can only be used for qualitative or semi-quantitative analyses.

A typical spectrometer for analysing the constituent wavelengths of the light emitted as a result of excitation of the sample is shown schematically in Fig. 77. The spectral lines are separated by the refraction of the light through the prism, usually of quartz, in the same way as Newton first observed the constituent colours in white light. By using a light path which is several metres in length, extremely complex spectra can be sufficiently resolved so that each emitted wavelength (i.e. spectral line) appears as a separate black line on the photographic plate, which in this case is used as the detector. Higher resolution, and hence greater separation of the spectral lines, can be achieved, if necessary, by using a diffraction grating instead of the quartz prism. However, with a diffraction grating, the wavelength range recorded is normally more restricted.

Since the complete spectrum associated with each element is unique, the elements present in the sample can be identified from the positions of the black lines on the photographic plate: the relationship between the wavelength and the position of the associated line being first established using standard samples containing known elements.

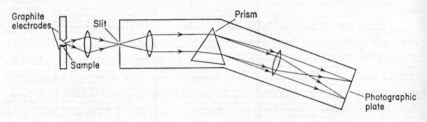

Figure 77. Schematic diagram showing the principal components of an optical emission spectrometer. The light emitted, as a result of the excitation of the sample, is focussed onto the spectrometer slit. After being refracted by the prism, the different wavelengths are focussed at different points along the photographic plate.

Subsequently one particular line for each element, selected to avoid overlap with other lines present on the plate, is normally used to determine the concentration of that element in the sample. A numerical evaluation of the degree of blackening of the chosen line is obtained using a photoelectric device, known as a microdensiometer. The degree of blackening is dependent on the intensity of the light at that wavelength and this is, in turn, proportional to the concentration of the associated element in the sample. However, because of peculiarities in the photographic process, the degree of blackening is not strictly proportional to the intensity of the light and consequently fairly elaborate calibration procedures are necessary in the initial setting-up of the equipment. The use of standard samples of known composition is essential and because the intensity of the light emitted by a particular element is effected by the presence of other elements, the standards must have a similar major element composition to that of the samples being analysed. Having established a calibration curve for the degree of blackening *versus* concentration for each element being studied, the characteristics of the electric discharge and the conditions under which the photographic plate is developed must be strictly controlled in order to obtain reproducible results over a long period.

In more sophisticated spectrometers, the intensity of the light at each wavelength is measured directly using a photomultiplier, in place of the photographic plate. Measurement of the intensity at successive wavelengths is achieved by rotating the prism. This technique is particularly rapid when the concentrations of only a few elements are required but it is, in many ways, less flexible for the analysis of the wide range of elements normally necessary in the study of archaeological artefacts.

Advantages and Limitations

Although optical emission spectrometry is not strictly non-destructive, the damage caused by extracting the necessary 5–100 mg sample is normally permissible, the main exceptions being coins and high quality ceramics. With metal artefacts, a small drilling is taken and the resulting hole is filled unobtrusively with wax. In this way, surface corrosion products can be removed and only the uncontaminated body of the artefact is analysed. With pottery, either a small chipping from a sherd fragment is used or a sample is taken from the base of the vessel using a diamond drill. Again the analysis of the body of pottery, without contamination by the glaze, is possible.

Analysis is confined to those elements which emit light with wavelengths greater than about 0·2 μm (i.e. 2000 Å) since ultra-violet light of shorter wavelength is strongly absorbed by air. Although this effectively precludes the analysis of many non-metal elements, there are some thirty to forty elements which can be analysed over a fairly wide range of concentrations using this technique. The lower concentration limit depends on the particular element under consideration but it is typically in the range from 10 to 100 ppm. Concentrations in excess of 10 per cent are difficult to estimate without the use of fairly elaborate dilution techniques. Again depending on the element considered and its concentration, the analyses are typically reproducible to within ± 10 per cent.

The provision of the initial calibration curves, necessary for quantitative analysis, is an extremely time-consuming operation. However, once this has been achieved, it is possible to analyse some forty artefacts in one week, the concentrations of at least ten elements being determined in this time.

Because of its considerable versatility and the fact that it is a long-established technique, optical emission spectrometry has been extensively used for the analysis of the minor and trace elements in a wide range of archaeological artefacts, including pottery, bronzes, glass and obsidian.

Atomic Absorption Spectrometry

In atomic absorption spectrometry, near ultra-violet or visible light with a sharply defined wavelength, which corresponds to the characteristic emission wavelength of the particular element chosen for analysis, is focussed onto the atomized sample. Since, for isolated atoms, absorption and emission occur at the same characteristic wavelength, the atoms of the chosen element absorb a proportion of the incident light; the energy associated with the light being transferred to the outer electrons which are consequently excited out of their ground state. The extent to which the light is absorbed therefore provides an estimate of the concentration of the chosen element in the sample.

Light of the characteristic wavelength is provided by a hollow cathode lamp; the sample, which is in solution, is atomized in a flame and the intensity of the emergent light beam, after absorption by the sample, is measured using a photomultiplier. A different lamp is required for each characteristic wavelength so that the analysis of each element necessitates a separate measurement.

Experimental Procedures

The samples for analysis, which vary in weight from 10 mg to 1 g depending on the concentrations of the elements under consideration, must first be taken into solution. Acqua regia is normally used for metals while, in the case of non-metallic materials (e.g. pottery, flint), the powdered samples are dissolved in a mixture of hydrofluoric and perchloric acids. A few millilitres of this solution are aspirated to form a fine spray which is then carried into a suitable flame (e.g. air/acetylene, nitrous oxide/acetylene) where the solution is effectively atomized.

A hollow cathode lamp, whose cathode is made from or lined with the element under analysis, provides light of the required characteristic wavelength. As shown schematically in Fig. 78, the light from the lamp is focussed onto the central portion of the flame. During its passage through the flame, atoms of the element under analysis absorb a proportion of the light. The emergent beam is focussed onto a slit and passed through a monochromator which filters out the characteristic wavelength from the background light. The intensity at this wavelength is then measured using a photomultiplier which is attached to a meter or recorder. This intensity (I_T) is compared with the intensity (I_0), at the characteristic wavelength, of the light transmitted in the absence of the atomized sample. The extent of the absorption, which

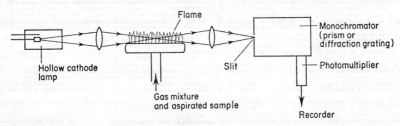

Figure 78. Schematic diagram showing the principal components of an atomic absorption spectrometer. The light from the hollow cathode lamp is focussed onto the flame. After the absorption by the sample atoms in the flame, the light is focussed onto the monochromator slit and the intensity at the characteristic wavelength is measured with the photomultiplier.

depends on the concentration of the chosen element in the sample, is normally specified in terms of the absorbance (A) which is given by

$$A = \log \frac{I_0}{I_T}$$

For the analysis of further elements, the process is repeated using different hollow cathode lamps.

For quantitative analysis, calibration with solutions containing known amounts of the chosen elements is necessary since the theoretically linear relationship between concentration and absorbance (A) is obeyed only approximately. In addition, the possibility of a modification to the concentration–absorbance relationship, as a result of chemical interference from other constituents of the sample, must be considered. For example, anions, such as phosphate and sulphate ions, can form chemical compounds with the alkaline earth metals (e.g. calcium, magnesium), thus reducing the absorption by these elements. Alternatively the absorption by the chosen element can be increased in the presence of a second more readily ionized element since only *atoms* absorb the characteristic wavelength and the presence of additional ions serves to increase the ratio of atoms to ions for the chosen element.

Advantages and Limitations

In considering the advantages and limitations of atomic absorption spectrometry, comparison with optical emission spectrometry is relevant since these two methods of analysis have many features in common. In requiring the removal of a small sample from the artefact, neither method is strictly non-destructive. Similarly, the range of elements which can be analysed is essentially the same for each method and they are both best suited to the analysis of the minor and trace constituents.

The optimum concentration range for the chosen element in the *solution* used for atomic absorption spectrometry is typically 1–10 ppm (i.e. about 1–10 μg/ml). Therefore, in order to analyse an element which is present in the *sample* at a concentration of 10 ppm, about 100 mg of sample must be dissolved to produce 1 ml of solution. Consequently, the lower concentration limit for analysis depends, to a large extent, on the amount of sample which is available. Similarly, to analyse an element which is present in the sample at concentrations in excess of 50 per cent, about 10 mg of sample must be dissolved in 1 l of solvent. At these high dilutions, the problem of contamination can become severe and therefore the method is not normally satisfactory for the analysis of the major elements.

The analyses obtained using atomic absorption spectrometry tend to be more accurate (typically about ± 2 per cent) than those obtained with optical emission spectrometry, especially when the d.c. arc method is employed in the latter case. However, in comparison with optical emission spectrometry, atomic absorption spectrometry suffers from two disadvantages. Firstly, the separate measurement required for the analysis of each element tends to make the method rather time-consuming when a large number of elements are being studied. Secondly, for the analysis of non-metallic materials (e.g. pottery, stone artefacts), the samples must first be dissolved in a mixture of hydrofluoric and perchloric acids which is somewhat unpleasant to use. Consequently, the application of atomic absorption spectrometry to the study of archaeological artefacts has been confined mainly to the analysis of non-ferrous metals (e.g. copper alloys), although the method has also proved to be valuable for the analysis of flint artefacts.

X-ray Fluorescence Spectrometry

In X-ray fluorescence spectrometry, the specimen to be analysed is irradiated with primary X-rays which displace electrons from the inner orbits of the constituent atoms. The resultant vacant inner electron energy levels are immediately filled by electrons from the outer orbits and the energy released in this process appears as secondary or fluorescent X-rays with wavelengths (λ) in the range from 2×10^{-5} to 2×10^{-4} μm (Fig. 62). Each element emits secondary X-rays at several characteristic and sharply defined wavelengths which depend on its atomic number (Z) and which are given, in the case of the more important $K(\alpha)$ and $L(\alpha)$ radiations, by the relationships:

$$\lambda_K(\mu m) = \frac{0.12}{(Z-1)^2} \qquad (9.1)$$

$$\lambda_L(\mu m) = \frac{0.65}{(Z-7.4)^2} \qquad (9.2)$$

Consequently, the determination of the constituent wavelengths of the secondary X-rays provides the basis for identifying the elements present in the specimen while the intensity of the X-rays at a particular wavelength provides an estimate of the concentration of the associated element.

The primary exciting X-rays are obtained from either a high-voltage X-ray tube or a series of radioactive sources. The characteristic secondary X-rays are separated into their constituent wavelengths using a diffracting crystal and are then detected with either a scintillation or a proportional counter. Alternatively, in the non-dispersive spectrometer, both the detection of the X-rays and the determination of their wavelengths is achieved, without prior separation, using a semiconductor counter. A further development, of particular importance for the study of archaeological artefacts, is the X-ray milliprobe (p. 272) which analyses a small area of the specimen, approximately 1 mm in diameter.

Experimental Procedures

A typical X-ray fluorescence spectrometer is shown schematically in Fig. 79. The spectrometer components must be enclosed in a lead chamber in order to shield the operator from stray X-rays and in some instruments, this chamber is maintained under high vacuum conditions. Provided that the archaeological artefact is sufficiently small for it to be contained within the spectrometer chamber, it can be analysed directly without the prior removal of a small sample. The continuous spectrum of primary X-rays, which is used to excite the specimen, is produced by a high voltage X-ray tube operating, typically, at 50 kV. This primary radiation emerges from the X-ray tube through a thin beryllium window and is incident on the surface of the specimen at an angle of approximately 45 degrees. The characteristic secondary X-rays from the specimen can only reach the diffracting crystal (e.g. lithium fluoride or quartz) via the first collimator which therefore precisely defines the angle, θ, between this incident radiation and the crystal surface. The spacing, d, between the crystal lattice planes is of the same order of magnitude as the X-ray

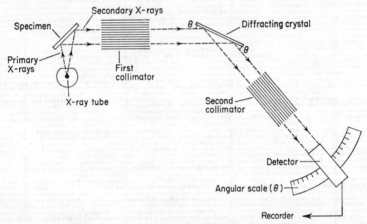

Figure 79. Schematic diagram showing the principal components of an X-ray fluorescence spectrometer.

wavelength and therefore, for a given wavelength (λ), appreciable reflection (i.e. diffraction) occurs only when the angle, θ, satisfies the Bragg condition:

$$n\lambda = 2d \sin \theta \tag{9.3}$$

where n is an integer (i.e. 1, 2, 3, etc.).

The detector is positioned so that it is at the same angle, θ, with respect to the crystal surface and the second collimator prevents scattered radiation from the crystal from reaching the detector. The characteristic secondary X-rays are therefore only detected when their wavelength satisfies the Bragg condition. In order to determine the constituent wavelengths of the secondary X-rays emitted by the specimen, the crystal is rotated and a system of mechanical gears ensure that the incident radiation and the detector are always at the same angle with respect to the surface of the diffracting crystal. The detector, which is typically either a scintillation or a gas proportional counter, produces an electrical pulse for each incident X-ray photon. Therefore the plot of the number of pulses *versus* the angle, θ, consists of a series of peaks (Fig. 80). The positions of these peaks, in terms of θ, indicate the constituent wavelengths of the secondary X-rays (equation 9.3) and hence the elements present in the specimen. Similarly the peak heights provide a measure of the intensity of the X-rays at these wavelengths and hence the concentrations of the associated elements in the specimen.

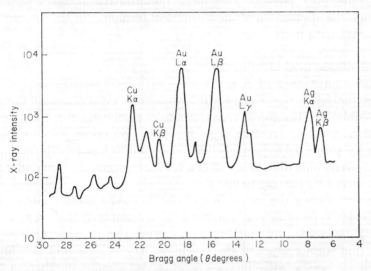

Figure 80. X-ray fluorescence spectrum for a gold–silver–copper alloy: X-ray intensity (i.e. number of pulses per second) *versus* Bragg angle (i.e. wavelength). The principal characteristic fluorescent X-ray wavelengths (Lα, Lβ, etc.) for gold (Au), silver (Ag) and copper (Cu) are marked.

In an alternative system, referred to as the *non-dispersive* X-ray fluorescence spectrometer, the diffracting crystal is dispensed with and the secondary X-rays emitted by the specimen are detected directly using a semiconductor counter (e.g. lithium-drifted germanium). In this case the amplitude of the electrical pulse produced by each incident X-ray photon is proportional to the energy of the photon and therefore inversely proportional to its wavelength (equation 7.2). The electrical pulses are analysed electronically using a multi-channel pulse analyser, each channel of which only accepts pulses with amplitudes between set limits. A plot of the intensity of the secondary X-rays *versus* wavelength is therefore obtained directly and can be interpreted as previously in order to provide a quantitative analysis of the specimen. Since, with this system, no collimators are required, a far higher proportion of the secondary X-rays emitted by specimen reach the detector. Consequently a weaker source of primary exciting X-rays can be employed and the high voltage X-ray tube can be replaced by radioactive sources (e.g. ^{3}H, ^{241}Am, ^{57}Co).

For quantitative analysis, calibration with standards, which closely resemble the specimen in terms of major-element composition, is normally essential. However, with the non-dispersive spectrometer, it is sometimes possible to achieve quantitative analyses directly, through the application of the theoretical formulae for the interaction of X-rays with matter.

Advantages and Limitations

A major advantage of X-ray fluorescence spectrometry is that the direct analysis of the artefact, without prior removal of a small sample, is possible and therefore, except for a faint discolouration, the method is entirely non-destructive. The discolouration occurs when glass or glaze are subjected to prolonged radiation but fortunately the majority of this darkening disappears after a few days, while the remainder can be removed by heating to 200°C.

In considering the suitability of the method for the analysis of a particular type of artefact, it must be remembered that X-rays are strongly absorbed by matter and therefore the analysis relates only to a thin surface layer of the specimen. The thickness of this layer, which decreases with increasing effective atomic number of the material, is typically in the range from 20 to 200 μm. Consequently X-ray fluorescence spectrometry is ideally suited for the analysis of the glaze on pottery whilst, because of corrosion and surface enrichment effects (p. 337), it is not normally suitable for metal analyses.

The range of elements that can be analysed is limited by the fact that X-rays are also absorbed by air. The absorption increases rapidly with increasing wavelength (i.e. decreasing energy) and therefore, from equations (9.1) and (9.2), it can be seen that the characteristic secondary X-rays from elements with low atomic numbers will be most strongly absorbed. In practice, the low limit is about $Z = 22$ (i.e. titanium) whilst there is no upper limit to the atomic number of detectable elements. Furthermore, by evacuating the spectrometer chamber, measurements can be extended down to magnesium with an atomic number of 12. In contrast to optical emission and atomic absorption spectrometry, X-ray fluorescence spectrometry is most satisfactory for the analysis of the major and minor constituents in the specimen. However, depending on the material and particular element being analysed, the concentrations of trace elements, as low as 10–100 ppm, can also be determined.

Inaccuracies in the non-destructive X-ray fluorescence analysis of archaeological artefacts are principally associated with the diverse sizes and shapes encountered. This problem is particularly severe with spectrometers employing a difffracting crystal since this requires a parallel beam of secondary X-rays. A parallel beam is achieved through the use of the first collimator which inevitably absorbs a large proportion of the secondary X-rays emitted by the specimen. Therefore, in order to obtain a reasonably large signal to background "noise" ratio, a comparatively large area of the specimen, typically 1 cm in diameter, must be irradiated with primary X-rays. For accurate quantitative analyses, this area should be flat and should be the same size as that of the calibration standards. In addition, both specimen and standards should be placed in the spectrometer in identical positions and at similar angles with respect to the collimator and primary X-ray beam. With many archaeological artefacts, it is impossible to satisfy these conditions and significant errors in the resulting analytical data can therefore arise. These difficulties are less pronounced in the case of the non-dispersive spectrometer since, by dispensing with the diffracting crystal, the geometry of the system is far simpler. These inaccuracies, together with the fact that only a thin surface layer of the artefact is analysed, have tended to limit the use of *non-destructive* X-ray fluorescence spectrometry, glazes and glass (i.e. man made glass and obsidian) being the principal materials studied.

Further applications of X-ray fluorescence spectrometry are, however, possible when the removal of a small sample from the artefact is permitted. In the case of metal artefacts, a drilling is dissolved in a suitable acid and a measured amount of the solution is dried on a filter paper which is then used for the analysis. Similarly, in the case of pottery, between 100 mg and 2 g of the sherd are ground to a fine powder which, with the addition of a suitable flux, is then fused to form a glass bead with uniform composition. Although this approach to X-ray fluorescence analysis is no longer strictly non-destructive, it possesses the significant advantage, in comparison to optical emission and atomic absorption spectrometry, that the recording of the secondary X-ray spectrum and the sample-changing can be fully automated. Therefore, having established the necessary calibration curves, large numbers of samples can be rapidly analysed for several elements to an accuracy which is normally better than ± 5 per cent. The method, in this partially-destructive form, is not however suitable for the analysis of coins but in this case, the X-ray fluorescence milliprobe provides an important alternative approach.

X-ray Milliprobe

In the X-ray milliprobe (Fig. 81), the primary exciting X-rays are

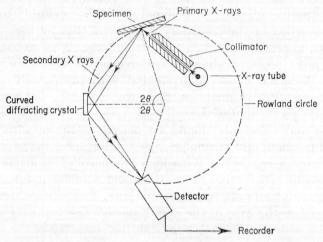

Figure 81. Schematic diagram showing the principal components of an X-ray milliprobe. With the specimen (point source), curved diffracting crystal and detector lying on the Rowland circle, the secondary X-rays with a characteristic wavelength satisfying the Bragg condition (equation 9.3) are focussed directly onto the detector.

collimated into a narrow beam, typically less than 1 mm in diameter. Secondary X-rays are emitted from the specimen, as previously, but in this case they originate from what is effectively a point source. Consequently by using a curved diffracting crystal, in place of the flat crystal used previously, secondary X-rays, whose wavelength satisfies the Bragg condition (equation 9.3), can be focussed directly onto the detector without the use of any further collimators. Although the integrated primary X-ray energy falling on the specimen is much lower with this system than with the standard spectrometer, the proportion of the secondary X-rays that are detected is very much greater and therefore a comparable signal to background noise ratio is achieved.

The specimen is located outside the spectrometer chamber and is separated from it by a thin Milar window which permits sufficient evacuation of the chamber for the analysis of elements with atomic numbers above about 14 (i.e. silicon). In order that the appropriate characteristic secondary X-rays are focussed onto the detector for all Bragg angles, θ, a fairly complex mechanical system is necessary since, in addition to the rotation of the crystal and detector, the distances between the point source on the specimen, the crystal and the detector must be altered. A suitable mechanical system, together with the theory for curved diffracting cyrstals, is described by Banks and Hall (1963).

Since the specimen is outside the spectrometer, artefacts of practically any size and shape (e.g. a large pottery vessel or a painting) can be analysed while, because the area analysed is very small, surface unevenness or curvature does not seriously affect the accuracy of the analytical data. Specific areas on the surface can be selected for analysis by means of an optical system, the binocular eyepieces of which are located on the front panel of the spectrometer. It is therefore possible to analyse, for example, particular pigments in a painting or glaze, separately from their surroundings. In this respect, the milliprobe represents a compromise between the standard X-ray fluorescence spectrometer and the electron probe microanalyser (p. 278); its major advantage over the latter instrument being the fact that elaborate specimen preparation is not necessary.

A further important application of the milliprobe is for the analysis of the major constituents in coins. In this case, the surface layer, at the point irradiated with the primary X-rays, can be removed without noticcablc damage to the coin. Consequently, analysis of the interior of the coin is possible, thus partially overcoming the problems of corrosion and surface enrichment associated with the conventional X-ray fluorescence analysis of metal artefacts.

Neutron Activation Analysis

In contrast to the preceding techniques, which involve the excitation of the atomic electrons, neutron activation analysis involves the excitation of the atomic nuclei. This excitation is achieved by bombarding the specimen with slow neutrons which interact with the

atomic nuclei of the constituent elements, transforming them into
unstable radioactive isotopes. These radioactive isotopes then decay
to form stable isotopes, the half-life for the decay process varying
from a fraction of a second to thousands of years, depending on the
particular radioactive isotope involved. Associated with the decay of
the radioactive isotope is the emission of gamma rays whose energies
are typically in the range from 0·1 to 2 MeV (Fig. 62). In discussing
gamma rays, it is more usual to refer to the energy carried by each

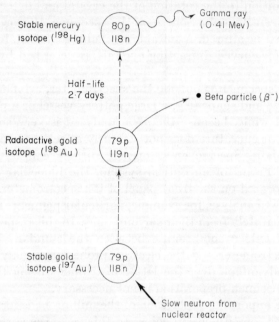

Figure 82. Neutron activation analysis: nuclear reactions involved in the emission of a
gamma ray whose energy (0.41 MeV) is effectively characteristic of the element, gold.
The numbers in the circles refer to the number of protons (p) and neutrons (n) in the
associated nuclei.

gamma ray photon rather than to the wavelength, the relationship
between energy and wavelength being given by equation (7.2). The
gamma rays have sharply-defined energies which are ultimately
characteristic of the particular element excited by the slow neutrons.
Consequently, the determination of the energies of the gamma rays
emitted by the specimen provides the basis for identifying its constituent elements while the intensity of the gamma rays at a particular
energy provides an estimate of the concentration of the associated
element.

The nuclear reactions, which link the original stable nuclei to the ultimate emission of characteristic gamma rays, are somewhat complex. For example, in the case of gold (Fig. 82), the original stable gold isotope (^{197}Au) is first transformed into the radioactive gold isotope, ^{198}Au, as a result of the neutron bombardment. The radioactive gold then decays, with a half-life of 2·7 days, to an excited state of the stable mercury isotope, ^{198}Hg, with the emission of a beta particle. The characteristic gamma ray, with an energy of about 0·41 MeV, is finally emitted when the mercury nucleus assumes its unexcited ground state, a process which is effectively instantaneous. Alternatively, the original stable isotope may first be transformed into a radioactive isotope of a different element, as in the case of nickel (^{58}Ni) which is converted to the radioactive cobalt isotope, ^{58}Co, with the emission of a proton. Furthermore, in many cases, the final stable nuclei, in assuming their unexcited ground states, can emit gamma rays at more than one sharply defined energy.

The neutron flux is normally provided by a nuclear reactor, although mobile neutron sources can be used. The characteristic gamma rays are subsequently detected and their energies determined using either a scintillation or semiconductor counter.

Experimental Procedures

For irradiation in the nuclear reactor, the specimens are placed in a metal can, typically 3 cm in diameter and 10 cm in height. Small specimens, such as coins and faience beads, can be irradiated and analysed directly without the prior removal of a small sample. However, in the case of larger specimens, such as pottery and stone artefacts, which cannot be accommodated in the standard cans, it is normally necessary to remove a sample approximately 50–100 mg in weight. The neutron dose, to which the specimens are subjected, depends on the elements present and their concentrations. Typical reactors provide a neutron flux of approximately 10^{12}–10^{13} neutrons cm^{-2} s^{-1} and radiation times ranging from a few minutes to several hours are employed.

Instead of a reactor, mobile neutron sources, such as a plutonium–beryllium source housed in a paraffin-filled Howitzer, can be used (Gordus, 1967). Their application is, however, more limited since they can only provide fluxes in the range from 10^3 to 10^6 neutrons cm^{-2} s^{-1}.

The gamma rays emitted by the specimen, subsequent to the neutron activation, can be detected using a scintillation counter. This typically consists of a crystal of sodium iodide, containing a small amount of thallium, which is placed in optical contact with a photo-multiplier and carefully shielded from external light. A percentage of the gamma rays are absorbed in the crystal and their energy is con-verted into visible light, each absorbed gamma ray photon producing a short pulse or flash of light. The light pulse is detected with the photo-multiplier which provides a corresponding electrical pulse at its out-put. The amplitude of the electrical pulse is proportional to the inten-sity of the light pulse which is, itself, proportional to the energy of the gamma ray photon. The electrical pulses are, typically, analysed electronically using a multi-channel pulse analyser, each channel of which only accepts pulses with amplitudes between set limits. Hence a plot of the number of gamma ray photons counted *versus* gamma ray energy is obtained. The gamma ray spectrum consists of a series of peaks whose positions along the energy axis indicate the elements present in the specimen and whose heights provide a measure of the concentrations of these elements.

An alternative detector, which has been developed during the past ten years, is the semiconductor counter which is typically a lithium-drifted germanium crystal. The mechanism for detection, in this case, is the production of free charge carriers (i.e. ionization) when the gamma rays are absorbed by the crystal. An electrical pulse is again associated with each absorbed gamma ray photon and the amplitude of the pulse is proportional to the energy of the photon. The electrical pulses are analysed as with the scintillation counter, a typical gamma ray spectrum being shown in Fig. 83. A major advantage of the semi-conductor counter, as compared to the scintillation counter, is that it has a much higher energy resolution and therefore the peaks, corre-sponding to gamma rays of particular energies, are much narrower. With the semiconductor counter, the peak half-widths are typically about 3 keV whereas with the scintillation counter they are as much as 50 keV. Consequently, the difficulty of overlapping peaks, which occurs when a large number of elements are present in the specimen, is considerably reduced by using a semiconductor counter. In addition, the peaks are more clearly distinguishable from the background gamma ray counts associated with Compton scattering, in which only a fraction of the energy of the gamma ray photon is absorbed by the detector. Therefore, lower concentrations can be determined with the semiconductor counter.

The length of time, which should elapse between the neutron

activation in the nuclear reactor and the measurement of the gamma ray spectrum, depends on the half-lives of the radioactive isotopes being studied. In practice, more than one spectrum is normally measured for each specimen. Data on the short-lived isotopes is obtained from measurements made as soon after irradiation as possible while the long-lived isotopes are more easily studied after several weeks have elapsed.

For quantitative analysis, calibration with standards of known composition is again necessary and in addition, standards must be included

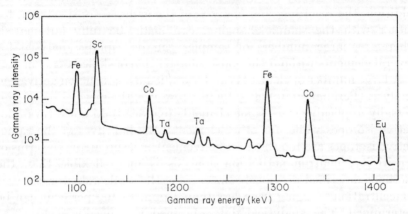

Figure 83. Gamma ray spectrum (partial) for a typical pottery sample, obtained using a high resolution semiconductor counter: gamma ray intensity (i.e. number of pulses per second) *versus* energy. The characteristic gamma ray energies associated with iron(^{59}Fe), scandium (^{46}Sc), cobalt (^{60}Co), tantalum (^{182}Ta) and europium (^{152}Eu) are marked.

with each batch of specimens in order to monitor variations in the neutron flux that occur within the reactor. For the analysis of minor and trace elements, the calibration is easier than for the preceding methods since, provided the matrix (i.e. the major element composition) remains reasonably constant, the gamma ray intensity is directly proportional to the concentration over a fairly wide range of concentrations. However, for the analysis of major elements, as in the determination of the silver content of silver coins, the situation is more complex. As a result of the progressive absorption of the neutrons as they pass through the specimen, the gamma ray intensity, in this case, also depends upon the thickness of the specimen and therefore somewhat specialized calibration techniques are necessary.

Advantages and Limitations

A major advantage of neutron activation analysis is that, in the case of small artefacts, direct analysis without the prior removal of a sample is possible. The method is therefore entirely non-destructive, provided, of course, that the specimen is not "over-irradiated". If an excessive neutron dose was used, the resulting radioactivity could be such that it would not be safe to handle the specimen for many years.

A further merit of the neutron activation method is that it provides an analysis of the *entire* specimen, rather than merely the thin surface layer which is analysed with X-ray fluorescence spectrometry. In addition, the recording and analysis of the gamma ray spectrum, together with the sample-changing, can again be fully automated. Therefore, large numbers of samples can be rapidly analysed for several elements without the constant attention of skilled personnel.

A large number of elements can be studied using neutron activation analysis (Perlman and Asaro, 1969). However, the method is not universally applicable since some elements (e.g. lead) do not form radioactive isotopes while, for other elements, the half-lives of the radioactive isotopes are too short for convenient measurement. In terms of sensitivity, neutron activation analysis is more flexible than the methods described previously since, using the semiconductor counter, concentrations ranging from less than 1 ppm to 100 per cent can be determined. The analytical data obtained is typically accurate to better than ± 5 per cent.

Because it is non-destructive and provides an analysis of the entire specimen, the neutron activation method has been extensively used to determine the concentrations of the major and minor elements in coins. In addition, with the development of the semiconductor counter, the method is now being used to determine the concentrations of the minor and trace elements in a wide range of materials, including pottery, flint, obsidian, glass and faience.

Electron Probe Microanalyser

The electron probe microanalyser involves the combination of the techniques of scanning electron microscopy (p. 246) with those of X-ray fluorescence spectrometry. In this instrument, the specimen to be analysed is irradiated with a fine electron beam instead of the beam of primary X-rays used in the standard X-ray fluorescence spectrometer. As before, the inner electrons of the constituent atoms are excited and secondary X-rays, whose wavelengths are characteristic of the particular element excited, are emitted. The intensity of the secondary X-rays, at a particular wavelength, is again dependent on the concentration of the associated element in the specimen.

The electron beam is focussed onto a small area of the specimen, approximately 1 μm in diameter, and the position of the beam can be changed so that it systematically scans the surface of the specimen. It is therefore possible to determine the variations in concentration, over the specimen surface, of the elements selected for analysis. With respect to the size of the area analysed, the electron probe microanalyser represents an important extension to the facilities provided by the X-ray milliprobe.

Experimental Procedures

A typical arrangement for an electron probe microanalyser is shown schematically in Fig. 84. The electrons are generated by means of a

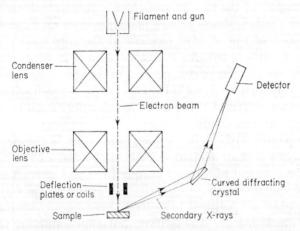

Figure 84. Schematic diagram showing the principal components of the electron probe microanalyser.

heated filament and are accelerated through about 30 kV, in order to provide a high energy electron beam which is directed towards the specimen. The beam is then passed through a series of magnetic lenses which serve to demagnify its diameter so that the irradiated area of the specimen is approximately 1 μm in diameter. The characteristic secondary X-rays, emitted by the specimen, are separated into their constituent wavelengths using a diffracting crystal and are detected with, for example, a gas proportional counter. Since these X-rays originate from what is effectively a point source, a curved diffracting crystal can be used and the X-rays are focussed directly onto the detector without the need for collimators. As previously, the Bragg angles (θ), at which the secondary X-rays are detected, establish their wavelengths and hence the elements present in the specimen. Similarly, the intensity of the X-rays at a particular angle (i.e. wavelength) provides a measure of the concentration of the associated element.

The scanning system consists of a set of magnetic deflection coils or electrostatic deflection plates, which are incorporated within the final lens assembly and serve to systematically deflect the electron beam over the specimen surface in a raster-like pattern. The diffracting crystal is set at the Bragg angle appropriate to the specific element chosen for analysis and the electrical output from the detector is used to control the brightness of the spot on the screen of a cathode ray tube. This spot scans the cathode ray tube screen in synchronism with the scanning of the specimen surface by the electron beam. An enlarged "image" of the specimen surface is therefore displayed on the screen and the brightness at any point provides an indication of the concentration of the selected element at the corresponding point on the specimen (Plate 20). An optical system is incorporated into the instrument so that the particular area of the specimen being analysed can be readily identified. As in the case of the electron microscope, the entire electronoptic and X-ray detection assembly must be maintained under high-vacuum conditions.

The preparation of specimens for examination in the electron probe microanalyser is more elaborate than in the case of the X-ray milliprobe. The removal of a small sample from the artefact is normally necessary and for accurate quantitative analysis, the surface of the specimen must be polished in order to remove any surface relief in excess of about 0·1 μm. In addition, for non-conducting materials, a thin metal film, about 10^{-2} μm in thickness, must be applied to the surface in order to carry away the electric charge deposited by the electron beam and thus maintain the specimen at earth potential.

For quantitative analysis, calibration with standards of known composition is necessary. However, in comparison with the situation for conventional X-ray fluorescence spectrometry, the factors which relate the concentrations to the X-ray intensities can be more easily calculated on a theoretical basis for the electron probe microanalyser. It is therefore possible, in many instances, to use pure elements as standards or alternatively compounds, whose composition differs considerably from that of the specimen under analysis, can be employed.

Applications

In spite of its considerable potential, the electron probe microanalyser has not, to date, been extensively used in the examination of archaeological artefacts. Possible applications (Hornblower, 1962), some of which have been exploited, include the identification and analysis of small inclusions in pottery, glass, stone artefacts and metals. In addition, the technique can be used to study the phenomenon of surface enrichment in metals (p. 337) and the nature of the bonding at the interface between two different metals (p. 236). In this case, sections cut perpendicular to the surface or interface are examined and the distribution of selected elements is established with a resolution of about 1 μm.

A further important application of electron probe microanalysis is in the study of the pigments used in paintings: this, of course, includes those paintings which are primarily of interest to the art historian rather than the archaeologist. In this case, a section, perpendicular to the surface and removed using a hypodermic needle, is examined and where several layers of paint are present, each layer, which may be only a few microns in thickness, can be analysed separately. Alternatively, the relationship between the pigments and the material (e.g. plaster), to which they have been applied, can be investigated.

In considering the possible uses of the electron probe microanalyser, it must be remembered that the technique is not strictly non-destructive since a small sample, typically a few millimetres in diameter, must be removed from the artefact. Further, as in the case of conventional X-ray fluorescence spectrometry, the analysis is only representative of a thin surface layer of the specimen, a few microns in thickness. Finally, it should be noted that the range of elements which can be analysed (i.e. elements with atomic number greater than 12) and the lower detection limits (i.e. 100–1000 ppm) are also comparable to those associated with X-ray fluorescence spectrometry.

Beta Ray Backscattering

As discussed in the context of the scanning electron microscope (p. 246), when electrons are incident on a specimen, some are effectively absorbed while others are backscattered and emerge from the surface of the specimen. This elastic backscattering is due to the interaction between the negative charge of the electrons and the charge carried by the nuclei of the constituent atoms. Therefore, the percentage of the electrons backscattered depends on the atomic number (Z) of the elements present in the surface layer of the specimen. Consequently, when a specific element of high atomic number (e.g. lead: $Z = 82$) is known to be present in a matrix of low atomic number elements, the concentration of this element can be estimated, non-destructively, by measuring the number of electrons that are backscattered.

In the beta ray backscatter (Fig. 85), a collimated beam of electrons (or positrons), approximately 5 mm in diameter, is provided by a weak radioactive beta source (e.g. ^{204}Tl or ^{35}S). The specimen under investigation is placed at an angle of 45° to the beam and the backscattered beta particles are counted using a Geiger counter. The

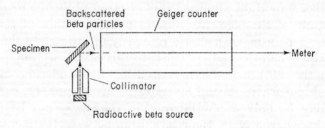

Figure 85. Schematic diagram of the beta ray backscatterer.

associated electronics can be powered by a small battery so that, as well as being cheap to produce, the complete apparatus is extremely portable and can therefore be readily taken to museums for the immediate examination of artefacts.

The beta ray backscatterer has been successfully used for the determination of the lead contents of glasses and glazes (Emeleus, 1960), calibration with standard glasses containing known concentrations of lead being necessary. The instrument is only sensitive to lead contents in excess of about 5 per cent. However, this is not normally a serious limitation since the primary aim is to distinguish between a glass or glaze to which lead has been added deliberately as a major constituent and similar material, of a non-leaded type, in which lead is present only as a minor or trace constituent.

An inherent and significant limitation of the beta ray backscatterer is that it is unable to identify the specific element responsible for the backscattering. Therefore, it cannot, for example, distinguish between a small concentration of lead ($Z = 82$) and a high concentration of an element with a medium atomic number (e.g. tin: $Z = 50$). Furthermore, when examining glazes, the number of backscattered beta rays will also depend on the thickness of the glaze, unless this is greater than about one-quarter of the beta particle range. This problem can be partially overcome by using the low energy beta rays (170 keV) from radioactive sulphur (^{35}S) for which the range is approximately 150 μm. Alternatively, as in the determination of the thickness of the gilt layer (i.e. gold: $Z = 79$) on a Buddha statue, direct use can be made of the dependence between the number of backscattered beta rays and the thickness of the high atomic number surface layer.

Specific Gravity Determinations

The measurement of specific gravity (i.e. the ratio of the density of the substance to the density of water) provides a useful non-destructive method for determining the composition of binary alloys (i.e. mixtures of two metals). For example, by comparing the specific gravity of a gold coin with that of pure gold (specific gravity = 19·3), the concentration of the alloying component in the coin can be determined provided that this can be assumed to be *either* silver (specific gravity = 10·5) *or* copper (specific gravity = 8·9).

The specific gravity is determined by weighing the specimen first in air and then suspended in a suitable liquid, whose specific gravity (S_1) at the operating temperature is known. The specific gravity of the specimen (S) is given by:

$$S = \frac{W_a}{(W_a - W_1)} \times S_1$$

where W_a and W_1 are the weights in air and the liquid respectively. Water (density = 0·998 g cm^{-3} at 20°C) is an obvious choice of liquid. However, organic liquids which have a higher specific gravity, a lower surface tension and a higher boiling point are now favoured.

The percentage of component A, in a binary alloy containing metals A and B, can be determined from the measured specific gravity, S, using the relationship:

$$\%A = \left(\frac{S_A S - S_A S_B}{S_A S - S_B S}\right) \times 100$$

where S_A and S_B are the specific gravities of the pure A and B metals respectively. Alternatively, a more precise relationship, which takes into account the variation in the crystal lattice spacing due to changes in the composition of the alloy, can be used. However, in this case, it is necessary to first establish a calibration curve for specific gravity *versus* the percentage of metal *A*, using alloys of known composition.

Because it is both non-destructive and provides an analysis of the entire artefact, specific gravity determinations have been extensively used for the analysis of coins made from gold–silver alloys (Hughes and Oddy, 1970). In ideal circumstances, the error in the determination of the gold content can be less than ± 1 per cent. However, the presence of a third metal (e.g. copper) can considerably reduce the accuracy since 5 per cent of copper in a gold–silver alloy will result in a 2 per cent lowering of the gold content as determined by the specific gravity method. Therefore, in considering ternary alloys (i.e. mixtures

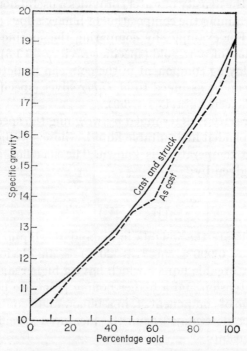

Figure 86. Specific gravity data for gold–silver alloy discs containing known percentages of gold. The data for the "as-cast" discs show irregularities due to the porosity associated with gas bubbles. However after hammering the discs at red-heat (i.e. cast and struck), the specific gravity data form a smooth curve, indicating that the hammering has eliminated the porosity.

of three metals), it is normally necessary to determine the concentration of one of the alloying components independently using, for example, neutron activation analysis (Das and Zonderhuis, 1964).

The presence of gas bubbles in cast metal artefacts is a further potential source of error since the associated porosity will lower the measured specific gravity with a consequent lowering of the estimated gold content. However, the comparison of the specific gravity data for standard alloys after casting with that after subsequent hammering at red heat (Fig. 86) suggests that gas bubbles will not normally be present in "worked" artefacts, such as struck coins. Finally, the necessity of removing surface corrosion products, which will also lower the measured specific gravity, must be emphasized.

X-Ray Diffraction

In contrast to the preceding techniques which involved the determination of the chemical composition (i.e. concentrations of the constituent elements) of artefacts, X-ray diffraction is used to identify the mineral phases and chemical compounds present in archaeological artefacts. In addition, the X-ray diffraction data can provide information on the mechanical and thermal treatments to which metal artefacts were subjected during their fabrication.

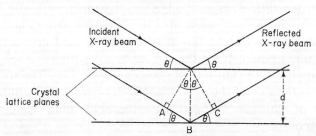

Figure 87. Diagram illustrating the Bragg relationship for X-ray diffraction. The path difference between reflections from successive lattice planes $= AB + BC = 2d \sin \theta = n\lambda$ (equation 9.3).

For X-ray diffraction measurements, the specimen is bombarded with a beam of *monochromatic* X-rays (i.e. X-rays with a sharply-defined wavelength). Although the fundamental process that occurs when X-rays strike a crystal is one of scattering or diffraction, it is more convenient to discuss the interaction in terms of reflection. The reflection is similar to that of light from a mirror (i.e. angle of reflection = angle of incidence), except that X-rays penetrate below the surface of the crystal and are reflected from the successive atomic layers in the crystal lattice (Fig. 87). A maximum in the reflected X-ray intensity therefore occurs at that angle for which the contributions from successive planes are in phase. This condition is expressed by the Bragg relationship (equation 9.3) which effectively states that, for a maximum reflected intensity, the path difference for successive reflections must equal a whole number of wavelengths.

A crystalline specimen will consequently produce a series of reflected X-ray intensity maxima, referred to as the diffraction pattern, at angles (θ) which are determined by the spacings (d) between the crystal lattice planes of its constituent minerals. Therefore, by studying this diffraction pattern, the minerals present in the specimen can be identified. It should be noted that the fundamental processes involved in X-ray diffraction are identical to those associated with the diffracting crystal employed in the X-ray fluorescence spectrometer (p. 268). The difference is that, in this case, monochromatic X-rays are employed and the crystal lattice spacings are determined whereas, in the X-ray spectrometer, the lattice spacing of the diffracting crystal is known and the wavelengths of the incident secondary X-rays are determined.

Powder-diffraction Method

In the powder-diffraction method, a small sample, typically between 5 and 10 mg in weight, must first be removed from the artefact. The sample is ground to a fine powder and formed into a thin rod, about 0·2 mm in diameter, either by mixing it with a suitable gum or by inserting it into a thin-walled glass capillary tube. The rod is then mounted on the axis of the cylindrical X-ray camera (Fig. 88), around the inside of which is wrapped a photographic film, and is rotated about its axis.

X-rays from a high-voltage X-ray tube are collimated and filtered to produce a beam of monochromatic radiation which is directed onto the sample rod. Crystal lattice planes with a specific spacing (d) give reflections along the surface of a cone with semi-angle 2θ (equation 9.3) since, in a finely powdered rotating sample, these lattice planes exist at all orientations with respect to the incident X-ray beam. This cone of X-rays impinges on the film in a pair of arcs. Reflections from planes with other spacings produce further pairs of arcs and therefore a series of dark arcs, referred to as the diffraction pattern, appears on the processed photographic film (Plate 24). From measurement of the

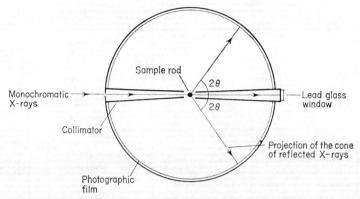

Figure 88. Schematic diagram of an X-ray power-diffraction camera. The axis of the sample rod is perpendicular to the plane of the paper. The cone of reflected (i.e. diffracted) X-rays, associated with a specific lattice spacing, forms a pair of arcs at its intersection with the film.

distances between pairs of arcs, the associated crystal lattice spacings can be calculated and by comparing this data with the lattice spacings for known minerals, which are listed in appropriate tables, the minerals present in the specimen can be identified. Furthermore, since the degree of blackening of the arcs depends on the intensity of the reflected X-rays, some indication of the concentrations of the associated minerals is obtained.

The sensitivity of the powder X-ray diffraction method, for the detection of a small amount of a particular mineral in a specimen, depends very much on the mineral concerned. A well-crystallized mineral, for which a particular reflection happens to be very strong (e.g. quartz, calcite), can often be detected at the 1 per cent level whereas for poorly crystallized minerals, concentrations in excess of 10 per cent may be necessary.

The powder X-ray diffraction method has been extensively used in the study of pottery to identify the clay minerals, the high-temperature phases produced during firing and the mineral inclusions incorporated into the clay matrix. In addition, the method has been employed for the identification of pigments, for the study of the corrosion products formed on the surface of metals and in the examination of stone artefacts.

Back Reflection Diffraction Method

The back reflection diffraction method is used primarily to obtain information on the mechanical and thermal treatments to which

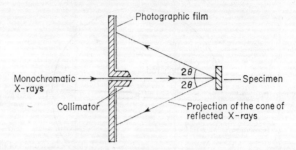

Figure 89. Schematic diagram of an X-ray back reflection diffraction camera. The cone of reflected (i.e. diffracted) X-rays, associated with a specific lattice spacing, forms a circular ring at its intersection with the film.

metal artefacts were subjected during fabrication. A narrow beam of monochromatic X-rays is directed onto the surface of the artefact (Fig. 89) which, in this case, can be studied directly without prior removal of a small sample. Back-reflection occurs at angles which are determined by the crystal lattice spacings in the specimen and the reflected X-rays are detected at a flat photographic film placed a few centimetres from the specimen. When a large number of small crystal grains are present in the area irradiated, the reflections associated with a specific lattice spacing occur along the surface of a cone, as in the case of the powder diffraction method, and a continuous circular ring is observed on the processed film. However, when a few large grains are present, the reflections only occur at a few points along the surface of the cone and the circular ring, observed on the film, has a broken or spotty appearance.

Hence, by studying the structure of the diffraction rings associated with specific lattice spacings, information can be obtained on the microstructure of the metal and, by inference, on the fabrication techniques employed in its manufacture. For example, an artefact which has been subjected to cold-working will produce continuous circular diffraction rings since cold-working results in the fragmentation and distortion of the crystal grains. However, if the artefact had been subsequently annealed, the diffraction rings would be broken and spotty since the annealing process results in the growth of large undistorted crystal grains.

Infra-red Absorption Spectrometry

In infra-red absorption spectrometry, infra-red radiation in the wavelength range from 2·5 to 16 μm (Fig. 62) is focussed onto the specimen which can be a solid, liquid or gas. The molecules or groups of atoms in the specimen are in continuous motion, vibrating at frequencies which are characteristic of the particular atomic groups present. Therefore if the frequency of the infra-red radiation is the same as the vibration frequency of an interatomic bond, associated with the specimen, the radiation is absorbed: the relationship between the frequency and the wavelength for electromagnetic radiation is given by equation (7.1). Similarly infra-red radiation, at frequencies which are not matched by those of interatomic bonds, passes through the specimen without absorption. Hence measurement of the extent of the absorption at each wavelength in the 2·5–16 μm range provides information on the interatomic bonds associated with the specimen

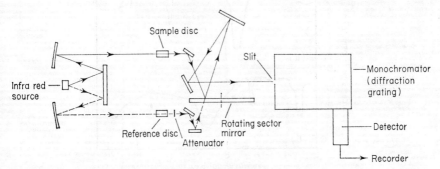

Figure 90. Schematic diagram showing the principal components of an infra-red absorption spectrometer. When the reflecting half of the rotating sector mirror is in position (as in diagram), the sample beam (solid line) is focussed onto the monochromator slit while when the transmitting half is in position, the reference beam (dashed line) is focussed onto the slit. Mirrors, rather than lenses, are used throughout the optical system in order to avoid absorption of the infra-red radiation.

and this can be used to identify the mineral phases and chemical compounds, both inorganic and organic, that are present.

For the examination of archaeological artefacts, a small sample, a few milligrams in weight, must first be removed. Typically, the sample is ground to a fine powder and is blended with approximately 1 g of high-purity potassium bromide. This mixture is then pressed in a vacuum die to form a small clear disc.

A typical spectrometer for measuring the infra-red absorption spectrum of the sample is shown schematically in Fig. 90. A continuous spectrum of infra-red radiation is provided by either a heated nichrome strip or a Nernst filament source. Using a system of mirrors, the radiation from the source is split into two beams, one of which is focussed through the sample disc and the other through a reference disc made from potassium bromide without the addition of any sample. The two beams are then recombined using a rotating sector mirror and are focussed onto the monochromator slit. The monochromator, consisting typically of a diffraction grating, disperses the infra-red radiation into its constituent wavelengths and this dispersed radiation is finally detected using a Golay cell, bolometer or photoconductive cell. As a result of the rotating sector mirror, a difference in the absorption of radiation between the sample and reference discs gives rise to an alternating electrical signal from the detector. This electrical

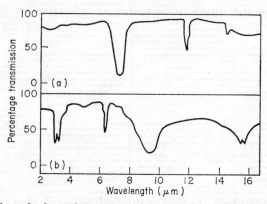

Figure 91. Infra-red absorption spectra for (a) calcite ($CaCO_3$) and (b) gypsum ($CaSO_4.2H_2O$): percentage transmission of infra-red radiation *versus* wavelength. The first two absorption peaks for the gypsum are associated with the water of crystallization.

signal powers a servomotor which drives an attenuator into the reference beam until the two beams are of equal intensity. By connecting a pen mechanically to the attenuator, a record of the percentage transmission by the sample *versus* wavelength (i.e. the infra-red absorption spectrum) is obtained.

Although the assignment of the various absorption bands to specific interatomic bonds in a solid can be extremely difficult, the identification of the chemical compounds in an archaeological specimen is frequently possible through the comparison of the observed infra-red absorption spectrum with those for known materials (Fig. 91). A semi-quantitative determination of the concentrations of the chemical compounds present is also possible, after calibration with standards of known composition.

Infra-red absorption spectrometry is, in many ways, less versatile for the identification of inorganic mineral phases than X-ray diffraction techniques and, to date, has been mainly employed in the study of paint pigments. However, in comparing these two techniques, it should be appreciated that they tend to be complimentary. Infra-red absorption spectrometry is extremely sensitive to short-range crystalline order, such as exists in poorly crystallized minerals, whereas X-ray diffraction relies on long-range ordering and the periodic repetition of the atomic planes throughout the crystal lattice, such as exists in well-crystallized minerals. Furthermore, infra-red absorption spectra provide information of the state of any water present in the specimen (i.e. absorbed water, water of crystallization and chemically combined hydroxyl water, OH^-).

In addition to the study of mineral phases, infra-red absorption spectrometry is particularly valuable for the examination of archaeological artefacts derived from certain organic materials, such as amber, and for the identification of the minor components (e.g. adhesives, varnishes, binding media) employed in the fabrication of artefacts.

Mössbauer Spectroscopy

The Mössbauer effect (Wertheim, 1964) refers to the *recoil-free* emission of gamma rays from excited nuclei formed in a radioactive source and their subsequent absorption by nuclei of the same isotope in the specimen under examination. The Mössbauer spectrum, which is obtained by varying the energy of the incident gamma rays, provides information on the immediate crystallographic environment of the isotope in the specimen. In the context of archaeological artefacts, the Mössbauer spectrum associated with the iron isotope, ^{57}Fe, is of particular interest and is used to study the iron-bearing minerals present in the artefacts. The technique is, in some ways, analogous to atomic absorption spectrometry in that this involves the absorption of visible light of characteristic wavelength through the excitation of the outer electrons of constituent atoms in the specimen whilst Mössbauer spectroscopy involves the absorption of gamma rays of characteristic energy through the excitation of the atomic nuclei.

Normally when an excited nucleus returns to its ground state with the emission of a gamma ray (e.g. in neutron activation analysis), a small proportion of the available energy is lost to the recoiling nucleus, the effect being analogous to the recoil of a gun when a bullet is fired. The energy of the emitted gamma ray is therefore slightly less than the nuclear transition energy (i.e. the energy difference between the ground and excited states of the nucleus). Similarly when a nucleus is excited out of its ground state through the absorption of a gamma ray, some energy is transferred to the crystal lattice and therefore the energy of the absorbed gamma ray is slightly greater than the nuclear transition energy. Consequently, the energies of the emitted and absorbed gamma rays associated with a particular isotope are slightly different (Fig. 92), the separation being typically less than 1 eV. In addition, since both the emitting and absorbing atoms are in thermal motion, the

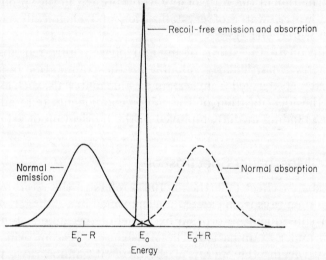

Figure 92. The energy spectrum associated with the emission and absorption of gamma rays by a nucleus for both the normal process and the recoil-free Mössbauer effect. E_0 equals the nuclear transition energy and R equals the recoil energy transmitted to the nucleus. The width and height of the recoil-free spectrum is not drawn to the same scale as the normal spectrum.

associated gamma rays exhibit a slight spread in energy, which is again normally less than 1 eV.

This situation contrasts with the Mössbauer effect in which gamma rays are emitted and absorbed without the transfer of any energy to the crystal lattice. In these recoil-free processes, the gamma ray energies are equal to the nuclear transition energy and, therefore, there is no difference between the energies of the emitted and absorbed gamma rays (Fig. 92). Furthermore, the spread in the energies of the associated gamma rays is very much reduced, being typically less than 10^{-6} eV. The Mössbauer effect can only occur when the nuclear transition energy is so small that the recoil energy, which would be available, is insufficient either to dislodge atoms from their crystal lattice sites or to contribute to the energy of the lattice vibrations (i.e. thermal energy or phonons). Recoil-free emission and absorption of gamma rays therefore only occurs in the case of a limited number of isotopes, of which the iron isotope, ^{57}Fe, is particularly appropriate.

In the study of iron-bearing minerals in archaeological artefacts, the radioactive cobalt isotope, ^{57}Co, provides the gamma ray source. This isotope decays to an excited state of the stable iron isotope, ^{57}Fe, which then assumes its unexcited ground state with recoil-free emission of gamma rays with an energy of 14·4 keV. These gamma rays are directed onto the specimen under examination, which is typically a few hundred milligrams in weight, and the intensity of the radiation, after absorption by the ^{57}Fe nuclei in the specimen, is measured using either a scintillation or semiconductor counter (Fig. 93). The energy of

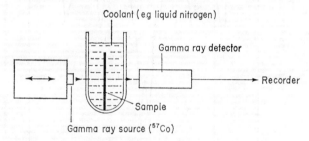

Figure 93. Schematic diagram showing the principal components of a Mössbauer effect spectrometer. The gamma ray source is mounted on a trolley which can be moved at various velocities with respect to the sample.

the incident gamma rays is varied over a range of about 10^{-5} eV by moving the source relative to the specimen at various velocities up to about 1 cm s^{-1}, the change in energy of the gamma rays occurring as a result of the Doppler effect. It is thus possible to obtain a plot of the percentage transmission of the gamma rays by the specimen *versus* gamma ray energy (i.e. velocity of the source), which is referred to as the Mössbauer spectrum.

The basic parameters which are obtained from the Mössbauer spectrum for the ^{57}Fe isotope (Fig. 94) are the width of the absorption peak at half its maximum height, the isomer shift, the quadrupole splitting and the magnetic field splitting. The isomer shift, which depends on the electron charge density around the nuclei, refers to the displacement of the main absorption peak with respect to the fundamental gamma ray energy associated with the source (i.e. zero source velocity). The quadrupole splitting refers to the splitting of the main absorption peak into two components and provides an indication of the electric field gradient at the nuclei. The magnetic field splitting refers to the presence of subsidiary absorption peaks on either side of the main peak and is due to the interaction between the nuclear magnetic dipole moments and the internal magnetic field associated with ferrimagnetic iron minerals. These four parameters provide information on the local crystallographic symmetry around the iron atoms in the specimen and hence provide the basis for distinguishing between paramagnetic and ferrimagnetic phases and between the different oxidation states (i.e. ferrous Fe^{2+} or ferric Fe^{3+}) for iron. In addition,

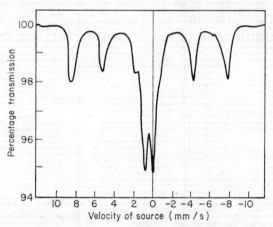

Figure 94. Mössbauer spectrum for a typical pottery sample: percentage transmission of gamma rays (i.e. normalized counting rate) *versus* velocity of source (i.e. gamma ray energy).

the extent of the absorption (i.e. the peak heights) provides an indication of the relative concentrations of the various iron-bearing minerals in the specimen.

Mössbauer spectroscopy has been used in the study of pottery in order to obtain information on both the iron-bearing minerals present in the clay and the firing conditions (i.e. temperature and kiln atmosphere) employed in its manufacture. In addition, it has been suggested (Herzenberg, 1970) that the technique could be of assistance in the identification of the geographical sources of the obsidian used to make artefacts. For the study of iron-bearing minerals, it should be appreciated that Mössbauer spectroscopy is, in many ways, more versatile than X-ray diffraction techniques since, as with infra-red absorption spectrometry, the Mössbauer effect is extremely sensitive to short-range order and is therefore particularly appropriate for the study of poorly crystallized minerals.

Thermal Analysis

In the present context, the term, thermal analysis, is used to cover the various observable physical and chemical changes that occur when a specimen is heated from room temperature to approximately 1000°C. Although not necessarily establishing their precise identity, these techniques do provide some information on the minerals present in the specimen since the effects observed during heating depend on the mineralogical and structural changes that occur. With regard to the examination of archaeological artefacts, thermal techniques have been mainly used to obtain information on the firing temperatures employed in the manufacture of pottery.

Differential Thermal Analysis

Differential thermal analysis provides information on the endothermic (i.e. absorption of heat) and exothermic (i.e. evolution of heat) reactions that occur when pottery is heated. These reactions indicate the presence of specific minerals (e.g. clay minerals, calcite) which in turn can provide an estimate of the original firing temperature of the pottery.

The technique involves simultaneously heating a powdered sample of the pottery, typically 100 mg in weight, and an equal volume of an inert material. The two samples are placed symmetrically in the separate compartments of an alumina block and are heated to approximately 1000°C in an electric furnace at a controlled, reproducible rate of about 400°C per hour. The difference in temperature between the two samples is measured by means of a differential thermocouple which consists of two linked junctions, one in the pottery sample and the other in the inert material. A plot of the temperature difference *versus* the actual temperature of the pottery sample can therefore be obtained automatically using a suitable recorder: a higher temperature in the pottery sample is indicative of an exothermic reaction occurring while a lower temperature indicates an endothermic reaction.

A hypothetical differential thermal analysis curve, which illustrates the principal reactions that can occur in a pottery sample, is presented in Fig. 95. The broad endothermic peak in the 100–200°C range is associated with the loss of absorbed water while the broad exothermic peak in the 250–500°C range is associated with the combustion of organic material. The well-defined endothermic peak at about 600°C is due to the loss of chemically-combined hydroxyl water by the clay minerals while the exothermic peak at about 950°C is due to the formation of high-temperature mineral phases (e.g. mullite, spinel), derived from the dehydroxylated clay minerals. Finally, the endothermic peak at about 850°C is due to the decomposition of calcite (i.e. calcium carbonate), a mineral which is present in many pottery samples.

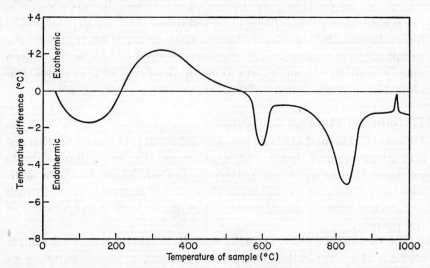

Figure 95. Hypothetical differential thermal analysis curve illustrating the principal reactions that can occur in a pottery sample: temperature difference between pottery sample and inert sample *versus* temperature of pottery sample.

The appearance of these various endothermic and exothermic peaks, during the differential thermal analysis of pottery, provides an indication of the *maximum* temperature to which the pottery was originally fired in antiquity. For example, the presence of the endothermic peak associated with the dehydroxylation of clay minerals indicates that hydrated clay minerals remain in the pottery and that the original firing temperature was below between 500 and 700°C. The precise temperature, at which the loss of the chemically-combined water would have occurred during firing in antiquity, depends on the actual clay minerals present (i.e. kaolinite, montmorillonite or illite) and on the heating rate employed in the kiln. Similarly, the presence of the endothermic peak associated with the decomposition of calcite indicates that the firing temperature was below between 750 and 850°C, the precise temperature at which decomposition would have occurred again depending on the heating rate and atmospheric conditions prevailing in the kiln.

Although of value in some instances, it must be emphasized that this technique for estimating the firing temperature has somewhat limited application since the majority of pottery samples only exhibit the uninformative low temperature peaks associated with loss of absorbed water and combustion of organic material.

Thermogravimetric Analysis

Thermogravimetric analysis involves studying the loss in weight of a sample when it is heated at a controlled, reproducible rate to approximately 1000°C, a specially designed thermobalance being employed.

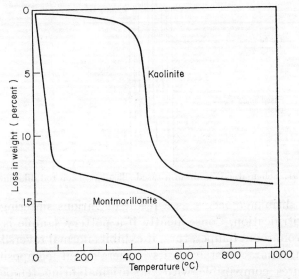

Figure 96. Thermogravimetric curves for typical clay minerals, showing the loss in weight due to the loss of inter-layer water (100°C) and the loss of chemically-combined hydroxyl water (500–700°C).

In the case of pottery, loss in weight can occur in the 100–200°C range due to the loss of absorbed water and in the 500–700°C range due to the dehydroxylation of the clay minerals (Fig. 96).

The occurrence of a significant loss in weight in the latter temperature range, during the thermogravimetric analysis of pottery, therefore indicates that hydrated clay minerals remain in the pottery and that the original firing temperature was below between 500 and 700°C. As in the case of differential thermal analysis, this method is mainly appropriate to the study of pottery fired at low temperatures.

Thermal Expansion Measurements

The thermal expansion method for determining the original firing temperature of pottery is based on the assumption that, when clays

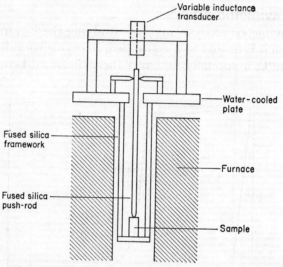

Figure 97. Schematic diagram of a fused silica extension rod dilatometer.

are fired, shrinkage occurs as a result of various sintering processes, such as vitrification. Consequently if a pottery sample is heated up steadily from room temperature, it exhibits normal reversible thermal expansion, characteristic of its mineralogical composition, until temperatures comparable with the original firing temperature are reached. With a continued increase in temperature, the pottery then begins to contract because, superimposed on the reversible expansion, there is an irreversible shrinkage associated with the resumption of sintering: that is, the firing of the pottery is being continued beyond the point reached during the original firing in antiquity. The temperature at which a net shrinkage is first observed should therefore provide an indication of the original firing temperature of the pottery.

Thermal expansion measurements can be made using the fused silica extension rod dilatometer shown schematically in Fig. 97. A sample, which is typically a parallelepiped with dimensions $2.5 \times 1.0 \times 1.0$ cm, is cut from the pottery sherd and is mounted on the fused silica framework. The dilatometer assembly is then heated in a tubular electric furnace at a controlled, reproducible heating rate of about 200°C per hour. The changes in length of the specimen are transmitted to the variable inductance transducer via the fused silica push-rod, changes in lengths of the fused silica framework being compensated by equivalent changes in length of the push-rod. The electrical output from the transducer is fed to the Y axis of an X–Y recorder and the voltage from the thermocouple, which is used to measure the temperature of

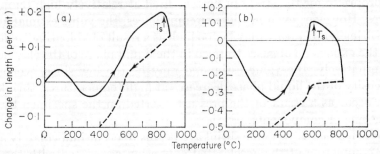

Figure 98. Thermal expansion curves during heating (solid line) and cooling (dashed line) for typical pottery samples. (a) Post-mediaeval pottery: $T_S = 870$°C. (b) Saxon pottery: $T_S = 625$°C.

the specimen, is fed to the X axis. A plot of the change in length of the specimen *versus* temperature is thus obtained automatically, changes in length of less than 0·2 μm being readily detected.

A typical thermal expansion curve for pottery is presented in Fig. 98a. The contraction starting at about 100°C is due to the loss of absorbed water while the accelerated expansion occurring at approximately 570°C is caused by the α–β phase inversion of the quartz present in the pottery. Finally, due to the resumption of sintering, a net irreversible shrinkage begins to occur at, in this case, approximately 870°C, measurement of this shrinkage temperature (T_S) being accurate to within ±5°C. In order to establish the relationship between the original firing temperature (T_F) and the observed shrinkage temperature (T_S), the specimen is refired, while still mounted in the dilatometer, for one hour at a temperature, T_F^*, which is typically about

50°C higher than T_S (Tite, 1969). After cooling, the specimen is re-heated and the new shrinkage temperature (T_S^*), associated with the refiring, is determined. The original firing temperature can then be estimated using the relationship:

$$(T_F - T_S) = (T_F^* - T_S^*) \tag{9.4}$$

Provided that vitrification (i.e. the appearance of a viscous liquid phase in the clay body) occurred during the original firing in antiquity, the values obtained for the firing temperature, using equation (9.4), are typically accurate to within $\pm 30°C$. Depending on the concentration of "fluxing" impurities in the clay, vitrification commences somewhere in the range 700–950°C. Therefore, the thermal expansion method is, in contrast to the preceding thermal methods, particularly appropriate for the study of pottery fired at relatively high temperatures. However, even in these circumstances, the value estimated for the firing temperature may be too high as a result of "bloating", caused by the expansion of gases trapped in the liquid phase of the clay body. Alternatively, the value estimated may be too low since, when the viscosity of the liquid phase decreases at high temperatures, shrinkage can occur as a result of the pressure exerted on the specimen by the dilatometer components.

When a net irreversible shrinkage begins to occur immediately after the completion of the accelerated expansion associated with the α–β quartz inversion (Fig. 98b), it is unlikely that the vitrification range for the clay was reached during the original firing. In these circumstances, the original firing temperature cannot be satisfactorily estimated using equation (9.4) and the thermal expansion data provide no precise information on the firing temperature. Instead it is merely possible to suggest that the firing temperature was either less than 500°C or in the 500–700°C range, depending on whether or not hydrated clay minerals are shown, by some other technique (e.g. differential thermal analysis, X-ray diffraction), to be present in the pottery.

Colour Analysis

The colours exhibited by pottery sherds are extremely diverse and are determined by a large number of inter-related factors. In the first place, the colour depends on the nature of the clay used; the iron oxide content, the amount of organic matter present or added and the texture being of particular importance. Secondly, the colours observed in pottery made from a particular clay vary dramatically according to the firing temperature, the duration of the firing and the atmospheric conditions (e.g. oxidizing, reducing) employed in its manufacture.

The colour of pottery sherds has therefore frequently been studied in an attempt to obtain information on the firing conditions employed in antiquity (Matson, 1955). One approach has been to refire the sherds in various atmospheres (oxidizing, reducing, reducing followed by oxidizing) to progressively higher temperatures and thus establish the temperature at which a change in the original colour first occurs. Alternatively, samples of a local clay, which was thought to have been that used in antiquity to produce the pottery, have been fired in various atmospheres to temperatures in the range 500–1000°C and the resulting colours have been compared with those of the pottery sherds under examination. However, as a result of the obvious complexity of the relationship between colour and firing conditions, the interpretation of the data obtained from either of these methods is normally extremely difficult and precise, unambiguous information on the firing conditions employed in antiquity is therefore frequently unobtainable.

Isotopic Analysis

For the great majority of chemical elements, the relative abundance of their isotopes is the same regardless of where the elements are found in the Earth's crust. For example, the copper in natural minerals always contains the same proportions of ^{63}Cu and ^{65}Cu while silver always contains the same proportions of ^{108}Ag and ^{109}Ag. However, the relative abundance of the isotopes of certain elements vary significantly depending on the origin of the material in which they are found. In addition to the radioactive isotopes and their decay products which provide the basis for the various methods of age determination, the relative abundance of the lead isotopes in metals and glass, the oxygen isotopes in glass and the oxygen, together with carbon, isotopes in mollusc shells are of particular interest in the context of archaeological material.

The relative abundance of the isotopes of the chosen element is determined using a mass spectrometer, the general principles of which have been described on p. 92. Lead samples are typically taken into solution and deposited as lead hydroxide on the spectrometer filament, from which lead ions are then obtained by the surface ionization method. Although, for convenience of handling, a few milligrams of sample are normally employed, satisfactory measurements can be made using as little as 10–20 μg of lead; accuracies of about 0·1 per cent being achieved for the lead isotopic ratios. For the study of the oxygen isotopes in glass, about 40 mg of the glass are first heated with fluorine gas and hydrogen fluoride at 450°C for 8 hours. The oxygen, which is released as a result of the reaction with the fluorine, is then converted to carbon dioxide by reacting with an electrically heated carbon rod. The carbon dioxide is ionized in the mass spectrometer and its oxygen isotopic ratio is determined to an accuracy of about 0·02 per cent. In the study of mollusc shells, carbon dioxide is liberated from the calcium carbonate of the shell by the action of phosphoric acid: this gas is then ionized and both the oxygen and carbon isotopic ratios are determined. The method requires less than 1 mg of shell and an accuracy of approximately 0·01 per cent can be achieved.

Table 21. Lead isotope ratios for lead ores from different mining regions (after Brill, 1970)

	Greece (Laurion)	England (Derbyshire)	Spain (Rio Tinto)
$^{207}Pb/^{206}Pb$	0·8307	0·8465	0·8598
$^{208}Pb/^{206}Pb$	2·0599	2·0814	2·102
$^{204}Pb/^{206}Pb$	0·05297	0·05413	0·05479

Four stable lead isotopes exist of which three, ^{206}Pb, ^{207}Pb and ^{208}Pb, are the ultimate decay products of the radioactive series associated with ^{238}U, ^{235}U and ^{232}Th respectively, while the fourth, ^{204}Pb, is not connected with any known nuclear decay scheme. Because of this association with radioactive decay, lead ores, which were deposited during different geological periods and were derived from different source rocks, can exhibit distinctly different isotopic abundances. For example, the lead ores from Greece, England and Spain, three important mining areas in antiquity, can be readily distinguished from one another on the basis of their isotopic ratios (Table 21). Consequently, measurement of the relative abundance of the four isotopes in lead from archaeological artefacts can provide information on the source of the ore from which the lead was smelted. In addition to metallic lead, the technique is applicable to other metals (e.g. bronze, silver) containing lead as an impurity as well as to glass, glazes and pigments. An important feature of the technique is the fact that the isotopic ratios, unlike the concentrations of minor and trace elements determined by chemical analysis, do not depend on the method of smelting.

The two stable isotopes of oxygen, which are normally of interest, are ^{16}O and ^{18}O, the heavier ^{18}O isotope occurring in nature in the ratio of about 1 to 500 with respect to the ^{16}O isotope. Although the two isotopes are identical in their chemical behaviour, they are, as a result of their different masses, susceptible to isotopic fractionation and therefore the $^{18}O/^{16}O$ ratio varies according to the material in

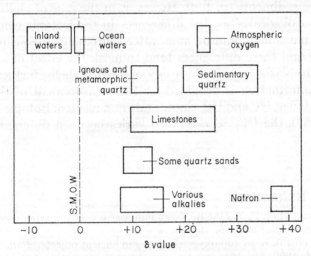

Figure 99. Variation in the $^{18}O/^{16}O$ ratio for various natural materials, including the raw materials (quartz sand, lime and alkali) used in making glass. The δ-value is the deviation in parts per thousand of the $^{18}O/^{16}O$ ratio from s.m.o.w. (i.e. standard mean ocean water).

which the oxygen occurs. This effect is particularly significant in the case of oxygen because the difference between the two atomic masses (i.e. 2 a.m.u.) represents a large percentage of the total atomic mass (i.e. 16 or 18 a.m.u.) and in addition, oxygen occurs in forms that readily interchange with one another. The range of variation in the $^{18}O/^{16}O$ ratio for representative natural materials is illustrated in Fig. 99 where the ratio is expressed in terms of the δ-value: that is, the deviation in parts per thousand of the $^{18}O/^{16}O$ ratio for the sample under consideration from that of an accepted standard sample, designated as standard mean ocean water. Thus the $^{18}O/^{16}O$ ratio for standard mean ocean water has a value of zero on the scale of δ-values.

The $^{18}O/^{16}O$ ratios for the raw materials (i.e. quartz sand, lime and alkali) used in the manufacture of glass, which typically contains between 40 and 50 per cent by weight of oxygen, exhibit significant variations. Therefore oxygen isotopic ratio data for glass can be used to provide an index for classifying ancient glass and possibly to suggest the geographical source of the raw materials.

In addition, the oxygen isotopic analysis of mollusc shells found on archaeological sites can provide information on, and assist in the identification of, the aquatic environment in which the molluscs grew. The general principles are similar to those associated with the study of deep sea sediments (p. 106). However, in the case of mollusc shells from archaeological sites, the differences in the isotopic composition of the various inland and oceanic water sources are the primary consideration and these differences tend to mask the effect of long-term temperature variations. In the study of mollusc shells, further supplementary information is provided by the measurement of the stable carbon isotopes, ^{12}C and ^{13}C, since, again as a result of isotopic fractionation (p. 80), the $^{13}C/^{12}C$ ratio also varies between different natural waters.

References

Banks, M. and Hall, E. T. (1963). X-ray fluorescent analysis in archaeology: the milliprobe. *Archaeometry* 6, 31–36.

Brill, R. H. (1970). Lead and oxygen isotopes in ancient objects. *Phil. Trans. R. Soc. Lond.* A269, 143–164.

Das, H. A. and Zonderhuis, J. (1964). The analysis of electrum coins. *Archaeometry* 7, 90–97.

Emeleus, V. M. (1960). Beta ray backscattering: a simple method for the quantitative determination of lead oxide in glass, glaze and pottery. *Archaeometry* 3, 5–9.

Gordus, A. A. (1967). Quantitative non-destructive neutron activation of silver in coins. *Archaeometry* 10, 78–86.

Herzenberg, C. L. (1970). Mössbauer spectroscopy as an instrumental technique for determinative mineralogy. *In* "Mössbauer Effect Methodology." (Ed. I. J. Gruverman), Vol. 5, pp. 209–230. Plenum Press, New York.

Hornblower, A. P. (1962). Archaeological applications of the electron probe microanalyser. *Archaeometry* 5, 108–112.

Hughes, M. J. and Oddy, W. A. (1970). A reappraisal of the specific gravity method for the analysis of gold alloys. *Archaeometry* 12, 1–12.

Matson, F. R. (1955). Ceramic archaeology. *Am. ceram. Soc. Bull.* 34, 33–44.

Perlman, I. and Asaro, F. (1969). Pottery analysis by neutron activation. *Archaeometry* 11, 21–52.

Tite, M. S. (1969). Determination of the firing temperature of ancient ceramics by measurement of thermal expansion: a reassessment. *Archaeometry* **11**, 131–143.

Wertheim, G. K. (1964). "Mössbauer Effect: Principles and Applications." Academic Press, New York and London.

Zussman, J. (Ed.) (1967). "Physical Methods in Determinative Mineralogy." Academic Press, London and New York.

10

Physical Methods of Analysis
—Applications

In the study of archaeological artefacts, the physical methods of analysis, which were described in Chapter 9, are used to assist in identifying the raw materials from which the artefacts were made and in establishing the geographical source of these raw materials, as well as to obtain information on the techniques used in their fabrication.

In the present context, the identification of the geographical source of the raw materials normally involves the chemical analysis for the minor and trace elements, the pattern of concentrations of these elements being used to characterize a group of artefacts made from raw materials from a particular source. Subsequently, through the comparison of the concentration patterns of the artefacts with those of samples from known sources, it is sometimes possible to establish the precise geographical location of the actual source of the raw materials used to make the artefacts. In order for this method of identifying sources to be successful, it is obviously essential that the pattern of concentrations of minor and trace elements varies between different geographical sources of the raw materials while remaining essentially unchanged throughout any one source. In addition, no significant changes in the concentration patterns for the constituent raw materials should occur either during the fabrication of the artefact or during its subsequent burial in the ground.

The relevance of these three main areas of investigation, together with the associated problems and the most appropriate physical methods of analysis (Table 15), are discussed in the context of stone artefacts (p. 307), pottery (p. 314), metal artefacts (p. 328), glass, glaze and faience (p. 345), paint pigments (p. 355), and artefacts derived from biological material (p. 358). Typical examples of the application of these techniques, which provide an indication of the archaeological significance of the data obtained, are described for each type of artefact.

Stone Artefacts

The primary aim, in the physical examination of stone artefacts, is the identification of the geographical sources of rocks used. Chemical analysis for the minor and trace elements has therefore been used to establish the source of fine-textured, homogeneous rocks and volcanic glasses, such as flint and obsidian respectively, which are not made amenable to petrological examination. Chemical analysis is not, however, particularly appropriate in the case of igneous and metamorphic rocks since these are more readily characterized, and their sources identified, on the basis of their constituent mineral phases. Similarly, although employed in the study of jade (p. 224), the identification of these mineral phases by means of X-ray diffraction (powder method) is less useful for characterization than petrological examination since the size, shape and arrangement of the mineral grains in the rock also provide essential diagnostic features.

Flint

Since the damage caused by the removal of a small sample is normally permissible, the four generally applicable physical methods of chemical analysis (p. 260 to p. 278) can, in principle, all be used for the analysis of flint artefacts. However, as a result of the suppressive effect of the high silica content on the spectral lines of the other elements, optical emission spectrometry is relatively insensitive and suffers from poor reproducibility. Atomic absorption spectrometry is more satisfactory with respect to sensitivity and reproducibility but does necessitate both the preparation of a finely powdered sample and its subsequent solution in a mixture of hydrofluoric and perchloric acids. Neutron activation analysis therefore provides the most satisfactory technique for the analysis of flint artefacts since, in addition to requiring the minimum amount of sample preparation, its sensitivity (less than 0·1 ppm) is particularly appropriate to the determination of the low concentrations of the trace elements present in flint.

Sieveking et al. (1970) and Aspinall and Feather (1972) have carried out a preliminary study of flint artefacts from some of the major axe factories and flint mines in southern Britain and continental Europe which were in operation during the Neolithic and Early Bronze ages. The flint, studied in this case, occurs as bands and nodules in the Cretaceous chalk and the trace elements, which provide the basis for characterization, are probably associated with the non-carbonate materials (e.g. quartz, clay minerals and heavy minerals) which were present in the original chalk. These non-carbonate materials would have been incorporated into the flint as it was being formed by the replacement of the calcium carbonate by silica. Differences in the trace element concentrations are therefore probably due to the variations, both lateral and vertical, in the distribution of the non-carbonate materials in the chalk.

Sieveking *et al.* employed, principally, atomic absorption spectrometry and used the concentrations of four elements (iron, aluminium,

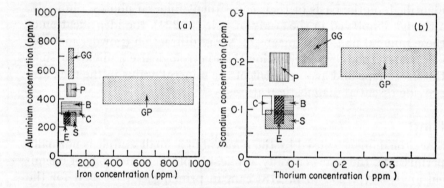

Figure 100. Trace element concentrations (mean value ±1 standard deviation) for flint from seven major axe factories and mines in southern Britain and continental Europe. (a) Atomic absorption spectrometry (after Sieveking *et al.*, 1970). (b) Neutron activation analysis (after Aspinall and Feather, 1972).
  Key to sites: B, Black Patch, Sussex; C, Cissbury, Sussex; E, Easton Down, Hants.; GG, Grimes Graves, Norfolk; P, Peppard, Oxon.; GP, Grand Pressigny, France; S, Spiennes, France.

magnesium and potassium) in order to characterize the different flint groups while Aspinall and Feather employed neutron activation analysis and studied fifteen elements, including several rare earth elements (e.g. cerium, ytterbium, samerium, lanthanum). From some typical results, which are presented in Fig. 100, it can be seen that a wide range of concentrations for each element is associated with any one group of flint artefacts. In addition, considerable inhomogeneity was, in some cases, found to exist within a single flint artefact. As a result of these inhomogeneities, it is doubtful whether a particular flint mining site can be satisfactorily characterized on the basis of the concentrations of one or two elements, a possible exception being the Grand Pressigny flints with their high iron, chromium and thorium concentrations. However, by examining the overall *pattern* of concentrations, either qualitatively or on a strict statistical basis, it was normally possible, in this preliminary study, to distinguish between flint artefacts derived from the various sites with a considerable degree of confidence. The main difficulty was to distinguish between flint from the Cissbury and Black Patch sites which, being geographically close together, exhibited essentially similar concentration patterns. In addition, it seemed probable that flint from different geological strata at the same site (e.g. Grimes Graves) exhibited different concentration patterns.

Consequently, by extending the number of mining and factory sites examined and by subsequently analysing artefacts from occupation sites, it should be possible, in the future, to establish the trading pattern for flint artefacts during the Neolithic and Early Bronze ages. However, in view of the very large number of flint sources and the trace element inhomogeneities within a particular source, this will be much more difficult than in the case of those stone artefacts which can be characterized by petrological examination (p. 222).

Obsidian

In contrast to the situation for flint, optical emission spectrometry provides satisfactory analytical data for obsidian and has therefore been extensively used, the damage caused by the removal of a small sample for analysis normally being permissible. Neutron activation analysis is equally suitable for the examination of obsidian and has the advantage that the system can be automated to provide limited analytical data on a large number of samples in a comparatively short time. Satisfactory results have also been obtained with X-ray fluorescence spectrometry in which either powdered samples or, when the surfaces were reasonably flat, solid samples were employed.

The characterization of obsidian sources on the basis of the concentrations of the minor and trace elements is somewhat easier than in the case of flint sources. In the first place, there is a relatively small number of obsidian sources which provide suitable material for the manufacture of artefacts and secondly, since obsidian is a volcanic glass which solidified from the molten state, the minor and trace element concentrations are comparatively uniform throughout a particular obsidian source. However, the data provided by a single physical method of chemical analysis is not always adequate to distinguish between different sources and it is therefore sometimes necessary to obtain data on the concentrations of further elements using a second method of chemical analysis.

Renfrew *et al.* (1966 and 1968) used optical emission spectrometry to analyse samples from known obsidian sources in the Near East and

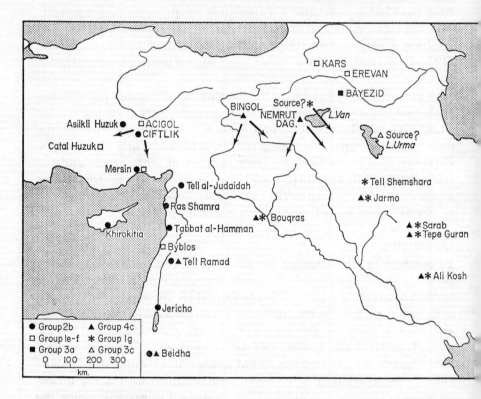

Figure 101. Sketch map of the Near East showing the principal obsidian sources (capital letters) and the settlement sites on which obsidian from these sources was employed during the seventh and sixth millennia BC (after Renfrew *et al.*, 1968).

obsidian artefacts from Near Eastern sites (Fig. 101) spanning the period from the Upper Palaeolithic through to the Bronze Age. On the basis of the concentrations of barium and zirconium, it was possible to define six major groups of obsidian (Fig. 102), confirmation of these groupings being provided by analytical data for other elements.

The two principal sources of obsidian in Cappodicia (southern Anatolia) are near to Acigöl and Çiftlik and belong to separate groups, that is 1e–f and 2b respectively. In eastern Anatolia (Armenia), the situation is however more complex. The obsidian sources at Nemrut

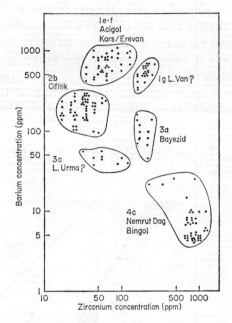

Figure 102. Barium and zirconium concentrations for obsidian samples from the Near East showing the division of the obsidian into six major groups. Each dot represents a single sample of obsidian (after Renfrew *et al.*, 1966).

Dağ and Bingöl both belong to group 4c and cannot be distinguished on the basis of the available analytical data. Similarly the two sources in the Kars and Erevan regions both belong to group 1e–f and, furthermore, cannot be distinguished from the Cappodician source near to Acigöl. In addition, the locations of the sources associated with groups 1g and 3c have not been established although the geographical distributions of the artefacts suggest that they are near to Lake Van and Lake Urmia respectively. Therefore, for eastern Anatolia, it is only group 3a that represents a single obsidian source whose location, near to Bayezid, is known. Having thus characterized the major obsidian sources, it was then possible to study the early development and extent of the obsidian trade in the Near East.

Although small quantities of obsidian were transported over distances of a few hundred kilometres from the Cappodician and eastern Anatolian sources during the Upper Palaeolithic, the quantities were such that they could readily have been acquired by a semi-nomadic people during the normal course of events. However, it is clear from characterization studies that, with the development of settled farming communities in the 7th and 6th millennia BC, more organized systems for the supply and exchange of obsidian were involved. The pattern of trade and supply from the sources in the Near East is illustrated in Fig. 101 while further insight into the mechanics of the obsidian trade is obtained from a more detailed consideration of the quantities of obsidian used at the various sites (Renfrew *et al.*, 1968). In Fig. 103,

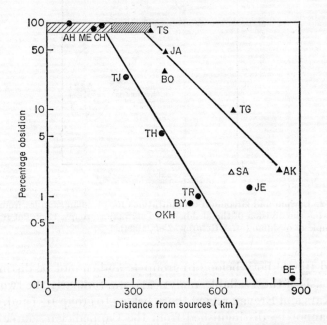

Figure 103. Variation in the percentage of obsidian in the total chipped stone industry with distance from the source for the Near East during the seventh and sixth millennia BC. Circles represent sites in the Levant and triangles those in the Zagros area. Less accessible sites, such as SA (in the hills) and KH (overseas in Cyprus), are represented by open symbols. Shaded areas indicate the *supply zones* (i.e. greater than 80 per cent of obsidian) and the straight lines show the approximate exponential fall-off in the percentage of obsidian in the *contact zones* (after Renfrew *et al.*, 1968).

Key to sites (see Fig. 101): *Zagros:* TS, Tell Shemsharah; JA, Jarmo; BO, Bouqras; TG, Tepe Guran; AK, Ali Kosh; SA, Sarab. *Levant:* AH, Asilki Hüyük; CH, Catal Hüyük; ME, Mersin; TJ, Tell al-Judaidah; TH, Tabbat al-Hammam; TR, Tell Ramad; BY, Byblos; JE, Jericho; BE, Beidha; KH, Khirokitia.

the percentage of obsidian in the total chipped stone industry is plotted on a logarithmic scale against the distance of the site from the source of the obsidian used. From this presentation, it can be seen that, for both the Levant (supplied from Cappodician sources) and the Zagros area (supplied from eastern Anatolian sources), sites within a distance of about 300 km from the source were well supplied with obsidian while outside this zone the percentage of obsidian falls off steeply. It is therefore reasonable to consider the distribution of obsidian in terms of a *supply zone*, within which the obsidian workers were themselves willing and able to travel the 300 km to the sources to obtain the raw material, and a *contact zone*, through which the obsidian was passed from village to village in a succession of exchange transactions, the quantity of obsidian becoming smaller with increasing distance from the supply zone. In proposing this model for the obsidian trade, Renfrew *et al.* (1968) emphasize that it need not imply any formal organization. Furthermore, it must be appreciated that there is no reason to suppose that obsidian was the only material traded or necessarily the most important. However, the obsidian trade does provide direct evidence that there was a widespread traffic in commodities and, by implication, in ideas during the Neolithic period in which the development of agriculture and the establishing of settled communities took place.

Renfrew *et al.* (1965) similarly investigated the obsidian in the Aegean. In this case, some difficulties arose because the obsidian from sources on the island of Melos exhibited the same pattern of trace element concentrations as that from sources on the island of Giali, 240 km east of Melos. Furthermore, both resembled, in their composition, obsidian from the Tokaj region of Hungary and from the Anatolian source near Acigöl (group 1e–f). In an attempt to overcome these problems, obsidian samples from these sources were subjected to fission track analysis (Durrani *et al.*, 1971). This technique, which is described on page 99, provides a date for the volcanic eruption in which the obsidian was formed as well as a value for the uranium content of the obsidian sample. From the results presented in Table 22, it can be seen that obsidian is available from successive eruptions in the case of the Aegean and Anatolian sources. However, samples from the Aegean, Hungarian and Anatolian sources can be clearly differentiated on the basis of both age and uranium content. Subsequently, obsidian artefacts from the Mesolithic site at the Franchthi Cave in southern Greece were investigated and on the basis of the fission track data, it was established that they came from either the Melian or Gialian sources, Hungarian and Anatolian sources being excluded. This conclusion was of particular interest since it provided positive evidence for maritime travel by the beginning of the 7th millennium BC and carried the history of seafaring back a thousand years.

Table 22. Fission track data for obsidian samples (after Durrani et al., 1971)

Obsidian sample[a]	Age (m.y.)	Uranium content[b] (ppm)
Hungarian		
Borsod	$3 \cdot 86 \pm 0 \cdot 24$	8·6
Borsod	$3 \cdot 37 \pm 0 \cdot 27$	8·9
Central Anatolian		
Acigöl	$1 \cdot 95 \pm 0 \cdot 33$	3·5
Acigöl	$8 \cdot 14 \pm 0 \cdot 59$	9·0
Aegean		
Giali	$2 \cdot 01 \pm 0 \cdot 26$	11·1
Giali	$8 \cdot 04 \pm 0 \cdot 65$	4·1
Melos	$8 \cdot 95 \pm 0 \cdot 94$	4·7
Melos	$8 \cdot 54 \pm 0 \cdot 73$	4·8
Melos	$8 \cdot 35 \pm 0 \cdot 72$	4·9
Melos	$2 \cdot 36 \pm 0 \cdot 53$	9·1
Franchthi cave (S. Greece)		
Sample 1	$8 \cdot 48 \pm 0 \cdot 55$	4·6
Sample 2	$8 \cdot 82 \pm 0 \cdot 57$	4·1
Sample 3	$9 \cdot 33 \pm 0 \cdot 60$	4·4

[a] Except for the obsidian artefacts from the Franchthi cave, the samples were collected from known obsidian sources.
[b] The errors in the values for the uranium contents are approximately ± 10 per cent.

Further obsidian characterization studies include the investigation of sources and artefacts in the western United States and Central America using neutron activation analysis (Gordus et al., 1967) and X-ray fluorescence spectrometry (Stevenson et al., 1971) and the investigation of obsidian from the south-west Pacific (New Guinea, British Solomon Islands) using optical emission spectrometry (Ambrose and Green, 1972).

Pottery

In the case of pottery, physical methods of analysis provide information both on the geographical source for the raw materials used

(Peacock, 1970) and on the firing conditions (i.e. temperature and atmosphere) employed in its manufacture.

Chemical analysis for the minor and trace elements has been extensively used to study both fine-textured pottery and pottery tempered with quartz sand since these wares are not amenable to characterization by petrological examination (p. 225). Although X-ray diffraction (powder method) has also been employed for characterization (Young and Whitmore, 1957), the data obtained on the mineral phases present is less useful than that from petrological examination which, in addition, provides information on the size, shape and arrangement of the mineral grains. Similarly the use of Mössbauer spectroscopy for the characterization of clay sources (Gangas *et al.*, 1971) is limited by the fact that the iron-bearing minerals present in the pottery depend on the firing conditions, as well as on the mineralogical composition of the original clay. However, both X-ray diffraction and Mössbauer spectroscopy are of value in studying the firing conditions employed in the manufacture of the pottery and, in conjunction with thermal analysis, provide information which supplements that obtained from petrological examination.

Source of Raw Materials

Optical emission spectrometry has, in the past, been extensively employed for the chemical analysis of pottery, the damage caused by the removal of a small sample normally being permissible. However, it seems probable that, in the future, this technique will be increasingly replaced by either neutron activation analysis, in which semiconductor counters with high sensitivity and resolution are employed, or by X-ray fluorescence spectrometry, in which homogeneous pellets made from powdered pottery are analysed.

The characterization of clay sources on the basis of the concentrations of minor and trace elements is rather more difficult than in the case of obsidian sources and possibly even the flint sources. Firstly, in any area, there is likely to be a large number of potential clay sources and the variation in the chemical compositions of these sources is likely to be fairly small. From Table 23, which shows the mean concentrations of selected elements in pottery from diverse regions around the world, it can be seen that, of the elements listed, only chromium shows a range of variation approaching one order of magnitude. Secondly, any particular clay source exhibits some inhomogeneity in chemical composition. Thirdly, changes in the

METHODS OF PHYSICAL EXAMINATION IN ARCHAEOLOGY

chemical composition of the original clay may have occurred as a result of the addition of tempering material, the volatilization of certain elements during firing and the post-burial migration of certain soluble and mobile elements.

Table 23. Concentrations of selected elements, determined using neutron activation analysis, in pottery from diverse sources (after Harbottle, 1970)

Pottery source	Concentration (ppm)						
	Cobalt	Chromium	Europium	Iron	Scandium	Thorium	Hafnium
Devon	17	91	0·97	5·4%	21	7·7	—
Mexico	36	730	1·65	6·9%	27	14	—
Knossos	59	792	1·17	8·8%	33	11·2	4·0
Mycenae	47	441	1·27	7·9%	32	11·9	3·7
S. Arabia	26	850	1·04	5·8%	28	4	2·8

In order to characterize the different pottery groups, it is therefore necessary to analyse for several minor and trace elements and these elements should be chosen with considerable care. For example, by analysing pottery sherds taken from various levels in a Bronze Age pit, Freeth (1967) has shown that the concentrations of calcium and manganese can depend on the depth at which the sherd was buried (Table 24). Since this pottery was tempered with shell (i.e. calcium

Table 24. Variation in the composition of pottery sherds as a result of burial conditions (after Freeth, 1967)

Position in pit	Concentration (per cent)		
	Calcium	Manganese	Iron[a]
Upper layer	6·1 ± 4.0	0·22 ± 0·11	15·7 ± 3·2
Lower layer	18·5 ± 13·0	0·34 ± 0·18	16·7 ± 5·2

[a] In contrast to the situation for calcium and manganese, there is no significant difference between the iron contents of sherds from the upper and lower layers of the pit.

carbonate) which, after conversion to calcium oxide during firing, would have absorbed water during burial to form calcium hydroxide, it is thought that the increase in calcium content with depth reflects the decreasing effectiveness, in dissolving and removing calcium hydroxide from the sherds, of the percolating water with increasing depth. In contrast, the increase in the manganese content with depth is thought to be due to the preferential deposition, after burial, of this element in those sherds in the lower levels of the pit. Poole and Finch (1972) have similarly studied the suitability for characterization of certain elements in terms of both their volatility during firing and their solubility during burial. By comparing the analytical data for samples taken from the exterior surface, interior surface and the core of a sherd, they showed that, of the elements selected for analysis, the concentrations of zirconium, rubidium, strontium, titanium and nickel are probably unaffected by firing or burial and are therefore suitable for characterization while the concentrations of zinc and sulphur will be less reliable.

In addition to the problems of volatility and solubility, it must be further appreciated that the different patterns of concentrations obtained for two groups of pottery could arise from the addition of different types of tempering material rather than from the use of different clays. Similarly, the addition of temper must also be considered when comparing the chemical compositions of the pottery and possible clay sources. Consequently it is desirable to supplement the chemical analysis by petrological examination and thus establish whether or not temper has been added to the clay, even though it is frequently not possible to identify the geographical source of the temper by this latter technique.

Although the pattern of minor and trace element concentrations can normally be used to group together pottery made from clay from a particular source, it is often more difficult to locate and identify the *actual* clay source used. Therefore instead of characterizing the sources of the raw material, as in the case of flint or obsidian, it is more usual to first characterize the products of the various relevant kiln sites. Alternatively, when kiln sites are not available, the geographical distribution of the particular pottery group identified by chemical analysis is used to define the approximate area in which the clay source must be located. It is consequently clear that characterization by chemical analysis provides less precise information on the source of the clay than can be achieved in the case of pottery which can be characterized by petrological examination. However, the chemical analysis approach is applicable to a far wider range of pottery since, as indicated on page 225, petrological characterization is normally only feasible when distinctive igneous and metamorphic rock fragments are present in the pottery.

Applications. The study of Romano-British mortaria using optical emission spectrometry represents one of the first attempts to characterize pottery on the basis of the minor and trace element concentrations (Richards and Hartley, 1960; Hartley and Richards, 1965). Pottery samples from a large number of kiln sites, distributed throughout England, were first analysed in order to provide reference groups of known geographical origin, some typical analytical data being presented in Fig. 104. Although, in distinguishing the products of dif-

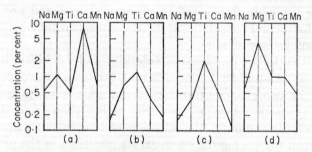

Figure 104. Average concentrations of five elements for groups of Romano-British mortaria from typical kiln sites (N.B. manganese concentrations are multiplied by 10). (a) Colchester, Essex. (b) Hartshill, Warwicks. (c) South Carlton, Lincs. (d) Wilderspool, Cheshire (after Hartley and Richards, 1965).

ferent kiln sites, the overall pattern of concentrations must normally be considered, a number of general regional traits emerged. For example, there is a relatively high calcium (Ca) concentration in the pottery from East Anglia (e.g. Colchester), a relatively high magnesium (Mg) concentration in the pottery from north-western England (e.g. Wilderspool) and a relatively high titanium (Ti) concentration in the Lincolnshire pottery (e.g. South Carlton). Having established the characteristic pattern of concentrations for the pottery from each kiln site, mortaria found on domestic and military sites can be studied in order to define the extent of the trade from the different production centres. In addition, since mortaria are frequently marked with the name of the potter who made them, it is possible to trace the movement of the individual potters between the various kiln sites. For example, since the three distinct fabrics used by the potter, G. ATTIVS MARINVS, were shown, on the basis of the analytical data, to fall into the groups established for Colchester (Essex), Radlett (Hertfordshire) and

Hartshill (Warwickshire), it was concluded that this potter produced mortaria at those three widely separated centres.

An extremely important study of Minoan and Mycenaean painted pottery, current in Aegean area and beyond between about 1500 and 1100 BC, has also been carried out using optical emission spectrometry (Catling *et al.*, 1963; Catling and Millett, 1965a). During the period of widest distribution (i.e. *circa* 1400–1200 BC), there was a remarkable degree of homogeneity both in the shapes and painted decoration of the pottery made by the Aegean potters and therefore the possibility of obtaining analytical criteria for distinguishing pottery from the various sources was investigated. More than a thousand pottery sherds from over fifty sites on the Greek mainland, Crete and throughout the eastern Mediterranean have been analysed and on the basis of the pattern of concentrations for nine elements, it has been possible to characterize some eighteen separate pottery groups. The ranges of the concentrations obtained for Mycenaean pottery manufactured in the Peloponnese (Group A) and the Minoan pottery manufactured at Knossos on Crete (Group B) are presented in Fig. 105 and

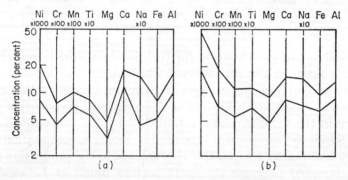

Figure 105. Ranges of concentrations of nine elements for (a) Mycenaean pottery from the Peloponnese (Group A) and (b) Minoan pottery from Knossos on Crete (Group B) (after Catling and Millett, 1965b).

from this it can be seen that there is no overlap between the two groups for the nickel (Ni), chromium (Cr) and magnesium (Mg) concentrations. Confirmation of the validity of these two *primary* groups was obtained from the neutron activation analysis of selected sherds (Harbottle, 1970). In providing data on elements present at concentrations of less than 100 ppm, this technique was essentially complimentary to optical emission spectrometry with which elements in the concentration range 100 ppm to 10 per cent were analysed (Table 25). The previously established groups (A and B) retained their homogeneity when elements present at these lower concentration levels were included in the characterization pattern and the difference in the concentrations of cobalt (Co) provided a further clear-cut distinction between the two groups.

Table 25. Comparison of the elements analysed in Greek pottery using optical emission spectrometry and neutron activation analysis (after Harbottle, 1970)

Concentration range	Elements analysed	
	Optical emission spectrometry	Neutron activation analysis
≥ 10 per cent	Ca, Al	
1–10 per cent	Mg, Fe	Fe
0·1–1 per cent	Na, Ti	
0·01–0·1 per cent	Cr, Mn, Ni	Cr, Ni
10–100 ppm		Co, Sc
1–10 ppm		Eu, Cs, Th, Hf, Ta

In contrast to the situation for the Romano-British mortaria, an adequate series of kiln sites was not available for the investigation of Mycenaean and Minoan pottery and therefore the production centres had to be defined on the basis of the geographical distribution of the pottery in the various groups established by the concentration patterns. Similarly, comparison between the chemical composition of the pottery and that of the possible clay sources in the production region was attempted only for Group D pottery found at Lefkandi and Amarinthos on the island of Euboea (Catling and Millett, 1969). In this case, a sample of clay from the modern brick-factory at Lefkandi was found to have the same concentration pattern as that for the Group D pottery and also as that for pottery of the eighth century BC from Chalkis in Euboea. Therefore, so far as this western area of Euboea is concerned, potters have evidently continued to use clay of the same composition group from at least the fourteenth century BC until the present day.

Having established the concentration patterns for the two major production centres (i.e. Group A—Mycenaean pottery from the Peloponnese and Group B—Minoan pottery from Knossos), it was then possible, on the other Mediterranean sites, to distinguish between locally-made pottery and that imported from these two centres. These results clearly established that, during the period 1400 to 1200 BC, the Mycenaeans were involved in extensive mercantile trade, exporting pottery to the Aegean islands of Melos, Chios and Rhodes as well as to Syria (Tell Atchana), Egypt (Tell el Amarna) and Cyprus. Furthermore, the much smaller quantity of exports from Knossos suggested that Minoan Crete had been supplanted by Mycenaean Greece as the major mercantile power in the east Mediterranean during this period.

The results for Cyprus (Catling and Millett, 1965a) were of compelling interest since it had previously been suggested that Mycenaean potters had migrated to Cyprus soon after 1400 BC and had settled in several of the richer towns where their workshops produced pottery that was indistinguishable in appearance from contemporary productions in the Peloponnese. However, the fact that the Mycenaean pottery found on Cyprus belonged to Group A and exhibited a different concentration pattern to that of locally-produced imitations of Mycenaean pottery (Groups L and M), clearly established that it was produced in the Peloponnese and imported to Cyprus. Similarly the diversity of the imported material (Groups A, B, F and H) found on Melos was of interest in that it provided a just reflection of its commercial importance midway between Crete and Greece and of the fact that it was an obvious staging port for ships travelling to and from the east Mediterranean.

A related investigation involved the analysis, using optical emission spectrometry, of a group of stirrup jars, bearing inscriptions in the linear B script and found at Thebes (Catling and Millett, 1965b). One aspect of the current controversy (Palmer, 1961) about relations between Crete and Greece in the period 1400–1200 BC and the proliferation of the linear B script during this period has been centred on these inscribed stirrup jars and consequently information on their place of manufacture is of particular interest. The Mycenaean and Minoan pottery groups, which had already been established, provided the basis for the investigation, the principal modification being the ability to subdivide the Group B pottery in terms of its germanium content. Previously Catling et al. (1963), had found that a large percentage of the pottery from Thebes appeared to have the same chemical composition as pottery manufactured at Knossos. Although it was possible that the Theban pottery had been imported from Knossos, it seemed more likely that the clay sources at Thebes and Knossos had similar compositions. This hypothesis was subsequently confirmed by a more detailed study of the optical emission spectrometry data which revealed that the pottery found at Thebes (Group B*) contained a very small quantity of germanium (about 10 ppm) while germanium was absent from the Knossos pottery (Group B).

In contradiction to the earlier subjective views, the analysis of the Theban stirrup jars (Fig. 106) excluded the possibility of their manufacture at Knossos or elsewhere in central Crete (Group B). Instead it

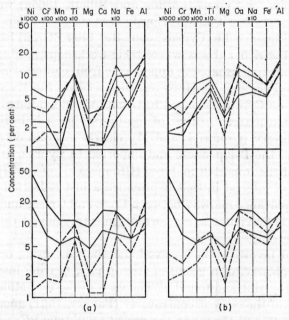

Figure 106. Comparison of the concentration ranges of nine elements for Theban stirrup jars (dashed lines) and Minoan pottery from Crete (solid lines). (a) Stirrup jars I (12 jars) compared with Group F pottery (upper) from East Crete and Group B pottery (lower) from Knossos. (b) Stirrup jars II (6 jars) compared with Group O pottery (upper) from East Crete and Group B pottery (lower) from Knossos (after Catling and Millett, 1965b).

was shown that eastern Crete (Groups F and O) was the most probable source of the majority of the jars while others came from the Peloponnese (Group A) and Thebes itself (Group B*). The archaeological interpretation of these results is difficult because of uncertainties concerning the date of the Theban stirrup jars and they neither confirm nor disprove the recent hypothesis (Palmer, 1961) that the palace of

Knossos was destroyed at about 1200 BC rather than at the previously accepted date of 1400 BC. However, the analytical data does provide clear proof that the linear B script was being used and trading communities existed at sites in Crete, other than Knossos, sometime during the period 1400–1200 BC. Although these results, and even the premises on which this method of characterizing pottery groups is based, have been questioned by Raison (1968), these criticisms have been more than adequately answered by Catling and Millett (1969).

Further recent pottery characterization studies include the investigation of Roman Samian pottery from France and Italy using X-ray fluorescence spectrometry (Picon *et al.*, 1971); the neutron activation analysis of pottery from a selection of British medieval kiln sites (Aspinall *et al.*, 1968) and the correlation of British post-medieval pottery with European kiln-site material using X-ray fluorescence spectrometry (Poole and Finch, 1972).

Technology

In the context of ceramic technology, the major application of the physical methods of analysis is in the determination of the firing temperatures employed in the manufacture of the pottery. The firing temperatures of ancient pottery are of interest because they provide information on the performance of the kilns used and on the technological capabilities of the potters. Apart from its immediate archaeological significance, this information is valuable when full-scale replicas of excavated pottery kilns are built and fired in order to acquire further data on the technology and economics of pottery production in antiquity (Mayes, 1961 and 1962). In addition, since the smelting and casting of copper requires temperatures in excess of 1000°C, a knowledge of the temperatures which could be produced by the ancient potters is relevant when considering the early stages in the development of metallurgy.

The firing temperature of ancient pottery is normally estimated either through studying those minerals which are altered during firing by means of X-ray diffraction and differential thermal analysis, as well as by petrological examination (p. 228), or from thermal expansion measurements. In principle, this latter approach should provide a more precise value for the firing temperature than that based on a "mineralogical temperature scale" which can only indicate an upper or lower limit for the firing temperature.

Perinet (1960) has studied pottery of the sixth to second century BC from the Mediterranean area using X-ray diffraction. Since calcareous clay was used to make this pottery, it was possible to estimate the firing temperatures employed (Table 26) by identifying the calcium alumino-silicates (gehlenite-$2CaO.Al_2O_3.SiO_2$; anorthite-$CaO.Al_2O_3.2SiO_2$; wollastonite-$CaO.SiO_2$) which had been formed during firing by reactions between the clay and the calcium carbonate. The major hazard involved in estimating the firing temperature from the presence

Table 26. Firing temperatures for calcareous pottery from the Mediterranean area, estimated on the basis of the mineral phases present (after Perinet, 1960)

Mineral phases present	Estimated firing temperature (°C)
Calcite	500–800[a]
Gehlenite	820–840
Gehlenite + anorthite	840–900
Anorthite + gehlenite + wollastonite	950–1000
Anorthite	1000–1050

[a] The lower limit of 500°C is based on the absence of hydrated clay minerals (e.g. kaolinite) from the pottery, while the upper limit is based on the fact that calcite starts to decompose in the temperature range 750–850°C.

or absence of calcium alumino-silicates and other high temperature crystalline phases, such as mullite ($3Al_2O_3.2SiO_2$) and cristobalite (SiO_2), is the fact that the temperature at which they are formed depends on the chemical composition of the pottery. Factors, such as the relative proportions of calcium carbonate and clay minerals, the type of clay mineral and the presence of "fluxing" impurities, can affect the temperature at which specific mineral phases are formed by as much as 100°C. It is therefore advisable to repeat the X-ray diffraction measurements after refiring the pottery at temperatures below and above the estimated firing temperature. Then, if the estimated firing temperature is valid, further mineralogical changes will be observed after refiring at the higher temperatures but not after refiring at the lower temperatures.

Bimson (1969) has also employed X-ray diffraction to identify the high-temperature crystalline phases in pottery but, in this case, used the data for classifying the different types of ceramic body and thus distinguishing between the various hard-paste and soft-paste porcelains produced in Europe after the sixteenth century AD. The characteristic mineral in hard-paste porcelains, stonewares and high-fired earthenwares was shown to be mullite. In contrast, whitlockite $(Ca_3(PO_4)_2)$ was typical of those soft-paste porcelains containing bone-ash and enstatite $(MgO.SiO_2)$ was typical of those containing soapstone while the glassy-frit type of soft-paste porcelains generally contained wollastonite.

Tite (1969) has used the thermal expansion method to determine the firing temperatures employed in the manufacture of a selection of pottery with a wide range of provenance and age. The firing temperatures for those pottery sherds, for which a net irreversible shrinkage was observed at temperatures in excess of 700°C, were determined on the basis of equation (9.4), a refiring time of one hour being employed. In these cases, the firing temperature should be regarded as that *constant* temperature which, if maintained for one hour, would have produced about the same amount of sintering as was actually achieved during the original firing, in which the technique of heating to a peak temperature, followed by immediate cooling, would probably have been employed. In contrast, when a net shrinkage was observed below 700°C, the thermal expansion data did not provide a satisfactory estimate of the firing temperature. However, since X-ray diffraction and differential thermal analysis established that these sherds did not contain hydrated clay minerals, it was suggested that their firing temperatures must have been in the range 500–700°C. Similarly when the sherds were shown to contain calcite, it was suggested that their firing temperature must have been less than 800°C: the irregular expansion and contraction exhibited by these sherds preventing any more precise estimate of the firing temperature.

The firing temperatures estimated by means of this combination of thermal expansion measurements and mineralogical examination are presented in Table 27. From this, it can be seen that firing temperatures ranging from 500°C to 1200°C were used in the manufacture of ancient pottery and that low or high firing temperatures were not necessarily confined to particular periods or parts of the world. For example, the firing temperatures employed during the Roman period ranged from 500–700°C for coarse pottery, such as amphora and black burnished ware, to 1000–1200°C for the high-class Samian ware. The

Table 27. Firing temperatures for pottery, estimated on the basis of thermal expansion measurements (after Tite, 1969)

Provenance[a]	Archaeological data		Estimated firing temperature[b] (°C)
	Period/age	Type	
Mersin, Turkey	Neolithic	—	750–820
Byblos, Lebanon	Neolithic	—	< 800
Arpachiyak, Iraq	Chalcolithic	Halaf ware	970–1050†
Chagar Bazar, Syria	Chalcolithic	Halaf ware	< 800
Al 'Ubaid, Iraq	Bronze Age	'Ubaid ware	1140–1180
Ur, Iraq	Bronze Age	'Ubaid ware	1070–1110
Hala Sultan Tekke, Cyprus	c. 1300 BC	Mycenaean ware	940–1000†
Myrtou, Cyprus	c. 1300 BC	Local copy of Mycenaean ware	1030–1070†
Al Mina, Turkey	c. 500 BC	Greek Attic ware	1000–1100
Al Mina, Turkey	c. 500 BC	Greek Attic ware	940–1010†
Catterick, Yorks.	Roman	Spanish amphora	500–700
Castor, Hunts.	Roman	Black burnished ware	500–700
Bainbridge, Yorks.	Roman	Calcite gritted ware	< 800
Stibbington, Hunts.	Roman	Grey ware	900–960†
Hartshill, Warwicks. (K)	Roman	Mortarium	900–950
Hartshill, Warwicks. (K)	Roman	Mortarium	950–990
Catterick, Yorks.	Roman	Colour coated ware	910–980
Catterick, Yorks.	Roman	Central Gaulish Samian	1020–1090
Catterick, Yorks.	Roman	South Gaulish Samian	1100–1150
Baston, Lincs.	Saxon	—	500–700
Ipswich, Suffolk	Saxon	Thetford ware	920–960†
Laverstock, Wilts. (K)	Mediaeval	—	750–820
West Cowick, Yorks. (K)	Mediaeval	—	940–990†
Pottersbury, Northants. (K)	c. 1650 AD	—	910–950
Halifax, Yorks. (K)	c. 1650 AD	—	910–950
China	Sung dynasty	Porcelain	1070–1140*
China	Sung dynasty	Celadon	1070–1190*
China	—	Porcelain: provincial	970–1060*
China	Ching dynasty	Porcelain	960–1050*

[a] With the exception of the Chinese porcelain, the provenance refers to the archaeological site at which the pottery sherd was found. Where the pottery has obviously been imported to the site, this is indicated in the archaeological data (e.g. Greek Attic ware found in Turkey, Mycenaean ware found in Cyprus, etc.). (K) is used to indicate those sherds which were obtained from the kiln site at which they were manufactured.

[b] The asterisk (*) indicates those firing temperatures which could be too low as a result of the presence of a low viscosity liquid phase and the dagger (†) indicates those which could be too high as a result of bloating.

high firing temperatures (1050–1200°C) employed in the manufacture of the Ubaid pottery from Al Ubaid and Ur are of particular interest since they indicate that the ceramic technology had achieved the refractory conditions, necessary for the smelting and casting of copper and bronze, at the period and in the region where significant developments in metallurgical technology were in progress. Furthermore, these firing temperatures are consistent with an earlier suggestion (Tobler, 1939), based on petrological examination, that some Ubaid pottery found at Tepe Gawra in Iraq had been fired to 1200°C. Also of interest is the fact that similar firing temperatures (950–1050°C) were used in the production of both Mycenaean pottery itself and the locally-produced imitations found in Cyprus.

Table 28. Mössbauer spectrum parameters for pottery and clay samples from Cheam, Surrey (after Cousins and Dharmawardena, 1969)

Sample	Mössbauer parameters (mm/s)		
	Isomer shift	Quadrupole splitting	Peak width at half-height
Pottery	0·10	0·94	{0·69 {0·65
Clay: unfired	0·17	0·60	{0·59 {0·61
Clay: fired at 800°C (10 h)	0·15	1·44	0·93
Clay: fired at 1000°C (6 h)	0·06	0·79	0·54

Cousins and Dharmawardena (1969) have investigated the possibility of obtaining further data on the firing temperatures, employed in the manufacture of pottery, from the study of the Mössbauer spectra associated with the iron-bearing minerals present in the pottery. They measured the Mössbauer spectra associated with clay samples which have been fired at different temperatures and showed that the parameters (e.g. isomer shift, quadrupole splitting and peak width at half-height), defining the Mössbauer spectrum, varied regularly with increasing firing temperature. They therefore suggested that, if the source of the clay used to make the pottery was known, the firing temperature for the pottery could be estimated by comparing its spectrum with those for clay samples which had been fired to various known temperatures. Results for a mediaeval sherd from Cheam (Surrey) and for fired samples of a local clay are presented in Table 28 and from these, it can be tentatively inferred that the firing temperature for the pottery was between 800 and 1000°C. Furthermore, since the Mössbauer spectrum provides information on the oxidation state of the iron present in the pottery, it has also been possible to obtain data on the atmospheric conditions prevailing during firing. For example, in the case of a pottery sherd with a red surface layer and a black interior, Cousins and Dharmawardena established that, in the surface layer, iron was present in the oxidized state (Fe^{3+}) whereas iron was present in both the oxidized (Fe^{3+}:27 per cent) and reduced (Fe^{2+}:73 per cent) states in the black interior. Consequently it can be inferred that this sherd was fired in an oxidizing atmosphere but that the firing was not continued for a sufficient length of time to oxidize the iron throughout the body of the pottery.

Metal Artefacts

In the study of metal artefacts, physical methods of chemical analysis (Caley, 1964) are of primary importance and have been used to determine the compositions of the metal alloys and to provide information on the geographical sources of the raw materials (Tylecote, 1970). In addition, isotopic analysis has been used to assist in the identification of lead sources while the electron probe microanalyser and the back reflection method of X-ray diffraction have provided information on the techniques employed in the fabrication of artefacts which has supplemented that obtained from metallographic examination (p. 230). The choice of analytical technique and the inferences that can be made from the composition of the alloy depend on both the particular metal or alloy and the type of artefact under consideration. Consequently copper and bronze artefacts, iron and steel artefacts, lead and coins are discussed separately in the following sections.

Copper and Bronze Artefacts

Optical emission spectrometry has normally been employed for the chemical analysis of copper and bronze artefacts, the damage caused by the removal of a small sample being permissible in most cases. However, it seems probable that, in the future, atomic absorption spectrometry will provide an alternative, and probably more accurate, technique. Because of the presence of surface corrosion products, the data obtained from X-ray fluorescence spectrometry tends to be somewhat unreliable while neutron activation analysis is not normally feasible because of the comparatively large size of the artefacts.

In the first place, the analysis of the major and minor elements in copper and bronze artefacts is of considerable importance in estab-

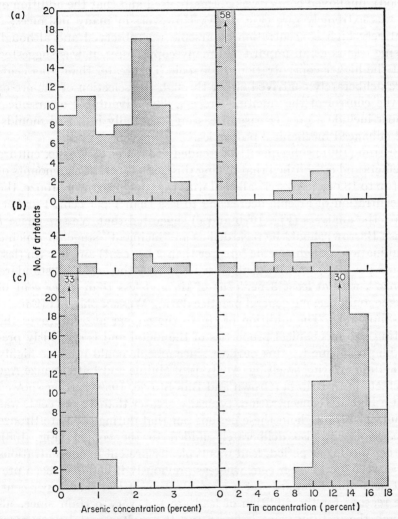

Figure 107. Histograms showing the variation in the concentrations of arsenic and tin in the alloys used to make copper/bronze artefacts during the Early Bronze Age in the British Isles. (a) Pre-Wessex (i.e. Beaker) period. The tin concentrations for the majority of the artefacts in the histogram range per 0–2 cent are less than 0·01 per cent (after Coghlan and Case, 1957). (b) Wessex phase I (Bush Barrow). (c) Wessex phase II (Camerton–Snowshill) and Arreton hoards (after Britton, 1961).

lishing the developments that occurred in the composition of the alloy employed by the ancient metalworkers. For example, in a study of the beginnings of metallurgy in the British Isles, Coghlan and Case (1957) showed that, during the period before the Wessex culture (i.e. Beaker period), unalloyed copper was normally used and that the addition of tin was extremely rare (Fig. 107a). However, in many instances, a relatively high concentration of arsenic was observed and although arsenic occurs as an impurity in many copper ores, it was suggested that the higher concentrations of arsenic (i.e. greater than 2 per cent) were deliberately contrived either through the selection of the ore or by the control of the smelting process. The advantages of arsenical copper include a greater ease of casting, especially in closed moulds, and enhanced mechanical properties.

Britton (1961) subsequently extended the study to Wessex culture artefacts and established that during this period increasing amounts of tin (up to 18 per cent) were alloyed with the copper to form bronze, the concentration of arsenic decreasing to less than 1 per cent. Furthermore, the analyses (Fig. 107b and c) suggested that Wessex phase I (Bush Barrow) should be regarded as an "incipient" stage, in which a combination of high arsenic (greater than 2 per cent) and low tin (less than 8 per cent) was frequently used and that the use of a "standard bronze", with at least 8 per cent of tin and less than 1 per cent of arsenic, only became general practice during Wessex phase II (Camerton-Snowshill). The addition of tin to the copper also improves the casting and mechanical properties of the metal and is obviously preferable to arsenic for this purpose since arsenic could produce highly toxic fumes during smelting. Analysis of Middle and Late Bronze Age artefacts from Britain (Brown and Blin-Stoyle, 1959) further showed that a high tin concentration, typically greater than 12 per cent, was maintained throughout these periods but that during the Late Bronze Age, lead was also deliberately added to the copper (Fig. 108). During this latter period, lead was typically present in concentrations of between 4 and 7 per cent whereas previously it had only been present as a minor impurity at a concentration of less than 1 per cent. The reasons for the addition of lead are not very certain since, although the melting point is lower and the molten metal flows more easily, the mechanical properties of the leaded alloy are inferior to those of the plain tin bronze. It is therefore possible that the use of lead may reflect a desire to economize on the amount of copper and tin required to make the bronze.

In addition to the determination of the composition of the alloy, analysis for the minor and trace elements in copper and bronze artefacts can, in principle, provide the basis for characterizing and distinguishing between the various ore sources used in antiquity. In the techniques of extracting copper available to prehistoric man, impurities from the ore would regularly persist in the smelted metal. Furthermore, it is unlikely that the addition of tin would greatly alter the pattern of minor and trace constituents and therefore, even with a

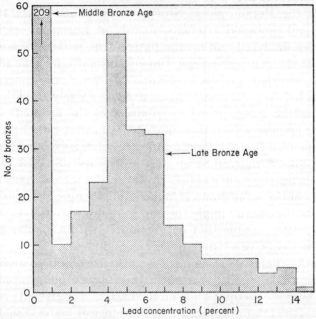

Figure 108. Histogram showing the difference between the lead concentrations in bronzes of the British Middle and Late Bronze Ages (i.e. lead concentrations of less than and greater than 1 per cent respectively) (after Brown and Blin-Stoyle, 1959).

true bronze, most of the impurities can be reasonably assigned to the copper. However, the various impurities present in the ore are carried over into the metal, during smelting, in different proportions and these proportions are to some extent dependent on the method of extraction employed. Thus all the silver and gold, the majority of the arsenic, antimony and bismuth and a high proportion of the nickel and lead survive the smelting process. Further obstacles to the characterization of ore sources by means of chemical analysis include inhomogeneity in the chemical composition of ore from a particular source, the similarity in the composition of ores from different sources and the use, particularly during the Middle and Late Bronze Ages, of scrap metal which could have been derived from several different ore sources. The difficulties associated with the characterization of copper and bronze artefacts on the basis of the pattern of minor and trace element concentrations are therefore somewhat greater than those associated with the equivalent characterization of obsidian, flint and pottery.

The most comprehensive programme of analyses of copper and bronze artefacts is probably that being carried out by the Arbeitsgemeinschaft für Metallurgie at Stuttgart (Junghans *et al.*, 1960 and 1968). Several thousand artefacts, mainly of European origin, have already been analysed and on the basis of the pattern of concentrations of five elements (arsenic, antimony, bismuth, nickel and silver), twelve characteristic groups were initially defined, the concentration boundaries between the groups being fixed on a solely statistical basis. By plotting the geographical distribution of the artefacts in these groups, the main concentrations of each group were established and it was then inferred that if a large number of artefacts of a certain group are found, for example, in Spain, this represents a Spanish group derived from a nearby source of ore. However, if a second concentration of artefacts of the same group is found in another geographical region, this does not necessarily imply the import of raw materials or artefacts since it is quite possible that an ore source with a similar chemical composition exists, or existed, in this second region.

The Stuttgart classification has been criticized on both archaeological and scientific grounds. Waterbolk and Butler (1965) consider that, in establishing the groups purely on the basis of a statistical evaluation of the analytical data, significant archaeological factors, such as the typology of the artefacts, have been ignored. By including archaeological factors and slightly modifying the concentration boundaries between the analytical groups, they feel that a simpler and more meaningful classification can sometimes be achieved. In contrast, Slater and Charles (1970) consider that the use of the bismuth concentrations in the characterization of the different groups can be dangerous since this element has an extremely low solubility in copper. It therefore tends to segregate out from the copper during the solidification of the molten metal and is not necessarily uniformly distributed throughout the artefact. This non-uniformity in the bismuth concentration was observed when a series of laboratory-cast bronze axes were subjected to multiple sampling, the bismuth concentration varying between 0·072 (± 0·001) and 0·084 (± 0·001) per cent for different samples taken from a typical axe. Consequently, when the bismuth concentration for an artefact is based on the analysis of a single sample, incorrect classification is possible in the case of those artefacts whose bismuth concentrations are close to the values for the boundaries between the different analytical groups (e.g. 0·16, 0·08, 0·02 and 0·008 per cent bismuth).

In spite of the difficulties inherent in the characterization of ore sources and the more specific criticisms of the Stuttgart classification, there is no doubt that the characterization of copper and bronze artefacts, on the basis of the minor and trace element concentrations, has made a significant contribution to the understanding of the development of metallurgy, especially with respect to the Early Bronze Age (Coles, 1969). However, it is equally clear that it will be extremely difficult to locate and identify the *actual* ore sources used. First, it is probable that, in many cases, ore was obtained from sources which have now been exhausted. Secondly, ore from sources within a fairly small geographical region can exhibit several different concentration patterns. For example, Tylecote (1970) has shown that the various Irish ores, analysed by Coghlan et al. (1963), correspond to the characteristic concentration patterns associated with at least four of the twelve groups initially defined by the Stuttgart team. It is, perhaps, some consolation that those Stuttgart groups which contain no artefacts emanating from the British Isles are not represented among the Irish ores.

Iron and Steel Artefacts

The quantitative chemical analysis of iron and steel presents considerable difficulties because of both the extensive corrosion that has normally occurred and also the inhomogeneity of the remaining metal. There is consequently far less analytical data available for iron and steel artefacts than in the case of copper and bronze artefacts. Optical emission and atomic absorption spectrometry again provide the most satisfactory physical methods for the determination of the concentrations of many minor and trace elements. However, for the analysis of impurities, such as carbon, phosphorus and sulphur, these methods must be supplemented by standard chemical methods.

The carbon concentration of the artefact should, in principle, provide the basis for distinguishing between wrought iron, cast iron and steel. However, in view of the non-uniform distribution of carbon in most early artefacts, metallographic examination (p. 238) provides more precise information on the iron–carbon alloy present and on the techniques (i.e. carburization, quenching and tempering) used in the fabrication of the artefact. The phosphorus concentration is also of technological interest since a high phosphorus concentration (e.g. 0·4 per cent) tends to harden the iron directly while, at the same time, making hardening by means of carburization more difficult. In addition, the concentration of nickel can be used to identify those rare artefacts fashioned from meteoric iron since this iron normally contains more than 5 per cent of nickel, in contrast to the concentrations of less than 0·1 per cent associated with the majority of iron smelted from ores.

The possibility of characterizing and identifying the iron ore sources used in antiquity, by means of minor and trace element analysis, has also been investigated. For example, Haldane (1970) has studied a selection of pre-Roman ironwork from Somerset and, on the basis of the pattern of concentrations of eight elements, was able to distinguish four separate groups of iron artefacts. The values for the calcium, magnesium and lead concentrations for one group suggested an ore source in the central Mendip region while the high manganese concentration for a second group suggested that the ore could have originated in the proximity of the Dolomitic Conglomerate, which extends along the south face of the Mendips. In spite of this limited success, the existence of a large number of iron ore sources in many regions means that unambiguous characterization will always be extremely difficult. Furthermore, as a result of the large number of available sources, trade in iron ore will have been less extensive than in the case of copper ore and therefore the characterization results will tend to be less significant.

Lead

Isotopic analysis has been the principal technique employed to obtain information on the source of the ore from which the lead, incorporated into a wide range of archaeological artefacts, was smelted. Although many of the problems associated with the characterization of metal ore sources by means of the minor and trace element concentrations still exist in this case, characterization by isotopic analysis has the specific advantage that the isotopic ratios are unchanged as a result of the smelting processes.

Brill and Wampler (1967) have carried out an extensive programme of isotopic analyses of lead ores and lead artefacts. The data for the ores and for lead artefacts, which were known to have been made from lead derived from specific mining areas, indicated that four reasonably well defined groups of lead ores (L, E, S and X) can be distinguished on the basis of the isotopic ratios, $^{208}Pb/^{206}Pb$ and $^{207}Pb/^{206}Pb$ (Fig. 109). Group L contains ores mined at Laurion in Greece; group E contains ores mined in Britain during the Roman period; group S includes ores from southern Spain, Sardinia and Wales, while group X can be

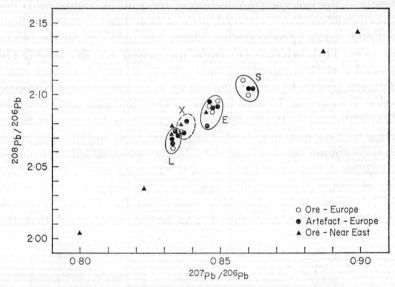

Figure 109. Lead isotope ratios for lead ores and lead artefacts produced from ores of known origin. The solid and dashed lines define the approximate isotopic limits for the four empirical lead ore groups (i.e. L, E, S and X). The increase in the values for the isotopic ratios is associated, in general terms, with the increasing geological age of the ore deposits (after Brill and Wampler, 1967).

tentatively assigned to ores mined in Italy. In addition, lead ores from the Near East, and particularly those from Egypt, span the entire range of isotopic compositions and in many cases, the values for their isotopic ratios fall within the four major groups. This isotopic data for essentially known ore sources provides the basis for identifying the source of the lead ore used in a wide range of artefacts. However, positive identification of the ore source is not normally possible from isotopic composition alone since ores from widely separated regions can exhibit the same isotopic ratios when they are located in geologically similar environments (e.g. ore deposits of the same geological age). Therefore assistance from the archaeological evidence itself must be sought when a positive identification is required. On the other hand, fairly conclusive negative statements can be made on the basis of the isotopic data. For example, although lead with the isotopic composition of group S could have been derived from ore mined in Spain, Sardinia or Wales, it certainly could *not* have been smelted from ore mined at Laurion in Greece (Group L).

In addition to the study of metallic lead artefacts, Brill (1970) has determined the isotopic composition of the lead in bronze coins and statues as well as that of the lead, present as an intentional ingredient, in red and yellow opaque glasses. The results obtained for the bronze coins (Fig. 110), which date from the period 350 BC to AD 310, suggested that the majority of the lead was derived from ores mined at Laurion (group L) and in Britain or some unidentified European location (group E). It was further noted that the isotopic ratios (^{208}Pb/^{206}Pb and ^{207}Pb/^{206}Pb) for the lead from Laurion tended to increase with decreasing age of the bronze artefacts and this may reflect variations among the ores from the different layers which were opened up at different times in the history of the Laurion mines. In the study of the glasses, a Mesopotamian ore source, for which the ^{208}Pb/^{206}Pb ratio is exceptionally high with respect to the ^{207}Pb/^{206}Pb ratio (Fig. 110), was identified and it was further established that this

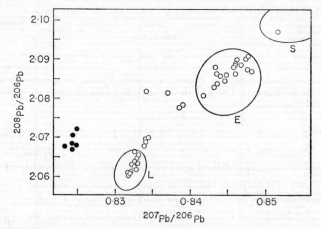

Figure 110. Lead isotope ratios for samples of lead extracted from bronze coins (open circles) and Mesopotamian red and yellow opaque glasses (solid circles). The solid lines define the approximate isotopic limits for the three empirical lead ore groups (i.e. L, E and S) (after Brill, 1970).

source was used over a period of more than 1000 years, extending from the fifteenth century BC up to Hellenistic times.

Further possible applications of isotopic lead analysis include the study of glazes, pigments and cosmetics as well as the analysis of the trace concentrations of lead in silver and gold artefacts. The high sensitivity of the technique (10–20 μg of lead) is particularly important in the latter case since, for silver and gold artefacts containing 0·1 per cent of lead, only 10 mg of metal would be required for analysis.

Coins

The criteria for selecting the most appropriate physical method of chemical analysis for the study of coins (Hall and Metcalf, 1972) are somewhat different to those considered in the case of the majority of other types of artefact. First, the analysis normally involves the determination of the concentrations of only three elements (i.e. gold, silver, copper) in what are nominally classified as either gold, silver or copper coins. Secondly, because of the small size and intrinsic value of the coins, the damage caused by the removal of the small sample, required for optical emission or atomic absorption spectrometry, is not normally permitted. Thirdly, because of surface enrichment phenomena, the chemical composition determined from the analysis of the surface of the coin is not necessarily representative of the original alloy used in the manufacture of the coin.

Surface enrichment (Hall, 1961; Condamin and Picon, 1964 and 1965) is the term used to describe the higher concentration of silver with respect to copper and the higher concentration of gold with respect to both silver and copper which is observed at the surface, as compared to the interior, of many ancient coins (Fig. 111). Surface enrichment can occur as a result of the corrosion (i.e. oxidation) and removal from the surface of the less chemically stable elements (i.e. less noble elements), copper being less stable than silver which, in turn, is less stable than gold. Diffusion effects, arising either from the concentration gradient produced by corrosion or from an internal stress gradient, can also contribute to the surface enrichment phenomena. Although the processes involved are not, as yet, fully understood, it is clear that the analysis of the enriched surface layer will not provide valid data on the composition of the original alloy. It is therefore essential either to remove this enriched layer before analysis or to employ a technique which provides data on the mean chemical composition of the entire coin. However, even with this latter approach, misleading results can still be obtained when extensive oxidation has occurred. For example, Condamin and Picon (1964) have shown that, for some Roman denarii (silver–copper alloy), the mean silver concentration was significantly higher than the silver concentration of the non-oxidized interior of the coin (e.g. 81 per cent silver compared to 71 per cent), which is presumably representative of the original alloy.

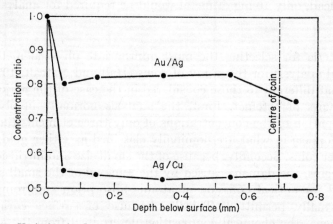

Figure 111. Variation in the concentration ratios (normalized to unity at the surface) for gold to silver (Au/Ag) and silver to copper (Ag/Cu) with the depth below the surface for a Roman coin made from a silver–copper alloy (after Condamin and Picon, 1965).

In view of the requirement for the completely non-destructive analysis of the entire coin and the fact that coins can be readily accommodated in a nuclear reactor, neutron activation analysis has been extensively used in the study of coins. In order to determine the absolute concentrations of the major components from the measured gamma ray intensities, the development of specialized calibration techniques (Wyttenbach and Hermann, 1966; Gordus, 1967) has been necessary since, as a result of the progressive absorption of the activating neutrons as they pass through the coin, the measured intensity also depends on the thickness of the coin. With the more recent development of the milliprobe, X-ray fluorescence spectrometry has been increasingly employed for the analysis of coins. Although this technique only provides data for a thin surface layer, the X-ray milliprobe is capable of analysing a specified area less than 1 mm in diameter and it is therefore possible to remove the enriched surface layer at the point chosen for analysis without causing noticeable damage to the coin. In practice, measurements, interspersed with the progressive removal of the surface layer, are normally continued until no further change in the composition of the alloy can be detected. In the case of coins made from binary alloys (e.g. gold–silver, copper–silver), the concentrations of the two major components can be satisfactorily determined by means of specific gravity measurements, average values for the entire coin again being obtained. However, in considering ternary alloys (e.g. copper–silver–gold), the concentration of at least one component must be independently determined using either neutron activation analysis or the X-ray milliprobe.

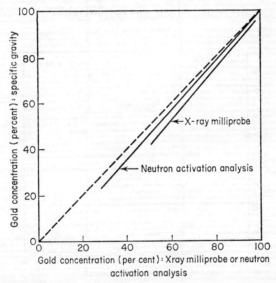

Figure 112. Comparison of the results obtained for the gold concentrations in gold–silver coins using specific gravity measurements, neutron activation analysis and the X-ray milliprobe. The solid lines represent the "best fitting straight lines" for the experimental data and the diagonal dashed line represents the situation for coincidence of the data obtained by the three methods (after Oddy, 1972).

A detailed comparison of the analytical data provided by these three physical methods, as well as that provided by standard wet chemical analysis, has been undertaken for silver–copper coins (Schweizer and Friedman, 1972) and for gold–silver coins (Oddy, 1972). These comparative programmes established that small systematic differences do exist between the data obtained from the various methods (Fig. 112) but that these differences would not normally be sufficient to invalidate the analytical data provided by any one of the available methods.

Applications. In the analysis of coins, the determination of the concentrations of the major components is of primary importance in that it provides direct information on the fineness of the alloy used at different periods and can therefore reveal any debasement of the coinage that occurred. Furthermore, having established the characteristic composition of the alloy used during a particular period, it is then possible to identify those modern forgeries which do not exhibit this composition. In addition, in the study of silver coins, the determination of the concentration of gold, which existed as a minor or trace element in the silver ore and which would not have been removed during smelting in antiquity, can sometimes provide information on the source of the silver ore which was employed.

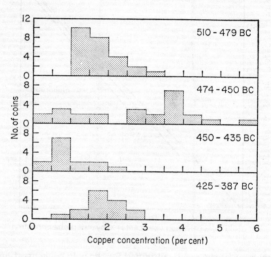

Figure 113. Histograms showing the variation in the copper concentrations in Greek silver coins minted at Syracuse at different periods during the fifth century BC (after Kraay and Emeleus, 1962).

Kraay and Emeleus (1962) employed neutron activation analysis in order to determine the concentrations of copper and gold in Greek silver coins of the sixth and fifth centuries BC. Since the concentration of copper reflects both the efficiency of the smelting processes used in refining the silver and the debasement of the coinage through the deliberate addition of copper, the interpretation of the analytical data for copper was sometimes difficult. However, it was established that a high standard of purity, with the silver containing less than 1 or 2 per cent of copper, could normally be achieved and therefore clear differences in the copper concentration between one issue and another were normally interpreted in terms of the deliberate addition of copper. For example, systematic fluctuations in the copper concentration were observed for coins minted at Syracuse during the fifth century BC (Fig. 113) and these were thought to reflect changes in the local political and economic situation. In particular, the high copper concentration in coins minted during the period 474–450 BC could be associated with the weakening position of the Syracusan tyrants prior to their expulsion in 460 BC, while the subsequent tendency towards a purer silver may have been due to the influence of the democratic government which succeeded them. In contrast to these fluctuations in the copper concentration which may have passed unnoticed by the general public, a somewhat different type of debasement was shown to have occurred in Macedonia during the fifth century BC, where two distinct forms of the same denomination (i.e. the tetrobol) were minted. The first, on which the horse on the obverse bears a rider, contained less than 0·2 per cent of copper while the second, on which the horse is without a rider, contained between 5 and 20 per cent of copper. In this case there was obviously no attempt at subterfuge and instead it seems probable that the high copper content coins were produced as a token coinage for internal trade, thus freeing the pure silver coins for the more profitable foreign trade.

From the consideration of the gold concentrations in the coins, Kraay and Emeleus also obtained considerable information on the sources of the ore from which the various Greek cities extracted their silver. For example, comparison of the gold concentrations for Athenian coins minted during the sixth and fifth centuries BC (Fig. 114a and b) clearly indicated that the ore was obtained from different sources during these two periods. Since the Athenian mines at Laurion are known, from literary evidence, to have been exploited during the fifth century BC, it seems probable that the low gold concentration in the fifth century coins is characteristic of ore from Laurion whereas, prior to the fifth century, Athens was obtaining its silver ore from some other source. Similarly the gold concentrations in coins minted at Corinth during the fifth century BC (Fig. 114c) suggest that Corinth was obtaining some, but by no means all, her silver from Athenian sources. This result does not however necessarily imply direct trading relations between Corinth and Athens since quantities of Athenian coinage could have been obtained through trade in other parts of the Mediterranean area and subsequently melted down in Corinth.

Hawkes *et al.* (1966), employed the X-ray milliprobe in the study of Dark Age coinage from Western Europe and have, in particular, investigated the change-over from a gold to a silver coinage which occurred during the second half of the seventh century AD, possibly as a result of gold scarcity arising from the eclipse of the Byzantine

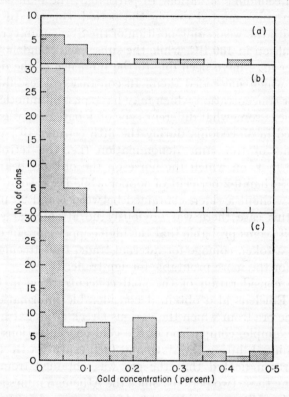

Figure 114. Histograms showing the variation in the gold concentrations in Greek silver coins minted at (a) Athens during the sixth century BC (Wappenmünzen), (b) Athens during the fifth century BC (Owls) and (c) Corinth during the fifth century BC (Ravel periods II and III) (after Kraay and Emeleus, 1962).

contact with Western Europe. The concentrations of gold and silver in the coins are presented in Fig. 115; the groups, which span the period from the second half of the sixth to the beginning of the eighth century AD, being arranged in an essentially chronological order. The existence of comparatively well-defined groups, particularly at gold concentrations of 25–30, 42–47 and 55–60 per cent (i.e. Groups IV, V and VII), suggested that the fall in the gold content of the coinage was not a gradual decline but a stepped reduction. Furthermore, since the percentages for these three groups are centred on gold contents of two-sevenths (28·5 per cent), three-sevenths (43 per cent) and four-sevenths (57 per cent), it is possible that the alloy was determined in siliquae and that the *theoretical* gold content of the coins were 2, 3 and 4 siliquae by weight, as compared to the 7 siliquae weight for this type of coin when minted from pure gold.

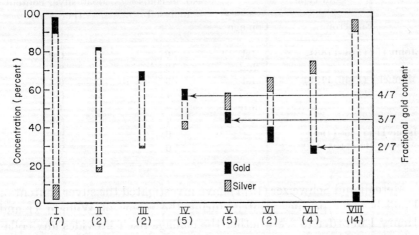

Figure 115. Concentration ranges for gold and silver in Dark Age coins from western Europe. The groups (I–VIII), which span the period from the second half of the sixth to the beginning of the eighth century AD, are arranged in an essentially chronological order, the number of coins in each group being given in the brackets (after Hawkes *et al.*, 1966).

Hendy and Charles (1970), using a standard wet method of chemical analysis, have investigated the variation in the concentration of silver in the copper–silver alloy employed in production of Byzantine trachy during the twelfth century AD. Their results (Table 29) indicated that the silver content of the coins decreased as the century progressed and that this decrease was the most probable explanation for the devaluation (by a factor of about 4) of the trachy, with respect to the precious-metal coinage, which was known to have occurred during this period. Furthermore, the data for the silver content showed that the bullion values (i.e. value based on the weight of silver) of the early coins (e.g. John II and Manuel) was lower than their original face value by a factor of about 2·5 but that, for those early coins remaining in circulation at the end of the century, the situation would have been reversed.

Therefore the drastic clipping of the early coins which, from the evidence in coin hoards, was known to have occurred during the reign of Alexius III, was probably aimed at reducing their bullion value and thus removing this obviously anomalous situation.

Table 29. Silver concentrations in twelfth-century Byzantine trachy (after Hendy and Charles, 1970)

Coin type		No. of coins analysed	Mean silver content (per cent)
Emperor	Coinage		
John II (1118–1143)	1st	6	6·0
	2nd	16	8·7
Manuel I (1143–1180)	1st	9	6·7
	2nd	7	8·2
	3rd	4	4·9
	4th	7	5·6
Isaac II (1185–1195)	—	6	2·8
Alexius III (1195–1203)	—	6	2·4

Metcalf and Schweizer (1971) have investigated the silver content of English silver pennies minted during the reigns of William II and Henry I in order to see whether the coinage itself provides any collaborative evidence for the very clear references, in written sources, to debasement and forgery of the coinage during this period. Particular consideration was given to the incident in 1124 AD when, on the instructions of Henry I, the moneyers were summoned from all over England to come to Winchester and were deprived of their right hands and their testicles; this brutal mutilation being justified on the grounds that they had fraudulently debased the coinage and had thus caused a collapse in confidence. The silver concentrations in a selection of coins, minted in the period (1087–1125) prior to the mutilation of the moneyers, was determined using the X-ray milliprobe and this data was compared with the silver content for coins minted in the preceding period (1050–1087). The results (Fig. 116) indicated that the range and distribution of silver contents was essentially the same in both periods, the average silver content being about 93 per cent. Although the number of coins available for analysis was insufficient to prove conclusively that fraudulent debasement of the coinage had not occurred prior to the mutilation of the moneyers, the data does suggest that the loss of confidence in the coinage was more probably due to a general economic and monetary recession, possibly precipitated by the King's overseas expenditure.

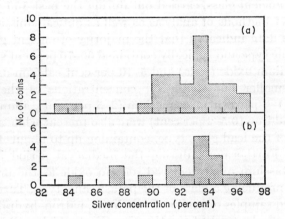

Figure 116. Histograms showing the variation in the silver concentrations in English silver pennies minted during the periods (a) 1050–1087 AD and (b) 1087–1125 AD (after Metcalf and Schweizer, 1971).

Glass, Glaze and Faience

Glass, glaze and faience are each produced by fusing finely ground quartz sand (i.e. silica, SiO_2) with various modifying oxides (e.g. oxides of sodium, potassium, calcium and lead) which reduce the melting point of the silica from 1710°C to less than 1000°C. Glass and glaze have an essentially similar range of compositions, the principal distinction being that glass is used by itself to form artefacts whereas glaze is supported by a pottery body. Faience is however somewhat different since it is a composite material made by coating a core of powdered quartz with a vitrous glaze.

In the study of glass, glaze and faience, chemical analysis is again of primary importance and has been used to establish the different regional and chronological production traditions and to provide information on the raw materials employed. Supplementary data on the raw materials used in the manufacture of glass has been obtained from oxygen isotopic analysis while chemical analysis and X-ray diffraction (powder method) have been employed in the investigation of the colorants used in glass and glaze.

Glass

Turner (1956a) has assembled and critically examined the chemical analyses of ancient glass, carried out during the past 150 years using standard wet methods of analysis as well as optical emission spectrometry. This data indicated that the majority of ancient glass was of the soda–lime type and typically contained 60–70 per cent silica, 10–20 per cent sodium oxide (soda) and 5–10 per cent calcium oxide (lime). However, smaller but significant concentrations of the oxides of potassium (1–3 per cent), magnesium (2–5 per cent), aluminium (1–5 per cent) and iron (0·5–2 per cent) were also present while a few specimens were of the lead glass type, containing up to about 40 per cent lead oxide. Furthermore, during the mediaeval period in Western Europe, potassium oxide replaced sodium oxide as the predominant alkali, thus producing a glass of the potash–lime type. Turner (1956b) also analysed samples of sand and alkali (i.e. natron–hydrated sodium carbonate and plant ash) from the Near East which could have been used for glass-making and established that, in addition to silica and soda, these materials would have provided the lime, potash, magnesia, alumina and iron oxide found in ancient soda–lime glass. This result was consistent with the recorded recipes for glass-making which prescribed two major constituents, sand and alkali, and normally make no reference to the deliberate addition of lime.

Sayre and Smith (1961), using optical emission spectrometry, flame photometry and colorimetry, have analysed several hundred specimens of ancient glass which represented a cross-section of the glass produced in the Middle East, Africa and Europe from the inception of hollow glass manufacture during the second millennium BC to about the tenth century AD. The principal emphasis was placed on the common types of clear glass and on the basis of the concentrations of five elements (magnesium, potassium, manganese, antimony, lead), it was possible to identify five main categories of ancient glass (Fig. 117). With the exception of the Islamic lead-glass (Group V), the groups represented minor variations in the basic soda–lime type of glass, the range of concentrations of silica, sodium oxide and calcium oxide being similar in each case. The reasons for the variations in the magnesium and potassium concentrations are not yet understood, although it is possible that they reflect changes in the types of raw materials utilized. In contrast, since antimony and manganese act as decolorants, suppressing the coloration associated with the iron oxide present in the glass, it seems probable that these elements were deliberately added to produce a clear glass. Although significant concentrations (0·3 per cent) of antimony are present in some glass produced in the Mediterranean area and the Near East during the period from the fifteenth to the seventh century BC (Group I), the consistent use of

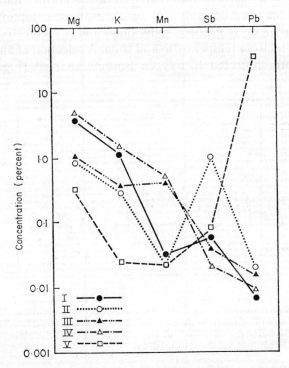

Figure 117. Average concentrations of various metal oxides in the five main categories of Western ancient glass. Group I (15 specimens): Mediterranean area and Near East, *circa* fifteenth to seventh century BC. Group II (34 specimens): Mediterranean area and Near East, *circa* sixth century BC to fourth century AD. Group III (73 specimens): Roman, Byzantine and Dark Age glass, *circa* fourth century BC to ninth century AD. Group IV (66 specimens): early Islamic glass, *circa* eighth to tenth century AD. Group V (6 specimens): Islamic lead-glass, circa eighth to tenth century AD (after Sayre and Smith, 1961).

antimony as a decolorant did not occur until about the sixth century BC (Group II). In some areas (e.g. Mesopotamia), antimony continued to be used during the ascendancy of Rome. However, further west (e.g. Syrian coastal cities, Egypt and Italy), manganese replaced antimony as the principal decolorant during the Roman period (Group

III). Furthermore manganese remained in use as a decolorant in European glass produced during the Dark Ages, in Byzantine glass and in Islamic soda–lime glass (Group IV).

Brill (1970a) has investigated the possibility of classifying ancient glass on the basis of its oxygen isotopic ratio, $^{18}O/^{16}O$ (i.e. δ-value). Measurements on glass manufactured in the laboratory indicated that the δ-value for glass depends only on the isotopic composition of the original ingredients (e.g. silica, soda, lime) and is unaffected by variations in the melting temperature and time. A selection of ancient glass was therefore subjected to oxygen isotopic analysis (Fig. 118) and

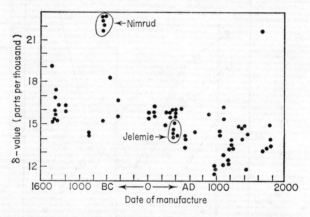

Figure 118. Oxygen isotope ratios ($^{18}O/^{16}O$) for a selection of ancient glass, the data points associated with glass from Jelemie and Nimrud being encircled. The δ-value is the deviation, in parts per thousand, of the $^{18}O/^{16}O$ ratio for the glass from that for standard mean ocean water (after Brill, 1970a).

although no clear regional or chronological classifications were achieved, the δ-values could sometimes be used to distinguish between glasses manufactured from different raw materials even when their chemical compositions were identical. In addition, the isotopic data supported the hypothesis that the glass from the fourth century AD factory of Jelemie in western Galilee was manufactured from ingredients closely resembling the nearby Belus River beach sand, with its attendant shell hash (i.e. lime) and the natron (i.e. soda) from Wadi Natroun in Egypt. In this case, the δ-values for the glass itself (Fig. 118) were in close agreement with the values calculated, using a simple additive relationship, from the isotopic data for these assumed ingredients (silica, δ = 10·93: lime, δ = 29·02: soda, δ = 39·77). Finally, the extremely high δ-values for the eighth to seventh century BC glass from Nimrud indicated that some rather exceptional raw materials were being employed and that chert, flint or quartzite pebbles, rather than quartz sand, may have provided the source of silica (see Fig. 99).

The analytical data for ancient glass, assembled by Turner (1956a), also provides a general picture of the principal metal ions employed as colorants. For example, depending on its concentration, iron produces green to opaque black glass; cobalt produces a deep blue glass and nickel produces a drab green glass. Depending on the atmospheric conditions and the composition of the glass, a blue, green or red colour is obtained from copper, a purple colour results from the addition of small amounts of manganese while the presence of manganese can also modify and suppress (i.e. decolorant) the colours produced by other metal ions.

Brill (1970b) has examined the amber, red and yellow stains applied to the surface of Islamic lustre glass manufactured during the period from the ninth to the eleventh century AD. X-ray diffraction studies indicated that the amber stain was caused by colloidal particles of metallic silver, that the red stain was due to metallic copper and that the yellow stain contained only cuprous oxide (Cu_2O). It was therefore suggested that the amber stain was produced by painting a silver salt on the surface of the glass and then firing under reducing conditions and that the red stain was similarly produced using a copper salt. However the production of the yellow stain would have been somewhat more difficult since the reduction must be stopped at the intermediate state of cuprous oxide and not be allowed to continue to the formation of metallic copper. Furthermore, the growth of the cuprous oxide grains must be arrested at a sufficiently small particle size so that they exhibit a yellow colour rather than the bright red colour characteristic of cuprous oxide in bulk phase or larger-grained dispersions. The production of the red and yellow stains on the Islamic lustre glass was also contrasted with the colorants employed in red and yellow opaque glasses, coloured throughout and manufactured from an early stage in the history of glass-making. In the opaque glasses, it has been established using X-ray diffraction and chemical analysis that the red colour was produced by precipitating out, frequently in the presence of lead oxide, crystalline dispersions of cuprous oxide while the yellow colour was produced by a suspension of lead antimonate ($Pb_2Sb_2O_7$) or a lead–tin oxide ($PbSnO_3$).

Newton (1971) has used the X-ray fluorescence milliprobe to determine the chemical composition of the strongly coloured decoration applied to the surface of some Iron Age glass beads. The aim of this study, which is at present only in its preliminary stages, is to investigate the hypothesis that the more sophisticated coloured glass was manufactured in bulk at a few specialist centres and was subsequently used, at a large number of sites, to decorate glass beads which had been made locally by the less-skilled resident glass-workers. If this hypothesis is correct, the compositions of the coloured decoration on beads from widely scattered sites could be identical even though the compositions of the locally-made beads themselves are very different. For these analyses, the X-ray milliprobe is particularly appropriate since, as a result of the small penetration (about 50 μm) of the X-rays, the surface decoration can be analysed without interference from the body glass. Furthermore, because of the small area analysed, specific areas of colour can be selected for analysis.

Glaze

In the study of glazes, physical methods of chemical analysis have been used to distinguish between lead glazes and alkali–silicate glazes (e.g. soda–lime, potash–lime), to identify the metallic oxides employed as colorants and to obtain information on the geographical sources of the associated metal ores. The identification of the colorant on the basis of the actual colour of the glazes is frequently not possible since the colour produced by a specific metallic oxide depends on the atmospheric conditions during firing and the type of glaze employed. For example, depending on its concentration in the glaze, iron oxide produces a yellow, red or brown colour when fired under oxidizing conditions whereas under reducing conditions, it produces a green glaze. Similarly, under oxidizing conditions, copper oxide gives a green colour in a lead glaze and a blue colour in an alkali–silicate glaze while under reducing conditions it produces a red glaze.

X-ray fluorescence spectrometry is ideally suited to the analysis of glazes since, as a result of the small penetration of the X-rays, the glaze can be analysed separately and without interference from the clay body of the pottery. Optical emission spectrometry, although employed in some instances, is less satisfactory since the glaze must be carefully scraped from the surface of the pottery and some contamination by the clay body is almost inevitable.

Frierman (1970) used X-ray fluorescence spectrometry to analyse the glaze on a selection of Near Eastern pottery produced during the period from the ninth to the fourteenth century AD and has shown that both lead and alkali–silicate glazes had been employed. In addition, considerable information on the glaze colorants (e.g. copper, iron, cobalt, manganese) was obtained. Musty and Thomas (1962), using optical emission spectrometry, have analysed, semi-quantitatively, both the glaze and clay body of a range of mediaeval pottery (mainly thirteenth century AD) from England and the Continent. In this case, the analytical data indicated that lead glazes had normally been used and that the tin concentration in the glaze could sometimes provide a basis for distinguishing between the pottery from the different kiln sites. It was further suggested that the use of powdered solder or pewter to produce the lead glaze might account for the presence of tin.

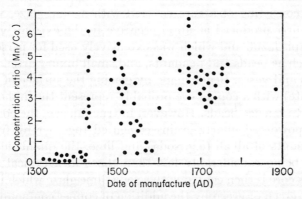

Figure 119. Concentration ratios for manganese to cobalt (arbitrary units) in the blue cobalt pigment used in the decoration of Chinese blue-and-white porcelain manufactured during the period 1300 to 1900 AD (after Young, 1956).

Young (1956) employed X-ray fluorescence spectrometry in order to determine the ratio of the manganese to cobalt concentrations in the blue cobalt pigment used in the decoration of Chinese blue-and-white porcelain which had been manufactured over a period of several centuries from about 1300 AD onwards. Since it was known that the cobalt ores occurring in China contain a high proportion of manganese while those occurring in Persia and the Near East are essentially manganese-free (Garner, 1956), it was possible, on the basis of the analytical data (i.e. Mn/Co ratio), to distinguish between the blue pigment derived from native Chinese cobalt ore and that derived from cobalt ores imported from Persia. Although variations in the quality of the blue colour had previously been ascribed to the use of imported ore for the more refined pieces and the use of native ore for the less refined ones, no correlation between the quality of the colour and the source of the ore, as ascertained from the analytical data, was found. However, it was discovered that the use of imported and native cobalt ores varied on a definite chronological basis. From the analytical data presented in Fig. 119, it can be seen that only imported ores (low Mn/Co ratio) were used prior to 1425 AD, that during the period from 1425 to 1600 AD both imported and native (high Mn/Co ratio) ores were employed and that after about 1600 AD only native ore was used.

Faience

In the present context, the term, faience, is applied to the composite material, consisting of a core covered with a blue glaze, which was probably first produced as an alternative to the extremely rare blue mineral lapis lazuli and which was extensively used for personal ornaments, such as beads and pendants, and small luxury articles, such as statuettes and vases. Beads made by glazing the surface of soapstone (i.e. steatite) with a copper ore probably represent the immediate predecessors to faience beads. However, in true faience, the core consists of finely powdered quartz grains cemented together by fusion with small amounts of alkali (e.g. soda) and lime, the quantities of alkali and lime being considerably less than those in a typical soda–lime glass. This core is then coated with a soda–lime glaze which is coloured blue, blue-green or green by the addition of copper compounds.

Stone and Thomas (1956) have summarized the evidence for the early use and subsequent distribution of faience in the Near East and Europe. From this, it appears that faience was first produced in northern Mesopotamia during the fifth millennium BC and that the foundation of the subsequently supreme Egyptian faience industry was laid in the fourth millennium BC during the pre-dynastic Gerzean period. Although the use of faience became increasingly common during the third millennium BC, the major expansion of the faience industry occurred during the second millennium BC. The Egyptian faience industry probably reached its peak during the XVIIIth Dynasty (1580–1314 BC) while the manufacture of faience spread to Crete during the early part of the second millennium and, at a slightly later date, to the Greek mainland. The distribution of faience beads was not, however, restricted to regions having known manufacturing sites but extended, during the second millennium BC, throughout prehistoric Europe.

In the study of faience beads, physical methods of chemical analysis have been employed in an attempt to characterize the products of the known manufacturing regions and to establish whether the beads found in Europe were made locally or were imported from the Mediterranean area and Egypt. In the case of Britain, the distinction between local manufacture and imports is of particular interest since the occurrence of faience beads represents one aspect of the reasoning which links the Wessex culture with the Mycenaean world and which provides the basis for dating the Wessex culture to the period 1600–1400 BC (p. 189).

Stone and Thomas (1956), using optical emission spectrometry, analysed, on a semi-quantitative basis, a selection of faience beads from the Mediterranean world (e.g. Egypt, Crete and Malta), Britain (i.e. Wessex and Scotland) and central Europe. They concluded that the analytical data did not provide an unequivocal indication of the origin of the beads but, on the archaeological evidence, subscribed to the view that the beads found in Britain had been imported from the Mediterranean world, either via the Danube and the Rhine or along the Mediterranean and across France. However, Newton and Renfrew (1970) recently studied this analytical data using new statistical techniques and showed that it is possible to distinguish between the beads from Wessex and Scotland on the basis of the concentrations of tin, aluminium and magnesium (Fig. 120). Furthermore, only five of the Egyptian beads exhibit the concentration patterns associated with the Wessex and Scottish beads. On the basis of this re-interpretation of the analytical data, together with the fact that many British beads differ considerably in shape from the Egyptian beads, Newton and Renfrew suggested that the British beads were made locally, with at least two production centres (Wessex and Scotland) being in operation.

Aspinall et al. (1972), using neutron activation analysis, re-analysed the majority of the faience beads originally studied by Stone and Thomas and confirmed that the tin content of the British beads was significantly greater than that found in groups of beads from elsewhere. In addition, the analytical data indicated that significant composition differences existed between the various groups of beads when compared in terms of the concentrations of scandium, caesium, silver, cobalt, antimony and strontium. Since the amounts of glaze remaining on the beads varied considerably and since the neutron activation analysis provided data representing the combined concentration pattern for the core and the glaze, the composition of the glaze itself was considered in terms of the ratio of the concentrations of tin and copper

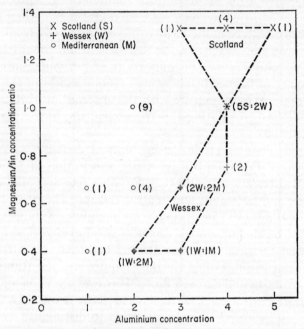

Figure 120. Magnesium/tin concentration ratio *versus* aluminium concentration for a selection of faience beads, the number of beads associated with each point being given in the brackets. The concentration scale, 0, 1, 2, 3, 4 and 5, represents concentrations of less than 0·001, 0·001–0·01, 0·01–0·1, 0·1–1, 1–10 and 10–100 per cent respectively (after Newton and Renfrew, 1970).

(Fig. 121) rather than in terms of the absolute concentrations of these elements. The high tin–copper ratios observed in the case of the British beads were surprising since copper ores normally contain only trace concentrations of tin. Furthermore, the tin–copper ratios in

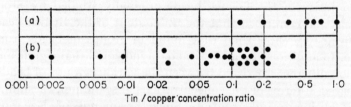

Figure 121. Tin/copper concentration ratios for faience beads from (a) Scotland and Wessex and (b) Egypt, XVIIIth and XIXth Dynasties (after Aspinall *et al.*, 1972).

bronzes, whose use as the colouring material in the glaze has been suggested, are normally less than 1 to 6 (p. 330).

Although the published analytical data tends to support the hypothesis that the British faience beads were manufactured locally, rather than being imported from the Mediterranean world, the case for the local production of faience in Britain certainly cannot be regarded as proved. In view of the extremely small number of beads that have been analysed, it is quite possible that large numbers of Egyptian beads with compositions similar to the British beads do in fact exist. In addition, the relatively sudden appearance and disappearance of faience in Britain, compared with the long period of growth and development in Egypt, favours the alternative hypothesis that the beads were imported into Britain. Further analyses are therefore essential and in addition, the composition of the glaze, which can be most easily determined by means of X-ray fluorescence spectrometry, should be compared with that of the alloy used in the manufacture of bronze artefacts in the various regions.

Pigments and Paintings

The pigments used in antiquity (Forbes, 1965) were normally either naturally occurring minerals or artificially produced inorganic compounds. For example, ochres, umbers and siennas were obtained from earthy deposits containing ferric oxide as a colorant. In its hydrated form (i.e. limonite), iron oxide is yellow but it is easily dehydrated to form the red oxide (i.e. haematite). In addition to these more or less pure iron oxides which provided the yellow and red ochres, browner colours (umbers and siennas) were obtained using iron oxides containing small amounts of black manganese dioxide. Green pigments were obtained from either the copper carbonate, malachite, or the iron-bearing clay mineral, glauconite, while the copper carbonate, azurite, provided a blue pigment. In addition, an artificial blue pigment (Egyptian blue) was prepared by fusing quartz and lime with a copper ore as a colorant, the resulting blue glass or frit being subsequently ground to a fine powder.

In order to ensure that the colour adhered to the surface being painted, the pigments were normally made into a paste with water or an organic medium, the two most common techniques, employed in antiquity for painting walls, being fresco and tempera. In the fresco technique, the pigments were mixed with lime and water and were applied to the surface of damp lime plaster. As a result of the chemical changes taking place in the plaster (i.e. carbonation of the calcium hydroxide to form calcium carbonate), the pigments became firmly attached to the plaster and a hard, durable painting resulted. In the tempera technique, the pigment was applied to the surface of the wall as a suspension in an organic medium, such as vegetable gum or proteinaceous material (e.g. egg-yolk). In addition to these two techniques, wax was used as the medium for the pigments in some parts of the world while, more recently, drying oils (e.g. linseed) which set hard on exposure to the atmosphere have been employed as the medium.

The physical examination of pigments and paintings therefore involves the identification of both the minerals used as pigments and the binding medium in which the pigments were applied to the surface being painted. Information is thus obtained on the range of pigments and painting techniques employed in different parts of the world at different periods in time.

Physical methods of chemical analysis can be used to determine the chemical composition (i.e. concentrations of the constituent elements) of the pigments and on the basis of this data, it is frequently possible to identify the actual mineral or chemical compound employed as the pigment (Cesareo *et al.*, 1972). Because of the small penetration of X-rays, X-ray fluorescence spectrometry is particularly appropriate for the analysis of paint pigments, the X-ray milliprobe being employed when it is necessary to analyse specified small areas of colour. In addition, the electron probe microanalyser can be used to study the distribution in depth of the pigment or to separately analyse superimposed layers of pigments. X-ray diffraction (powder method) or infra-red absorption spectrometry can also be used to identify the minerals and chemical compounds employed as pigments; the information on the crystalline structure, which is provided by these techniques, being essential in the situation where several pigments exhibit similar chemical compositions. For example, infra-red absorption spectrometry is particularly appropriate for the classification of the various types of ochres since it provides information on the state of hydration on which the colour of the iron oxide depends.

Giovanoli (1969) employed several physical techniques in the investigation of provincial Roman wall painting. X-ray fluorescence spectrometry established that copper was the significant element in the blue pigment and iron in the red, yellow, brown and green pigments; the calcium, which was present in all the pigments, being associated with the lime plaster and binding medium. X-ray diffraction showed that Egyptian blue (calcium copper silicate) had been used as the blue pigment and haematite as the red pigment, while the green pigment was identified as glauconite on the basis of the similar concentration profiles obtained for iron and potassium (Fig. 122) when the distribution of the pigments in depth was studied using the electron probe microanalyser. The pigment distribution revealed by the

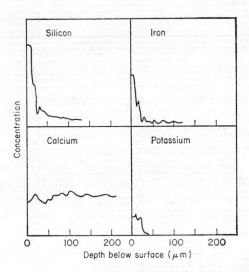

Figure 122. Concentration profiles (arbitrary units) for the four major elements in the green pigment (glauconite) employed in a provincial Roman wall painting (after Giovanoli, 1969).

electron probe microanalyser also showed that, although the majority of the pigments were applied as thin homogeneous layers (about 20 μm in thickness), the blue colour consisted of a thick (about 60 μm) and fairly heterogeneous pigment layer. It was therefore suggested that, whereas the fresco technique had been employed for the majority of the painting, the blue pigment had been mixed with some additional, but unidentified, binding medium.

Fleming *et al.* (1971) have investigated wall paintings, made on terracotta and purporting to be Etruscan, which had appeared on the Swiss and American art markets in the past ten years. In this case, the analysis of the pigments established that materials, which had only become available during comparatively recent times, had been used in many instances. For example, X-ray diffraction indicated that the yellow-brown pigment was Naples yellow (lead antimonate) and that the black pigment was magnetite (magnetic iron oxide) while, on the basis of the infra-red absorption spectrum, the red pigment was identified as English red, an iron oxide produced by heating iron sulphate with limestone. This data on the pigments therefore provided strong confirmation for the thermoluminescent dates (p. 128) which also indicated that these terracottas were modern imitations of the Etruscan materials.

In spite of the problems associated with the progressive deterioration and chemical changes that occur in the case of organic materials, infra-red absorption spectrometry, chromatography and microchemical tests can sometimes be used to identify the organic binding media employed in paintings. For example, de Silva (1963) devised a series of microchemical and paper chromatography tests for distinguishing between vegetable gums, proteinaceous material and drying oils while Kühn (1960) employed infra-red absorption spectrometry in the study of the medium used in some Egyptian Fayum mummy portraits which had been painted on wood. In the latter case, it was possible to distinguish between beeswax and Punic wax (beeswax containing salts of fatty acids) as well as differentiating between paintings in which the wax and tempera (i.e. vegetable gum) techniques had been employed.

Amber and Mollusc Shells

Apart from the minor organic components, such as adhesives, varnishes and binding media, amber and mollusc shells are the principal types of biological material employed in the fabrication of artefacts which are amenable to investigation by means of the physical methods of *analysis*, as opposed to microscopic examination.

Amber

Amber is a fossil tree resin, typically of coniferous origin, which was widely used in antiquity to make beads and similar small objects. Extensive deposits of amber (succinite) exist in the Baltic Sea region but amber of similar composition is also found in France, England, Rumania, Hungary and Sicily. Although employed in northern Europe during the Neolithic period, the major spread in the use of amber occurred during the Bronze Age. It has been suggested that Baltic amber was traded south to the Mycenaean world during this period, supposedly precise trade routes between the Baltic and the eastern Mediterranean having been defined. Since these amber trade routes are fundamental to the assumption that the Mycenaean world exerted a strong influence on northern Europe during the Bronze Age, it is obviously essential to establish unequivocally that Baltic amber, rather than the more local amber sources, was used to produce the artefacts found in the eastern Mediterranean.

Although early chemical analyses (Helm, 1877) suggested that Baltic amber could be distinguished from other types of amber on the basis of the succinic acid content, subsequent investigations of the formation of amber (Rottländer, 1970) have shown that succinic acid is a normal oxidation product of amber and that its concentration does not, therefore, provide a satisfactory parameter for characterizing amber sources. Beck *et al.* (1965) have studied the infra-red absorption spectra associated with amber and have shown that Baltic amber exhibits a highly characteristic absorption pattern in the 8·0 to 9·0 μm spectral range (Fig. 123) which is due to the carbon–oxygen

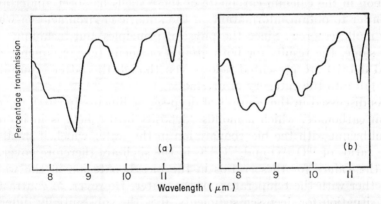

Figure 123. Infra-red absorption spectra for (a) Baltic amber and (b) Sicilian amber (after Beck *et al.*, 1965).

single bond stretching of saturated aliphatic esters. Although it should normally be possible to distinguish between Baltic and non-Baltic European amber on the basis of this absorption pattern, the variations that occur in the absorption spectra for different specimens of Baltic amber, as a result of the deterioration (i.e. oxidation) of the amber, could cause some difficulties. More recently, Mills and Gough (1972) have employed gas chromatography in the study of amber and have shown that, on the basis of its characteristic gas-chromatogram,

Baltic amber (i.e. succinite) can be distinguished with considerable assurance from other types of amber (e.g. Sicilian, Rumanian).

It is therefore apparent that, as a result of their different botanical origins and degrees of fossilization (Langenheim, 1969), the various types of amber possess sufficient differences in their chemical components for them to be characterized and distinguished by means of infra-red absorption spectrometry and gas chromatography. However, until a more complete characterization of the various amber sources has been achieved and the amber artefacts from the Mediterranean region have been positively assigned to these sources, the amber trade routes proposed for the Bronze Age must be regarded as a hypothesis, rather than an established fact.

Mollusc Shells

The mollusc shells found on archaeological sites include those which were used to make ornaments (e.g. beads and bangles) and those which remained purely as food debris. Isotopic analysis of the oxygen and carbon in the calcium carbonate of these shells has been undertaken in order to obtain information on the aquatic environment in which the molluscs grew. Since the physical principles and techniques are the same, the results for both groups of shells (i.e. ornaments and food debris) are presented below even though the latter group does not fall into the category of artefacts.

As discussed in the context of deep-sea sediments (p. 107), the calcium carbonate, which a mollusc deposits in its shell, is in isotopic equilibrium with the bicarbonate ion in the water which it inhabits. The ratios of $^{18}O/^{16}O$ and $^{13}C/^{12}C$ in the shell are therefore governed by the values for these ratios in the bicarbonate ion in the water, together with the temperature of the water. However, in contrast to the situation for deep-sea sediments, it is the substantially different isotopic compositions of the various natural waters which are of primary importance in the study of mollusc shells from archaeological sites, rather than variations in the temperature of the water. The variation in the $^{18}O/^{16}O$ ratio occurs because water molecules containing ^{18}O are heavier than those containing ^{16}O and therefore have a slightly lower chance of evaporating into the atmosphere. Consequently water vapour in the atmosphere, and therefore both rain water and fresh water sources (e.g. rivers, lakes), are slightly depleted in ^{18}O compared to sea water. In terms of the δ-values, the bicarbonate ion in fresh water exhibits negative values (e.g. $\delta^{18}O \approx -10$

part per thousand) while in sea water, $\delta^{18}O$ is zero or slightly positive in the case of high salinity water. The factors governing the variation in $^{13}C/^{12}C$ ratio are more complex. However, it can normally be assumed that the $\delta^{13}C$ value for the bicarbonate ion in sea water is slightly positive while, as a result of the incorporation of isotopically light carbon derived from the decomposition of plant matter, the $\delta^{13}C$ value for the bicarbonate in river water is negative (e.g. $\delta^{13}C \approx -12$ parts per thousand).

Shackleton and Renfrew (1970) undertook the isotopic analysis of *Spondylus* shells, which were used as personal ornaments during the Neolithic period, in order to ascertain whether the shells originated in Mediterranean or the Black Sea. From the isotopic data obtained for shells found on settlement sites in northern Greece, the Balkans and central Europe (Table 30), it was apparent that, in spite of their di-

Table 30. Oxygen isotopic data for *Spondylus* shells from Neolithic sites (after Shackleton and Renfrew, 1970)

Site[a]	$\delta^{18}O$ (parts per thousand)
Tell Goljanio Delschevo	−1·06
Tell Goljanio Delschevo	+0·04
Tell Goljanio Delschevo	−0·71
Sitagroi	−0·27
Sitagroi	−0·97
Sitagroi	−0·55
Sitagroi	−0·17
Gradeshnitsa	−1·21
Vinča	−0·91

[a] Tell Goljanio Delschevo is near the Black Sea coast of Bulgaria. Sitagroi is in northern Greece, lying some 40 km from the Aegean Sea coast. Gradeshnitsa in northeast Bulgaria and Vinča in Yugoslavia are both more than 200 km from the sea.

verse archaeological origins, the shells fell within a single oxygen isotopic grouping. Assuming that the growth of the shells occurred during the summer at temperatures between 19° and 24°C, their oxygen isotopic ratios are consistent with water of isotopic composition, $\delta^{18}O \approx +0·6$ parts per thousand (equation 4.4). Alternatively, if winter growth at temperatures between 12° and 17°C is assumed, then the data for the shells is consistent with water of isotopic composition, $\delta^{18}O \approx -1$ part per thousand). Comparison of this data with the published isotopic analyses for Mediterranean water ($\delta^{18}O \approx +1\cdot2$ parts per thousand) and Black Sea water ($\delta^{18}O \approx -2\cdot5$ parts per thousand) suggested a Mediterranean origin for all the *Spondylus* shells studied. Confirmation of this hypothesis was provided by the isotopic analysis of modern shells from the Black Sea for which $\delta^{18}O$ values in the range $-1\cdot6$ to $-4\cdot5$ parts per thousand were obtained, this wide range reflecting the variations in temperature that occurred during the growth of the shells. Furthermore, the possibility that, during the Neolithic period, the isotopic composition of the Black Sea was closer to that of the Mediterranean could be rejected since, up to approximately 8000 years ago, the Black Sea was largely filled with glacial meltwater and was isolated from the Mediterranean. Glacial meltwater is deficient in ^{18}O, so that, if anything, the $\delta^{18}O$ value for the Black Sea would have been more negative during the Neolithic period.

The oxygen isotopic analyses therefore established, fairly conclusively, that the *Spondylus* shells originated in the Aegean and were subsequently traded as far afield as the Black Sea. An interesting feature of this *Spondylus* trade was the fact that, in contrast to the obsidian trade in the Near East (p. 310), the quantities of shells found did not decrease exponentially with the distance from their Aegean source; finds being at least as common on sites near to the Black Sea as on those in northern Greece. Consequently the straightforward down-the-line trading mechanism postulated for the obsidian trade was regarded as inappropriate and a different model, referred to as "prestige chain exchange", was proposed. In this trading process, it is visualized that an essentially uniform distribution was achieved as a result of prestige goods, such as *Spondylus* shells, being exchanged on a basis of balanced reciprocity rather than being expended or utilized in daily life.

Shackleton (1970) also employed isotopic analysis in the study of cockles shells remaining as food debris on the Neolithic settlement site of Nea Nikomedeia in Greece. Since the site is sufficiently distant from the present coastline to have dissuaded prehistoric man from carrying back shell-fish before eating them, it was hoped that the isotopic data would provide information on the water body near to site in the Neolithic period. The isotopic analysis of the successive growth increments in a selection of shells indicated that the cockles had lived in an extremely variable environment. For example, the values for $\delta^{18}O$

and $\delta^{13}C$ for sample N from a typical shell (Fig. 124a) implied growth in more or less undiluted Mediterranean water while, at the opposite extreme, the deficiency in ^{18}O and ^{13}C in sample B implied growth in a mixture of approximately one part sea water and two parts river water (i.e. fresh water). Furthermore, the variation in δ-values was cyclic, the data for the shell, represented in Fig. 124a, extending through two

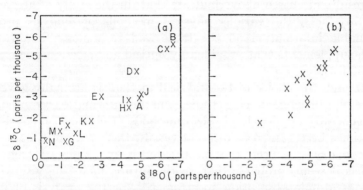

Figure 124. Oxygen and carbon isotopic ratios (i.e. $^{18}O/^{16}O$ and $^{13}C/^{12}C$ respectively) for cockle shells from the Neolithic settlement site of Nea Nikomedeia in Greece. (a) Data for the successive growth increments on a single shell, the samples being lettered from the edge (A) inwards to (N). (b) Data for the outer growth layer from a selection of different shells. The δ-values are the deviations, in parts per thousand, of the ratios for the shell from those for standard mean ocean water (after Shackleton, 1970).

complete years of growth. It was therefore suggested that, during the Neolithic period, the water body near to the site was freely connected with the sea as an estuary. In the dry summer season, the water would have had the salinity of the open sea (sample N) while in winter, the salinity would have been reduced (sample B) by river inflow resulting from heavy rainfall.

In addition to the information obtained on the aquatic environment of the site, the season of the year at which the shell-fish were collected and eaten could be inferred from the isotopic data for the outer growth layer. For example, in the case of the shell represented in Fig. 124a, the data (sample A) suggested collection in the spring after the low salinity of the previous winter. Further, the deficiency in ^{18}O and ^{13}C in the outer growth layers of the majority of the shells, which were analysed (Fig. 124b), indicated that the shell-fish were normally collected and eaten during the winter and spring. Although a greater number of shells must be analysed before a reliable assessment of the situation can be made, the available data does suggest that the main occupation of the settlement occurred during the winter and spring and that it was deserted during the summer when the cattle were taken to higher ground away from the estuary.

Conclusions

The results discussed above indicate that, in the study of archaeological artefacts, the various physical methods of analysis provide invaluable information on the trade and technology in antiquity which supplements that provided by optical and electron microscopy (Chapter 8).

Although the choice of the physical method is normally governed by the type of artefact being studied and the information required, the four generally applicable physical methods of chemical analysis can sometimes be regarded as alternatives. In the past, optical emission spectrometry has been the most extensively employed technique whereas it seems probable that, in the future, increasing use will be made of atomic absorption spectrometry for the analysis of metal artefacts and of X-ray fluorescence spectrometry or neutron activation analysis in the case of non-metallic artefacts. However, optical emission spectrometry will continue to provide a valuable method of analysis while it must be emphasized that these four methods tend to provide essentially complimentary data with respect to both the elements and concentrations which can be studied. Furthermore, the choice of the method of analysis will continue to be determined, in part, by the availability of the necessary equipment.

Through the characterization of the raw materials and the identification of the geographical sources from which they were obtained, the physical methods of examination (i.e. microscopy and analysis) can provide direct and indisputable proof that the transport of goods and materials from one region to another was taking place. Furthermore, this information, in turn, provides a clear indication of the contacts that existed between different cultural groups in antiquity. In describing this transport of goods and materials as "trade", the term is employed in its widest possible sense (i.e. the reciprocal traffic, exchange or movement of goods and materials through peaceful human agency) and does not necessarily imply the existence of full-time professional traders deriving their livelihood or sustenance entirely from these exchanges. Therefore, having established the existence of trade by means of the physical methods of examination, it is then necessary to try to obtain some understanding of the mechanisms involved in the trading system. A quantitative evaluation of the amount of material traded (i.e. the prehistoric "trade statistics") is of considerable assistance in establishing possible models, the contact and supply zones for the obsidian trade (p. 312) and the prestige chain exchange model for the *Spondylus* trade (p. 362) being typical examples. However, since trade is essentially a two-way process, the complete description of the trading system also requires the documentation of the reciprocal trade. This is frequently more difficult to achieve while any notion of the relative values of the commodities being exchanged inevitably remains hypothetical.

Through the identification of the major constituents used in the manufacture of artefacts and the elucidation of the techniques employed in their fabrication, the physical methods of examination provide an indication of the stage of technological development achieved by the cultural group under consideration. This information can again help to establish whether or not contact existed between different cultural groups. In particular, the detailed comparison of the alloys and fabrication techniques, employed by the early copper and bronze metal-workers in different parts of the world, could assist in determining whether the development of metallurgy in the Balkans and Iberia was inspired through "contact" with the technologically more advanced societies in the Near East or whether metallurgy was independently invented in these regions (p. 186).

The documentation of trade and the development of new technologies is also of considerable importance when attempting to *explain* the cultural developments that occurred in antiquity. Obviously the clear indications of intercultural contact, which are provided by this documentation, are of fundamental importance when explaining cultural change in terms of external influences arising from diffusion, migration or invasion. However, since trade and technology are major components in the aggregate of systems which constitute a culture, their documentation is also relevant to the explanation of cultural changes in terms of the internal interactions of the economic subsystems (Binford, 1965). For example, Renfrew (1969) has suggested that the inception of a bronze metallurgy and the development of trade were the principal reasons for the "urbanization" and increased cultural sophistication which occurred in the Aegean region (e.g. Troy, Lerna, Phylakopi) during the later part of the third millennium BC. He further suggested that the correlation between metallurgical development and the growth of trade was due to the fact that the metallurgy created both a commodity which was worth trading and increased wealth which produced new needs requiring trade for their fulfilment. These views are, however, contrary to much current opinion which explains the "urbanization" in terms of either the effect of influences from outside the Aegean region or an increase in agricultural efficiency and population brought about by the introduction of metal tools. In this situation, where opposing explanations for cultural change have been proposed, the detailed documentation of trade and the development of metallurgy would be of considerable interest.

In the future, improvements in the existing physical methods of analysis and the development of new methods can be expected while more sophisticated statistical techniques will undoubtedly be employed for handling the analytical data obtained. However, these developments will probably be of less significance than the additional information on trade and technology which will be obtained from the examination of an ever-increasing range of archaeological artefacts using currently available techniques.

References

Stone Artefacts

Ambrose, W. R. and Green, R. C. (1972). First millennium BC transport of obsidian from New Britain to the Solomon Islands. *Nature* **237**, 31.

Aspinall, A. and Feather, S. W. (1972). Neutron activation analysis of prehistoric flint mine products. *Archaeometry* **14**, 41–53.

Durrani, S. A., Khan, H. A., Taj, M. and Renfrew, C. (1971). Obsidian source identification by fission track analysis. *Nature* **233**, 242–245.

Gordus, A. A., Fink, W. C., Hill, M. E., Purdy, J. C. and Wilcox, T. R. (1967). Identification of the geological origins of archaeological artefacts: an automated method of Na and Mn activation analysis. *Archaeometry* **10**, 87–96.

Renfrew, C., Cann, J. R. and Dixon, J. E. (1965). Obsidian in the Aegean. *Ann. Br. Schl Archaeol. Athens* **60**, 225–247.

Renfrew, C., Dixon, J. E. and Cann, J. R. (1966). Obsidian and early cultural contact in the Near East. *Proc. prehist. Soc.* **32**, 30–72.

Renfrew, C., Dixon, J. E. and Cann, J. R. (1968). Further analysis of Near Eastern obsidians. *Proc. prehist. Soc.* **34**, 319–331.

Sieveking, G. de G., Craddock, P. T., Hughes, M. J., Bush, P. and Ferguson, J. (1970). Characterization of prehistoric flint mine products. *Nature* **228**, 251–254.

Stevenson, D. P., Stross, F. H. and Heizer, R. F. (1971). An evaluation of X-ray fluorescence analysis as a method for correlating obsidian artifacts with source location. *Archaeometry* **13**, 17–25.

Pottery

Aspinall, A., Slater, D. N. and Mayes, P. (1968). Neutron activation analysis of Medieval ceramics. *Nature* 217, 388.

Bimson, M. (1969). The examination of ceramics by X-ray powder diffraction. *Stud. Conserv.* 14, 83–89.

Catling, H. W. and Millett, A. (1965a). A study in the compositional patterns of Mycenaean pictorial pottery from Cyprus. *Ann. Br. Schl Archaeol. Athens* 60, 212–224.

Catling, H. W. and Millett, A. (1965b). A study of the inscribed stirrup-jars from Thebes. *Archaeometry* 8, 3–85.

Catling, H. W. and Millett, A. (1969). Theban stirrup-jars: questions and answers. *Archaeometry* 11, 3–20.

Catling, H. W., Richards, E. E. and Blin-Stoyle, A. E. (1963). Correlations between composition and provenance of Mycenaean and Minoan pottery. *Ann. Br. Schl Archaeol. Athens* 58, 94–115.

Cousins, D. R. and Dharmawardena, K. G. (1969). Use of Mössbauer spectroscopy in the study of ancient pottery. *Nature* 223, 732–733.

Freeth, S. J. (1967). A chemical study of some Bronze Age sherds. *Archaeometry* 10, 104–119.

Gangas, N. H. J., Kostikas, A., Simopoulos, A. and Vocotopoulou, J. (1971). Mössbauer spectroscopy of ancient Greek pottery. *Nature* 229, 485–486.

Harbottle, G. (1970). Neutron activation analysis of potsherds from Knossos and Mycenae. *Archaeometry* 12, 23–34.

Hartley, K. F. and Richards, E. E. (1965). Spectrographic analysis of some Romano–British mortaria. *Bull. Inst. Archaeol. Lond.* 5, 25–43.

Mayes, P. (1961). The firing of a pottery kiln of Romano-British type at Boston, Lincs. *Archaeometry* 4, 4–30.

Mayes, P. (1962). The firing of a second pottery kiln of Romano-British type at Boston, Lincs. *Archaeometry* 5, 80–92.

Palmer, L. R. (1961). "Mycenaeans and Minoans." Faber and Faber, London.

Peacock, D. P. S. (1970). The scientific analysis of ancient ceramics: a review. *Wld Archaeol.* 1, 375–389.

Perinet, G. (1960). Contribution de la diffraction des rayons X à l'évaluation de la température de cuisson d'une céramique. *Trans. 7th Intern. Ceram. Congress*, 371–376.

Picon, M., Vichy, M. and Meille, E. (1971). Composition of the Lezoux, Lyon and Arezzo Samian ware. *Archaeometry* 13, 191–208.

Poole, A. B. and Finch, L. R. (1972). The utilization of trace chemical composition to correlate British post-medieval pottery with European kiln site materials. *Archaeometry* 14, 79–91.

Raison, J. (1968). "Les Vases à Inscriptions Peintes de l'Age Mycénien et leur Contexte Archéologique." Incunabula Graeca XIX, Centro di Studi Micenei, Universita di Roma.

Richards, E. E. and Hartley, K. F. (1960). Spectrographic analysis of Romano–British pottery. *Nature* 185, 194–196.

Tite, M. S. (1969). Determination of the firing temperature of ancient ceramics by measurement of thermal expansion: a reassessement. *Archaeometry* 11, 131–143.

Tobler, A. J. (1939). "Excavations at Tepe Gawra." Vol. II, Appendix H, pp. 159–162. University Museum, Philadelphia.

Young, W. J. and Whitmore, F. E. (1957). Analysis of Oriental ceramic wares by non-destructive X-ray methods. *Far Eastern Ceram. Bull.* 9, 1–27.

Metal Artefacts

Brill, R. H. (1970). Lead and oxygen isotopes in ancient objects. *Phil. Trans. R. Soc. Lond.* A269, 143–164.

Brill, R. H. and Wampler, J. M. (1967). Isotope studies of ancient lead. *Am. J. Archaeol.* 71, 63–77.

Britton, D. (1961). A study of the composition of Wessex culture bronzes. *Archaeometry* 4, 39–52.

Brown, M. A. and Blin-Stoyle, A. E. (1959). A sample analysis of British Middle and Late Bronze Age material, using optical spectrometry. *Proc. prehist. Soc.* 25, 188–208.

Caley, E. R. (1964). "The Analysis of Ancient Metals." Pergamon Press, New York.

Coghlan, H. H. and Case, H. (1957). Early metallurgy of copper in Ireland and Britain. *Proc. prehist. Soc.* 23, 91–123.

Coghlan, H. H., Butler, J. R. and Parker, G. (1963). "Ores and Metals." Royal Anthropological Instit. Occasional Paper No. 17.

Coles, J. M. (1969). Metal analyses and the Scottish Early Bronze Age. *Proc. prehist. Soc.* 35, 330–344.

Condamin, J. and Picon, M. (1964). The influence of corrosion and diffusion on the percentage of silver in Roman denarii. *Archaeometry* 7, 98–105.

Condamin, J. and Picon, M. (1965). Notes on diffusion in ancient alloys. *Archaeometry* 8, 110–114.

Gordus, A. A. (1967). Quantitative non-destructive neutron activation analysis of silver in coins. *Archaeometry* 10, 78–86.

Haldane, W. (1970). A study of the chemical composition of pre-Roman ironwork from Somerset. *Bull. Hist. Metallurgy Group* 4, 53–66.

Hall E. T. (1961). Surface-enrichment of buried metals. *Archaeometry* 4, 62–66.

Hall, E. T. and Metcalf, D. M. (Eds.) (1972). "Methods of Chemical and Metallurgical Investigation of Ancient Coinage." Royal Numismatic Society Special Publication Series, London.

Hawkes, S. C., Merrick, J. M. and Metcalf, D. M. (1966). X-ray fluorescent analysis of some Dark Age coins and jewelry. *Archaeometry* 9, 98–138.

Hendy, M. F. and Charles, J. A. (1970). The production techniques, silver content and circulation history of the twelfth-century Byzantine trachy. *Archaeometry* 12, 13–21.

Junghans, S., Sangmeister, E. and Schröder, M. (1960). "Metallanalysen kupferzeitlicher und frühbronzezeitlicher Bodenfunde aus Europa (SAM 1)." Berlin.

Junghans, S., Sangmeister, E. and Schröder, M. (1968). "Kupfer und Bronze in der frühen Metallzeit Europas (SAM 2)." Berlin.

Kraay, C. M. and Emeleus, V. M. (1962). "The Composition of Greek Silver Coins: analysis by neutron activation." Ashmolean Museum, Oxford.

Metcalf, D. M. and Schweizer, F. (1971). The metal contents of the silver pennies of William II and Henry I (1087–1135). *Archaeometry* 13, 177–190.

Oddy, W. A. (1972). The analysis of gold coins—a comparison of results obtained by non-destructive methods. *Archaeometry* 14, 109–117.

Schweizer, F. and Friedman, A. M. (1972). Camparison of methods of analysis of silver and gold in silver coins. *Archaeometry* 14, 103–107.

Slater, E. A. and Charles, J. A. (1970). Archaeological classification by metal analysis. *Antiquity* 44, 207–213.

Tylecote, R. F. (1970). The composition of metal artefacts: a guide to provenance? *Antiquity* 44, 19–25.

Waterbolk, H. T. and Butler, J. J. (1965). Comments on the use of metallurgical analysis in prehistoric studies. *Helinium* 5, 227–251.

Wyttenbach, A. and Hermann, H. (1966). A quantitative non-destructive analysis of silver coins by neutron activation. *Archaeometry* 9, 139–147.

Glass, Glaze and Faience

Aspinall, A., Warren, S. E., Crummett, J. G. and Newton, R. G. (1972). Neutron activation analysis of faience beads. *Archaeometry* 14, 27–40.

Brill, R. H. (1970a). Lead and oxygen isotopes in ancient objects. *Phil. Trans. R. Soc. Lond.* **A269**, 143–164.

Brill, R. H. (1970b). Chemical studies of Islamic luster glass. In "Scientific Methods in Medieval Archaeology." (Ed. R. Berger), pp. 351–377. University of California Press, Los Angeles.

Frierman, J. D. (1970). Physical and chemical properties of some medieval Near Eastern glazed ceramics. In "Scientific Methods in Medieval Archaeology." (Ed. R. Berger), pp. 379–388. University of California Press, Los Angeles.

Garner, H. G. (1956). The use of imported and native cobalt in Chinese blue-and-white. *Oriental Art* 2, 48–50.

Musty, J. W. G. and Thomas, L. C. (1962). The spectrographic examination of English and Continental medieval glazed pottery. *Archaeometry* 5, 38–52.

Newton, R. G. (1971). A preliminary examination of a suggestion that pieces of strongly coloured glass were articles of trade in the Iron Age in Britain. *Archaeometry* 13, 11–16.

Newton, R. G. and Renfrew, C. (1970). British faience beads reconsidered. *Antiquity* 44, 199–206.

Sayre, E. V. and Smith, R. W. (1961). Compositional categories of ancient glass. *Science* 133, 1824–1826.

Stone, J. F. S. and Thomas, L. C. (1956). The use and distribution of faience in the ancient East and prehistoric Europe. *Proc. prehist. Soc.* 22, 37 84.

Turner, W. E. S. (1956a). Studies in ancient glasses and glassmaking processes. Part IV. The chemical composition of ancient glasses. *J. Soc. Glass Technol.* 40, 162–186 (T).

Turner, W. E. S. (1956b). Studies in ancient glasses and glassmaking processes. Part V. Raw materials and melting processes. *J. Soc. Glass Technol.* 40, 277–300 (T).

Young, S. A. (1956). An analysis of Chinese blue-and-white. *Oriental Art* 2, 43–47.

Pigments and Paintings

Cesareo, R., Frazzoli, F. V., Mancini, C., Sciuti, S., Marabelli, M., Mora, P., Rotondi, P. and Urbani, G. (1972). Non-destructive analysis of chemical elements in paintings and enamels. *Archaeometry* 14, 65–78.

de Silva, R. H. (1963). The problem of the binding medium particularly in wall paintings. *Archaeometry* **6**, 56–64.

Fleming, S. J., Jucker, H. and Riederer, J. (1971). Etruscan wall-paintings on terracotta: a study in authenticity. *Archaeometry* **13**, 143–167.

Forbes, R. J. (1965). Paints, pigments, inks and varnishes. In "Studies in Ancient Technology." Vol. III, pp. 210–264. Brill, Leiden.

Giovanoli, R. (1969). Provincial Roman wall painting investigated by electron microscopy. *Archaeometry* **11**, 53–59.

Kühn, H. (1960). Detection and identification of waxes, including Punic wax, by infra-red spectrography. *Stud. Conserv.* **5**, 71–81.

Amber and Mollusc Shells

Beck, C. W., Wilbur, E., Meret, S., Kossove, M. and Kermani, K. (1965). The infra-red spectra of amber and the identification of Baltic amber. *Archaeometry* **8**, 96–109.

Helm, O. (1877). Notizen über die chemische und physikalische Beschaffenheit des Bernsteins. *Archiv Pharmacie* **11**, 229–246.

Langenheim, J. (1969). Amber, a botanical inquiry. *Science* **163**, 1157–1169.

Mills, J. S. and Gough, L. J. (1972). Composition of Baltic amber. Conference Abstracts: Archaeometry and Archaeological Prospection. Res. Lab. Archaeol. Oxford.

Rottländer, R. C. A. (1970). On the formation of amber from pinus resin. *Archaeometry* **12**, 35–52.

Shackleton, N. J. (1970). Stable isotope study of the palaeoenvironment of the Neolithic site of Nea Nikomedeia, Greece. *Nature* **227**, 943–944.

Shackleton, N. J. and Renfrew, C. (1970). Neolithic trade routes re-aligned by oxygen isotope analyses. *Nature* **228**, 1062–1065.

Conclusions

Binford, L. R. (1965). Archaeological systematics and the study of culture process. *Am. Antiquity* **31**, 203–210.

Renfrew, C. (1969). Trade and culture process in European prehistory. *Cur. Anthropol.* **10**, 151–169.

Author Index

Italics indicate pages where references are listed at the end of chapters

A

Abdulla, A. B., 252, *254*
Aitchison, L., *213*
Aitken, M. J., 7, 8, 21, 38, 44, 49, *56*,
  58, *74*, 115, 117, 120, 122, 128, *132*,
  139, 142, 147, 148, *164*
Alcock, L., 45, *56*
Alldred, J. C., 22, *56*
Allen, I. M., 236, *255*
Ambrose, W. R., 314, *366*
Arai, T., 148, *165*
Arnold, J. R., 76, 83, *129*
Asaro, F., 278, *304*
Aspinall, A., 31, 39, 40, *56*, 307, 308,
  323, 353, 354, *366*, *367*, *369*
Atkinson, R. J. C., 8, 50, *56*
Attix, F. H., 115, *132*

B

Baker, M. J., 82, *130*
Banks, M., 273, *304*
Bannister, B., 68, *74*
Bauer, L. A., 139, *164*
Baxter, M. S., 82, *130*
Baynes-Cope, A. D., 152, *166*
Bean, C. P., 34, *56*
Beck, C. W., 359, *370*
Begg, E. L., 64, *75*
Berger, R., 84, *129*, 148, 149, *165*
Bimson, M., 324, *367*
Binford, L. R., 4, *6*, 365, *370*
Bishop, W. W., 169, *193*
Blanchard, R. L., 129, *132*

Blin-Stoyle, A. E., 319, 321, 330, 331,
  367, *368*
Bowie, S. H. U., 152, *166*
Boyd, C. A., 115, *132*
Boyle, R., 114, *132*
Braidwood, R. J., 182, *193*
Brewster, D., 161, *165*
Brill, R. H., 105, *131*, 161, 162, 163,
  165, 302, *304*, 334, 335, 336, 348,
  349, *368*, *369*
Britton, D., 329, 330, *368*
Brothwell, D., *213*, *214*, 251, 252, *254*
Brown, M. A., 330, 331, *368*
Bucha, V., 84, 86, *130*, 143, 144, 148,
  149, *164*
Burlatskaya, S. P., 148, *165*
Burton, D., 68, *75*
Bush, P., 307, 308, *366*
Butler, J. J., 332, *369*
Butler, J. R., 333, *368*

C

Caley, E. R., 328, *368*
Callow, W. J., 82, *130*
Campbell Smith, W., 224, *254*
Cann, J. R., 310, 311, 312, 313, *366*
Carson, H. H., 8, *56*
Case, H., 329, 330, *368*
Catling, H. W., 319, 320, 321, 322, 323,
  367
Cesareo, R., 356, *369*
Chaplin, R. E., *214*
Charles, J. A., 236, 238, *254*, *255*, 332,
  343, 344, *368*, *369*

Childe, V. G., 4, *6*, 185, *193*
Christodoulides, C., 129, *132*
Claringbull, G. F., 152, *166*
Clark, A. J., 31, 50, 51, *56*
Clark, J. G. D., 4, *6*, 58, *75*, 169, *193*, 179, 180, *193*
Coghlan, H. H., 236, 239, *254*, 329, 330, 333, *368*
Colani, C., 34, 38, *56*
Coles, J. M., 169, 174, *193*, 333, *368*
Condamin, J., 337, 338, *368*
Cousins, D. R., 327, *367*
Cox, A., 140, *165*
Craddock, P. T., 307, 308, *366*
Crummett, J. G., 353, 354, *369*
Curtis, G. H., 94, 99, 104, *131*, 170, 172, 173, *193*

D

Dabrowski, K., 50, *56*
Damon, P. E., 86, *130*
Daniels, F., 115, *132*
Darling, A. S., 251, *254*
Das, H. A., 285, *304*
Davidson, C. F., 152, *166*
DeBlois, R. W., 34, *56*
Dharmawardena, K. G., 327, *367*
Dimbleby, G. W., 3, *6*, 72, *75*, *214*
Dixon, J. E., 310, 311, 312, 313, *366*
Douglass, A. E., 69, *75*
Durrani, S., 104, *131*, 313, 314, *366*
Dunlop, D. J., 135, *165*

E

Edmunds, F. H., 152, *166*
Edwards, I. E. S., 84, *130*
Emeleus, V. M., 282, *304*, 340, 342, *368*
Emiliani, C., 107, 108, 109, 111, 112, 113, *131*, *132*
Ericson, D. B., 107, 113, 114, *131*, *132*, 168, *193*
Evans, C., 159, 160, *165*
Evans, J. G., 72, *75*
Evens, E. D., 223, 226, *254*
Evernden, J. F., 94, 99, 104, *131*, 170, 172, 173, *193*
Ewing, M., 107, 113, *131*

F

Feather, S. W., 307, 308, *366*
Ferguson, C. W., 69, *75*
Ferguson, J., 307, 308, *366*
Finch, L. R., 317, 323, *367*
Fink, W. C., 314, *366*
Fitch, F. J., 97, 98, *131*
Flannery, K. V., 183, *193*
Fleischer, R. L., 99, 101, 104, 105, *131*
Fleming, S. J., 115, 117, 118, 120, 128, *132*, 357, *370*
Fletcher, J. M., 177, *193*
Folgheraiter, G., 134, *165*
Forbes, R. J., 355, *370*
Foster, E., 34, *56*
Francis, P. D., 19, *57*
Frazzoli, F. V., 356, *369*
Frechen, J., 172, 173, *193*
Freeman, I. L., 250, *254*
Freeth, S. J., 316, *367*
Fremlin, J. H., 129, *132*
Friedman, A. M., 339, *369*
Friedman, I. I., 154, 155, 156, 158, *165*
Frierman, J. D., 350, *369*
Frischknecht, F. C., 7, *56*
Fryd, C. F. M., 152, *166*
Funkhouser, J., 64, *75*

G

Gangus, N. H. J., 315, *367*
Garner, H. G., 351, *369*
Geer, G. de, 70, *75*
Geiss, J., 111, *132*
Gentner, W., 92, 104, *131*
Giertz, V., 69, *75*
Giovanoli, R., 356, 357, *370*
Glass, B., 113, 114, *132*, 168, *193*
Glass, J. A., 113, 114, *132*, 168, *193*
Godwin, H., 181, 182, *193*
Goksu, H. Y., 129, *132*
Goodyear, F. H., *213*
Gordus, A. A., 275, *304*, 314, 338, *366*, 368
Gough, L. J., 359, *370*
Grasty, R. L., 93, *131*
Gray, P. H. K., 252, *254*
Green, R. C., 314, *366*
Grinsell, L. V., 223, 226, *254*

H

Hackens, T., 34, *56*
Haldane, W., 334, *368*
Hall, E. T., 273, *304*, 337, *368*
Han, M. C., 115, *133*
Hansen, R. O., 64, *75*
Harbottle, G., 316, 319, 320, *367*
Harcourt, R., 252, *254*
Haring, A., 80, *130*
Harold, M. R., 147, *164*
Harrison, C. G. A., 141, *165*
Harrison, R. G., 252, *254*
Hartley, B. R., 53, *56*
Hartley, K. F., 318, *367*
Hartshorne, N. H., 215, *255*
Haury, E. W., 148, 149, *165*
Hawley, H. N., 142, 147, *164*
Hawkes, J., 4, *6*
Hawkes, S. C., 342, 343, *368*
Healy, J. F., 251, *254*
Heezen, B. C., 107, 113, 114, *131*, *132*, 168, *193*
Heidenreich, R. D., 242, *255*
Heizer, R. F., 314, *366*
Helm, O., 359, *370*
Hendy, M. F., 238, *255*, 343, 344, *368*
Hermann, H., 338, *369*
Herzenberg, C. L., 294, *304*
Hesse, A., 7, *56*
Hey, M. H., 152, *166*
Higgs, E. S., 169, 174, 183, *193*, *213*
Hill, M. E., 314, *366*
Hirooka, K., 148, *165*
Hodges, H. W. M., *213*, *214*, 228, *255*
Hodson, F. R., 3, *6*
Hofman, U., 250, *255*
Hole, F., 183, *193*
Hood, H. P., 161, 162, 163, *165*
Horn, W., 177, *193*
Hornblower, A. P., 281, *304*
Howell, M., 35, *56*
Huber, B., 69, *75*
Hughes, M. J., 284, *304*, 307, 308, *366*
Hurst, J. G., 148, *165*
Huxtable, J., 126, *133*

I

Ichikawa, Y., 115, *132*
Irwin-Williams, C., 64, *75*

Isaac, G. Ll., 4, *6*, 169, *193*
Ito, H., 148, 165

J

Janssens, P. A., *214*
Jarman, M. R., 183, *193*
Jasinska, M., 129, *132*
Jewell, P. A., 3, *6*
Johnson, F., 177, *193*
Johnson, N. M., 129, *132*
Joseph, A., 128, *132*
Jucker, H., 357, *370*
Junghans, S., 332, *368*

K

Katsui, Y., 158, *165*
Kawai, N., 148, *165*
Keiller, A., 223, *255*
Kellaway, G. A., 223, *255*
Keller, G. V., 7, *56*
Kendall, D. G., 3, *6*
Kenyon, K. M., 182, *193*
Kermani, K., 359, *370*
Khan, H. A., 104, *131*, 313, 314, *366*
Kharkar, D. P., 64, *75*
Koenigswald, G. H. R. von, 104, *131*
Koezy, F. F., 111, *132*
Kondo, Y., 158, *165*
Kossove, M., 359, *370*
Kostikas, A., 315, *367*
Kraay, C. M., 340, 342, *368*
Kuhn, H., 358, *370*
Kulp, J. L., 111, *132*
Kume, S., 148, *165*

L

Langan, L., 23, *56*
Langenheim, J., 360, *370*
Leakey, L. S. B., 104, *131*, 169, *193*
Leakey, M. D., 169, *193*
Le Borgne, E., 12, *56*
Le Gros Clark, W. E., 152, *166*
Lerman, J. C., 84, *130*
Libby, W. F., 76, 78, 83, *129*, *130*
Lingenfelter, R. E., 87, *130*
Linington, R. E., 8, 46, 49, 50, 51, 52, *56*, *57*

Lippolt, H. J., 92, 104, *131*, 172, 173, *193*
Long, W. D., 155, 156, *165*
Longin, R., 81, *130*
Lucas, A., *214*
Lynam, J. T., 31, 39, 40, *56*

M

Malde, H. E., 64, *75*
Mancini, C., 356, *369*
Marabelli, M., 356, *369*
Maryon, H., 241, *255*
Matson, F. R., 301, *304*
May, J., 47, *57*
Mayes, P., 3, *6*, 323, *367*
Mayneord, W. V., 122, *133*
McDougall, D. J., 115, *132*
Meggers, B. J., 159, 160, *165*
Meille, E., 323, *367*
Mejdahl, V., 115, *132*
Meret, S., 359, *370*
Merrick, J. M., 342, 343, *368*
Merwe, N. J. van der, 82, *130*
Metcalf, D. M., 337, 342, 343, 344, 345, *368*
Michels, J. W., 159, *166*
Miller, J. A., 93, 97, 98, *131*
Millett, A., 319, 320, 321, 322, 323, *367*
Mills, J. S., 359, *370*
Milojčić, V., 178, *193*
Mitchell, J. G., 94, *131*
Molleson, T., 252, *254*
Momose, K., 148, *165*
Montagu, M. F. A., 151, *166*
Mook, W. G., 84, *130*
Moorey, P. R. S., 128, *132*
Mora, P., 356, *369*
Moss, H. M., 128, *132*
Mullins, C., 13, 35, 38, *57*
Musson, C. R., 38, *57*
Musty, J. W. G., 351, *369*

N

Nachasova, I. E., 148, *165*
Nagata, T., 148, *165*
Nechaeva, T. B., 148, *165*
Néel, L., 135, *165*
Nesbitt, L. B., 34, *56*
Neustupný, E., 4, *6*, 83, *130*

Newton, R. G., 161, 162, 164, *166*, 349, 353, 354, *369*
Niewiadomski, T., 129, *132*
Nishimura, S., 105, 106, *131*

O

Oakley, K. P., 150, 151, 152, 153, *166*
Oddy, W. A., 284, *304*, 339, *369*
Opdyke, N. D., 113, 114, *132*, 168, *193*

P

Palmer, L. R., 321, 322, *367*
Palmer, L. S., 30, *57*
Parasnis, D. S., 7, *57*
Parker, G., 333, *368*
Peacock, D. P. S., 225, 226, 227, 228, *255*, 315, *367*
Penniman, T. K., 236, *255*
Perinet, G., 324, *367*
Perlman, I., 278, *304*
Picon, M., 323, 337, 338, *367*, *368*
Piggott, S., 181, 189, *193*, 223, 226, *254*, *255*
Plesters, R. J., 152, *166*
Poole, A. B., 317, 323, *367*
Poole, J. B., 68, *75*
Price, P. B., 99, 101, 104, 105, *131*
Purdy, J. C., 314, *366*

Q

Quitta, H., 127

R

Radley, J. M., 122, *133*
Raison, J., 323, *367*
Ralph, E. K., 28, *57*, 115, *133*
Rayment, D. L., 250, *254*
Reed, R., 68, *75*
Rees, A., 8, *56*
Rees, A. I., 47, *57*
Reid, J., 115, 117, 120, *132*
Renfrew, C., 4, *6*, 104, *131*, 186, 187, 188, 189, 191, *193*, *194*, 310, 311, 312, 313, 314, 353, 354, 361, 365, *366*, *369*, *370*

Rice, C. B. F., *213*
Richards, E. E., 318, 319, 321, *367*
Richter, K., 153, 154, 166, 172, 173, *194*
Riederer, J., 357, *370*
Rosenfield, A., *214*, 217, *255*
Rosholt, J. N., 11, *132*
Rotondi, P., 356, *369*
Rottländer, R. C. A., 359, *370*
Rusakov, O. M., 148, *165*

S

Sangmeister, E., 332, *368*
Sasajima, S., 148, *165*
Saunders, D. F., 115, *132*
Sayre, E. V., 346, 347, *369*
Schaeffer, O. A., 64, *75*
Schove, D. J., 87, *130*
Schröder, M., 332, *368*
Schulman, E., 69, *75*
Schweizer, F., 339, 344, 345, *368, 369*
Sciuti, S., 356, *369*
Scollar, I., 43, *57*
Shackleton, N. J., 109, 112, 113, 114, *132*, 361, 362, 363, *370*
Shaw, T., 177, *194*
Shepard, A. O., *214*, 225, *255*
Schrager, A. M., 230, *255*
Sieveking, G. de G., 307, 308, *366*
Silva, R. H., de., 358, *370*
Simopoulos, A., 315, *367*
Slater, D. N., 323, *367*
Slater, E. A., 332, *369*
Smellie, D. W., 18, *57*
Smith, R. L., 154, 155, 156, 158, *165*
Smith, R. W., 346, 347, *369*
Solecki, R. S., 182, *194*
Stacey, F. D., 135, 138, *165*
Stevenson, D. P., 314, *366*
Stock, R., *213*
Stone, J. F. S., 352, 353, *369*
Strahm, C., 90, *130*
Stross, F. H., 314, *366*
Stuart, A., 215, *255*
Stuiver, M., 85, *130*
Suess, H. E., 82, 83, 84, 86, 89, 90, *130*
Szabo, B. J., 64, *75*

T

Taj, M., 104, *131*, 313, 314, *366*
Tarhov, E. N., 148, *165*
Tauber, H., 85, *130*
Taylor, R. E., 148, 149, *165*
Tchelidze, Z. A., 148, *165*
Thellier, E., 135, 143, 148, *165*
Thellier, O., 135, 143, *165*
Thomas, H. H., 223, *255*
Thomas, H. L., 177, *194*
Thomas, L. C., 351, 352, 353, *369*
Thornton, P. R., 246, *255*
Tite, M. S., 13, 21, 35, 38, 44, 53, *56, 57*, 115, 117, 120, 123, *132, 139*, 300, *304*, 325, 326, *367*
Tobler, A. J., 327, *368*
Trigger, B. G., 1, *6*
Turekian, K. K., 64, *75*
Turner, C., 113, 114, *132*
Turner, R. C., 122, *133*
Turner, W. E. S., 346, 349, *369*
Tylecote, R. F., *214*, 328, 333, *369*

U

Ucko, P. J., 128, *132, 214*
Urbani, G., 356, *369*

V

Vichy, M., 323, *367*
Vocotopoulou, J., 315, *367*
Vogel, J. C., 84, *130*
Vokehok, H. L., 110, *132*
Vries, A. E. de, 80, 83, 87, *130*
Vries, H. de., 80, 87, *130*

W

Wailes, B., 45, *57*
Wait, J., 39, *57*
Walker, R. M., 99, 101, 104, 105, *131*
Wallis, F. S., 223, 226, *254, 255*
Walton, A., 82, *130*
Wampler, J. M., 334, 335, *368*
Wangersky, P. J., 111, *132*
Warren, S. E., 353, 354, *369*
Waterbolk, H. T., 332, *369*
Waters, G. S., 19, *57*
Weaver, G. H., 142, 147, *164, 165*

Webster, G., 8, *56*
Weiner, J. S., 152, *166*
Werner, A. E. A., 152, *166*
Wertheim, G. K., 291, *305*
West, R. G., 70, 71, *75*, 171, *194*
West, S., 135, *165*
Whitmore, F. E., 315, *368*
Wilbur, E., 359, *370*
Wilcox, T. R., 314, *366*
Willis, E. H., 177, *193*
Wollin, G., 107, 113, *131*
Wright, A. E., 47, *57*
Wyttenbach, A., 338, *369*

Y

Yashawa, K., 148, *165*
Young, S. A., 147, *164*, 351, *369*
Young, W. J., 315, *368*

Z

Zagniv, G. F., 148, *165*
Zimmerman, D. W., 115, 117, 118,
    120, 126, 127, *132*, *133*
Zonderhuis, J., 285, *304*
Zussman, J., *213*, 257, *304*

Subject Index

A

Absorbance, 265
Adhesives, 211
Aerial photography, 7–8, 46, 50, 55
Alloys, 233–234, 239
Alpha particles, 110–111, 116–118, 122
Aluminium, 308, 319–320, 353–354
Amber, 210–211, 358–360
Amphibole, 217–218, 221, 224–225
Angle of declination (see Earth's magnetic field direction)
Angle of dip (see Earth's magnetic field direction)
Annealing, 101, 104, 233–236, 288
Anorthite, 324
Antimony, 210, 331–332, 346–347
Apatite, 150–154
Archaeomagnetism (see Magnetic dating)
Arsenic, 329–332
Astatic magnetometer, 146–147
Atomic absorption spectrometry, 201, 264–267, 271, 291
    flint, 307
    metals, 328, 333
Atomic number, 248, 251–252, 267, 270–271, 273, 282–283
Azurite, 355

B

Barium, 310–311
Barrows, 50, 181–182
Beaker culture, 4, 181–182, 192, 229, 330

Beestonian glacial, 113, 173
Beta particles, 78–79, 110–111, 116–118, 282–283
Beta ray backscatterer, 202, 281–283
Binding media, 211, 355–356
Birefringence, 157, 219–221
Bismuth, 331–333
Black-body radiation, 120
Bloating, 300, 326
Blocking temperature, 136–137
Bloomery process, 238
Bluestones (Stonehenge), 223
Bones
    chemical dating, 66–67, 150–154
    radiocarbon dating, 81
    radiography, 213, 252–254
    thermoluminescent dating, 65, 129
    uranium decay series dating, 64
Bragg relationship, 268, 280, 285–286
Bristlecone pines (see Dendrochronology)
Bronze, 184, 233 (see also Metal artefacts: non-ferrous)
Bronze Age
    amber, 358–360
    faience, 353–355
    historical dates, 184–186, 188–191
    metallurgy, 184–189, 236, 329–333
    pottery, 229, 316–317, 326–327
    radiocarbon dates, 185–191
Brunhes polarity epoch, 140–142
Byzantine coins, 238, 343–344

C

Calcite, 97, 119, 218, 222, 229, 287, 290, 296–297, 316, 324–325
Calcium, 265, 316–317, 319–320, 334, 356–357
Calcium carbonate (see Calcite)
Calcium fluoride, 115, 122
Callabrian stage, 168–169
Carbon-14 dating (see Radiocarbon dating)
Carbon exchange reservoir, 77–78, 82–88
Carbon isotopic analysis, 302, 304, 360–364
Carburization, 238–240, 334
Cassiterite, 218
Cathodoluminescence, 249
Cementite, 239, 241
Chalk, 14–15, 46, 222
Characterization of raw materials, 206–207, 306 (see also Stone artefacts, Metal artefacts, Pottery, etc.)
Charcoal, 61, 81–82, 127–128
Chemical analysis, 201–202, 257–260, 306 (see also Atomic absorption spectrometry, Neutron activation analysis, Optical emission spectrometry and X-ray fluorescence spectrometry)
Chemical dating of bone, 66–67, 150–154, 172–173
Chert, 67, 349
Chromatography, 203–206, 210–211, 358–359
Chromium, 309, 315–316, 319–320
Cleavage planes, 218–219
Cobalt, 316, 320, 349, 351–352
Coins
  alloy composition, 209, 340–345
  characterization of ore, 341–342
  fabrication, 238, 251
  lead isotope analysis, 336
  location, 33–34
Cold-working, 232–236, 251, 288
Collagen, 68, 81, 150
Collared Urns, 229
Collimator, 268, 270–272
Colour analysis, 300–301

Compton scattering, 276
Computors, 3, 42–43, 55
Copper
  alloys, 184, 233–234
  analysis, 283–284, 301, 337–341
  colorant, 349–352, 355 (see also Metal artefacts: non-ferrous)
Copper Age (see Bronze Age)
Coprolites, 212
Cosmic rays, 77–78, 86–87, 117–118
Cristobalite, 324
Cromerian interglacial, 173–174
Cultivation of plants (see Farming economy)
Cuprous oxide, 349
Curie temperature, 11, 136–137, 145
Cyclotron resonance, 93–94

D

Damescene steel, 241–242
Dark Age
  coins, 342–343
  glass, 347–348
  metallurgy, 240–241
  pottery, 126, 326
Dead Sea scrolls, 68
Deep sea sediments, 63–64, 106–114, 172–173, 304
  oxygen isotopic temperatures, 107–109, 112–113
  temperature sensitive foraminifera, 107, 113–114
Dendrites, 233–234, 251
Dendrochronology, 68–70, 83–85, 90, 161
Detrital remanent magnetism, 110, 141
Diamond, 114
Differential thermal analysis, 295–297, 300, 325
Diffracting crystal, 268–269, 271–273, 279–280, 286
Diffraction, 199 (see also Electron and X-ray diffraction)
Diffusion (cultural), 1, 4, 58–59, 185, 188–189, 191–192, 365
Diffusion (physical), 96–97, 155, 234, 337
Dilatometer, 299
Dolerite, 222–223

Dolomite, 218
Domestication of animals (see Farming economy)
Doppler effect, 293
Double refraction (see Birefringence)

E

Earth's magnetic field direction, 138
  effect on magnetic anomalies, 18
  polarity reversals, 110, 140–141, 170
  secular variation, 65, 138–140, 142–143, 147–148
Earth's magnetic field intensity, 138
  diurnal variation, 19
  effect on ^{14}C production, 86, 150
  secular variation, 66, 140, 143–146, 148–150
Eddy currents, 32–34
Egyptian blue, 355, 357
Electrodes, 29, 40, 261
Electromagnetic radiation, 197–198
Electromagnetic surveying, 8, 32–39, 45–46, 55
  applications, 45–46
  detection depth, 37–38
  response to soil, 35–39
Electrons
  backscattered, 246–248
  diffraction, 245–246
  secondary emission, 246–248
  wavelength, 197–198, 242–243
Electron microscopy, 196, 200, 242–252, 278
Electron probe microanalyser, 202, 249, 273, 278–281
  metals, 238, 251
  pigments, 210, 357
Electrum, 251
Endothermic reactions, 295–297
Enstatite, 325
Environment, 2, 4, (see also Pollen analysis, Pleistocene and Postglacial climates)
Etching, 102, 230–232
Etruscan cemeteries, 50–51
Eutectic, 234, 236–239
Exothermic reactions, 295–297
Experimental earthworks, 3
Experimental kilns, 3, 323

F

Faience, 209–210, 352–355
Farming economy, 72, 178–184, 211–212, 313
Felspar, 96–99, 119, 217–218, 221–223, 225
Ferrimagnetism, 9–10, 135
Ferrite, 238–239
Fibres, 212
Fired clay structures (see Pottery kilns)
Firing temperatures (see Pottery)
Fission track dating, 63, 99–106, 168
  results, 104–106, 170, 313–314
  spontaneous fission decay constant, 100–101, 105
  statistical errors, 102–103
  uranium concentration, 125, 313–314
Flame photometry, 92, 122
Flint artefacts
  characterization, 208, 222–223, 307–309
  thermoluminescent dating, 65, 129
Flint mines, 181–182
Fluorine dating (see Chemical dating of bone)
Fluxgate magnetometer, 22–23
Foraminifera (see Deep sea sediments)
Forgeries, 128, 340, 357–358
Fossil fuel effect, 82–83
Fresco painting, 355–357

G

Gabbro, 222, 225–226
Galena, 218
Galley Hill skeleton, 151–152
Gamma rays, 116–118, 122–123, 197–198, 202, 252, 274, 291–293
Gas proportional counter, 79, 269, 279
Gehlenite, 324
Geiger counter, 79, 151, 282
Geophysical prospecting (see Electromagnetic, Induced polarization, Magnetic and Resistivity surveying)
Germanium, 276, 321–322
Gippingian glacial, 173
Glacial climatic sequence: nomenclature, 172 (see also Pleistocene chronology and climate)

Glacial deposits, 14–15, 32, 73, 106, 112–114, 171, 173, 223 (*see also* Varves)
Glass, 209–210
    colorants, 349–350
    composition, 346–348
    fission track dating, 63, 101–102, 104–105
    isotopic analysis, 302–304, 336–337, 348–349
    surface layer counting, 67, 161–164
    thermoluminescent dating, 129
Glauconite, 355, 357
Glaze, 209–210, 350–352
Glow curve, 120–122
Gneiss, 221–222
Golay cell, 290
Gold
    alloys, 233–234, 251
    analysis, 274, 283–285, 331, 337–339, 341–343 (*see also* Metal artefacts: non-ferrous)
Granite, 25–26, 208, 222
Gravel, 14, 26, 32, 70, 157
Greek (Classical)
    coins, 251, 340–342
    pottery, 250, 326
Grog, 228–229
Gypsum, 218, 290

H

Haematite, 9–12, 135–137, 145, 250, 355, 357
Half-life: definition, 60
Heavy mineral analysis, 226–228
Heidelberg man, 174–175
Henge monuments, 50, 181–182, 189–190 (*see also* Stonehenge)
Historical chronologies, 58, 78, 84, 168, 177–179, 184–186, 188–191
Hollow cathode lamp, 264–265
Homo habilis, 170
Homo sapiens, 2, 64, 175, 212
Hornblende, 96–97, 218
Hoxnian interglacial, 113–114, 173
Hydration layer dating of obsidian, 67, 154–160, 177
Hydroxyl water, 150–151, 291, 296

I

Igneous rocks, 24, 208, 221–222, 225–226
Illite, 218, 250, 296
Induced polarization surveying, 8, 39–41
Infra-red absorption spectrometry, 202, 210, 288–291, 294, 358–359
Interatomic bonds, 289–290
Interference colours, 220–221
Invasions, 1, 4, 181, 365
Ionium dating, 63–64, 110–111
Ipswichian interglacial, 113, 173–174
Iron
    analysis, 308–309, 316, 319–320
    colorant, 349–351, 355–358
    location of artefacts, 9, 24, 42–43, 50
    Mössbauer spectroscopy, 202, 293–294, 315, 327–328
    radiocarbon dating, 82
    (*see also* Metal artefacts: ferrous)
Iron Age
    cemeteries (location), 50–51
    glass, 349–350
    hill-forts (location), 7, 43–46, 55
    metallurgy, 239–240, 334
    pottery, 126, 225–226
Iron smelting furnaces, 53
Islamic glass, 346–349
Isomer shift, 293
Isotopic analysis, 203, 301–304 (*see also* Carbon, Lead *and* Oxygen isotopic analysis)
Isotopic enrichment, 80
Isotopic fractionation, 80, 108, 303–304

J

Jade axes, 224, 307

K

Kaolinite, 97, 218, 296–297, 324
Kyanite, 227–228

L

Lasers, 261
Leaching, 67, 125, 161, 316–317

Lead, 210, 278, 282–283, 330–331, 334, 346–347, 350–351
Lead antimonate, 349, 358
Lead isotopic analysis, 62, 203, 209, 301–303, 334–337
Lime, 161, 209, 346, 348, 352, 355–357
Limestone, 14, 25–26, 32, 115, 153, 222, 225
Limonite, 218, 355
Linear B script, 321–323
Lithium fluoride, 115, 268
Los Millares culture, 185
Lowestoftian glacial, 173, 223
Luminescent centre, 115–116, 249

M

Maghaemite, 9–10, 12–13
Magnesium, 210, 265, 271, 308, 318–320, 334, 346–347, 353–354
Magnetic dating, 65–66, 134–150, 177
    direction measurements, 110, 138–143, 147–148, 170
    intensity measurements, 86, 140, 143–146, 148–150
Magnetic domains, 10–12, 135–137
Magnetic field intensity anomalies, 9, 15–19, 24, 42–53
Magnetic field reversals (see Earth's magnetic field direction)
Magnetic lens, 242, 279
Magnetic surveying, 8–25, 41–56
    applications, 43–53
Magnetic susceptibility of soils, 11–15, 38, 49
Magnetic viscosity (see Viscous remanent magnetism)
Magnetite, 9–13, 135–137, 145, 250, 358
Magnetometers, 18–23, 146–147
Malachite, 218, 355
Manganese, 210, 316–317, 319–320, 334, 346–349, 351–352
Martensite, 239
Mass spectrometer, 92–93, 108, 111, 203, 301–302
Matuyama polarity epoch, 140–142, 170
Mediaeval period
    coins, 344–345
    dendrochronology, 69

deserted villages (location), 7, 50
    glass, 346
    magnetic dating, 74, 147–148
    pottery, 326–328, 351
    radiocarbon dating, 176–177
Megalithic tombs, 50, 184–186, 188–189
Metal artefacts: ferrous
    characterization of ores, 334
    fabrication, 239–242
    radiography, 253
Metal artefacts: non-ferrous, 209
    alloy composition, 329–330, 354–355
    characterization of ores, 331–333
    fabrication, 236–238, 287–288
    (see also Coins and Lead isotopic analysis)
Metal detectors, 8, 32–35, 50
Metallographic microscopy, 199, 209, 230–242
    ferrous metals, 239–242
    non-ferrous metals, 188, 236–238
Metallurgical microscope (see Metallographic microscopy)
Metallurgy: early development, 4, 178, 181, 184–189, 192, 323, 327, 365–366
Metamorphic rocks, 24, 221–222, 225–226
Mica, 96–97, 217–218, 221–222
Microradiography (see Radiography)
Migration, 1, 4, 176, 192, 365
Minoan
    metallurgy, 236–238
    pottery, 319–323
Mollusc shells
    climatic indicators, 72
    isotopic analysis, 210, 302–304, 360–364
    radiocarbon dating, 81
    thermoluminescent dating, 129
Monochromator, 265, 290
Montmorillonite, 218, 296–297
Mössbauer spectroscopy, 202–203, 209, 291–295, 315, 327–328
Mousterian culture, 174–175
Mullite, 296, 324–325
Multi-channel pulse analyser, 269, 276
Multidomain grains (see Magnetic domains)

Mummies, 213, 252–253
Mycenaean civilization, 4, 185, 189–
  191
  amber, 358–359
  faience, 353–355
  pottery, 319–323, 326–327

N

Native copper, 184–185, 188, 232
Natron, 345, 348
Neanderthal man, 174–175
Neolithic period
  camps (location), 46
  flint artefacts, 307–309
  historical dates, 178–179
  mollusc shells, 361–364
  pottery, 225, 228–229, 326
  obsidian artefacts, 312–313
  radiocarbon dates, 90, 127, 179–184
  stone axes, 223–225
  thermoluminescent dates, 127
Nernst filament lamp, 289
Neutron activation analysis, 201, 273–
  278, 285
  coins, 338–339
  faience, 353–354
  flint, 307–308
  pottery, 319–320
Neutrons, 77–78, 82, 94–95, 100–102,
  273, 275
Nickel, 317, 319–320, 331–332, 334
Nicol prism, 217
Nitrogen dating (see Chemical dating
  of bone)
Nuclear reactor, 101, 275
Nuclear transition energy, 292
Nuclear weapon testing, 82–83
Numerical aperture, 200

O

Obsidian artefacts
  characterization (chemical analysis),
    208, 222, 309–313, 365
  characterization (fission track), 104,
    313–314
  fission track dating, 63, 101–102,
    104
  hydration layer dating, 67, 154–160

Ocean temperatures (see Deep sea
  sediments)
Olivine, 217, 221
Omegatron, 93–94
Optical bleaching, 119, 129
Optical emission spectrometry, 201,
  260–264, 266, 271
  faience, 353
  flint, 307
  glass, 346
  glaze, 350
  metals, 328, 333
  obsidian, 309–311
  pottery, 318–320, 322
Optical microscopy, 102, 157, 162,
  196, 198–199, 212 (see also Metallographic and Petrological microscopy)
Oxygen isotopic analysis
  deep sea sediments, 64, 107–109
  glass, 210, 302–304, 348–349
  mollusc shells, 210, 302–304, 360–
    364

P

Palaeolithic chronology (see Pleisto-
  cene chronology)
Palaeomagnetism, 135, 150
Palaeopathology, 212–213, 253
Parchment, 67–68
Partition coefficient, 204
Pattern welding, 240–241
Pearlite, 239, 242
Petrological microscopy, 97, 199, 208–
  209, 215–230
  pottery, 224–230
  stone artefacts, 222–224
Phase contrast microscopy, 199
Phonons, 293
Phosphate ion, 150, 265
Phosphorus, 333–334
Photomultiplier, 79, 119–120, 249,
  263, 265, 276
Photons, 197, 269, 276
Pigments, 210, 355–358
Piltdown man, 152–153
Planck's constant, 197
Plane polarized light, 217, 219–221
Pleichroism, 219

Pleistocene chronology, 73, 168–176
  chemical dating of bones, 153–154, 172–173
  deep sea sediments, 111–114, 172–173
  fission track dating, 104
  magnetic dating, 140–141, 170
  pollen analysis, 72, 173
  potassium-argon dating, 97–99, 169–173
  radiocarbon dating, 171–176
  thermoluminescent dating, 126–127
Pleistocene climate, 158, 167
  deep sea sediments, 64, 111–114, 172–173
  effect on ^{14}C production, 87–88
  molluscs, 72
  pollen analysis, 70–72, 171
Pliocene, 167–169, 171
Pluvial phases, 167
Polarizing microscope (see Petrological microscopy)
Pollen analysis, 70–72, 85, 171, 181, 212
Porcelain, 325–326, 351–352
Postglacial climate, 70–72, 167
Potash, 161, 209, 346
Potassium, 210, 308, 346–347, 357
Potassium-40, 62, 65, 116–117, 122 (see also Potassium-argon dating)
Potassium-argon dating, 2, 62–63, 90–99
  age spectra, 95–99
  ^{40}Ar/^{39}Ar method, 94–96
  results, 97–99, 104, 113, 141, 169–170, 172–173
Pottery, 208–209
  characterization (chemical analysis), 228, 315–323
  characterization (petrology), 225–228
  detection of forgeries, 128, 357–358
  fabrication, 228–229, 250
  firing atmosphere, 229–230, 328
  firing temperature, 229, 250–251, 295–301, 323–328
  fission track dating, 63, 102, 105–106
  magnetic dating, 66, 135, 143–146, 148–150
  thermoluminescent dating, 64–65, 115–128
Pottery kilns
  experimental, 3, 323
  location, 38, 51–53
  magnetic dating, 65–66, 142–143, 147–148
Protactinium/ionium dating, 110–111
Proton gradiometer, 21–22
Proton magnetometer, 19–21
Pulsed induction meter, 34–35, 38–39
Pumice, 96–99, 104
Pyrite, 218
Pyroxene, 217–218, 221, 224

Q

Quadrupole splitting, 293–294
Quartz, 67, 116, 119, 128, 217, 221–225, 287, 299, 303
Quartz sand, 208–209, 226–228, 303, 345, 349
Quenching, 239–240, 334

R

Radiation dosimetry, 115, 122
Radioactive decay
  general principles, 59–61
  statistical errors, 79–80
Radiocarbon dating, 2, 61, 76–90, 127–128, 139, 150, 153, 158, 176–177
  corrections to radiocarbon dates, 89–90, 168, 183–184, 186, 191
  half-life, 78, 88
  results, 113, 126–127, 171–176, 179–191
  statistical errors, 79–80, 88–89
Radiography, 196, 200, 213, 252–254
Radiowaves, 197–198
Radon emanation, 124–125
Rare earth elements, 308, 316, 320
Relative chronologies, 58–59, 67, 72–73, 151
Remanent magnetism (see Detrital, Thermo- and Viscous remanent magnetism)
Replicas, 244
Resistivity anomalies, 26–28, 30–32, 40–41, 46–50, 54
Resistivity meters, 28–29

Resistivity of soils, 25–26
Resistivity surveying, 8, 25–32, 41–51,
    53–55
  applications, 46–47, 49–50
  electrode configurations, 26–27, 29–
    31
Resolution (microscopy), 199–200, 243,
    248
Roman period
  glass, 347–348
  magnetic dating, 74, 147–148
  metallurgy, 240
  pottery, 227–228, 250, 318–319,
    325–326
  pottery kilns (location), 53
  towns (location), 47–49, 55
  villas (location), 47
  wall painting, 356–357
Rubidium, 317
Rubidium vapour magnetometer, 23

S

Sandstone, 25–26, 208, 222, 225
Scandium, 308, 316, 320
Scanning electron microscope (see Elec-
    tron microscopy)
Schist, 221–222
Scintillation counter, 79, 122, 247,
    269, 275–276, 293
Secular variation, 138 (see also Earth's
    magnetic field direction and in-
    tensity)
Seismic surveying, 8–9
Semiconductor counters, 247, 269,
    276, 293
Sheffield plate, 236–237
Shrinkage temperature
  parchment, 67–68
  pottery, 298–300
Siderite, 218
Silicon, 260, 273, 357
Silver
  alloys, 233–234
  analysis, 277, 283–284, 331–332,
    337–339, 342–345, 349 (see also
    Metal artefacts: non-ferrous)
Single domain grains (see Magnetic
    domains)
Skins, 212

Smenkhkare, 253
Soapstone, 352
Social hierarchy, 178, 192
Soda, 161, 209, 346, 348, 352
Sodium, 319–320
Sodium iodide, 279
Soils (see Magnetic susceptibility and
    Resistivity of soils)
Sorbite, 239
Source of raw materials (see Charac-
    terization of raw materials)
Specific activity, 78, 83
Specific gravity measurements, 202,
    283–285, 339
Spinner magnetometer, 147
Spondylus shells, 361–362, 365
Spontaneous fission (see Fission track
    dating)
Standard deviation, 79–80, 102–103
Steel, 238–239 (see also Metal artefacts:
    ferrous)
Stirrup jars, 321–323
Stone artefacts, 208, 222–224, 307 (see
    also Flint and Obsidian artefacts)
Strontium, 317
Succinite (see Amber)
Sulphate ion, 265
Sulphur, 317, 333
Sumerian metallurgy, 184–185
Sun-spot activity, 87
Supralinearity, 123–124, 126
Surface enrichment, 270, 273, 337–
    338
Swanscombe skull, 151–152, 175
Swords, 239–242, 253

T

Technology, 3–4, 206–207, 365 (see also
    Metal artefacts, Pottery, etc.)
Temper, 208, 224–226, 228–229, 317
Tempera painting, 355–356
Tempering, 239–240, 334
Thermal analysis (see Differential ther-
    mal analysis, Thermal expansion
    measurements and Thermogravi-
    metric analysis)
Thermal expansion measurements,
    298–300, 325–327
Thermogravimetric analysis, 297–298

Thermoluminescent dating, 64–65, 114–129, 177
  authenticity testing, 128
  results, 126–127
Thermoremanent magnetism, 10–11, 24, 135–137 (*see also* Magnetic dating)
Thorium
  analysis, 308–309, 316, 320
  decay series, 62, 65, 116–117, 122, 302
Tin, 283, 329–330, 351, 353–354
Titanium, 270, 317–320
Tourmaline, 227–228
Trade, 3–4, 206, 223–226, 228, 309, 312–314, 318, 321–323, 341, 358–360, 362, 364–365
Tree ring dating (*see* Dendrochronology)
Tuff, 97–99, 169, 208, 223, 225
Tutankhamun, 252–253
Twinned crystals, 221, 235

U

Unetice culture, 188–189
Uranium decay series, 62, 302
  dating of bone, 64
  dating of deep sea sediments, 64, 110–111
  fission track dating, 101–104
  thermoluminescent dating, 65, 116–117, 122, 125
  uranium-lead dating, 153
Urban development, 178, 365–366

V

Varnishes, 211
Varve counting, 70, 85–86
Villafranchian fauna, 167
Viscous remanent magnetism, 38–39, 136–137
Vitrification, 298, 300

Volcanic deposits, 51, 73
  fission track dating, 63, 102, 104
  magnetic dating, 65, 140–141, 170
  potassium-argon dating, 62–63, 90–99, 104, 169–170, 172–173

W

Wax, 356, 358
Weichselian glacial, 113, 171, 174
Wessex culture, 4, 182, 185–192, 329–330, 353–354
Whitlockite, 325
Wollastonite, 324–325
Wood
  dendrochronology, 68–70
  optical microscopy, 212
  radiocarbon dating, 61, 81, 127–128
Wrought iron, 238 (*see also* Metal artefacts: ferrous)

X

X-rays, 201–202, 249, 252, 267, 285–287
X-ray diffraction: back reflection, 287–288
X-ray diffraction: powder, 151, 153–154, 202, 285–287, 291, 294
  glass, 349
  pigments, 210, 357–358
  pottery, 209, 300, 315, 323–325
  stone artefacts, 307
X-ray fluorescence spectrometry, 201, 267–273, 278, 281, 286, 350, 355–356
X-ray milliprobe, 272–273, 279–280, 338–339, 349–350

Z

Zinc sulphide, 122
Zinjanthropus, 170
Zircon, 63, 102, 105–106, 227
Zirconium, 310–311, 317

Index of Sites

A

Abingdon, 182
Acigöl, 310–311, 313–314
Ali Kosh, 183, 310, 312
Al Mina, 326–327
Al 'Ubaid, 326
Amarinothos, 320
Amesbury, 182
Arminghall, 182
Arpachiyak, 326
Asilki Hüyük, 310, 312
Athens, 341–342
Auvernier, 90

B

Bainbridge, 326
Bardown, 53
Barnsley Park, 47
Baston, 326
Bayezid, 310–311
Beidha, 310, 312
Belius River, 348
Bingöl, 310–311
Black Patch, 182, 308–309
Bolonia, 49
Borsod, 314
Bouqras, 310, 312
Burford, 182
Burton Fleming, 50
Byblos, 310, 312, 326

C

Cadbury Castle, 14, 45–46

Carn Brea, 226
Castle-an-Dinas, 45
Castor, 326
Catal Hüyük, 310, 312
Catterick, 326
Cernavoda, 187–188
Cerveteri, 51
Chagar Bazar, 326
Chalkis, 320
Cheam, 327
Chippenham, 182
Chorrera, 159–160
Çiftlik, 310–311
Cissbury, 182, 308–309
Colchester, 14, 318
Corfe Mullen, 226
Corinth, 341–342

D

Dane's Camp, 44–45
Dhimini, 187
Dolni Vestonice, 126–127
Dragonby, 47–49

E

Easton Down, 182, 308
Eifel, 173
Erevan, 310–311
Eutresis, 187–188
Ezero, 187–188

F

Franchthi Cave, 313–314

Fussell's Lodge, 182

G

Galley Hill, 151–152
Giali, 313–314
Gradeschnitsa, 361
Grand Pressigny, 308–309
Great Langdale, 223–224
Grime's Graves, 182, 308–309
Grimston, 143
Gwithian, 226

H

Hacilar, 128, 183
Hala Sultan Tekke, 326
Haldon, 226
Hambledon, 182
Hartshill, 53, 318–319, 326
Hazard Hill, 182, 226
Heidelberg, 174
Hembury, 181–182, 225–226
High Peak, 182, 226

I

Ichkeul, 153

J

Jamestown, 163
Jarmo, 183, 310, 312
Jelemie, 348
Jericho, 182–183, 310, 312

K

Karanova, 187–188
Kars, 310–311
Khirokitia, 310, 312
Kingston, Massachusetts, 163
Knaphill, 182
Knossos, 187, 319, 321–323

L

Lake of Clouds, 85
Lake Rudolf, 73, 97–99, 169
Lake Urma, 310–311

Lake Van, 310–311
Laurion, 302, 335–336, 341
Laverstock, 326
Lefkandi, 320
Lerna, 187, 365
Les Matignons, 46
Lion Point, 182
Los Millares, 185, 188–189

M

Macedonia, 341
Madmarston, 14, 44
Maiden Castle, 226
Malvern Hills, 225
Mancetter, 53
Melos, 313–314, 321
Mendips, 334
Mersin, 183, 310, 312, 326
Minnesota, 85–86
Mycenae, 189–191
Myrtou, 326

N

Nea Nikomedeia, 183, 362–364
Nemrut Dağ, 310–311
Nimrud, 348–349
Nishapur, 162–163
North Elmham, 14
Nutbane, 182

O

Olduvai, 99, 104, 169–170
Owlesbury, 14

P

Peppard, 308
Peterborough, 53
Phylakopi, 365
Piltdown, 152–153
Port Royal, 163
Pottersbury, 326
Prescelly Mountains, 223

R

Rainsborough, 44

Ras Shamra, 183, 310
Rio Grande, 225
Rio Tinto, 302
Robin Hood's Ball, 226

S

Saliagos, 187
Sarab, 310, 312
Sardis, 162–163
Shanidar Cave, 182
Sheffield, 236
Sitagroi, 186–188, 361
South Carlton, 318
South Street, 182
Spiennes, 308
Stanton Harcourt, 50
Stibbington, 326
Stonehenge, 181–182, 189–190, 223
Swanscombe, 151–152
Syracuse, 340–341

T

Tabbat al Hamman, 310, 312
Tarquinia, 49, 51
Taruga, 53
Tell al-Judaidah, 310, 312
Tell Atchana, 321
Tell el Amarna, 321
Tell Goljanio Delschevo, 361
Tell Halaf, 183
Tell Ramad, 310, 312

Tell Shemshara, 310, 312
Tepe Gawra, 327
Tepe Guran, 310, 312
Tepe Serab, 183
Thebes, 321–322
Troy, 178, 185–186, 188, 365

U

Ur, 326–327

V

Verulamium, 49
Vinca, 178, 185, 187–188, 361

W

Wadi Natroun, 348
Wattisfield, 182
West Cowick, 143, 326
White Mountains, 68, 73
Wilderspool, 318
Winchester, 14
Windmill Hill, 46, 181–182, 226

Y

York River, 163

Z

Zagros Mountains, 185
Zawi Chemi Shanidar, 185